Holt Literature & Language Arts

Second Course

TEACHER'S EDITION

UNIVERSAL ACCESS Interactive Reading

- **Word Analysis, Fluency, and Systematic Vocabulary Development**
- **Reading Comprehension**
- **Literary Response and Analysis**

HOLT, RINEHART AND WINSTON

A Harcourt Classroom Education Company

Austin · New York · Orlando · Atlanta · San Francisco · Boston · Dallas · Toronto · London

Credits

Editorial

Project Director: Kathleen Daniel
Editor: Amy Fleming
Managing Editor: Mike Topp
Manager of Editorial Services: Abigail Winograd
Senior Product Manager: Don Wulbrecht
Editorial Staff: Brenda Sanabria, Susan Kent Cakars, Steven Fechter,
Rob Giannetto, Kerry Johnson, Dan Unger
Project Administration: Elizabeth LaManna
Editorial Support: Renée Benitez, Louise Fernandez, Soojung Christine Han,
Bret Isaacs, Laurie Muir
Editorial Permissions: David Smith, Carrie Jones
Conceptual Framework and Writing: e2 Publishing Services, Inc.

Art, Design, and Production

Director: Athena Blackorby
Senior Design Director: Betty Mintz
Series Design: Proof Positive/Farrowlyne Associates, Inc.
Design and Electronic Files: Proof Positive/Farrowlyne Associates, Inc.
Photo Research: Proof Positive/Farrowlyne Associates, Inc.
Production Manager: Catherine Gessner

Printed in the United States of America
ISBN 0-03-065098-4

2 3 4 5 6 32 05 04 03 02

Contents

• SECTION ONE •
GUIDE TO TEACHING *INTERACTIVE READING* 1

CHAPTER 1   Structures: Patterns of Meaning

Standards Focus

Vocabulary Development 1.2   Understand the most important points in the history of the English language, and use common word origins to determine the historical influences on English word meanings.

Reading Comprehension 2.2   Analyze text that uses proposition and support patterns.

Literary Response and Analysis 3.2   Evaluate the structural elements of the plot (for example, subplots, parallel episodes, climax), the plot's development, and the way in which conflicts are (or are not) addressed and resolved.

Reading Strategy: "Somebody Wanted But So"

CHAPTER 2   Characters: Doing the Right Thing

Standards Focus

Vocabulary Development 1.2   Understand the most important points in the history of the English language, and use common word origins to determine historical influences on English word meanings.

Reading Comprehension 2.3   Find similarities and differences between texts in the treatment, scope, or organization of ideas.

Literary Response and Analysis 3.3   Compare and contrast motivations and reactions of literary characters from different historical eras confronting similar situations or conflicts.

CHAPTER 3   Being There: Setting

Standards Focus

Vocabulary Development 1.3   Use word meanings within the appropriate context, and show ability to verify those meanings by definition, restatement, example, comparison, or contrast.

Reading Comprehension 2.1 (Grade 6 Review)   Identify the structural features of popular media (for example, newspapers, magazines, online information).

Literary Response and Analysis 3.4   Analyze the relevance of the setting (for example, place, time, customs) to the mood, tone, and meaning of the text.

CHAPTER 6 Sound and Sense: Forms of Poetry

Standards Focus

Reading Comprehension 2.4 Compare the original text to a summary to determine whether the summary accurately captures the main ideas, includes critical details, and conveys the underlying meaning.

Reading Comprehension 3.1 Determine and articulate the relationship between the purposes and characteristics of different forms of poetry (for example, ballad, lyric, couplet, epic, elegy, ode, sonnet).

Reading Strategy: "Text Reformulation"

CHAPTER 7 Literary Criticism: The Person Behind the Text

Standards Focus

Vocabulary Development

1.1 Analyze idioms, analogies, metaphors, and similes to infer the literal and figurative meanings of phrases.

1.3 Use word meanings within the appropriate context, and show ability to verify those meanings by definition, restatement, example, comparison, or contrast.

Reading Comprehension 2.7 Evaluate the unity, coherence, logic, internal consistency, and structural patterns of text.

Literary Response and Analysis 3.7 Analyze a work of literature, showing how it reflects the heritage, traditions, attitudes, and beliefs of its author (biographical approach).

Reading Strategy: "Think-Aloud"

CHAPTER 8 Reading for Life

Standards Focus

Reading Comprehension 2.1 Compare and contrast the features and elements of consumer materials to gain meaning from documents (for example, warranties, contracts, product information, instruction manuals).

Reading Comprehension 2.5 Understand and explain the use of a complex mechanical device by following technical directions.

Reading Comprehension 2.6 Use information from a variety of consumer, workplace, and public documents to explain a situation or decision and to solve a problem.

Reading Strategy: "Close Reading"

• SECTION TWO •
ANSWER KEY TO PUPIL'S EDITION OF *INTERACTIVE READING* . 119

CHAPTER 1 Structures: Patterns of Meaning

CHAPTER 2 Characters: Doing the Right Thing

Generic Graphic Organizers

• SECTION FOUR •
TRANSPARENCIES FOR MODELING INSTRUCTION

Transparency 1: Somebody Wanted But So

Transparency 2: Comparison and Contrast

Transparency 3: Sketch to Stretch

Transparency 4: Save the Last Word for Me

Transparency 5: Charting Literary Devices

Transparency 6: Text Reformulation

Transparency 7: Think-Aloud

Transparency 8: Close Reading

To the Teacher

Interactive Reading will help your students master the art of reading. Various aspects of this program are designed to ensure success for various levels of readers.

How does *Interactive Reading* fulfill this promise? How does it empower students to understand great literature and to become contributing members of this "information age"?

Guiding Principles of the Program

The development of *Interactive Reading* was guided by several principles:

- Students need explicit and systematic instruction to develop strategies to unlock the meaning of literary and informational text.
- Students need explicit and systematic instruction with modeling for applying strategies to manageable text before moving on to more complex text.
- Students need opportunities to interact with the text in order to access the meaning and power of the printed word and develop positive attitudes toward reading.
- Students need to read a wide variety of material in order to become comfortable with the many text structures that they will encounter in the real world.
- In order to master the language arts standards, students need explicit and systematic instruction.
- To develop proficiency, students need sequenced materials that identify and introduce less complex elements before more complex elements.
- Students need scaffolded instruction, starting with strong guided support, building toward lighter support, and leading toward independence.

A Bridge to Learning and Mastery

Interactive Reading works as a bridge to *Holt Literature and Language Arts.* Its four-pronged approach—

- prepares students for reading the literary and informational selections in *Holt Literature and Language Arts.*
- provides support as they read the selections in *Holt Literature and Language Arts.*
- builds independence and provides further reading opportunities beyond *Holt Literature and Language Arts.*
- provides materials that can be used as primary texts for additional instructional time.

Structure of the Student Book

Q: **How does *Interactive Reading* prepare students to read the selections in *Holt Literature and Language Arts*?**

A: *Interactive Reading* prepares students for *Holt Literature and Language Arts* by providing—
- an overview of chapter contents.
- an engaging Practice Read with controlled vocabulary and sentence structure.
- a strategy that helps students read the Practice Read successfully and master the standards.
- annotations to guide students' interaction with the Practice Read and help them apply the strategy.
- a graphic organizer or chart for applying the strategy.
- support for vocabulary development, word knowledge, and decoding, as well as for comprehension and mastery of text structure.

Q: **How does *Interactive Reading* provide support as students read the selections in *Holt Literature and Language Arts*?**

A: *Interactive Reading* provides support for the selections in *Holt Literature and Language Arts* through the use of selection-specific graphic organizers. These graphic organizers offer students a visual means to organize, interpret, and understand what they read.

The graphic organizers offer—
- support for reading each literature and informational text.
- support for mastering the standards.
- a creative way to interact with texts.
- opportunities for informal assessment.

Q: How does *Interactive Reading* help students build independence and provide further reading opportunities beyond *Holt Literature and Language Arts?*

A: Research has shown that the more students read, the better they will read. In addition, the more they interact with text—asking questions, clarifying information, making connections—the better they will understand.

Interactive Reading provides—

- new literary and informational selections for interactive reading.
- material for further author study, so that students can learn more about and read more by their favorite authors.
- questions and comments to guide reading and help students interact with text.
- projects to explore related ideas and extend knowledge.
- materials that can be used as primary texts for additional instructional time.

Structure of the Teacher's Edition

The Teacher's Edition is divided into four sections:

Section One • Guide to Teaching *Interactive Reading*

The Guide to Teaching *Interactive Reading* provides instructional plans for each chapter. The instructional design is—

Start with the Strategy and Practice Read
- About the Strategy
- Introduce the Strategy
- Model the Strategy
- Apply the Strategy with the Practice Read
- Assess

Support the Selections in *Holt Literature and Language Arts*
- Apply the Strategy to Literary Texts
- Focus on Informational Texts
- Assess

Build Independence Through Interactive Selections
- Introduce
- Model
- Teach
- Assess and Extend

In addition, the instructional plans contain chapter objectives, reading standards focuses, teacher-to-teacher notes, and differentiating instruction notes.

Of course, aligning assessment and instruction is essential. Each instructional plan is accompanied by—

- Vocabulary Checks—to assess mastery of selection vocabulary and the vocabulary standard.
- Comprehension Checks—to assess mastery of comprehension, academic vocabulary, and the literary or informational standard.

Section Two • Annotated Edition of *Interactive Reading*

Reduced pages of the complete student edition appear here in the Teacher's Edition. For your convenience, all the answers are in place at point of use.

Section Three • Graphic Organizers

For each chapter, you will find graphic organizers that can be used over and over with the selections in that chapter.

The graphic organizers for reading strategies—
- help students apply the reading strategies.
- help students practice and master the literary standards.

The generic graphic organizers—
- help students practice and master the literary standards.
- help students practice and apply the informational standards.

Section Four • Transparencies for Modeling Instruction

Modeling is essential for effective instruction. Students benefit when specific strategies they are expected to use are clearly demonstrated. For each reading strategy, a corresponding transparency is provided for your use in modeling the strategy. Students can then apply the strategy to a Practice Read.

Interactive Reading: Success for All Your Students

Everything in this book—instructional plans, assessments checks, graphic organizers, transparencies for modeling—will help you ensure that all your students master the standards. This program will also help you help all your students develop the strategies they need to enter the new worlds they will discover through reading.

A Walk Through the Book
Guide to Teaching *Interactive Reading*

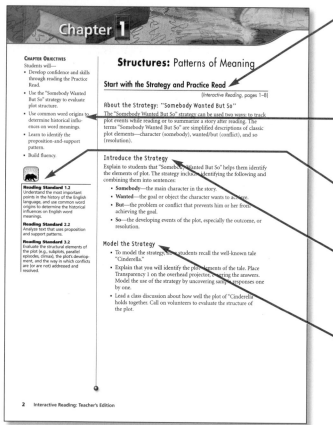

Start with the Strategy and Practice Read
The first part of each instructional plan introduces a strategy and applies it to a Practice Read.

Chapter Objectives
Objectives identify what students will learn in the chapter.

Reading Standards Focus
The reading standards to be mastered in the chapter are listed.

Introduce the Strategy
This section explains how to introduce the strategy. It shows what effective use of the strategy looks like.

Model the Strategy
This section provides transparencies of familiar folk stories for use in modeling strategies.

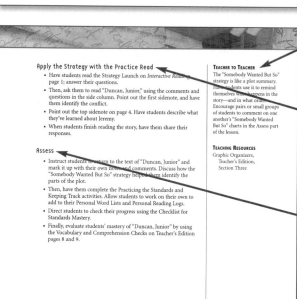

Teacher to Teacher
Notes provide classroom-friendly tips for using the strategy and teaching the standards.

Apply the Strategy with the Practice Read
This section provides a step-by-step approach for applying the strategy with the Practice Read.

Assess
This section provides multiple opportunities for informal and formal assessment.

Support the Selections in *Holt Literature and Language Arts*

The second part of the instructional plan moves students into *Holt Literature and Language Arts.* Here you are shown how to apply the strategy and use the graphic organizers.

Assess

This section provides various suggestions for assessment.

Chart

The chart lists selections in *Holt Literature and Language Arts* and their corresponding graphic organizers in *Interactive Reading.*

Build Independence Through Interactive Selections

The third part of the instructional plan provides lesson plans for the new interactive literary and informational selections in *Interactive Reading.*

Instructional Design

Each lesson plan follows the same instructional design: Introduce, Model, Teach, Assess and Extend.

Differentiating Instruction

You can reach all students using these tips for customizing the instruction.

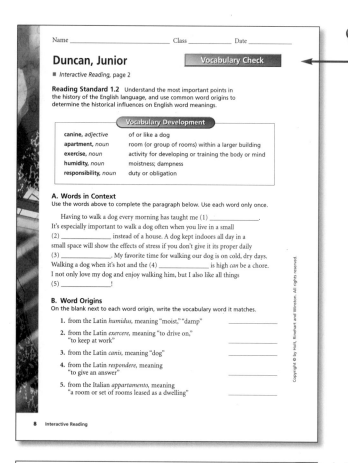

Name _____ Class _____ Date _____

Duncan, Junior

Vocabulary Check

■ *Interactive Reading,* page 2

Reading Standard 1.2 Understand the most important points in
the history of the English language, and use common word origins to
determine the historical influences on English word meanings.

Vocabulary Development

canine, *adjective*	of or like a dog
apartment, *noun*	room (or group of rooms) within a larger building
exercise, *noun*	activity for developing or training the body or mind
humidity, *noun*	moistness; dampness
responsibility, *noun*	duty or obligation

A. Words in Context
Use the words above to complete the paragraph below. Use each word only once.

Having to walk a dog every morning has taught me (1) _____.
It's especially important to walk a dog often when you live in a small
(2) _____ instead of a house. A dog kept indoors all day in a
small space will show the effects of stress if you don't give it its proper daily
(3) _____. My favorite time for walking our dog is on cold, dry days.
Walking a dog when it's hot and the (4) _____ is high *can* be a chore.
I not only love my dog and enjoy walking him, but I also like all things
(5) _____!

B. Word Origins
On the blank next to each word origin, write the vocabulary word it matches.

1. from the Latin *humidus,* meaning "moist," "damp"   _____

2. from the Latin *exercere,* meaning "to drive on,"
   "to keep at work"   _____

3. from the Latin *canis,* meaning "dog"   _____

4. from the Latin *respondere,* meaning
   "to give an answer"   _____

5. from the Italian *appartamento,* meaning
   "a room or set of rooms leased as a dwelling"   _____

8   Interactive Reading

Vocabulary Check

Blackline masters help you assess students'
understanding of selection vocabulary and
mastery of the vocabulary standard.

Name _____ Class _____ Date _____

Duncan, Junior

Comprehension Check

■ *Interactive Reading,* page 2

Reading Standard 3.2 Evaluate the structural elements of the
plot, the plot's development, and the way in which conflicts are
(or are not) addressed and resolved.

Academic Vocabulary

conflict	struggle between opposing forces
complication	event that makes the conflict harder to resolve
resolution	conclusion of a story, when the conflict has been settled

A. Circle the letter of the best response to each item below.

1. The main **conflict** in "Duncan, Junior" is between—
   A Jeremy and Duncan
   B Duncan and Duncan
   C Jeremy and his parents
   D Jeremy's parents and Duncan Junior

2. When Jeremy's mother tries to walk DJ in the snow, what
   complication arises?
   F DJ rushes out ahead of her.
   G Jeremy tries to pretend he's asleep.
   H Jeremy's father tells her not to do it.
   J DJ refuses to go out with her.

3. In the **resolution** of the plot of "Duncan, Junior"—
   A Jeremy finally tricks his parents into walking the dog again
   B the family shares equally in all the dog-related chores
   C Jeremy feels better about having to walk the dog every day
   D Jeremy decides it's time to get another dog

B. Imagine that the story has one more scene in it. In this new scene something
unexpected but good occurs. Describe what the scene might be.

_____

_____

_____

_____

Chapter 1   9

Comprehension Check

Blackline masters help you assess students'
comprehension of academic vocabulary
and the literary or informational standard.

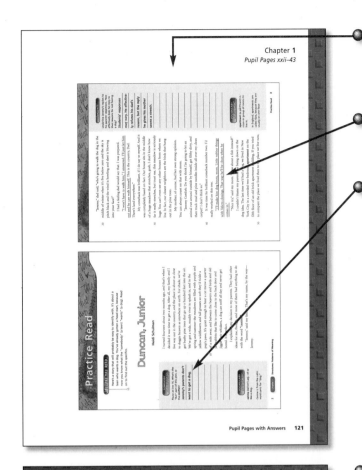

Pupil Pages with Answers 121

Teacher's Edition
The complete student edition of *Interactive Reading* is reproduced in convenient format.

Annotations
Selections are marked up to show suggested responses.

Answers
Answers and suggested responses are provided for every question.

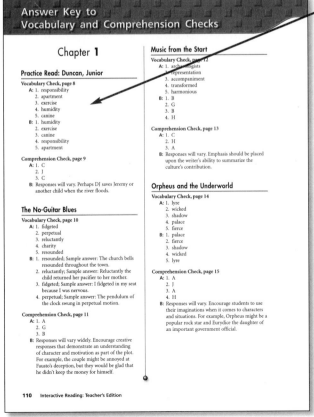

Answer Key to Vocabulary and Comprehension Checks

Chapter 1

Practice Read: Duncan, Junior

Vocabulary Check, page 8
A: 1. responsibility
2. apartment
3. exercise
4. humidity
5. canine
B: 1. humidity
2. exercise
3. canine
4. responsibility
5. apartment

Comprehension Check, page 9
A: 1. C
2. J
3. C
B: Responses will vary. Perhaps DJ saves Jeremy or another child when the river floods.

The No-Guitar Blues

Vocabulary Check, page 10
A: 1. fidgeted
2. perpetual
3. reluctantly
4. charity
5. resounded
B: 1. resounded; Sample answer: The church bells resounded throughout the town.
2. reluctantly; Sample answer: Reluctantly the child returned her pacifier to her mother.
3. fidgeted; Sample answer: I fidgeted in my seat because I was nervous.
4. perpetual; Sample answer: The pendulum of the clock swung in perpetual motion.

Comprehension Check, page 11
A: 1. A
2. G
3. B
B: Responses will vary widely. Encourage creative responses that demonstrate an understanding of character and motivation as part of the plot. For example, the couple might be annoyed at Fausto's deception, but they would be glad that he didn't keep the money for himself.

Music from the Start

Vocabulary Check, page 12
A: 1. archaeologists
2. representation
3. accompaniment
4. transformed
5. harmonious
B: 1. B
2. G
3. B
4. H

Comprehension Check, page 13
A: 1. C
2. H
3. A
B: Responses will vary. Emphasis should be placed upon the writer's ability to summarize the culture's contribution.

Orpheus and the Underworld

Vocabulary Check, page 14
A: 1. lyre
2. wicked
3. shadow
4. palace
5. fierce
B: 1. palace
2. fierce
3. shadow
4. wicked
5. lyre

Comprehension Check, page 15
A: 1. A
2. J
3. A
4. H
B: Responses will vary. Encourage students to use their imaginations when it comes to characters and situations. For example, Orpheus might be a popular rock star and Eurydice the daughter of an important government official.

Answer Keys to Vocabulary and Comprehension Checks
Answers and suggested responses to all blackline masters are provided.

Graphic Organizers

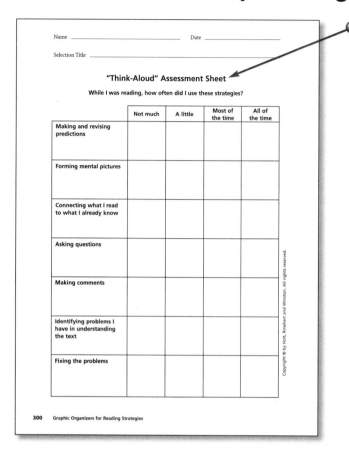

Graphic Organizers for Reading Strategies

A generic form of each strategy graphic organizer is provided so that students can apply this strategy to all selections in the chapter.

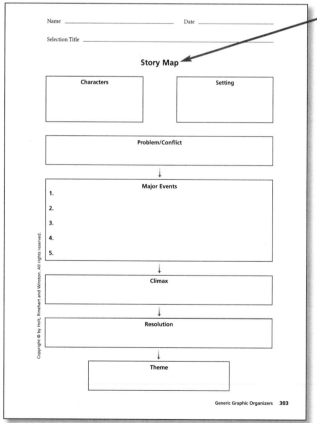

Generic Graphic Organizers

Additional generic organizers are also provided. Students can use these with the interactive selections or with any selection in the chapter.

Transparencies for Modeling

Strategy: Somebody Wanted But So

Transparency **1**

Cinderella

Somebody	Wanted	But	So
Cinderella	to go to the ball	her stepsisters made her stay home and clean the house	her fairy godmother came and gave Cinderella a pumpkin that turned into a coach
THEN			
Cinderella	to stay at the ball with Prince Charming	midnight struck—her gown turned to rags	she had to return to her house
THEN			
Prince Charming	to be reunited with Cinderella	he didn't know who she was or where she lived	Prince Charming found her by trying the glass slipper on the foot of every maiden in the land

Transparency for Modeling
A transparency for modeling instruction is provided for each reading strategy.

Section One

Instructional Materials

- VOCABULARY CHECKS

- COMPREHENSION CHECKS

- ANSWER KEY TO VOCABULARY
  AND COMPREHENSION CHECKS

- Develop confidence and skills through reading the Practice Read.

- Use the "Somebody Wanted But So" strategy to evaluate plot structure.

- Use common word origins to determine historical influences on word meanings.

- Learn to identify the proposition-and-support pattern.

- Build fluency.

Reading Standard 1.2
Understand the most important points in the history of the English language, and use common word origins to determine the historical influences on English word meanings.

Reading Standard 2.2
Analyze text that uses proposition and support patterns.

Reading Standard 3.2
Evaluate the structural elements of the plot (e.g., subplots, parallel episodes, climax), the plot's development, and the way in which conflicts are (or are not) addressed and resolved.

Structures: Patterns of Meaning

Start with the Strategy and Practice Read

(*Interactive Reading,* pages 1–8)

About the Strategy: "Somebody Wanted But So"

The "Somebody Wanted But So" strategy can be used two ways: to track plot events while reading or to summarize a story after reading. The terms "Somebody Wanted But So" are simplified descriptions of classic plot elements—character (somebody), wanted/but (conflict), and so (resolution).

Introduce the Strategy

Explain to students that "Somebody Wanted But So" helps them identify the elements of plot. The strategy includes identifying the following and combining them into sentences:

- **Somebody**—the main character in the story.

- **Wanted**—the goal or object the character wants to achieve.

- **But**—the problem or conflict that prevents him or her from achieving the goal.

- **So**—the developing events of the plot, especially the outcome, or resolution.

Model the Strategy

- To model the strategy, have students recall the well-known tale "Cinderella."

- Explain that you will identify the plot elements of the tale. Place Transparency 1 on the overhead projector, covering the answers. Model the use of the strategy by uncovering sample responses one by one.

- Lead a class discussion about how well the plot of "Cinderella" holds together. Call on volunteers to evaluate the structure of the plot.

Apply the Strategy with the Practice Read

- Have students read the Strategy Launch on *Interactive Reading* page 1; answer their questions.
- Then, ask them to read "Duncan, Junior," using the comments and questions in the side column. Point out the first sidenote, and have them identify the conflict.
- Point out the top sidenote on page 4. Have students describe what they've learned about Jeremy.
- When students finish reading the story, have them share their responses.

Assess

- Instruct students to return to the text of "Duncan, Junior" and mark it up with their own notes and comments. Discuss how the "Somebody Wanted But So" strategy helped them identify the parts of the plot.
- Then, have them complete the Practicing the Standards and Keeping Track activities. Allow students to work on their own to add to their Personal Word Lists and Personal Reading Logs.
- Direct students to check their progress using the Checklist for Standards Mastery.
- Finally, evaluate students' mastery of "Duncan, Junior" by using the Vocabulary and Comprehension Checks on Teacher's Edition pages 8 and 9.

TEACHER TO TEACHER

The "Somebody Wanted But So" strategy is like a plot summary. Have students use it to remind themselves what happens in the story—and in what order. Encourage pairs or small groups of students to comment on one another's "Somebody Wanted But So" charts in the Assess part of the lesson.

TEACHING RESOURCES

Graphic Organizers, Teacher's Edition, Section Three

TEACHER TO TEACHER

Try varying the "Somebody Wanted But So" work process for each literary selection in the chapter. You might have the whole class cooperate to compose one statement for "Broken Chain," based on their charts. Later, for "Flowers for Algernon," assign separate portions of Charlie's journal to small groups, and then have all students use their charts to compose a single statement for the whole novella. For "The Landlady," have students work independently; then, have them compare their charts with those of their peers.

Support the Selections in
Holt Literature and Language Arts

(Chapter 1, pages 4–81)

Interact with Literary Texts

- Before students begin to read each literary selection, remind them to use the "Somebody Wanted But So" strategy to follow and understand the plot.
- After students read each literary selection, have them complete the corresponding graphic organizer.

Interact with Informational Texts

- After students read each informational selection, have them complete the corresponding graphic organizer.

Assess

- Use the graphic organizers as alternate assessments.
- Photocopy and distribute the "Somebody Wanted But So" Chart in Section Three of the Teacher's Edition. Have students exchange their completed charts with a partner and evaluate each other's work.
- Discuss with students how the reading strategy helped them to understand the story line of literary texts.

Selections in *Holt Literature and Language Arts*	Graphic Organizers in *Interactive Reading*
Broken Chain, p. 7	**Plot Diagram,** p. 11
Road Warriors, Listen Up, p. 20	**Main-Idea Chart,** p. 12
Flowers for Algernon, p. 23	**Story Map,** p. 13
Memory a Matter of Brains and Brawn, p. 58	**Evaluation Chart,** p. 14
The Landlady, p. 62	**Foreshadowing Chart,** p. 15

Build Independence Through Interactive Selections

(Interactive Reading, pages 16–43)

The No-Guitar Blues
Gary Soto ▪ page 17

INTRODUCE

- Tell students that they are going to read another story by Gary Soto. Review "Broken Chain," and encourage them to summarize what they know about the author.
- Read the Author Study and Before You Read note aloud. Tell students that they will find more stories by Gary Soto in his two collections, *Baseball in April* and *Local News*.

MODEL

- Tell students to use the "Somebody Wanted But So" strategy to help them identify and evaluate the plot of this story.
- Have a volunteer read the first sentence of the story and the "Somebody Wanted But So" sidenote aloud. Ask students which words they labeled with the letters *S* and *W*.

TEACH

- Have students complete the rest of the story independently, writing their responses to the side-column notes in their books.
- Read the Fluency note aloud, and have volunteers demonstrate reading the dialogue passage aloud.
- Have students add the story to their Personal Reading Logs.

ASSESS AND EXTEND

- Photocopy and have students complete the "Somebody Wanted But So" Chart in Section Three of the Teacher's Edition.
- Use the Vocabulary Check on Teacher's Edition page 10 to evaluate mastery of the vocabulary standard.
- Use the Comprehension Check on Teacher's Edition page 11 to evaluate mastery of the literary standard.
- As an extension activity, assign the Project on author Gary Soto.

- **Learners Having Difficulty** Have students work with benchmark students or advanced learners to read the text; when a difficult passage appears, ask the student who understands what is happening in the story to rephrase the passage in simpler language.
- **Benchmark Students** The Spanish words and names in "The No-Guitar Blues" may pose a stumbling block for non-Spanish-speaking students in this or in any other group. Encourage Spanish speakers to help by offering the correct pronunciations.
- **Advanced Students** Encourage these learners to compare the plot of this story with that of "Broken Chain," or extend the reading by presenting a mini-lesson on Gary Soto and his works.

TEACHER TO TEACHER
By reading students' "Somebody Wanted But So" statements, you can quickly gain insight into thinking-skill problems such as generalizing, recognizing cause and effect, and distinguishing the main idea from details. One goal of the strategy is to help students get past the "and-then-this-happened" stage of plot comprehension by having them focus on complications, the conflict, and the effects of other characters on the plot. Frequent "Somebody Wanted But So" statements joined with the word *and* may indicate that students are still at an earlier stage of comprehension.

- **Learners Having Difficulty**
Slower readers may find it
difficult to follow the layout.
Help these learners determine
how the various sections and
features are related.

- **Benchmark Students** Invite
students to preview the illustrations and text features
before reading the text itself.
Discuss their impressions of
each topic in the selection,
and have them express what
they learned from the Before
You Read note.

- **Advanced Students** These
students can extend their
knowledge by reporting on
the origin of a modern musical instrument.

TEACHER TO TEACHER

Music is a topic that many students know about and in which
they may be interested. Write the
words *History of Music* on the
chalkboard. Have students
brainstorm a list of words that
come to mind as they consider
this topic. Create a word web as
they talk.

Music from the Start
Patricia Hunt-Jones ▪ page 28

INTRODUCE

- Tell students that they will read an overview of the history of
music around the world, from ancient times to the present. Review
ancient cultures, such as those of Egypt, Greece, and Rome, about
which students already know.

- Have students read the Before You Read note. Encourage them to
describe imaginatively and with details what it might have been
like to attend a concert in ancient Greece.

MODEL

- Read the first paragraph of the article aloud, and ask students to
respond to it. Ask why it might be interesting for all music lovers
to learn how music began.

- Have students read the first two text structure notes and follow the
directions. Point out that these notes help them understand how
the article is organized.

TEACH

- Allow students to read the rest of the selection independently,
using the sidenotes as a guide.

- If you have access to a slide library or can make your own color
transparencies, either would be an excellent way to supplement the
illustrations in the text.

ASSESS AND EXTEND

- Evaluate students' mastery of the selection by using the Vocabulary
and Comprehension Checks on Teacher's Edition
pages 12 and 13.

- As an extension activity, assign the Musical Time Line project.
Students might work in pairs to do the research and prepare their
time lines, perhaps adding illustrations.

Orpheus and the Underworld

retold by Mollie McLean and Anne M. Wiseman • page 36

INTRODUCE

- Tell students that they will now read an ancient Greek myth with an all-time favorite plot. The story of Orpheus is so memorable that it has been retold, rewritten, and made into movies over and over again. For instance, two film versions, made a generation apart, have set the tale in Brazil during carnival season.

- Have students read the Before You Read note. You might point out that in ancient cultures, people of great talent or achievement were often believed to be favored by the gods. So it seemed natural for such heroes to interact with gods in myths.

MODEL

- Remind students that they will be using the "Somebody Wanted But So" strategy for this story. Then, explain that "the Underworld" is the place where the ancient Greeks believed that souls went after death.

- Model the "Somebody Wanted But So" strategy using the notes in the side column to identify the **Somebody** and **Wanted** parts of the strategy. Point out specific words that led you to identify these elements, such as *Orpheus wanted to be with Eurydice.*

- Now model how students should identify the **But** and **So** elements. For example, "**But** Eurydice had died from a snake bite **So** Orpheus decides to go to Hades to find her."

TEACH

- Have students read the rest of the myth independently. Remind students to respond to the side-column questions and comments.

- Read the Fluency note aloud, and have volunteers take turns reading the passage aloud with suitable tones of voice.

ASSESS AND EXTEND

- Photocopy and have students complete the "Somebody Wanted But So" Chart in Section Three of the Teacher's Edition.

- Use the Vocabulary and Comprehension Checks on Teacher's Edition pages 14 and 15 to evaluate students' mastery of the standards.

- Assign the storyboard project as an extension activity. When all have finished, you could have groups combine their individual storyboards into master storyboards that include the entire plot.

DIFFERENTIATING INSTRUCTION
Orpheus and
the Underworld

- **Learners Having Difficulty** To avoid confusion, preview with students the place-names and the names of all the characters involved.

- **Benchmark Students** Text passages that include dialogue would be good places for these students to take turns reading aloud. Although students may already be reasonably fluent, this exercise will provide them with additional practice in reading with expression.

- **Advanced Students** Because myths change as they are retold over time, this selection offers a good opportunity for these learners to show their comprehension by paraphrasing or retelling the selection.

TEACHER TO TEACHER

After students have read the selection once or twice, have them use their "Somebody Wanted But So" Charts as the basis of their own retelling of the Orpheus myth.

Duncan, Junior

■ *Interactive Reading,* page 2

Reading Standard 1.2 Understand the most important points in the history of the English language, and use common word origins to determine the historical influences on English word meanings.

Vocabulary Development

canine, *adjective*	of or like a dog
apartment, *noun*	room (or group of rooms) within a larger building
exercise, *noun*	activity for developing or training the body or mind
humidity, *noun*	moistness; dampness
responsibility, *noun*	duty or obligation

A. Words in Context
Use the words above to complete the paragraph below. Use each word only once.

Having to walk a dog every morning has taught me (1) _____.
It's especially important to walk a dog often when you live in a small
(2) _____ instead of a house. A dog kept indoors all day in a
small space will show the effects of stress if you don't give it its proper daily
(3) _____. My favorite time for walking our dog is on cold, dry days.
Walking a dog when it's hot and the (4) _____ is high *can* be a chore.
I not only love my dog and enjoy walking him, but I also like all things
(5) _____!

B. Word Origins
On the blank next to each word origin, write the vocabulary word it matches.

1. from the Latin *humidus,* meaning "moist," "damp"   _____

2. from the Latin *exercere,* meaning "to drive on,"
   "to keep at work"   _____

3. from the Latin *canis,* meaning "dog"   _____

4. from the Latin *respondere,* meaning
   "to give an answer"   _____

5. from the Italian *appartamento,* meaning
   "a room or set of rooms leased as a dwelling"   _____

Duncan, Junior

■ *Interactive Reading,* page 2

Reading Standard 3.2 Evaluate the structural elements of the plot, the plot's development, and the way in which conflicts are (or are not) addressed and resolved.

Academic Vocabulary

conflict	struggle between opposing forces
complication	event that makes the conflict harder to resolve
resolution	conclusion of a story, when the conflict has been settled

A. Circle the letter of the best response to each item below.

1. The main **conflict** in "Duncan, Junior" is between—
   A Jeremy and Duncan
   B Duncan and Duncan
   C Jeremy and his parents
   D Jeremy's parents and Duncan Junior

2. When Jeremy's mother tries to walk DJ in the snow, what **complication** arises?
   F DJ rushes out ahead of her.
   G Jeremy tries to pretend he's asleep.
   H Jeremy's father tells her not to do it.
   J DJ refuses to go out with her.

3. In the **resolution** of the plot of "Duncan, Junior"—
   A Jeremy finally tricks his parents into walking the dog again
   B the family shares equally in all the dog-related chores
   C Jeremy feels better about having to walk the dog every day
   D Jeremy decides it's time to get another dog

B. Imagine that the story has one more scene in it. In this new scene something unexpected but good occurs. Describe what the scene might be.

_____

_____

_____

_____

The No-Guitar Blues

■ *Interactive Reading,* page 16

Reading Standard 1.2 Understand the most important points in the history of the English language, and use common word origins to determine the historical influences on English word meanings.

Vocabulary Development

perpetual, *adjective*	lasting or enduring forever
fidgeted, *verb*	moved in a restless, nervous, or uneasy way
reluctantly, *adverb*	unwillingly; grudgingly
charity, *noun*	voluntary giving of money or help to those in need
resounded, *verb*	filled with sound; echoed

A. Words in Context

Use the words above to complete the paragraph below. Use each word only once.

Fausto (1) _____ nervously as he sat in the strangers' house, staring at their (2) _____ clock. He accepted their money (3) _____. Feeling guilty, he went to church and put the twenty dollars they had given him in the collection basket for (4) _____. As if to reward him, that afternoon his grandfather gave him a guitarron, whose strong bass chords (5) _____ throughout the neighborhood.

B. Word Origins

On the blank next to each word origin, write the correct word from the Vocabulary Development box. Then, use each word in a sentence.

1. from the Latin *re-,* "again," + *sonere,* "to sound"   _____

_____

2. from the Latin *reluctari,* "to resist" or "to struggle against"   _____

_____

3. from the Middle English *fichen,* "to move restlessly"   _____

_____

4. from the Latin *perpetuus,* "continuous, uninterrupted"   _____

_____

The No-Guitar Blues

■ *Interactive Reading,* page 16

Reading Standard 3.2 Evaluate the structural elements of the plot, the plot's development, and the way in which conflicts are (or are not) addressed and resolved.

> ### Academic Vocabulary
>
> | | |
> |---|---|
> | **motivation** | reason for a character's actions |
> | **conflict** | struggle between opposing forces in a story |
> | **resolution** | conclusion of a story, when the conflict has been settled |

A. Circle the letter of the best response to each item below.

1. Which phrase from the story states Fausto's **motivation** to play the guitar?
   A "The moment Fausto saw the group Los Lobos . . . he knew exactly what he wanted to do with his life."
   B "His eyes grew large with excitement. . . ."
   C "Fausto decided to mow lawns to earn money. . . ."
   D "It was the happiest day of his life."

2. What **conflict** does Fausto face in trying to obtain a guitar?
   F He doesn't know where to get one.
   G He doesn't have enough money.
   H His parents don't listen to him.
   J He can't find the right one.

3. What role does Fausto's grandfather play in the **resolution** of the plot?
   A He convinces Fausto that having a guitarron is not important.
   B He gives Fausto his old bass guitarron.
   C He distracts Fausto by playing football with him.
   D He gives Fausto a job so that he can afford a guitar.

B. Suppose the owners of the dog that Fausto found eventually read this story. How do you think they would respond? Why?

_____

_____

_____

Music from the Start

■ *Interactive Reading,* page 28

Reading Standard 1.2 Understand the most important points in the history of the English language, and use common word origins to determine the historical influences on English word meanings.

Vocabulary Development

archaeologists, *noun*	scientists who study the remains of ancient cultures
representation, *noun*	image or a likeness
transformed, *verb*	changed the form or appearance of
harmonious, *adjective*	having musical tones combined to produce a pleasing effect
accompaniment, *noun*	music that is performed to accompany, or go with, the main part of a song

A. Words in Context
Use the words above to complete this paragraph. Use each word only once.

A group of (1) _____ discovered a beautiful picture of musicians from ancient Greece. It was a (2) _____ of flute and lyre players and a singer at a feast. The picture suggested that the instruments provided (3) _____ to the singer's voice. In one corner was a mythical creature who had been (4) _____ into a man with the head of a bull. Even he was singing happily to the (5) _____ music.

B. Word Origins
Using a dictionary, circle the letter of the word whose origin is most closely related to that of the boldface word.

1. **archaeologists**
   A archangels   B archaeology   C arches   D psychologists

2. **representation**
   F president   G present   H preserve   J sent

3. **transformed**
   A former   B form   C for   D changed

4. **accompaniment**
   F accomplish   G complaint   H companion   J pan

Music from the Start

■ *Interactive Reading,* page 28

Reading Standard 2.2 Analyze text that uses proposition and support patterns.

Academic Vocabulary

proposition	important idea or opinion offered for discussion
support	evidence that suggests that a statement is true

A. Circle the letter of the best response to each item below.

1. Which statement provides **support** for the proposition that people have been making music for more than ten thousand years?
   A The first stringed instruments were played about 3000 B.C.
   B Many instruments were created in Egypt between 1550 and 1080 B.C.
   C Archaeologists have discovered Chinese flutes from about 9000 B.C.
   D Ancient Greek philosophers Aristotle and Plato wrote about music.

2. What **proposition** is the second section of the article based on?
   F that all cultures make and appreciate music
   G that some modern instruments look much like the ancient versions
   H that Greek music is the foundation for much of Western music
   J that archaeologists have found evidence of ancient peoples who made music

3. What **support** does the writer give for her suggestion that musical instruments have changed over time?
   A Egyptian musicians transformed the harp into a twenty-string instrument.
   B Modern musicians play instruments somewhat like ancient ones.
   C Some instruments invented by the Aztecs and Incas, who lived in the West, resemble those of ancient Egyptians or Greeks, who lived in the East.
   D Instruments made of strong, hard materials tend to last a very long time.

B. Choose one of the cultures discussed in the article. Explain in your own words what that culture did to advance the creation of music and musical instruments.

_____

_____

_____

_____

Orpheus and the Underworld

■ *Interactive Reading*, page 36

Vocabulary Check

Reading Standard 1.2 Understand the most important points in the history of the English language, and use common word origins to determine the historical influences on English word meanings.

Vocabulary Development

palace, *noun*	official residence of a king or head of state
lyre, *noun*	small stringed instrument of the harp family
fierce, *adjective*	savage; violent; cruel
shadow, *noun*	feeling of gloom or depression
wicked, *adjective*	morally bad or wrong

A. Words in Context
Use the words above to complete each paragraph. Use each word only once.

Orpheus sang and played his (1) _____ as he traveled through the lower regions of Hades, where good people as well as people who had lived (2) _____ lives were found. As he observed the unhappy people in Hades, a (3) _____ fell upon Orpheus. The entrance to Pluto's dark (4) _____ was guarded by a (5) _____ three-headed dog named Cerberus, who finally let Orpheus through the gate. At last, Orpheus would see Pluto himself, the dark king of a dark and somber kingdom!

B. Word Origins
On the line next to each word origin, write the correct modern word.

1. from the Latin *palatium,* "house on the Palatine Hill in Rome where emperors lived" _____

2. from the Latin *ferox,* meaning "wild; arrogant" _____

3. from the Old English *sceaduw,* meaning "shade" _____

4. from the Middle English *wicke,* meaning "evil" _____

5. from the Greek and Latin *lyra,* meaning "stringed musical instrument" _____

Orpheus and the Underworld

■ *Interactive Reading, page 36*

Reading Standard 3.2 Evaluate the structural elements of the plot, the plot's development, and the way in which conflicts are (or are not) addressed and resolved.

Academic Vocabulary

conflict	struggle between opposing forces
climax	most exciting or suspenseful part of the plot when we know how the conflict will be resolved
resolution	end of the plot, when loose ends of the story are tied up
suspense	uncertainty a reader feels about what will happen next in a story

A. Circle the letter of the best response to each item below.

1. Orpheus is torn between wanting to obey Pluto and wanting to be sure Eurydice is following him. This statement describes the myth's—

    A conflict   **C** resolution

    B climax   **D** suspense

2. The **climax** of this myth occurs when—

    F Orpheus goes down to the underworld

    G Eurydice dies of snakebite

    H Orpheus drowns with Eurydice's name on his lips

    J Orpheus looks behind him to see if Eurydice is following him out of Hades

3. Which question is *not* a source of **suspense** in this myth?

    A How did Orpheus become a great musician?

    B Will Orpheus look back or not?

    C Will Eurydice be reunited with Orpheus?

    D What will Orpheus do after returning to the world of the living?

4. Which best describes the **resolution** of the story?

    F Readers are warned not to meddle with the power of the gods.

    G Through the power of music, the characters are happily reunited.

    H The hero travels, plays his lyre, and sings, but never again sings a love song.

    J Though there is grief, there is also beauty.

B. If you were going to update this myth, who would the main characters be?

_____

_____

CHAPTER OBJECTIVES

Students will—

- Develop skills and confidence through reading the Practice Read.

- Compare and contrast characters and their motivations.

- Find similarities and differences in the organization of ideas between texts.

- Understand common word origins.

- Build fluency.

Reading Standard 1.2
Understand the most important points in the history of the English language, and use common word origins to determine the historical influences on English word meanings.

Reading Standard 2.3
Find similarities and differences between texts in the treatment, scope, or organization of ideas.

Reading Standard 3.3
Compare and contrast motivations and reactions of literary characters from different historical eras who confront similar situations or conflicts.

Characters: Doing the Right Thing

Start with the Strategy and Practice Read

(*Interactive Reading,* pages 45–54)

About the Strategy: "Compare and Contrast"

One of the most important aspects of a literary selection is the author's success at characterization. Well-drawn characters, who perform logical acts with believable motivations, are an essential key to an effective, enjoyable piece of literature.

One interesting way to analyze the characters in a selection is to think about how the specific time period they inhabit in the selection affects their actions and motivations. A particularly effective way to see how specific time periods affect the characters is to compare characters from different time periods. To have students complete this kind of analysis, use the "Compare and Contrast" strategy.

Introduce the Strategy

Explain to students that considering the historical time period of a selection will help them understand why the characters in the selection do the things they do. Tell them that the importance of the time period can most clearly be seen when comparing similar characters from different selections that take place in different time periods. This analysis involves—

- Taking notes while reading the selection, using a comparison grid.

- Identifying key actions taken by the characters.

- Looking for the motivations behind the characters' actions.

- Analyzing how the historical time period affected the characters' motivations and actions.

Model the Strategy

- To model the reading strategy, place Transparency 2 on the overhead projector. Read the short biography of Davy Crockett to the class.

- When you're finished reading, read through the list of bulleted questions one by one. Allow time for class discussion following each question.

- Guide students to realize that people's actions are sometimes governed by the time and place in which they live. You may want to ask the class to provide further examples of people who fit this description.

- Then, tell students that they will be applying the "Compare and Contrast" strategy to the Practice Read.

Apply the Strategy with the Practice Read

- Have students read the Strategy Launch on *Interactive Reading* page 45. Discuss any questions they may have.

- Read the Before You Read note on page 46 for the class. Make sure students realize that they will be reading a second selection and making comparisons between the two.

- Tell students that they will be comparing and contrasting the two selections. Students can complete the Comparison Grid on page 54 as they read the selections, or they can read the selections through then complete the Grid upon review.

- Then, have students read "John Adams: The Forgotten Man," beginning on page 46, followed by the editorial "Do the Right Thing," beginning on page 51. Remind students to use the comments and questions in the side column to guide their reading.

- Have students work in pairs or in small groups to either complete the Comparison Grid or to review their completed grids.

Assess

- As an informal assessment, have students share their Comparison Grids with other partners and groups. Invite them to mention any especially insightful points presented.

- As a further assessment of how well students understood the John Adams selection, have them complete the Character Grid on page 53.

- Then, have students return to the selections, marking them up with questions and comments.

- Finally, evaluate students' mastery of the two selections using the Vocabulary Check on page 22 and the Comprehension Check on page 23 of the Teacher's Edition.

TEACHER TO TEACHER

Remind students that **comparing** involves ways in which two things are alike and that **contrasting** involves ways in which they are different. Even though **comparing** is often used to describe both relationships, students will probably understand the strategy best if they adhere to the classic definitions above.

TEACHING RESOURCES

Graphic Organizers,
    Teacher's Edition,
    Section Three

Support the Selections in
Holt Literature and Language Arts

(Chapter 2, pages 84–147)

Apply the Strategy to Literary Texts

- Before students read each selection, remind them to use the "Compare and Contrast" strategy as an aid to understanding. Have them show how characters, motivations, settings, and outcomes in each selection are similar to or different from others.
- Encourage them to compare the characters in each selection with characters from selections set in other historical periods.
- After reading, have them complete the corresponding graphic organizer for each selection.

Focus on Informational Texts

- After students read each informational selection, have them complete the matching graphic organizer in *Interactive Reading.*

Assess

- Use the graphic organizers in *Interactive Reading* as an alternative assessment.
- After students read each selection, pair them with partners or place them in small groups. Have them use the "Compare and Contrast" strategy to show similarities and differences in relevant parts of the selection.

Selections in *Holt Literature and Language Arts*	Graphic Organizers in *Interactive Reading*
from **Harriet Tubman: Conductor on the Underground Railroad**, p. 87	**What If? Chart**, p. 55
The Fugitive Slave Acts of 1793 and 1850, p. 101	**Venn Diagram**, p. 56
Barbara Frietchie, p. 107	**Character-Traits Cluster**, p. 57
Too Soon a Woman, p. 114	**Motivations Web**, p. 58
Union Pacific Railroad Poster; Home, Sweet Soddie, p. 122	**Comparison Chart**, p. 59
Mrs. Flowers, from *I Know Why the Caged Bird Sings, p. 130	**Problem-Resolution Chart**, p. 60
Mrs. Flowers's Recipes, p. 137	**Process Chart**, p. 61

Build Independence Through Interactive Selections

(Interactive Reading, pages 62–87)

New Directions

Maya Angelou • p. 63

Field Work

Rose Del Castillo Guilbault • p. 66

INTRODUCE

- Tell students that they will read two selections about people from different historical periods who faced similar difficulties. As they read, have them watch for similarities and differences in the characters' motivations and reactions.
- Read the Author Study note aloud. Then, tell students that they will find more stories and reflections by Maya Angelou in her autobiographical books *Wouldn't Take Nothing for My Journey Now* and *Life Doesn't Frighten Me.*

MODEL

- Read the first paragraph of "New Directions" aloud, and do the same for "Field Work." Then, ask students to predict the various difficulties that Annie Johnson and the narrator of "Field Work" will face in the rest of the story.
- Model for them one set of similarities and then one set of differences between the two women. Point out that they may use the same format for comparing and contrasting other story items as well.

TEACH

- Allow class time for students to read the selections independently. Remind students to use the sidenotes as a guide.
- Read the Fluency note aloud. Then, organize the class into small groups in which members take turns reading the final three paragraphs of "New Directions" aloud.
- Have students add these selections to their Personal Reading Logs.

ASSESS

- Have students work individually or in small groups to complete the Comparison Chart on *Interactive Reading* page 73 for Mrs. Johnson and the narrator of "Field Work." Discuss students' responses as a class.
- Use the Vocabulary Check on page 24 and the Comprehension Check on page 25 of the Teacher's Edition to evaluate students' mastery of the standards.

DIFFERENTIATING INSTRUCTION
New Directions;
Field Work

- **Learners Having Difficulty** Give these students a preview of each narrator by reading aloud a portion of each story before they begin reading.
- **Benchmark Students** Teach the vocabulary for "New Directions" and "Field Work" before these students read the stories. Then, based on these words, have these students anticipate what the characters will be like and what the selections will be about.
- **Advanced Students** These selections should pose no difficulty for advanced students. You might extend the Author Study project by having them turn their research into a multimedia presentation.

- **Learners Having Difficulty**
  This group may need extra help with the vocabulary and the idioms in this selection. You may want to teach the vocabulary first. Then, make a list of the idioms on the board and have students guess the meaning of each one.

- **Benchmark Students**
  Benchmark students might have problems with the format of this selection. Read the introductory paragraph aloud. Then, use a call-and-response method for reading each idiom and its definition. Try reading the idiom aloud, and have a volunteer read the definition—or vice versa.

- **Advanced Students**
  Advanced students should find this selection very enjoyable. As they read, encourage them to add other food-related idioms to the ones in their books.

TEACHER TO TEACHER

Give students some food-related words of your own, and invite them, either individually or in small groups, to recall or invent some additional "food" idioms. Have them use each one in a sentence. (Example: That excuse sounds **fishy** to me.)

You Took the Words Right Out of My Mouth . . .

Evan Morris ▪ p. 74

INTRODUCE

- Tell students that they will learn of some English idioms that use food names to describe nonfood situations. Explain that an *idiom* is an expression peculiar to the language and that suggests something different from its literal meaning.

- Share with students that Evan Morris, who calls himself "the word detective," is a newspaper columnist who writes about the English language and that these idioms are taken from some of his columns.

MODEL

- Direct students' attention to the first side-column note. Have students think about the title of the selection, and ask whether they've ever heard or used the idiom *You took the words right out of my mouth.* Be sure students know that it means that a speaker has just said what another person was about to say.

- Make sure students understand the glossary format of this selection. Read aloud the first idiom *a chicken in every pot,* and then read its meaning. Have students visualize voters in 1928—the year before the Great Depression began—and what the promise of a full cooking pot meant at that time.

TEACH

- As you discuss the remaining entries, point out other aspects of text structure that make the selection resemble a dictionary (examples: italicized words and phrases, Latin derivations, sentence fragments).

- Have students work in pairs to read and grasp the meaning of each idiom.

- Have students add their comments about the text to their Personal Reading Logs.

ASSESS AND EXTEND

- Use the Vocabulary Check on page 26 and Comprehension Check on page 27 of the Teacher's Edition to evaluate students' mastery of the standards.

- Use the Glossary Templates project as an extension activity.

Prometheus Steals Fire from Heaven

retold by Anne Terry White • page 79

Paul's Popcorn

Walter Blair • page 83

INTRODUCE

- Tell students that they will read two selections about heroic figures. One is Prometheus, a character from an ancient Greek myth who gave a great gift to the human race. The other is Paul Bunyan, a tall-tale hero of the American West. Ask the class what they already know about these two figures.
- Tell the class that a *myth* is a traditional story rooted in a particular culture. Myths usually involve gods and goddesses and often explain a belief or natural occurrence.
- Note that the accompanying story is a *tall tale,* a type of folk tale marked by humorous exaggeration.

MODEL

- Read the Before You Read note aloud. Then, write the following statement on the board: "Literature helps us to see the similarities and differences among people who live in different times and places. It helps us to know that we are not alone." Invite students to comment on this idea.
- Model how you would compare and contrast people who are living now, in the twenty-first century, with those who lived in ancient Greece, about 500 B.C. Use as guides their levels of civilization, the struggles of each group, and their hopes for the future. Ask students to offer additional comments.

TEACH

- Have students read both selections independently, using the side-column notes to guide their reading. Remind them to look for similarities and differences in the two main characters' motivations and reactions.
- After students finish reading, invite them to discuss the details they found most effective, interesting, and entertaining. Discuss which character was really a hero.

ASSESS

- As an informal assessment, have students complete the Contrast Chart on *Interactive Reading* page 87.
- Use the Vocabulary Check and Comprehension Check on pages 28 and 29 of the Teacher's Edition to check students' mastery of the standards.

DIFFERENTIATING INSTRUCTION
Prometheus Steals ◄━━► Fire from Heaven; Paul's Popcorn

- **Learners Having Difficulty** These two selections both contain some difficult vocabulary. "Paul's Popcorn" contains humor, a quality that these students might miss when they read. Help students with the vocabulary first, and then have them read along as you read aloud.

- **Benchmark Students** These students should have no difficulty with vocabulary in the two selections but might have trouble comparing and contrasting them. Suggest that they use a comparison grid or some other simple graphic organizer to do this.

- **Advanced Students** Advanced students might have fun dramatizing these selections or using "Paul's Popcorn" to make a cartoon comic strip.

TEACHER TO TEACHER
Students can have some fun reading "Paul's Popcorn" aloud. Have them try out folksy tones of voice, noticing which tones are most and least funny or appropriate for a tall tale.

John Adams: The Forgotten Man; Do the Right Thing: A Simple Plan ■ *Interactive Reading*, page 46

Reading Standard 1.2 Understand the most important points in the history of the English language, and use common word origins to determine the historical influences on English word meanings.

Vocabulary Development

nominated, *verb*	named as a candidate for something
patriots, *noun*	those who love and support their own country
unanimous, *adjective*	based on complete agreement
tyrant, *noun*	absolute ruler, especially one who is cruel

A. Words in Context
Use the words above to complete this paragraph.

Opinion was far from (1) _____ about what step the American colonists should next take in their conflict with England. Many (2) _____ agreed with Adams that a permanent break must be made. King George III, Adams and others claimed, was a (3) _____ who no longer deserved to rule the colonies. Adams finally resolved to seek a "declaration" of independence and (4) _____ Thomas Jefferson to write it.

B. Word Origins
For each vocabulary word listed below, think of another word that is related to that word in some way. Then, write a sentence for your new word. A dictionary will help you.

1. nominated *(page 46)* _____

_____

2. patriots *(page 47)* _____

_____

3. unanimous *(page 49)* _____

_____

4. tyrant *(page 50)* _____

_____

John Adams: The Forgotten Man; Do the Right Thing: A Simple Plan ■ *Interactive Reading*, page 46

Reading Standard 3.3 Compare and contrast motivations and reactions of literary characters from different historical eras.

Academic Vocabulary	
characterization	ways in which a writer reveals a character's personality
motivation	character's reasons for doing something

A. Circle the letter of the correct response to each item below.

1. Which of the following phrases is *not* part of the essay's **characterization** of John Adams?
   - **A** "He was short and pudgy and mostly bald."
   - **B** "He was a daydreamer, a prankster, a school-skipper."
   - **C** "John's cousin Samuel Adams called the incident the 'Boston Massacre.'"
   - **D** "Whatever flaws Adams had, no one who knew him ever doubted his honesty."

2. According to the essay, Adams acted as he did out of—
   - **F** love for his country
   - **G** interest in politics
   - **H** desire for peace
   - **J** pursuit of fame

3. Which statement *best* describes the **motivations** of John Adams and Ana, one of the girls at Rosemont High?
   - **A** Both believed in the importance of action.
   - **B** Both were suspicious of the rule of law.
   - **C** Both needed to be persuaded before joining a struggle.
   - **D** Both acted in solitary.

B. Write a paragraph for Ana's petition that explains her motivation.

_____

_____

_____

New Directions; Field Work
Interactive Reading, page 63

Reading Standard 1.2 Understand the most important points in the history of the English language, and use common word origins to determine the historical influences on English word meanings.

Vocabulary Development

domestic, *noun*	household servant
provisions, *noun*	stock of food and other supplies
ominous, *adjective*	of or serving as an omen; threatening; sinister
despondent, *adjective*	sad; dejected
stamina, *noun*	endurance; resistance to fatigue and illness
insidious, *adjective*	steadily treacherous; spreading slowly but with dangerous effects

A. Words in Context
Use the words above to complete this paragraph. Use each word only once.

The weary travelers knew they must keep from becoming (1) _____ over the (2) _____ weather and the lack of food. They had to keep going even after their (3) _____ had run out and they had only snow to eat. They needed to keep up their (4) _____ and the will to move onward. One woman, who had worked as a (5) _____, found some berries and made soup from boiled snow. It was better than nothing. No matter what happened, the travelers had to fight off the (6) _____ desire to lie down and sleep, aware that if they gave in, they would die.

B. Word-Origins Puzzle
Use a dictionary to solve these word-origin puzzlers. Write the vocabulary word whose origin is described in each puzzle.

1. I come from a Latin word with the prefix *in-* and the root *sedere.* I mean "treacherous." _____

2. My word contains the Latin prefix *de-,* meaning "away from," and the verb *sperare,* meaning "to hope." _____

3. My word comes from the Latin word *providere,* meaning "to look ahead" or "to provide for." _____

4. My root word is *domus,* which is Latin for "house." The word *domesticus* means "of the home" or "of the family." _____

New Directions; Field Work ■ *Interactive Reading, page 63*

Reading Standard 3.3 Compare and contrast motivations and reactions of literary characters from different historical eras who confront similar situations or conflicts.

Academic Vocabulary

motivation	reasons a character behaves in a certain way
inference	educated guess made on the basis of evidence
conflict	struggle between opposing characters or opposing forces

A. Circle the letter of the correct response to each item below.

1. Which is *not* one of the **motivations** that led to Mrs. Annie Johnson's business decision?

   A She wanted a career.

   B Her husband left her with two children to support.

   C She had very little money of her own.

   D She didn't want to work as a domestic.

2. Why does the narrator of "Field Work" need to make money?

   F to pay off a debt

   G to take a vacation

   H to buy a dress

   J to buy food

3. How does the narrator of "Field Work" plan to solve her **conflict**?

   A She protests against the harvest.

   B She opens a fruit stand.

   C She offers to help with the harvest.

   D She empties her savings account.

B. Suppose that Mrs. Johnson's story is taking place today. How might it be different? How might it be similar?

_____

_____

_____

_____

_____

Name _____ Class _____ Date _____

You Took the Words Right Out of My Mouth . . .

■ *Interactive Reading,* page 74

Reading Standard 1.2 Understand the most important points in the history of the English language, and use common word origins to determine the historical influences on English word meanings.

Vocabulary Development

prosperity, *noun*	good fortune; success
debatable, *adjective*	having strong points on both sides; worthy of debate
simulating, *adjective*	taking on the external appearance of something
inconsequential, *adjective*	unimportant; trivial
partisans, *noun*	persons who are unreasonably devoted to something

---

A. Words in Context
Use the words above to complete this paragraph. Use each word only once.

The good times and general (1) _____ in our nation today have renewed people's interest in food. Many ethnic foods have their (2) _____, who declare their favorite to be the tastiest food on earth. Which food is the tastiest, of course, is (3) _____ and arguing about it is a minor, (4) _____ pursuit. Yet, in a way, this interest in ethnic foods shows that many Americans *do* have good taste and are not simply (5) _____ the attitudes of gourmets.

B. Word Origins
Write the vocabulary word that matches a description of its parts.

1. A root meaning "favorable" or "successful" and a suffix meaning "the condition of being" _____

2. A root meaning "copy or imitate" _____

3. A root meaning "firm believer in a faction or cause" _____

4. A prefix meaning "not," a root meaning "follow along, to be important," and a suffix meaning "relating to" _____

5. A root meaning "fight using words" and a suffix meaning "capable of" _____

You Took the Words Right Out of My Mouth . . . ■ *Interactive Reading,* page 74

Reading Standard 2.3 Find similarities and differences between texts in the treatment, scope, or organization of ideas.

Academic Vocabulary

allusion	reference to a statement, a person, a place, or an event in history or current events
idiom	expression peculiar to a particular language that means something different from what it literally says

---

A. Circle the letter of the correct response to each item below.

1. Which **idiom** might you use to describe something not important?
   - **A** a chicken in every pot
   - **B** full of beans
   - **C** humble pie
   - **D** small beer

2. Which **idiom** might you use to describe something that is very simple to do?
   - **F** small beer
   - **G** feeling one's oats
   - **H** sour grapes
   - **J** easy as pie

3. Having a "chicken in every pot" means—
   - **A** being too full
   - **B** having food for everyone
   - **C** being overly busy
   - **D** having too much curiosity

4. Which word is an **allusion** to an old-time comic strip character?
   - **F** milquetoast
   - **G** tripe
   - **H** rhubarb
   - **J** feisty

5. To whom does the expression *sour grapes* apply?
   - **A** sloppy eaters
   - **B** sore losers
   - **C** good sports
   - **D** bad cheaters

B. Would the ideas in this column be presented more effectively if the column were organized differently? Explain.

_____

_____

_____

Prometheus Steals Fire from Heaven; Paul's Popcorn

■ *Interactive Reading,* page 79

Reading Standard 1.2 Understand the most important points in the history of the English language, and use common word origins to determine the historical influences on English word meanings.

Vocabulary Development

forethought, *noun*	planning beforehand
cunning, *noun*	skill in deception; slyness
quick-witted, *adjective*	nimble of mind; alert
irrigated, *verb*	supplied (land) with water by means of ditches or sprinklers
considerable, *adjective*	much or large
resources, *noun*	something that a country or state has and can use to its advantage

A. Words in Context

Use the words above to complete this paragraph. Use each word only once.

Prometheus, whose name means (1) _____, gave man the gift of fire. But Zeus was jealous of man's likeness to the gods, and used his (2) _____ to shape the first woman, Pandora. Because of her (3) _____ beauty and her great curiosity, Pandora would be a disaster. While ordinary humans (4) _____ the land and cared for the crops and other (5) _____, Epimetheus took Pandora for his wife. Although (6) _____ in some ways, Epimetheus and Pandora were very foolish.

B. Word Origins

Write the vocabulary word that best fits each clue below. Use a dictionary if you need help. You may also refer to the selection sidenotes.

1. I come from the Middle English *cunnen,* meaning "to know."

_____

2. I come from the Old English word *thoht,* meaning "thought."

_____

3. I come from the Old French verb *resourdre,* meaning "to relieve."

_____

Prometheus Steals Fire from Heaven; Paul's Popcorn

Comprehension Check

■ *Interactive Reading,* page 79

Reading Standard 3.3 Compare and contrast motivations and reactions of literary characters from different historical eras who confront similar situations or conflicts.

> ### Academic Vocabulary
>
> **character** person or animal in a story
> **motivation** reasons for a character's behavior

A. Circle the letter of the correct response to each item below.

1. Prometheus's **motivation** for giving humankind fire is—
   A to make them stronger than the gods
   B to make them superior to the animals
   C to get them in trouble with Zeus
   D to please his brother Epimetheus

2. The **character** Paul Bunyan can best be described as—
   F easygoing and confident   **H** foolish and curious
   G aggressive and cruel   **J** weak and cautious

3. Zeus's **motivation** in creating Pandora was to—
   A give the Titans a present to make up for overthrowing them
   B thank Prometheus for giving fire to human beings
   C make human beings equal to the gods
   D prevent human beings from rivaling the gods

B. Think of someone you would describe as a modern-day Prometheus or Paul Bunyan. Write a paragraph describing this person and explaining why the comparison fits.

_____

_____

_____

_____

_____

Being There: Setting

CHAPTER OBJECTIVES

Students will—

- Develop confidence and skills through reading the Practice Read.

- Use the "Sketch to Stretch" strategy to understand a story's setting.

- Clarify word meanings using appropriate context.

- Identify text structures of popular media.

- Build fluency.

Reading Standard 1.3
Use word meanings within the appropriate context, and show ability to verify those meanings by definition, restatement, example, comparison, or contrast.

Reading Standard 2.1 (Grade 6 Review)
Identify the structural features of popular media (e.g., newspapers, magazines, online information), and use the features to obtain information.

Reading Standard 3.4
Analyze the relevance of the setting (e.g., place, time, customs) to the mood, tone, and meaning of the text.

Start with the Strategy and Practice Read

(*Interactive Reading*, pages 89–96)

About the Strategy: "Sketch to Stretch"

Many students are better able to express things visually than in writing, especially when it involves describing a story's setting. Not only does "Sketch to Stretch" address the needs of these students, but it coaxes them into verbalizations by requiring them to explain their sketches orally and in writing. This is the "Stretch" part of the strategy, the most important part pedagogically. Of course, because getting students to draw pictures is not the goal, think of the sketch as an icebreaker that will eventually lead students to arrive at informed, thoughtful conclusions about what they read.

Introduce the Strategy

Explain to students that "Sketch to Stretch" will help them think about what a selection means to them. To use the strategy, students—

- Make a sketch that represents their interpretation of the setting of a scene from the story or the story as a whole.

- Review their sketch or sketches and ask themselves what the story is saying or how it makes them feel.

Model the Strategy

- To model the strategy, have students recall the story of Pinocchio, the puppet who eventually becomes a real boy.

- Tell students that you will show them a "Sketch to Stretch" picture that an eighth-grader drew to interpret the story. Note: This "Sketch to Stretch" does not involve a setting. It is used as an example.

- Place Transparency 3 on an overhead projector with the explanation of the drawing covered. Have students interpret the sketch and, afterward, reveal the explanation. Point out that the heart and the ice cream cone symbolize the forces of good and evil, which are both at work in the story.

- Discuss the sketch and explanation with students. Have them evaluate how effectively the sketch conveys the meaning of the story.

Apply the Strategy with the Practice Read

- Have students read the Strategy Launch on *Interactive Reading* page 89 and discuss their questions. Then, have them read "Lost and Found" beginning on *Interactive Reading* page 90. Remind students to use the comments and questions in the side column to guide their reading.

- After reading, have students turn to the graphic organizer on page 96 and use it to make "Sketch to Stretch" drawings for the story. Remind students not to draw literal pictures of the story's setting.

Assess

- Have students study one another's sketches and discuss what their elements represent. Discuss how well they feel they understand the sketching approach to interpreting stories.

- Encourage students to go back to the story and mark it up with their questions and comments.

- Finally, evaluate students' mastery of "Lost and Found" by using the Vocabulary Check and Comprehension Check on Teacher's Edition pages 36 and 37.

TEACHER TO TEACHER

Some students may agonize over what to draw. You may want to set a time limit for drawing, to steer students away from over-analyzing the story or its setting.

TEACHING RESOURCES

Graphic Organizers, Teacher's Edition, Section Three

Some students may produce only representational sketches because they have trouble thinking symbolically. Others may do so because it is easier. You may need to keep emphasizing the difference between illustrating a story and using images to suggest its meaning. Students who have difficulty with the strategy may benefit from working with partners who have a clearer understanding.

Support the Selections in *Holt Literature and Language Arts*

(Chapter 3, pages 150–207)

Apply the Strategy to Literary Texts

- Before students begin each literary selection, remind them that they will be using the "Sketch to Stretch" strategy to interpret it.
- As students read each selection, have them complete the corresponding graphic organizer in *Interactive Reading*.

Focus on Informational Texts

- After students read each informational selection, have them complete the corresponding graphic organizer in *Interactive Reading*.

Assess

- Use the graphic organizers in *Interactive Reading* as an alternative assessment.
- After students read each literary selection, you may wish to photocopy the "Sketch to Stretch" graphic organizer in Section Three of the Teacher's Edition. Have students form small groups to make and discuss "Sketch to Stretch" drawings. When the groups have done this, have them display all the participants' drawings together. Invite them to discuss how well, as a group, they have learned to convey story ideas symbolically.

Selections in *Holt Literature and Language Arts*	Graphic Organizers in *Interactive Reading*
In Trouble, p. 153	"Follow the Setting" Chart, p. 97
Fast, Strong, and Friendly Too, p. 163	"It Makes a Difference" Chart, p. 98
There Will Come Soft Rains, p. 168	"What's *Really* Going On?" Chart, p. 99
Destination: Mars, p. 178	Matching Chart, p. 100
The Circuit, p. 183	"Thought Bubbles" Frames, p. 101
Cesar Chavez: He Made a Difference, p. 192	What If? Chart, p. 102
Picking Strawberries: Could You Do It? p. 197	Conclusions Chart, p. 103

Build Independence Through Interactive Selections

(*Interactive Reading*, pages 104–135)

The Fog Horn

Ray Bradbury ▪ page 105

INTRODUCE

- Tell students that this is another Ray Bradbury story. This one has a topic different from the one in "There Will Come Soft Rain," but the stories share some of the same feelings.
- Guide the class through the Author Study and Before You Read notes. Ask students, "What might answer the sound of a fog horn?" Discuss student suggestions, and then have them read the story to learn the answer.

MODEL

- Tell students they will be using the "Sketch to Stretch" strategy in reading this story.
- Have students read the first paragraph, and then direct them to the first side-column note. Model a response to the note by having students underline the phrases "cold water" and "far from land." Ask volunteers to suggest other phrases and words in the paragraph that contribute to the story's mood.

TEACH

- Have students continue reading the story, noting their responses to the sidenotes in their books.
- Tell students they may make quick sketches as they read. Alternatively, they can wait until they've completed the selection, when they will use the graphic organizer to sketch.
- Have students add the story to their Personal Reading Logs.

ASSESS AND EXTEND

- Photocopy and have students complete the "Sketch to Stretch" graphic organizer in Section Three of the Teacher's Edition. Have students work in small groups to share and discuss their "Sketch to Stretch" drawings for "The Fog Horn." As an informal assessment, direct each group to submit a single drawing that they think captures the meaning of the story.
- Use the Vocabulary Check and Comprehension Check on pages 38 and 39 in the Teacher's Edition to check students' mastery of the standards.
- Assign the Author Profile project as an extension activity.

DIFFERENTIATING INSTRUCTION
The Fog Horn

- **Learners Having Difficulty** Have students read "The Fog Horn" with dictionaries at their sides to look up unfamiliar words. Because the story uses colorful words, phrases, and metaphors, students may have to read some passages more than once.

- **Benchmark Students** Have students pay attention to the way in which mood and tone are conveyed in the story. Suggest that students jot down words, phrases, sentences, and literary devices (such as metaphors) that they feel convey the story's mood and tone.

- **Advanced Students** McDunn made up a one-paragraph story "to try to explain why this thing [the sea animal] keeps coming back to the lighthouse every year." Have advanced students write their own one-paragraph stories that could replace McDunn's.

TEACHER TO TEACHER
Setting is such a powerful force in "The Fog Horn" that you might want to have students create two distinct drawings of the story: one an atmospheric illustration of the setting and the other a symbolic drawing expressing its meaning.

- **Learners Having Difficulty**
Review some facts necessary
for understanding the article.
For example, make sure students know where the sightings take place by having
them find Scotland on a world
map. Be sure they understand
time references such as *first
century* A.D.

- **Benchmark Students** Have
these students preview the
article and its subheadings.
Encourage them to use the
sidenotes as a reading guide.

- **Advanced Students**
Advanced students will have
no problems reading this article. You may want these students to learn more about this
topic by visiting the Web site
this text comes from:
http://www.pbs.org/wgbh/
nova/lochness/legend.html.

Birth of a Legend
Stephen Lyons • page 118

INTRODUCE

- Read the Before You Read note to the class. Have students discuss
what they know about the Loch Ness monster and other such
phenomena.

- Preview the text structure of the article with students, pointing out
the photos, captions, subheadings, extended quotations, and the
various features of a Web site. Ask volunteers how they access
information online.

MODEL

- Have students turn to the first page of the article. Draw their attention to the opening quote. Have students read and circle it. Suggest
to students that a clever opening quotation is a common feature of
popular articles such as this. The quotation serves to grab the readers' attention and make them want to read on.

- With students, go through the photos in the article. Have students
rate them from 1 to 4 on their level of interest and degree of usefulness, with 1 as the highest and 4 as the lowest. Ask the class what
other photos they might want to see in an article like this one.

TEACH

- Direct students to read the rest of the selection independently.

- Afterward, have students form small groups to revisit the article
and brainstorm conclusions based on the information it presents
along with their own prior knowledge. Then, have each group
examine its conclusions by searching in the text for evidence and
deciding which conclusions are valid.

ASSESS AND EXTEND

- Use the Vocabulary Check and Comprehension Check on Teacher's
Edition pages 40 and 41 to evaluate students' mastery of the
standards for this selection.

- Assign the Time Line project as an extension activity.

Greyling

Jane Yolen ▪ page 128

INTRODUCE

- Tell students that they will read a fantasy story with a seacoast setting. Ask volunteers to tell of other stories with that setting, and have them recall the mood of the setting.

MODEL

- Point out the Visualize note on page 128, and lead students to recognize details that reveal the story's setting.
- Help students understand that the couple's desire for a child may propel events in this story.

TEACH

- Have students read the story independently, responding to the side-column questions and comments. When they have completed the reading, have them respond to the tale's setting and mood.
- Invite volunteers to read the Fluency passage aloud, interpreting its emotion with a tone, pace, and modulation of voice that captures its meaning.
- Encourage students to add this story to their Personal Reading Logs.

ASSESS AND EXTEND

- Photocopy and have students complete the "Sketch to Stretch" graphic organizer in Section Three of the Teacher's Edition.
- As an informal assessment, encourage students to display and explain their sketches. You may also want the "audience" to evaluate how well these students have captured the essence of the story.
- Use the Vocabulary Check and Comprehension Check on pages 42 and 43 of the Teacher's Edition to evaluate students' mastery of the standards.
- Assign the Retelling Chart project as an extension activity.

DIFFERENTIATING INSTRUCTION
Greyling ↓

- **Learners Having Difficulty** This story is a simple one that should pose few difficulties for these students. Encourage them to read the story independently, using the sidenotes as a guide.

- **Benchmark Students** These students will probably encounter no problems with the story's plot or its vocabulary. To help students recognize how well the writer has brought to life the story's characters and setting, allow class time for student volunteers to read aloud portions of the story.

- **Advanced Students** Although this story has a simple plot, it can be read on many levels. You may want to have these students read the story through once for basic comprehension, then again to appreciate its themes and poetic uses of language.

TEACHER TO TEACHER

Students may produce their best results if they use "Sketch to Stretch" as a postreading strategy.

Lost and Found

■ *Interactive Reading,* page 90

Reading Standard 1.3 Use word meanings within the appropriate context, and show ability to verify those meanings by definition, restatement, example, comparison, or contrast.

Vocabulary Development

catapulted, *verb*	shot or launched from
distressed, *adjective*	troubled; anxious
ascended, *verb*	moved upward; climbed

A. Words in Context
Use the words above to complete this paragraph. Use each word only once.

Sander7 was amazed when the wallet (1) _____ toward him from above; had it hit him on the head, he might have thought he was dreaming. Sander7 opened the wallet, finding the owner's contact number. "Should I dial it?" he asked himself, but he already knew what he should do. Sander7 reached the owner easily and arranged to meet him and return the wallet. The owner was Christo4, and Sander7 wondered why he looked more (2) _____ than happy or grateful. But as they (3) _____ a set of moving stairs to the place where Christo4 worked, Sander7 sensed that he was on the verge of learning a strange new secret.

B. Sentence Composition
Use each vocabulary word in a sentence. Include context clues that would allow a reader to guess the word's meaning. Underline your context clues.

1. **catapulted:** _____

   _____

2. **distressed:** _____

   _____

3. **ascended:** _____

   _____

Lost and Found

■ *Interactive Reading,* page 90

Reading Standard 3.4 Analyze the relevance of the setting (for example, place, time, customs) to the mood, tone, and meaning of the text.

Academic Vocabulary

setting	time and place of a story, play, or narrative poem
mood	overall feeling of a work of literature
character	person or animal in a story, a play, or another literary work
sensory details	words that appeal to the senses

A. Circle the letter of the correct response to each item below.

1. This story is told from the point of view of which **character**?
   - **A** Christo4
   - **B** an unnamed character
   - **C** Sander7's father
   - **D** Sander7

2. This story takes place—
   - **F** in a big city
   - **G** on a space ship
   - **H** on Mars
   - **J** on Earth

3. The **mood** of the story might be described as—
   - **A** mysterious
   - **B** amusing
   - **C** horrifying
   - **D** romantic

B. Why is setting so important to this story? Explain your answer in a paragraph.

_____

_____

_____

_____

_____

_____

_____

_____

_____

The Fog Horn

■ *Interactive Reading,* page 105

Reading Standard 1.3 Use word meanings within the appropriate context, and show ability to verify those meanings by definitions, restatement, example, comparison, or contrast.

Vocabulary Development

verify, *verb*	confirm; prove to be true
immense, *adjective*	extremely large; vast; huge
subterranean, *adjective*	beneath the earth's surface; underground
primeval, *adjective*	of the earliest times and ages; ancient
abruptly, *adverb*	suddenly; unexpectedly

A. Words in Context
Use the words above to complete this paragraph. Use each word only once.

It rose from its lonely (1) _____ home, where it had lived for millions of years, an (2) _____ creature, larger than a house, with a sharp head on its long, arching neck. What ancient (3) _____ world had it come up from to enter ours, so technological, so arrogant, and so utterly unprepared for its rising? We waited, unmoving, until it saw us and (4) _____ descended again into the sea. Why did it leave so suddenly? Or better, why did it arrive? Perhaps it came only to (5) _____ that it was still the strongest, largest, and most amazing creature in the universe.

B. Restatement
Complete each statement with the appropriate vocabulary word.

1. If I must validate or confirm something, I must _____ it.

2. If a creature or a site is prehistoric, we might call it _____.

3. If something is really huge, it is _____.

4. If someone lives in a cave or in an underground grotto, we might describe the home as _____.

5. If you end a conversation hastily or without warning, you have ended it _____.

The Fog Horn

■ *Interactive Reading,* page 105

Reading Standard 3.4 Analyze the relevance of the setting to the mood, tone, and meaning of the text.

> ### Academic Vocabulary
>
> **setting** time and place of a story, play, or narrative poem
> **mood** overall feeling of a work of literature
> **theme** truth about life revealed in a work of literature

A. Circle the letter of the correct answer for each item below.

1. What is the **setting** of this story?
   A a lighthouse that is built at sea C a boat on the sea
   B a coastal town D a whaling village

2. The **mood** of the story can be best described as—
   F mysterious H playful
   G romantic J comic

3. Which of the following passages *best* conveys the **theme** of the story?
   A "Yes. It's an old world."
   B The Fog Horn was blowing steadily, once every fifteen seconds.
   C "That's life for you," said McDunn. "Someone always waiting for someone who never comes home."
   D It was as silent as the fog through which it swam.

B. How is the fog horn a character in this story? Explain.

_____

_____

_____

_____

_____

_____

_____

_____

Birth of a Legend

■ *Interactive Reading,* page 118

Reading Standard 1.3 Use word meanings within the appropriate context, and show ability to verify those meanings by definitions, restatement, example, comparison, or contrast.

Vocabulary Development

complied, *verb*	agreed; went along with
submerged, *verb*	plunged into water; sank
nonchalant, *adjective*	matter-of-fact; showing no concern or worry

---

A. Words in Context

Use the words above to complete this paragraph. Use each word only once.

We had no choice in the matter—we simply (1) _____ with the captain's orders. Even in our cabins, though, we could see what looked like the head of a giant lizard. We caught only a glimpse of this strange creature before it (2) _____ itself again. I looked around to see if the other passengers were nervous, but they appeared (3) _____. As a result, I, too, made an effort to look unconcerned.

B. Context Clues: Antonyms

Complete each item with the most appropriate word from the list above.

1. Joe was extremely worried, but I was _____ about the flu epidemic.

2. I was relieved to see Russell standing up in the water next to me; his head had been _____ for a mere moment.

3. Rather than risk getting in trouble, I _____ with the rules posted at the campsite.

Birth of a Legend

■ *Interactive Reading,* page 118

Reading Standard 2.1 (Grade 6 Review) Identify the structural features of popular media (for example, newspapers, magazines, online information), and use the features to obtain information.

Academic Vocabulary

caption	brief text that explains the contents of a picture
link	item or segment of text or graphics in an electronic document that connects to another Web site

A. Circle the letter of the best response to each item below.

1. You can use the **captions** in this article to learn—
    - **A** more about the scenes in the photographs
    - **B** which newspaper first ran an article about the Loch Ness monster
    - **C** how Loch Ness has changed over the years
    - **D** who claims to have seen "Nessie"

2. This article was originally published on the World Wide Web. Which **link** would you probably *not* find in the online version?
    - **F** sea creatures in mythology
    - **G** UFO sightings
    - **H** French folklore
    - **J** undersea life

3. The interview in this article takes place between—
    - **A** Moffat and Lyons
    - **B** Nova and White
    - **C** Campbell and White
    - **D** Mackintosh and Nova

B. Which structural features did you find most useful in "Birth of a Legend"? Explain.

_____

_____

_____

_____

_____

_____

Greyling

■ *Interactive Reading,* page 128

Reading Standard 1.3 Use word meanings within the appropriate context, and show ability to verify those meanings by definition, restatement, example, comparison, or contrast.

Vocabulary Development

kin, *noun*	relatives
roiling, *adjective*	stirred up; agitated
slough, *verb*	shed; get rid of
wallowed, *verb*	rolled about, as in mud or water

A. Words in Context
Use the words above to complete this paragraph. Use each word only once.

When the storm came, the penguins gathered all their (1) _____,
jumped down from the high rocks, and hid in the shelter of the overhang. The sea,
tossing and swelling, was (2) _____ from the violence of the wind. One
lone penguin still (3) _____ unsteadily in the water, unable to decide
where to go. Suddenly, a huge chunk of rock splashed into the bay. It just missed the
penguin. To anyone watching, it might seem as if the land had wanted to
(4) _____ off its loose parts.

B. Examples
Respond to each statement below by giving examples.

1. Name some of your **kin.**

_____

2. Name something that can be **roiling** that is *not* the sea.

_____

3. State something that an animal or a person might wish to
slough off.

_____

4. Name an animal that has **wallowed** in the mud.

_____

Greyling

■ *Interactive Reading,* page 128

Reading Standard 3.4 Analyze the relevance of the setting
to the mood, tone, and meaning of the text.

Academic Vocabulary

setting	time and place of a story, play, or narrative poem
mood	overall feeling of a work of literature
theme	truth about life expressed in a story

A. Circle the letter of the correct response to each item below.

1. The **setting** in which this story mostly occurs is best described as—
   A a hut   C the past
   B the seaside   D the imagination

2. If you visualize the **setting** of "Greyling," you will probably *not* see—
   F mountains   H gray cliffs
   G small huts   J the ocean

3. The **mood** at the beginning of this story is best described as—
   A calm and peaceful   C sad and lonely
   B dark and menacing   D sweet and nostalgic

4. Which line from the text best expresses the **theme** of "Greyling"?
   F "They searched up the beach and down, but they did not find the boy."
   G "His nets were full but his heart was empty, yet he never told his wife."
   H "Though my heart grieves at his leaving, it tells me this way is best."
   J "The fisherman's wife ran out of the hut, fear riding in her heart."

B. Imagine that you are Greyling. One year after you returned to the sea, you visit
your parents on land. What do you tell them?

_____

_____

_____

_____

_____

CHAPTER OBJECTIVES

Students will—

- Develop confidence and skills through reading the Practice Read.

- Use the "Save the Last Word for Me" strategy to identify and analyze theme.

- Identify main ideas, and connect them to other sources and related topics.

- Use word meanings in appropriate contexts.

- Verify word meanings through a variety of methods.

- Build fluency.

Reading Standard 1.3
Use word meanings within the appropriate context, and show ability to verify those meanings by definition, restatement, example, comparison, or contrast.

**Reading Standard 2.3
(Grade 6 Review)**
Connect and clarify main ideas by identifying their relationships to other sources and related topics.

Reading Standard 3.5
Identify and analyze recurring themes (e.g., good versus evil) across traditional and contemporary works.

We Still Believe

Start with the Strategy and Practice Read

(Interactive Reading, pages 137–148)

About the Strategy: "Save the Last Word for Me"

To help students identify the theme of a selection and to make sure the theme they identify is supported by the text, use the "Save the Last Word for Me" strategy. Use of this strategy not only helps students think about the theme, but also helps them develop confidence in their own judgments and conclusions.

Introduce the Strategy

Tell students they're going to learn to use a strategy called "Save the Last Word for Me." To use this strategy, students—

- Mark passages they find interesting or important as they read the text.

- Identify the most important passage and write it down.

- Write down why they chose that passage, listing at least two reasons for their choice.

- Read the passage, but *not* their reasons, to a small group.

- Listen to group members' responses to the passage.

- Read aloud their "last words," or reasons for their choice of passage.

Model the Strategy

- Place Transparency 4 on the overhead projector, and read the story aloud.

- Point out the boxed passage, and tell students that this might be the most important passage in the story.

- Then, point out the two reasons for choosing the passage, reading them aloud in turn.

- Discuss those reasons with the class. If a student offers a valid critique or a better reason for choosing the passage, accept his or her comments. Tell students that you now have arrived at the "last words" on why you feel this passage is important.

Apply the Strategy with the Practice Read

- Have students read the Strategy Launch on *Interactive Reading* page 137. Discuss any questions students may have.
- Then, have students read "The Wise Old Woman" and "Legacy II," beginning on *Interactive Reading* page 138. Tell students to use the comments and questions in the side column to guide their reading.
- Tell students to pay special attention to the "Save the Last Word for Me" notes that conclude each selection.
- Have students use their responses to the strategy sidenotes to complete "Save the Last Word for Me" cards on *Interactive Reading* page 148.

Assess

- Have students get together in groups and discuss their completed "Save the Last Word for Me" cards.
- Encourage students to go back to the selections and mark any questions and comments they may have.
- Evaluate students' mastery of "The Wise Old Woman" and "Legacy II" by using the Vocabulary Check on Teacher's Edition page 50 and the Comprehension Check on Teacher's Edition page 51.

TEACHER TO TEACHER

"Save the Last Word for Me" is essentially a postreading strategy, which makes it a good prewriting strategy, too. Encourage students to use their written responses as starting points for critical or responsive essays that you assign. You can easily narrow the focus to specific literary elements if you wish. Just mention the relevant literary element in your prompt for using the strategy. For example, instead of, "Pick your favorite passage," you might say, "Pick a passage that you think really shows the story's theme (or characterization or plot, and so on)."

TEACHING RESOURCES

Graphic Organizers, Teacher's Edition, Section Three

TEACHER TO TEACHER

Students' "Save the Last Word for Me" responses may stir them to want to keep discussing a work. However, if they keep discussing it, the written response is by definition no longer the last word! Create a psychological boundary between the reading of a "last word" card and further discussion. For example, take a break or turn to a different responder's card before returning to a freer discussion as a wrap-up.

Support the Selections in
Holt Literature and Language Arts

(Chapter 4, pages 210–347)

Apply the Strategy to Literary Texts

- Before students begin to read each literary selection, encourage them to use the "Save the Last Word for Me" strategy. Tell them that this strategy will help them focus on the theme.
- After students read each literary selection, have them complete the corresponding graphic organizer in *Interactive Reading*.

Focus on Informational Texts

- After students read each informational selection, have them complete the corresponding graphic organizer in *Interactive Reading*.

Assess

- Use the graphic organizers in *Interactive Reading* as an alternative assessment.
- You may want to photocopy and distribute the "Save the Last Word for Me" Cards that appear in Section Three of the Teacher's Edition. Have students discuss their completed charts.

Selections in *Holt Literature and Language Arts*	Graphic Organizers in *Interactive Reading*
The Diary of Anne Frank, p. 217	Theme Chart, p. 149
from The Diary of a Young Girl, p. 287	Words/Thoughts/Actions Chart, p. 150
Anne and Margot Frank, p. 291	Main-Idea Chart, p. 151
A Tragedy Revealed: A Heroine's Last Days, p. 295	"Main Idea and Examples" Chart, p. 152
Walking with Living Feet, p. 313	Details Organizer, p. 153
Camp Harmony; In Response to Executive Order 9066, p. 319	Side-by-Side Chart, p. 154
The Gettysburg Address, p. 330	Repetition Chart, p. 155
from I Have a Dream, p. 333	Allusion Listing, p. 156
from The Power of Nonviolence, p. 339	Main-Idea Note Cards, p. 157

Build Independence Through Interactive Selections

(*Interactive Reading*, pages 158–187)

Out of the Ghetto

Gerda Weissmann Klein • page 159

INTRODUCE

- Have students read the Author Study and Before You Read notes. Ask students to identify any other literary works about World War II and the Holocaust with which they are familiar.

MODEL

- Have students read the beginning of the selection, up until the "Save the Last Word for Me" side-column note. Ask a volunteer to read the note aloud.

- Remind students that an important part of the reading strategy is to note passages they find especially important or interesting. Later, they will review the passages they marked and use them as they think about the theme of the selection as a whole. Ask students to talk about which passages in this beginning section strike them as important or especially interesting.

TEACH

- Have students continue reading the selection independently or in small groups, reading aloud. Remind them to note their responses to the side-column notes in their books.

- After students have finished reading, divide the class into small groups. Have students discuss the passages they marked as part of the "Save the Last Word for Me" strategy.

- Have students add the title of this memoir to their Personal Reading Logs.

ASSESS AND EXTEND

- Photocopy the "Save the Last Word for Me" Cards in Section Three of the Teacher's Edition. Have students complete the cards; then, discuss their completed cards with a partner.

- Use the Vocabulary Check on Teacher's Edition page 52 to evaluate mastery of the vocabulary standard.

- Use the Comprehension Check on Teacher's Edition page 53 to evaluate mastery of the literary standard.

- To extend students' reading, have them complete the Museum Brochure project on *Interactive Reading* page 168.

DIFFERENTIATING INSTRUCTION
Out of the Ghetto

- **Learners Having Difficulty** There are at least two elements of "Out of the Ghetto" on which students might focus. One is the emotionally intense atmosphere of the story. Another is the story's theme. You might ask students, before they read, to keep these elements in mind.

- **Benchmark Students** One theme of this story is the question of how or why people can do terrible things to other people. Ask students to react, in a short essay, to the paragraph that begins "I know why." Do they share the viewpoint expressed in this paragraph?

- **Advanced Students** Have students gather in groups of three. Ask them to discuss what part or parts of the story made the strongest impression on them. They may focus on the emotional impact of the story, or they may discuss the theme of the story.

TEACHER TO TEACHER

In a narrative as stark and chilling as this, it would be hard to pick a passage that *didn't* work well with "Save the Last Word for Me." If students, after responding to one passage, still seem to need more practice with the strategy, try suggesting one or more of your own favorite passages to them to work with.

READING OPTION

Dramatization and dramatic reading are natural possibilities for "Out of the Ghetto" as for so many of the other selections in this chapter.

- **Learners Having Difficulty**
  Before students read, review with them the format of "An Anne Frank Scrapbook." Discuss the style of presentation of each part.

- **Benchmark Students** Review with students the various devices used in the selection to convey thoughts and feelings. Discuss whether these devices add to or take away from the subject matter.

- **Advanced Students** Have advanced students verify the information in this scrapbook by referring to other sources.

TEACHER TO TEACHER

Photographs from the Holocaust are often disturbing because of their gruesomeness. The ones in this selection are, for the most part, disturbing because of their normality. Lead students to focus their attention on even the most ordinary-seeming photos and to bear in mind the fates of the people in the photos. There's an underlying dramatic irony throughout: The Franks had no idea what was about to happen to them.

An Anne Frank Scrapbook

- page 169

INTRODUCE

- Tell students that they are going to look at photographs and read accompanying text of Anne Frank's life, beginning with a baby picture. Encourage students to predict the photo subjects that they are likely to see in the collection.

- Inform students that they can find a great deal more information about Anne Frank online at http://www.annefrank.com.

MODEL

- Model the process of viewing the photos and text. Direct students to the first photo, and read the heading, caption, and other text aloud. Ask a volunteer to comment on the effectiveness of such a photograph on our understanding of the tragic end to Anne's life.

TEACH

- Have students continue reading the text independently or aloud. Remind them to note their responses to the side-column notes.

- After students have finished reading, have them discuss their responses in small groups.

- Have students add the title of this selection to their Personal Reading Logs.

ASSESS AND EXTEND

- Have partners write main-idea paragraphs as directed on *Interactive Reading* page 179 to evaluate their understanding.

- Use the Vocabulary Check on Teacher's Edition page 54 to evaluate mastery of the vocabulary standard.

- Use the Comprehension Check on Teacher's Edition page 55 to evaluate mastery of the informational standard.

- To extend students' reading, have them complete the Web Page project on *Interactive Reading* page 180.

A Family in Hiding

Miep Gies with Alison Leslie Gold • page 181

INTRODUCE

- Tell students that they are already familiar with the characters in this selection. Remind them of what they have already read about Anne Frank. Ask volunteers for a brief review of the characters of Miep, Anne, and Anne's parents.

- Have students read the Before You Read note and discuss the possible viewpoint of Miep and her character as seen in previous selections.

MODEL

- Remind students to use the "Save the Last Word for Me" strategy as they read. Tell them that there won't be a side-column note addressing this strategy until they reach the end of the selection. As they read, students should mark passages that strike them as especially important or interesting.

- Have students read the first seven paragraphs and pause at the fourth side-column note. Discuss with students about how silent the Annex had to be by day and what that meant for the Franks' daily existence: having to live knowing that any noise they made would endanger their lives.

TEACH

- Have students continue reading the selection independently or in small groups aloud. Remind them to note their responses to the side-column notes in their books.

- After students have finished reading, divide the class into small groups. Have the groups discuss their responses. Have students especially discuss the passages that they marked as part of the "Save the Last Word for Me" strategy.

- Have students add the title of this selection to their Personal Reading Logs.

ASSESS AND EXTEND

- Photocopy and distribute the "Save the Last Word for Me" Cards in Section Three of the Teacher's Edition. Have students complete the cards and then discuss their completed cards with a partner.

- Use the Vocabulary Check on Teacher's Edition page 56 to evaluate mastery of the vocabulary standard.

- Use the Comprehension Check on Teacher's Edition page 57 to evaluate mastery of the literary standard.

- To extend students' reading, have them complete the Dramatic Scene project on *Interactive Reading* page 187.

DIFFERENTIATING INSTRUCTION
A Family in Hiding

- **Learners Having Difficulty** Students should look up any words with which they are unfamiliar. This story expresses a range of emotions, from happiness to fear. Ask students to pay attention to how the writer conveys these emotions.

- **Benchmark Students** Have a class discussion on the following. Through much of "A Family in Hiding," the Franks and their friends feel the happiness and warmth of socializing. Yet, at the story's end, Miep says the Franks are terrified. Is this possible? Can people really find moments of happiness under such terrifying circumstances? Isn't this a contradiction?

- **Advanced Students** Have students write a short essay in response to the following: Miep writes that the Franks "were in a prison, a prison with locks inside the doors." How can a prison have locks inside the doors? Interpret Miep's statement. How is the Franks' experience like and unlike being in conventional prison?

TEACHER TO TEACHER

Although the whole selection is compelling (and short), some paragraphs leap to mind as particularly suited for "Save the Last Word for Me" treatment. These are passages where narrator Miep reflects inwardly on her surroundings, such as when listening to the radio or to the church bell.

The Wise Old Woman; Legacy II ■ *Interactive Reading,* page 138

Reading Standard 1.3 Use word meanings within the appropriate context, and show ability to verify those meanings by definition, restatement, example, comparison, or contrast.

Vocabulary Development

decree, *verb*	order; rule
clustered, *verb*	gathered in a group
conquer, *verb*	defeat; get control of by winning a conflict
bewilderment, *noun*	state of confusion; puzzlement

A. Words in Context
Use words from the word box to complete the paragraph below.

The cruel young lord decided to (1) _____ that all old people must leave his village. One day a neighboring lord set out to (2) _____ the cruel young lord's village, with all its small houses (3) _____ together. The young lord talked with his advisers, but none could come up with a plan to defeat the enemy. Imagine the young lord's (4) _____ when an old woman came up with a way to defeat the invaders. The young lord soon changed his ways.

B. Find the Clues
Circle the context clues to each boldface word.

1. After the first **invasion** of the village, another attack came from another village across the hill.

2. The war between the villages brought **chaos:** The only order left was military order.

3. Some people think that war is always **immoral:** They think it is wrong to meet even violence with violence.

4. **Conquest** of land—conquering your enemy's territory—is normal in a world ruled by force.

The Wise Old Woman;
Legacy II ■ *Interactive Reading,* page 138

Reading Standard 3.5 Identify and analyze recurring themes (for example, good versus evil) across traditional and contemporary works.

Academic Vocabulary

theme	truth about life that is revealed in a literary work
recurring theme	theme that appears in many works of literature
conflict	struggle between opposing forces or characters in a story

A. Circle the letter of the correct response to each item below.

1. What **conflict** is at the center of the folk tale "The Wise Old Woman"?
   A A cruel lord wants to get rid of all old people in his village.
   B A young man must find his missing grandmother.
   C The old people of a village rebel against a cruel lord.
   D A lord attempts to change his villagers' dependence on farming.

2. Which of the following statements describes both the old woman in the folk tale and the grandfather in the poem "Legacy II"?
   F Both make life difficult for their children and grandchildren.
   G Both may not have formal education but are wise from experience.
   H Both are fleeing from political persecution.
   J Both are experienced in folk wisdom as well as "book" learning.

3. Which of the following is the *best* statement of the **recurring theme** in both the folk tale and the contemporary poem?
   A Trouble can sometimes come at us from all directions.
   B Conflict sometimes cannot be settled peacefully.
   C Education is important for young and old.
   D Wisdom can come from age and experience.

B. Restate the recurring theme in "The Wise Old Woman" and "Legacy II" in your own words. Is the theme important today? Explain your response.

_____

_____

_____

_____

Out of the Ghetto

■ *Interactive Reading,* page 159

Reading Standard 1.3 Use word meanings within the appropriate context, and show ability to verify those meanings by definition, restatement, example, comparison, or contrast.

Vocabulary Development

benediction, *noun*	blessing
desperation, *noun*	state of hopelessness or despair
reluctantly, *adverb*	unwillingly
enclosure, *noun*	closed-in place; area surrounded by a boundary or fence

A. Words in Context
Use words from the word box to complete the paragraph below.

Father raised his arms as if he were giving a (1) _____. He then bent down and embraced me. He began to pull away, and (2) _____ I let go. In my (3) _____, I couldn't help but imagine what was to happen to him. In what kind of (4) _____ would he be held, and would that be the worst of it?

B. Word Analogies
A word analogy is a comparison that follows the pattern, "_____ is to _____ as _____ is to _____." Choose the right word to complete each analogy below.

1. **Benediction** is to blessing as soldier is to _____.
   A priest   **B** peacemaker   **C** warrior   **D** army

2. Hope is to **desperation** as joy is to _____.
   F wealth   **G** happiness   **H** boredom   **J** sorrow

3. **Reluctantly** is to eagerly as wise is to _____.
   A learned   **B** owl   **C** foolish   **D** cunning

4. Open area is to **enclosure** as fire is to _____.
   F flames   **G** ice   **H** heat   **J** furnace

Out of the Ghetto

■ *Interactive Reading*, page 159

Reading Standard 3.5 Identify and analyze recurring themes (for example, good versus evil) across traditional and contemporary works.

Academic Vocabulary

theme	truth about life revealed in a literary work
recurring theme	theme that appears in many works of literature
climax	most exciting or tense moment in a story, when the outcome of the conflict is decided

A. Circle the letter of the correct response to each item below.

1. According to Gerda, why didn't the concentration-camp victims fight back?

   A They didn't have weapons.
   B They had faith in human beings.
   C They were fooled into obeying.
   D They were afraid of the Nazis.

2. At the **climax** of the action, what does Gerda's mother tell her?

   F "You hurt my hand."
   G "Be strong."
   H "Arthur's picture is in it."
   J "Today especially not."

3. Which of the following does *not* state a theme of "Out of the Ghetto"?

   A The main character in this story is Gerda.
   B Life is fragile and precious.
   C It's important to be strong in times of crisis.
   D Sharing experiences is a sign of humanity.

B. Explain how one of the themes of "Out of the Ghetto" is echoed in another literary work or movie.

_____

_____

_____

_____

_____

An Anne Frank Scrapbook

Vocabulary Check

■ *Interactive Reading,* page 169

Reading Standard 1.3 Use word meanings within the appropriate context, and show ability to verify those meanings by definition, restatement, example, comparison, or contrast.

Vocabulary Development

tolerance, *noun*	respect for views different from your own
haven, *noun*	safe place; refuge
in conjunction with	in cooperation with
debilitated, *adjective*	weakened; made feeble

A. Words in Context

Use words from the word box to complete the paragraph below.

In my (1) _____ state, there was nothing I could do but dream of a happier future. I imagined finding a (2) _____ where we could be safe. There we would live with others in a spirit of (3) _____. It would be a place where peace-loving people of all faiths and countries would live (4) _____ one another.

B. Restatement

Rewrite each sentence, restating each boldface word or phrase.

1. In times of trouble, people look for a **haven.**

_____

2. Why is **tolerance** important?

_____

3. The army, **in conjunction with** the marines, fought in World War II.

_____

4. After a long illness, the prisoner became more **debilitated.**

_____

An Anne Frank Scrapbook

■ *Interactive Reading,* page 169

Reading Standard 2.3 Connect and clarify main ideas by identifying their relationships to other sources and related topics.

Academic Vocabulary

main idea most important idea in a piece of nonfiction writing

purpose reason for doing something, such as writing a text

source text or person from which you get information

A. Circle the letter of the correct response to each item below.

1. Which of the following was *not* part of Anne Frank's **purpose** in keeping a diary?
   A to practice so that she might become a writer when she grew up
   B to have a place to put her deepest, most secret thoughts
   C to have something to do during the long, silent hours in the Annex
   D to show her mother, father, and sister what she really thought of them

2. Which of the following is the **main idea** of this scrapbook?
   F Anne Frank was born in a hospital on June 12, 1929.
   G The Frank family lived busy lives.
   H Millions of people died in Nazi concentration camps.
   J Anne Frank suffered a terrible death, but her early life was very normal.

3. This scrapbook is a good **source** of information about—
   A events in Anne's life
   B the renovation of the Anne Frank Museum
   C the childhood of Anne's father, Otto Frank
   D the later lives of the Franks' helpers

B. Where might you go to learn more about Anne Frank? Explain.

_____

_____

_____

_____

A Family in Hiding

■ *Interactive Reading,* page 181

Reading Standard 1.3 Use word meanings within the appropriate context, and show ability to verify those meanings by definition, restatement, example, comparison, or contrast.

Vocabulary Development

enthusiasm, *noun*	energetic interest
allotted, *verb*	handed out; given
insatiable, *adjective*	unable to be satisfied
reverberated, *verb*	echoed

A. Words in Context
Use words from the word box to complete the paragraph below.

As I hid in the basement, without a prayer for survival, my hope never once subsided, and my craving for life remained (1) _____. This small space, which I had been (2) _____ , apparently by fate, so unexpectedly brought forth wonderful feelings. My imagination raced. My heart and mind burst with (3) _____ for all that I had ever loved, both people and things. So loud did my inner voice yell that its sound (4) _____ inside my mind all during my confinement.

B. Word Substitution
Substitute the correct vocabulary word for each underlined word or phrase.

1. A meager bowl of thin, watery soup was <u>doled out</u> to each inmate.   _____

2. The Nazis, <u>never satisfied</u> in their quest for treasure, pulled the teeth of their victims to get the gold fillings.   _____

3. Anne Frank's <u>zest</u> for life did not disappear during her years of hiding.   _____

4. The cheers of the freed prisoners <u>pealed out</u> so loudly that I felt they could be heard for miles.   _____

A Family in Hiding

■ *Interactive Reading,* page 181

Reading Standard 3.5 Identify and analyze recurring themes (for example, good versus evil) across traditional and contemporary works.

Academic Vocabulary

theme	truth about life revealed in a work of literature
dramatic irony	situation in which the reader knows something that the characters don't know

A. Circle the letter of the correct response to each item below.

1. In Miep's chronological account of her night in the Annex, which event comes first?
   A Miep finally understands what it means to be a Jew hiding from the Nazis.
   B The "family" listens to the radio.
   C Miep brings nightclothes to work.
   D The Franks invite Miep to stay overnight.

2. Three things that kept Miep awake were the booming of the clock, the silence after each ringing, and—
   F doubts about whether she was doing the right thing
   G thick terror pressing on her like something physical
   H Anne's endless, eager questions about the outside world
   J Mr. Van Daan coughing with uncontrollable bursts

3. Which situation illustrates **dramatic irony**?
   A After many requests, Miep agrees to visit the Annex for an overnight stay.
   B Mrs. Frank's cooking is delicious, even in these conditions where food is short.
   C Miep says, "No fuss, please," to which Mr. Frank replies, "Of course not."
   D The radio news fills the Franks with hope, but we know they are doomed.

B. How would you state the theme of "A Family in Hiding"? In what other books or movies have you encountered that theme?

_____

_____

_____

Chapter 5

CHAPTER OBJECTIVES

Students will—

- Develop confidence through reading the Practice Read.
- Use the "Charting Literary Devices" strategy to identify and interpret literary devices and style.
- Analyze idioms, analogies, metaphors, and similes to infer the literal and figurative meanings of phrases.
- Identify examples of fallacious reasoning.
- Understand structure.
- Build fluency.

Reading Standard 1.1
Analyze idioms, analogies, metaphors, and similes to infer the literal and figurative meanings of phrases.

Reading Standard 2.8 (Grade 6 Review)
Note instances of fallacious reasoning in text.

Reading Standard 3.6
Identify significant literary devices (e.g., metaphor, symbolism, dialect, irony) that define a writer's style, and use those elements to interpret the work.

Imagine That! Literary Devices

Start with the Strategy and Practice Read

(Interactive Reading, pages 188–197)

About the Strategy: "Charting Literary Devices"

To help students identify and appreciate the style of an author, use the "Charting Literary Devices" strategy.

The "Charting Literary Devices" strategy gives students practice in identifying literary elements used by an author as they read a selection. After identifying the literary elements, students can then organize their thoughts and draw conclusions about how the use of the particular elements adds up to a particular writer's style.

Introduce the Strategy

Explain to students that identifying and appreciating the style of an author takes time. Tell them that a good way to go about analyzing literary elements and style is to use the "Charting Literary Devices" strategy. To use this strategy, students—

- Read through a selection, putting sticky notes next to passages that have a particular effect on them.
- Revisit the passages they marked up, and identify any specific patterns or literary devices the author used.
- Make connections between the literary devices identified and how those devices contributed to the plot, theme, or characterizations in the story or poem.

Model the Strategy

- Place Transparency 5 on the overhead projector. Have students follow along as you read the story.
- Point out the sticky notes to the side. Inform students that the notes were put there to indicate that the reader found those passages interesting.
- Then, draw students' attention to the notes at the bottom of the page. These notes were written after the reader revisited the passages with sticky notes.
- Read each bulleted item with students, and help them see the connections between literary devices and author's style.

Apply the Strategy to the Practice Read

- Have students read the Strategy Launch on *Interactive Reading* page 189. Discuss any questions they may have.
- Have students read "The Overhead Man," beginning on *Interactive Reading* page 190. Tell them to use the comments and questions in the side column to guide their reading. Have students pay special attention to the sidenotes highlighting the "Charting Literary Devices" strategy and to circle or highlight any other passages that have a special effect on them.
- After reading the selection through, have students fill out the Literary Devices Chart on *Interactive Reading* page 197.
- In pairs, have students exchange charts and suggest additions to one another. Then, have partners discuss what conclusions they can draw about the writer's style based on the entries in their charts.

Assess

- As a class, have student pairs volunteer their conclusions about the writer's style, based on their completed Literary Devices Chart and responses to the side-column notes. Point out any conclusions that do not appear to be based on a reasonable interpretation of a literary element in the selection.
- Have students go back to the story and mark any questions and comments they may have.
- Evaluate students' mastery of "The Overhead Man" by using the Vocabulary Check on Teacher's Edition page 64 and the Comprehension Check on Teacher's Edition page 65.

TEACHER TO TEACHER

Students may have difficulty drawing conclusions about the writer's style, even if they are able to identify specific literary elements. Suggest that students imagine how their reaction to the story would differ if a specific literary element were to be left out.

TEACHING RESOURCES

Graphic Organizers,
Teacher's Edition,
Section Three

TEACHER TO TEACHER

Encourage students to preview the accompanying graphic organizer before they read each selection. The graphic organizer will help them set a purpose for reading.

Support the Selections in
Holt Literature and Language Arts

(Chapter 5, pages 350–399)

Apply the Strategy to Literary Texts

- Before students start each literary selection, encourage them to use the "Charting Literary Devices" strategy to help them identify literary elements. Identifying literary elements will help them draw conclusions about a writer's style.
- After students read each literary selection, have them complete the corresponding graphic organizer in *Interactive Reading*.

Interact with Informational Texts

- After students read each informational selection, have them complete the corresponding graphic organizer in *Interactive Reading*.

Assess

- Use the graphic organizers in *Interactive Reading* as an alternative assessment.
- After students read each literary selection, photocopy and distribute the Literary Devices Chart in Section Three of the Teacher's Edition. Students can use the chart to record the literary elements they identify in the selection. They can then use their completed charts to draw conclusions about the writer's style.

Selections in *Holt Literature and Language Arts*	Graphic Organizers in *Interactive Reading*
The Tell-Tale Heart, p. 354	Irony Chart, p. 198
Edgar Allan Poe: His Life Revealed in His Work, p. 364	Fallacy Wheel, p. 199
Raymond's Run, p. 367	Literary Device Pie Chart, p. 200
Olympic Games *and* The Old Olympic Games: A Report, p. 379	Inference Chart, p. 201
My Mother Pieced Quilts, p. 383	Quilt of Literary Devices, p. 202
A Word is dead; The Word/La palabra, p. 390	Figurative Spokes, p. 203

Build Independence Through Interactive Selections

(Interactive Reading, pages 204–219)

The Bells

Edgar Allan Poe ▪ page 205

INTRODUCE

- Tell students that they are going to read another selection by Edgar Allan Poe, this time one of his most famous poems.
- Read the Author Study note aloud. Point out that Poe is one of the best-known American authors, whose work is enjoyed by ordinary readers as well as by literary experts. Students will probably read many stories and poems by Poe during their school careers.

MODEL

- Read the first stanza of the poem aloud. Then, direct students' attention to the first side-column note.
- Model a response to the note: "Repetition is one of the most common and most effective literary devices. Repetition is used often in poetry. Let me look back at this stanza and find examples of repetition." Have students circle the examples in their books as you or volunteers point them out.

TEACH

- Have students continue reading the poem independently. Remind them to note their responses to the side-column notes in their books.
- After students have finished reading, divide the class into small groups. Have the groups discuss their responses.
- Read the Fluency note aloud. Make sure students understand that the dashes, commas, and exclamation marks are key to capturing the rhythm of the poem.
- Have students write responses to this selection in their Personal Reading Logs.

ASSESS AND EXTEND

- Photocopy the Literary Devices Chart in Section Three of the Teacher's Edition. Have students fill out the chart with the literary devices they identified as they read the poem. Then, have them use their entries to draw conclusions about the writer's style.
- Use the Comprehension Check on Teacher's Edition page 66 to evaluate mastery of the literary standard.
- To find out more about Edgar Allan Poe's works, have students complete the Annotated List of Works project on *Interactive Reading* page 210.

DIFFERENTIATING INSTRUCTION
The Bells ↑

- **Learners Having Difficulty**
  Students may struggle to find the natural breaks in the poem as they read. Encourage students to read slowly and aloud, repeating lines as necessary until they ascertain meaning.

- **Benchmark Students**
  Remind on-level students to review the side-column notes and footnotes as they read.

- **Advanced Students**
  Encourage advanced students to make connections between this poem and other poems they read in this chapter.

TEACHER TO TEACHER

Have students brainstorm other situations about which a similar poem with a similar theme might be written. Possibilities include drums beating, a choir singing or an orchestra playing, a carpenter hammering, and so on.

READING OPTION

Students might enjoy reading the poem as a team, using an interrupted reading strategy. One student begins the poem, then another student jumps in at a natural break, followed by another student at the next break, and so on. You or a designated student can monitor the reading to make sure the interruptions are made at valid points.

from Beyond the Grave
Troy Taylor • page 211

- **Learners Having Difficulty**
The information in this selection is accessible, but some students may stumble over the vocabulary and the structure of some of the sentences. Preview the vocabulary with students, and encourage them to split up longer sentences to help them figure out their meaning.

- **Benchmark Students** This selection should pose no difficulty for benchmark students. Remind them to address the side-column notes as they read.

- **Advanced Students** Have advanced students offer their own explanations for the mysterious person in black. Students can exchange their explanations and assess the reasoning behind the explanation as valid or fallacious.

TEACHER TO TEACHER

Tell students that reviewing a selection for instances of fallacious reasoning is something they should do continuously and consistently. It is something they should keep in mind for almost every sentence of a nonfiction piece.

READING OPTION

Although nonfiction, this selection from *Beyond the Grave* reads as if it were a piece of fiction. Make sure students aren't tempted to skim and scan the piece as they might with other pieces of nonfiction. Encourage them to read the selection silently and then revisit it to review specific pieces of information.

INTRODUCE

- Tell students that they are going to read an essay on a special subject relating to Edgar Allan Poe: his burial in a Baltimore cemetery and the mysterious ritual that has developed at his gravesite.

- Have students read the Before You Read note and speculate on what modern mystery could possibly be connected with Poe's death.

MODEL

- Read the first three paragraphs of the selection aloud, pausing at the fourth side-column note.

- Have students circle the words that describe the visitor. You may wish to begin by pointing out "man" and "Dressed completely in black" to help students get started.

TEACH

- Have students read the rest of the selection independently, noting their responses to the side-column notes in their books.

- After students have finished reading, divide the class into small groups. Have the groups discuss their responses.

- Have students record their responses to this selection in their Personal Reading Logs.

ASSESS AND EXTEND

- Have students complete the chart on *Interactive Reading* page 214 to evaluate their understanding. Ask students to share their responses.

- Use the Vocabulary Check on Teacher's Edition page 67 to evaluate mastery of the vocabulary standard.

- Use the Comprehension Check on Teacher's Edition page 68 to evaluate mastery of the informational standard.

- As an extension project, have students complete the Baltimore Brochure project on *Interactive Reading* page 215.

A Dream Within a Dream/Life

Edgar Allan Poe/Naomi Long Madgett • page 216

INTRODUCE

- Tell students they are going to read two poems. The first is another poem by Edgar Allan Poe. The second is by a different author, Naomi Long Madgett, but it explores themes and uses images that are familiar to readers of Poe.

MODEL

- Read the first three lines of the poem aloud, calling on volunteers to repeat the three lines. Point out the rhyming words at the end of each line.

- Model how you might respond to the first sidenote: "I know that poems often evoke images and explore ideas, but these first two lines actually describe a very concrete action. If I read each line slowly, word by word, the meaning is quickly clear. In the first line, the speaker is simply kissing someone on the forehead. In the second line, the speaker is saying that he is leaving. The speaker is giving someone, probably his love, a kiss as he bids her goodbye."

TEACH

- Have students read the rest of "A Dream Within a Dream" independently, noting their responses to the side-column notes in their books. Then, have students go on to read "Life," again addressing the side-column notes.

- After students have finished reading, divide the class into small groups. Have the groups discuss their responses, especially to the "Charting Literary Devices" notes.

- Read the Fluency note aloud. Have students discuss how the sound of each poem helps contribute to its meaning.

- Have students write their responses to the two poems in their Personal Reading Logs.

ASSESS AND EXTEND

- Photocopy the Literary Devices Chart in Section Three of the Teacher's Edition. Have students fill out the chart with the literary devices they identified as they read the poems.

- Use the Comprehension Check on Teacher's Edition page 69 to evaluate mastery of the literary standard.

- To extend students' exposure to style, have them complete the Imitation of Style project on *Interactive Reading* page 219.

DIFFERENTIATING INSTRUCTION
A Dream Within a Dream; Life

- **Learners Having Difficulty** Although the individual lines of the poems are short, students may still have difficulty grasping the meaning of each line. Suggest that students pause after each line, checking vocabulary that they don't understand.

- **Benchmark Students** After reading the poems through, have benchmark students enhance their understanding by re-reading the poems aloud.

- **Advanced Students** After advanced students read the poems, invite them to write poems of their own on related themes, using similar literary devices.

TEACHER TO TEACHER

Have students picture in their minds who each poet is addressing. Thinking about who is being influenced and what point is being put across will broaden students' understanding of the poem.

The Overhead Man

■ *Interactive Reading,* page 190

Reading Standard 1.1 Analyze analogies, metaphors, and similes to infer the literal and figurative meanings of words.

Vocabulary Development

erupt, *verb*	burst forth
fuming, *adjective*	very angry
massive, *adjective*	enormous; large scale
consequences, *noun*	results of an action

A. Words in Context

Use words from the word box to complete the paragraph below.

When I arrived home and saw that the job had not been finished, I was (1) _____. I was so angry, I felt that I was going to (2) _____ like a volcano. Although I realized that it was a (3) _____ job, at least *some* progress should have been made. I swore that there would be (4) _____ for the mysterious character who had promised to fix my roof.

B. Analogies

An **analogy** is a comparison that is set up to follow a set pattern. A pair of words that have a specific relationship (synonyms, antonyms, part to whole) is given, along with an item from a second pair that shows the same relationship.

Complete each analogy below by writing a word or phrase that fits the meaning.

   1. Results is to _____ as mistakes is to errors.

   2. Tiny is to small as _____ is to big.

   3. Content is to _____ as carefree is to worried.

   4. Roar is to engine as _____ is to volcano.

The Overhead Man

■ *Interactive Reading,* page 190

Reading Standard 3.6 Identify significant literary devices (for example, metaphor, symbolism, dialect, irony) that define a writer's style, and use those elements to interpret the work.

Academic Vocabulary

simile	figure of speech that compares two unlike things, using the word *like* or *as*
metaphor	figure of speech that compares two unlike things, without using a word of comparison
dialect	way of speaking that is characteristic of a region or group of people

A. Circle the letter of the correct response to each item below.

1. Which passage from "The Overhead Man" contains a **simile**?
   - **A** When it was built back a hundred years ago, my house was a barn.
   - **B** I went back into the house, fuming.
   - **C** And, like a fever, it suddenly vanished . . .
   - **D** His face had turned a shade of hideous purple . . .

2. Which sentence from "The Overhead Man" contains a **metaphor**?
   - **F** His yellow eyes bulged at me like hideous egg yolks.
   - **G** The only thing holding him up there was the second rope, around his neck.
   - **H** The rest is a blur to me.
   - **J** "Mizz Derby," he said, with an oily smile.

3. Which statement below contains **dialect**?
   - **A** The drips were constant, never ending.
   - **B** "What can I do for ye, Mizz—"
   - **C** "This is outrageous!" I said.
   - **D** The feeling was like a fever.

B. "The Overhead Man" presents a theory about the effects of hatred. Explain that theory in your own words.

_____

_____

_____

The Bells

■ *Interactive Reading,* page 205

Reading Standard 3.6 Identify significant literary devices (for example, metaphor, symbolism, dialect, irony) that define a writer's style, and use those elements to interpret the work.

Academic Vocabulary

repetition	repeated use of words to achieve a literary effect
end rhyme	rhyming words at the ends of lines
alliteration	repetition of the same or similar consonant sounds in words that are close together
onomatopoeia	use of a word whose sound imitates its meaning

A. Circle the letter of the correct response to each item below.

1. Which of the following is an example of **onomatopoeia**?
   A icy
   B clanging
   C brute
   D paean

2. Which of the following is an example of an **end rhyme**?
   F Through the balmy air of night/How they ring out their delight!—
   G With a desperate desire,/And a resolute endeavor
   H Yet the ear, it fully knows,/By the twanging,
   J Feel the glory in so rolling/On the human heart a stone—

3. Which of the following is an example of **alliteration**?
   A From the jingling and the tinkling of the bells
   B In a clamorous appealing to the mercy of the fire,
   C What a tale of terror, now their turbulency tells!
   D All the heavens seem to twinkle

4. Which of the following is an example of **repetition**?
   F Of the rapture that impels
   G From the molten-golden notes
   H How they tinkle, tinkle, tinkle
   J What a tale their terror tells

B. Identify the four types of bells presented by Poe in "The Bells." Then, write a simile or metaphor of your own that describes each type of bell.

_____

_____

_____

from **Beyond the Grave**

■ *Interactive Reading,* page 211

Reading Standard 1.1 Analyze analogies, metaphors, and similes to infer the literal and figurative meanings of words.

Vocabulary Development

compelling, *adjective*	irresistibly interesting; captivating
tangible, *adjective*	able to be touched; actual or real
ritual, *noun*	ceremony
elusive, *adjective*	hard to capture or get hold of

A. Words in Context
Use words from the word box to complete the paragraph below.

The mystery was so (1) _____ I could not get it out of my mind. I decided I couldn't rest until I had found some (2) _____ evidence that would finally reveal the identity of the mysterious visitor. However, such evidence was proving maddeningly (3) _____. Would we never have an explanation for this strange (4) _____ that took place each year?

B. Analogies
An **analogy** is a comparison between two sets of words that have the same relationship. A pair of words that have a specific relationship (synonyms, antonyms, part to whole) is given, along with an item from a second pair that shows the same relationship.

Complete the following analogies with the vocabulary words from above.

1. Horrifying is to terrifying as captivating is to _____.

2. Cellar is to basement as ceremony is to _____.

3. Courteous is to polite as _____ is to actual.

4. Sly is to cunning as evasive is to _____.

from **Beyond the Grave**

■ *Interactive Reading,* page 211

Reading Standard 2.8 Note instances of fallacious reasoning
in text.

Academic Vocabulary

hasty generalization	conclusion from weak or insufficient evidence
false cause and effect	assumption that one thing caused another just because it happened before the other
either/or fallacy	assumption that there is only one solution to a problem or answer to a question
stereotyping	believing that all members of a group share the same traits

A. Circle the letter of the correct response to each item below.

1. Arguing that Jerome invited the photographer to the grave-
   yard because of the birthday party in 1983 is an example of—
   A hasty generalization   **C** false cause and effect
   B stereotyping   **D** either/or fallacy

2. Thinking that the people who are interested in Poe's gravesite
   are weird is an example of—
   F false cause and effect   **H** stereotyping
   G either/or fallacy   **J** hasty generalization

3. Which is an example of a **hasty generalization**?
   A The visitor in black might be many different individuals.
   B Jeff Jerome is the visitor in black.
   C Poe is buried in the Old Western Burial Ground.
   D The visitor leaves roses and cognac.

B. What conclusion do you draw about the visitor in black?

_____

_____

_____

A Dream Within a Dream; Life
■ *Interactive Reading,* page 216

Reading Standard 3.6 Identify significant literary devices (for example, metaphor, symbolism, dialect, irony) that define a writer's style, and use those elements to interpret the work.

Academic Vocabulary

analogy	comparison between two things to show how they are alike
imagery	use of language to evoke a picture or a sensation
symbol	person, place, thing, or event that has meaning in itself and that also stands for something more than itself

A. Circle the correct response to each item below.

1. Which of the following are symbols in "A Dream Within a Dream"?

   A dreams and kisses   **C** night and day

   B waves and sand   **D** hope and despair

2. Which line does *not* use **imagery** that appeals to the senses?

   F "I stand amid the roar/ of a surf-tormented shore."   **H** "And I hold within my hand/ Grains of the golden sand."

   G "Yet if hope has flown away/ In a night, or in a day"   **J** "Thus much let me avow/ You are not wrong."

3. What **analogy** does the author of "Life" make to describe the subject of the poem?

   A She compares childhood to a ticking watch.

   B She compares death to a sinking ship.

   C She compares infants to wild animals.

   D She compares life to a toy.

B. What symbols and imagery might you use in a poem that has a more optimistic view of the human condition?

_____

_____

_____

_____

_____

Sound and Sense: Forms of Poetry

CHAPTER OBJECTIVES

Students will—

- Develop confidence through reading the Practice Read.
- Use "Text Reformulation" to demonstrate the relationship between the purposes and characteristics of different forms of poetry.
- Clarify word meanings.
- Build fluency.

Reading Standard 2.4
Compare the original text to a summary to determine whether the summary accurately captures the main ideas, includes critical details, and conveys the underlying meaning.

Reading Standard 3.1
Determine and articulate the relationship between the purposes and characteristics of different forms of poetry (e.g., ballad, lyric, couplet, epic, elegy, ode, sonnet).

Start with the Strategy and Practice Read

(*Interactive Reading*, pages 221–230)

About the Strategy: Text Reformulation

Reformulating a text helps students understand similarities and differences among the various forms of poetry and prose. By deciding what to include in a reformulation, students will analyze a text. When putting text into a different form, students state ideas and information in another way. For example, the "Fortunately/Unfortunately" reformulation helps students identify positive and negative events. The "If/Then" reformulation helps them understand causes and effects.

Introduce the Strategy

Explain to students that "text reformulation" means writing the main elements of a selection in a different form. The strategy includes—

- Working in small groups or independently.
- Brainstorming possible new forms for the text of a poem.
- Selecting one of the patterned structures or a prose or poetry form for reformulation.
- Writing the reformulation.

Model the Strategy

- To model the strategy, place Transparency 6 on the overhead projector, showing the rhyme but neither of the reformulations. Read the rhyme aloud for students.
- Then, tell students that you have reformulated (rewritten) the rhyme as an "If/Then" sequence and then as a newspaper article. Model the first reformulation by suggesting that "**If** the cat fiddles, **then** the cow will jump over the moon." Ask volunteers to use the "If/Then" reformulation on the rest of the verse. Then, reveal the reformulation on the transparency.
- Have students suggest how the verse might be rewritten as a news story. After they have offered some examples, reveal the story on the transparency. Invite students' responses.

Apply the Strategy with the Practice Reads

- Have students read the Strategy Launch on page 221 and the Before You Read notes on pages 222 and 225. Discuss any questions that arise.
- Then, read "Skywriting" aloud as students follow along in their books. Read the first sidenote, and have a volunteer identify the audience. Then, read the third note, and have students suggest possible answers.
- Group students in pairs or in small groups to complete the sidenotes and write individual reformulations of the poem. Then, have them read "The Midnight Ride of Billy Dawes," following the same strategy. Encourage them to share their work with the group.

Assess

- Encourage the class to revisit the two poems, marking them up with their own questions and comments and highlighting information that they find important.
- Challenge students to assess their progress in restating poetry into other forms. Ask them what skills it takes to reformulate and what insights a reformulation provides.
- Evaluate students' mastery of "Skywriting" and "The Midnight Ride of Billy Dawes" by using the Comprehension Checks on Teacher's Edition pages 77 and 78.

TEACHER TO TEACHER

You might suggest reformulations to help students work on specific skills. For example, reformulating text into post-cards and headlines is a good strategy for identifying main ideas.

TEACHING RESOURCES

Graphic Organizers, Teacher's Edition, Section Three

Support the Selections in
Holt Literature and Language Arts

(Chapter 6, pages 402–465)

Apply the Strategy to Literary Texts

- Before students begin to read each selection, remind them of the goal and the method of the "Text Reformulation" strategy.

Focus on Informational Texts

- After students read each informational selection, have them complete the corresponding graphic organizer in *Interactive Reading*.

Assess

- After students read each literary selection, have them complete the accompanying graphic organizer on their own. Then, allow them to work in groups to compare and contrast their entries.
- Reading a poem aloud might also be used for informal assessment.

Selections in *Holt Literature and Language Arts*	Graphic Organizers in *Interactive Reading*
Valentine for Ernest Mann, p. 406	"Most Important Word" Graph, p. 231
Paul Revere's Ride, p. 410	Cause-and-Effect Chart, p. 232
The Cremation of Sam McGee; The Dying Cowboy; Maiden-Savin' Sam, p. 417	Story Map, p. 233
from Beowulf; Casey at the Bat, p. 428	Epic-Comparison Chart, p. 234
Summaries of "Casey at the Bat," p. 435	Summary-Event List, p. 235
Ode to Thanks; Birdfoot's Grampa; Ode to a Toad, p. 437	Cluster Map, p. 236
On the Grasshopper and the Cricket, p. 443	Line-by-Line Paraphrase, p. 237
O Captain! My Captain!, p. 447	Extended-Metaphor Chart, p. 238
I Hear America Singing; I, Too, p. 451	Venn Diagram, p. 239
Langston Hughes: A Biography; Langston Hughes: A Summary, p. 455	Summary-Notes Chart, p. 240

Build Independence Through Interactive Selections

(Interactive Reading, pages 241–259)

The Wreck of the Hesperus

Henry Wadsworth Longfellow • page 242

INTRODUCE

- Remind students that they may already be familiar with Henry Wadsworth Longfellow, having previously read "Paul Revere's Ride." Ask them to recall what they know about the poet from his brief biography.

- Read the Author Study and Before You Read notes aloud. Tell students that Longfellow was one of the first poets from the United States to be respected and admired internationally. In his time he was a beloved popular artist, much as the poet Toni Morrison and the director Steven Spielberg are today.

MODEL

- Read the first line of the second verse aloud, and ask a volunteer to put the line into logical order. Point out that such reverse order was commonly used in poetry during the nineteenth (and earlier) centuries.

- Call students' attention to the Own the Poem page in their textbooks, and model how a news article on the *Hesperus* tragedy might begin.

TEACH

- Have students read the poem and use the sidenotes for guidance. Then, tell them to write a news article about the story in the poem. Remind them that a reporter would make the scene as vivid as possible.

- Bring the class back together, and have volunteer groups read their news articles. Discuss the good points of each article, and allow the listeners to suggest scenes or wording to add.

- Read the Fluency note aloud. Encourage students to read several lines with various tones of voice, serious or tragically comedic, for particular scenes.

- Have students add the title of the poem to their Personal Reading Logs.

DIFFERENTIATING INSTRUCTION
The Wreck of the Hesperus

- **Learners Having Difficulty** Old-fashioned phrases and inverted word order will give some students trouble. You might want to alert them to these by previewing the poem with them and pointing out the unfamiliar phrases and inverted word order.

- **Benchmark Students** Because of its strong story line, rhythm, and rhyme scheme, this narrative poem is ideal for students to use in giving dramatic readings. The dialogue provides opportunities for them to really get into their roles.

- **Advanced Students** This selection should pose no problem for advanced learners. Encourage these students to compare and contrast the poem with "The Midnight Ride of Billy Dawes."

Have students work as a class to discuss the plot of the poem. Suggest that they look for examples of cause and effect or ways in which plot events affect each other. Challenge them to put these events into sentences that begin with *fortunately* or *unfortunately*.

ASSESS AND EXTEND

- Photocopy and distribute the Text Reformulation Chart in Section Three of the Teacher's Edition. Assign the Text Reformulation Chart to students, and assess the results.

- Have students evaluate their own progress using the Checklist for Standards Mastery.

- Use the Comprehension Check on Teacher's Edition page 79 to evaluate mastery of the comprehension standard.

- Assign the Author Profile as an extension activity, instructing students to complete the project individually. You might want to place Longfellow in a historical context: He lived and worked in New England in the 1840s and 1850s, one of the great periods of American literature.

Schooners

Edwin Tunis ▪ page 249

INTRODUCE

- Tell students that they will read a short nonfiction piece about schooners. The *Hesperus* was a type of schooner.
- Have students read the Before You Read note. Ask whether in reading "The Wreck of the Hesperus," they imagined a schooner as large or small, fast or slow.

MODEL

- Ask the question in the first sidenote. Guide students to recognize that the first half of the first sentence contains the main idea.

TEACH

- Have students read the rest of the article in pairs, following the side-column questions and writing their answers.
- Encourage students to jot notes about the text in the margins of their books. Allow time for students to look up any terms they are unfamiliar with.

ASSESS

- Photocopy and distribute the Venn diagram in Section Three of the Teacher's Edition to use as an informal assessment. Then, have students complete the material in Practicing the Standards.
- Have each student work individually to evaluate his or her progress by using the Checklist for Standards Mastery and to add to his or her Personal Word List and Personal Reading Log.
- Finally, evaluate students' mastery of the selection by using the Comprehension Check on page 80 of the Teacher's Edition.

DIFFERENTIATING INSTRUCTION
Schooners ◀▶

- **Learners Having Difficulty** Invite these students to study the pictures and captions before reading the texts. Elicit their impressions of what it might have been like to sail on one of these ships.

- **Benchmark Students** Ask students to compare and contrast the two types of schooners with reference to size, shape, number of sails, and so on.

- **Advanced Students** These students might be invited to use encyclopedias or the internet to research other types of schooners and to share this knowledge with the rest of the class.

TEACHER TO TEACHER
These passages are filled with detail, both technical and historical. As such, they provide a springboard for discussing what might be included in a summary and what might be left out. Don't hesitate to point to specific details as minor or unnecessary to include in a summary.

- **Learners Having Difficulty**
  At appropriate places in the
  text, have these students pause
  and reformulate the text into
  newspaper headlines. This will
  assure that they are understanding the material.
- **Benchmark Students** Have
  one or more volunteers read
  each poem aloud. One student
  can read the entire Langston
  Hughes poem, and one reader
  per stanza can read the Carl
  Sandburg poem.
- **Advanced Students** You may
  want to challenge advanced
  students to compare and contrast the way in which Hughes
  and Sandburg approach similar subject matter.

Lincoln Monument: Washington
Langston Hughes ▪ page 254
Mr. Longfellow and His Boy
Carl Sandburg ▪ page 255

INTRODUCE

- Tell students that they will read another poem by Langston Hughes,
  whose poetry they have already read in this chapter. Introduce Carl
  Sandburg, a modern American poet who, like Hughes and
  Longfellow, wrote verse that appealed to a large audience. Note that
  Sandburg was deeply interested in American culture and wrote a
  biography and several poems about Abraham Lincoln.
- Have students read the Before You Read note. Discuss ways of finding out more about Hughes and Sandburg, such as encyclopedias,
  biographies, and the Internet.

MODEL

- Note that students will use the "Text Reformulation" strategy for
  these poems.
- Read aloud the first line of Hughes's poem: "Let's go see old Abe."
  Ask students whether Hughes calls Lincoln *old Abe* because he
  believes that Lincoln is not important today—or whether he has
  some other reason. Discuss students' responses.
- Choose several lines of Sandburg's poem to read aloud. Ask students what the poet reveals about his attitude toward his country.

TEACH

- Have students read the two poems on their own, responding to the
  side-column questions and comments in their books. Allow time
  for students to share their comments.
- Then, assemble students in small groups to reformulate each poem
  in one of the formats you've given them. Walk among the groups
  to oversee their work and offer suggestions.
- When the groups have finished, bring them back together as a
  class. Have a volunteer from each group share the reformulations
  and answer questions from the other students.

ASSESS AND EXTEND

- Have students read and complete the Practicing the Standards sec-
  tion individually. Ask them also to add to their Personal Word Lists
  and Personal Reading Logs.
- Evaluate students' mastery of the selections by using the
  Comprehension Check on Teacher's Edition page 81.
- Assign the Poetry Dartboard project on page 259 in *Interactive
  Reading* as an extension of the lesson.

Skywriting

■ *Interactive Reading,* page 222

Reading Standard 3.1   Determine and articulate the relationship between the purposes and characteristics of different forms of poetry.

Academic Vocabulary	
stanza	group of lines in poetry that form a unit
lyric poem	poem that expresses the speaker's emotions or thoughts
narrative poem	poem that tells a story
speaker	voice that is talking in a poem

A. Circle the best answer to each item below.

1. How many **stanzas** does "Skywriting" have?
   A six   C four
   B five   D three

2. Which of the following statements about "Skywriting" is correct?
   F It is a narrative poem because it tells a story.
   G It is a lyric poem because it expresses the speaker's feelings.
   H It is a narrative poem because it has a speaker.
   J It is a lyric poem because it tells a story.

3. What does the **speaker** of "Skywriting" want to inspire readers to do?
   A build rockets   C write poems
   B explore basements   D rent billboards

B. Name your favorite lines in "Skywriting." Explain why you like them.

_____

_____

_____

_____

_____

_____

The Midnight Ride of Billy Dawes ■ *Interactive Reading,* page 225

Comprehension Check

Reading Standard 3.1 Determine and articulate the relationship between the purposes and characteristics of different forms of poetry.

Academic Vocabulary

purpose	writer's reason for writing
narrative poem	poem that tells a story
rhyme	repetition of accented vowel sounds and all sounds following them
stanza	group of lines in poetry that form a unit

A. Circle the letter of the best answer.

1. How would you describe the rhyme scheme of this poem?
   - **A** Every other word rhymes.
   - **B** There is no set rhyme.
   - **C** The second and fourth and the sixth and eighth lines rhyme.
   - **D** The second and fourth and the final two lines rhyme.

2. "The Midnight Ride of Billy Dawes" is a **narrative poem** because it—
   - **F** is long and historical
   - **G** puts Paul Revere in his place in history
   - **H** contains rhyme and rhythm
   - **J** tells a story

3. What is the first line of the **stanza** that tells what Paul Revere did for a living?
   - **A** "The answer, perhaps"
   - **B** "The lesson one learns"
   - **C** "Then the word leaked out"
   - **D** "I'm only a farmer"

B. Describe the poet's purpose in writing this poem.

_____

_____

_____

_____

_____

The Wreck of the Hesperus

Comprehension Check

■ *Interactive Reading,* page 242

Reading Standard 3.1 Determine and articulate the relationship between the purposes and characteristics of different forms of poetry.

Academic Vocabulary

narrative poem	poem that tells a story
elegy	poem expressing grief over loss
rhyme	repetition of accented vowel sounds and all sounds following them
simile	comparison of two unlike things using *like* or *as*

A. Circle the best answer to each item below.

1. What characteristics of a **narrative poem** are found in "The Wreck of the Hesperus"?
   A It has a story line.   **C** It has characters.
   B It has a conflict.   **D** All of the above

2. "The Wreck of the Hesperus" is a **narrative poem.** Why might it also be considered an **elegy**?
   F Almost any poem can be called an elegy.
   G It uses strong rhyme and meter.
   H It grieves for the deaths of the characters.
   J It is set in a sailing ship in the 1800s.

3. Which lines rhyme in each stanza of "The Wreck of the Hesperus"?
   A the first and third   **C** the second and fourth
   B the first and second   **D** the third and fourth

4. Which of these lines contains a **simile**?
   F "And the billows frothed like yeast"
   G "And a scornful laugh laughed he"
   H "The snow fell hissing in the brine"
   J "At day-break on the bleak sea-beach"

B. Rewrite stanzas 4 and 5 as a narrative paragraph in everyday English.

_____

_____

_____

Schooners

■ *Interactive Reading,* page 249

Reading Standard 2.4 Compare the original text to a summary to determine whether the summary accurately captures the main idea, includes critical details, and conveys the underlying meaning.

Academic Vocabulary

summary	restatement of the main idea and major details of a text
main idea	most important point in a text

A. Circle the letter of the best answer.

1. What is the best statement of the **main idea** of "Schooners"?
    A Schooners are used as much now as they ever were.
    B Over the years, schooners have been used for work, for war, and for play.
    C The Gloucester Fishing Schooner was a late model schooner.
    D Schooners are sailing ships.

2. Which detail best **supports** the idea that schooners were important during the nineteenth century?
    F All schooners have fore-and-aft sails.
    G Some schooners were designed "on the Bermuda mould."
    H Schooners were profitable in fishing, in the slave trade, and in privateering.
    J Schooners fished on the Grand Banks off the coast of New England.

3. Suppose you were to write a **summary** of "Schooners." Which detail below would *not* be used because it is not important?
    A All schooners have two or more masts.
    B Schooners in New England were originally used for fishing.
    C Baltimore Clippers were permitted to capture enemy ships in War of 1812.
    D The *Chausseur*'s captain was named Boyle.

B. Write a sentence in which you state one fact you learned from "Schooners."

_____

_____

_____

_____

Lincoln Monument: Washington; Mr. Longfellow and His Boy ■ *Interactive Reading,* page 254

Reading Standard 3.1 Determine and articulate the relationship between the purposes and characteristics of different forms of poetry.

Academic Vocabulary

repetition	repeated use of words or phrases to emphasize ideas or to create a musical effect
alliteration	repetition of consonant sounds at the beginnings of words that are close together
simile	comparison of unlike things that uses a word such as *like* or *as*
metaphor	comparison of unlike things that does not use words such as *like* and *as*
personification	comparison that gives human traits to something nonhuman

A. Circle the letter of the best answer.

1. The line "Sitting in the marble and the moonlight," contains an example of—

   A metaphor   **C** rhyme

   B simile   **D** alliteration

2. Identify the literary device that is featured in this passage: "Our hearts, our hope, are all with thee, / Our hearts, our hopes, our prayers, our tears . . ."

   F rhyme   **H** repetition

   G simile   **J** metaphor

3. What figurative language is used in this line quoted from Longfellow's poem: "Sail on, O Union, strong and great!"

   A personification **C** simile

   B idiom   **D** alliteration

B. Re-read "Mr. Longfellow and His Boy." In a sentence, tell what you think Sandburg's purpose was in writing it.

_____

_____

CHAPTER OBJECTIVES

Students will—

- Develop confidence and skills through reading the Practice Read.

- Use the "Think-Aloud" strategy to analyze literature, and speculate on how it reflects the author's heritage, attitudes, and beliefs.

- Use context clues to clarify word meanings.

- Understand idioms.

- Evaluate the unity and consistency of the structure of a text.

- Build fluency.

Reading Standard 1.1
Analyze idioms, analogies, metaphors, and similes to infer the literal and figurative meanings of phrases.

Reading Standard 1.3
Use word meanings within the appropriate context, and show ability to verify those meanings by definition, restatement, example, comparison, or contrast.

Reading Standard 2.7
Evaluate the unity, coherence, logic, internal consistency, and structural patterns of text.

Reading Standard 3.7
Analyze a work of literature, showing how it reflects the heritage, traditions, attitudes, and beliefs of its author (biographical approach).

Literary Criticism:
The Person Behind the Text

Start with the Strategy and Practice Read

(Interactive Reading, pages 260–271)

About the Strategy: "Think-Aloud"

The "Think-Aloud" strategy helps students comprehend the meaning of the text. Students will raise and answer questions, clarify meanings, make connections, and visualize scenes or characters. Pausing to think aloud gives students the opportunity to analyze how literature can reflect the heritage, attitudes, traditions, and beliefs of the author.

Introduce the Strategy

Tell students that the "Think-Aloud" strategy will help them analyze a work of literature and think about how it reflects the heritage, traditions, attitudes, and beliefs of its author. The strategy involves pausing during reading to make a comment on or ask a question about the text. Students' comments and questions may include—

- A question about something that is not understood.

- A prediction about what might happen next.

- A visualization of a scene or character.

- A comparison to another text or a personal experience.

- A statement of agreement or disagreement with something the writer states or something a character does.

Model the Strategy

- To model the strategy, have students recall the well-known tale "Little Red Riding-Hood."

- Tell students that you are going to model how to use "Think-Aloud" with part of the tale.

- Place Transparency 7 on the overhead projector. Have students follow along as you read the text of the tale, pausing at the appropriate points to read the "Think-Aloud" comments in the side margin.

- Discuss with students the different kinds of "Think-Aloud" comments represented on the transparency.

Apply the Strategy with the Practice Read

- Have students read the Strategy Launch on page 261 and the Before You Read note on page 262 in their books. Discuss any questions that arise.
- Then, have students read "It's About Time," which begins on page 262.
- Tell students to use the comments and questions in the side column to guide their reading.
- Remind students to pause, think, and comment when they come to "Think-Aloud" sidenotes. They may write their comments in their books or share comments with partners.
- After students finish reading the story, elicit their responses on how use of the strategy helped their understanding.
- Direct students to work in pairs to complete the Tally Sheets on page 271 in their books.

Assess

- Use the "Think-Aloud" Tally Sheets to evaluate students' use of the strategy.
- As students make progress in mastering "Think-Aloud," their comments should increase in sophistication, rising from the level of basic comprehension to that of interpretation. The biographical approach to literary criticism may appear in comments such as, "Does the author really think this?" or "Which side is the author on?"
- Have students return to the text of "It's About Time" and mark it with their own notes and comments.
- Have students complete the Practicing the Standards and Keeping Track activities. Students can work on their own to add to their Personal Word Lists and Personal Reading Logs.
- Have students check their progress using the Checklist for Standards Mastery.
- Evaluate students' mastery of "It's About Time" by using the Vocabulary Check on page 88 and the Comprehension Check on page 89 of the Teacher's Edition.

TEACHER TO TEACHER
When first using "Think-Aloud," students and teachers alike often err in the direction of making too many comments. This can prevent students from ever reaching the end of the assigned text. As you move around the room observing students' comments, inform students that they don't need to comment on everything. Connections, predictions, and comprehension problems provide good reasons for pausing to comment.

Support the Selections in
Holt Literature and Language Arts

(Chapter 7, pages 468–525)

Apply the Strategy to Literary Texts

- Before students begin to read each literary selection, remind them to use the "Think-Aloud" strategy to analyze the text.
- After students finish reading the text, ask them what questions they still have about the text that their thinking aloud did not answer.
- After students read each literary selection, have them complete the corresponding graphic organizer.

Interact with Informational Texts

- After students read each informational selection, have them complete the corresponding graphic organizer.
- Because many texts blend the types of organizational structure, and readers may differ in identifying these types, encourage students to share—and at times revise—their interpretations of how the informational text is organized.

Assess

- Use the graphic organizers as an alternative assessment.
- You may wish to photocopy and distribute the Think-Aloud Tally Sheet in Section Three of the Teacher's Edition to evaluate students' understanding of the literary selections.

Selections in *Holt Literature and Language Arts*	Graphic Organizers in *Interactive Reading*
Ribbons, p. 471	**Story-Events Ladder,** p. 272
Getting to the *Pointe*, p. 485	**Position Chart,** p. 273
The Treasure of Lemon Brown, p. 490	**Story Map,** p. 274
Little Walter, p. 503	**Idiom Map,** p. 275
A Smart Cookie/ Bien águila, p. 508	**"Most Important Word" Graph,** p. 276
Saying Yes, p. 514	**Dialogue-Essentials Cartoon,** p. 277

Build Independence Through Interactive Selections

(*Interactive Reading*, pages 279–305)

The Buried Treasure

Laurence Yep ▪ page 279

INTRODUCE

- Have students read the Author Study note. Remind students of Laurence Yep's story "Ribbons," which they read in *Holt Literature and Language Arts.* Ask a volunteer or two to recap that story briefly.

- Read the Before You Read note aloud. Brainstorm some ways in which folk tales with identical plots might vary with different cultural settings. (For example, characters' attitudes and responses to an event, such as the discovery of treasure, might be different; the lessons in the tales might be different.)

- Make sure students understand that although "The Buried Treasure" has been retold by Laurence Yep, it is a traditional Chinese folk tale.

MODEL

- Have students read the first two paragraphs; then, direct their attention to the first side-column note. Model a response to the sidenote query: "One son cares for business; the other does not. The younger son is also very generous, and people take advantage of him." Suggest to students that this information about the two sons, coming as it does at the beginning of the tale, is probably very important to remember in order to understand what happens and why in the rest of the tale.

- Remind students to use the "Think-Aloud" strategy as they read the rest of the folk tale.

TEACH

- Have students continue reading independently, responding to the sidenotes.

- Read the Fluency note aloud. Have different pairs of students perform the dialogue for the rest of the class. Invite students to suggest other passages that they would like to act out.

ASSESS

- Have students complete the Story-Attitude Chart on *Interactive Reading* page 286 to evaluate their understanding of how a writer sometimes expresses his or her attitudes and beliefs through his or her writing.

- Evaluate students' mastery of "The Buried Treasure" by using the Vocabulary Check and the Comprehension Check on pages 90 and 91.

DIFFERENTIATING INSTRUCTION
The Buried Treasure

- **Learners Having Difficulty** Student pairs who are using "Think-Aloud" may benefit from using a quiet corner or other separate area of the room so that they will not distract silent readers and will not be distracted by other students.

- **Benchmark Students** These students will be able to use the "Think-Aloud" strategy successfully, as individuals.

- **Advanced Students** Encourage these students to compare and contrast this story with "Ribbons" or to extend the reading by doing a research project about Laurence Yep.

TEACHER TO TEACHER

One key to making "Think-Aloud" work is to get students into the habit of doing it for themselves. Students should practice this strategy a couple of times a week. Students need use "Think-Aloud" for only five to ten minutes at a stretch, not for an entire period.

- **Learners Having Difficulty**
First, preview the article, pointing out its many textual features such as marginal notes, a drawing with matching photos, and even a comic strip. Then, read the first paragraph or two of the main text aloud for these learners.

- **Benchmark Students**
Encourage these students to answer the sidenotes as they read. Then, have them reread the article to be sure they understand its main points.

- **Advanced Students** Have these students propose alternative ways of structuring the information in the article.

TEACHER TO TEACHER

When reading the main article, emphasize connections of time and place to help students follow the text. Pause to paraphrase transitions; for example, "OK, we just learned about the ancient king named Midas who ruled in what is now Turkey. Now we're reading about how modern scientists flew there from the United States to find his remains."

The Funeral Banquet of King Midas

John Fleischman • page 287

INTRODUCE

- Tell students that they are going to read a magazine article about how scientists uncovered the truth behind an ancient myth.
- Have students read the Before You Read note. Ask whether any students have heard of King Midas or of the Midas Touch or the Golden Touch. Have volunteers briefly summarize the myth of the Golden Touch, or do so yourself.

MODEL

- Have a world map or a globe available, if possible, to give students a broader context in which to set the map of Phrygia.
- Have students read the first two paragraphs aloud; then turn back to the Identify note. Have volunteers cite the evidence from the text that tells that King Midas was an actual historical figure. (The Assyrians as well as the ancient historian Herodotus wrote about him.) Help students appreciate the logical structure of these first two paragraphs. In the first, the familiar "mythical" King Midas is mentioned. The second paragraph builds on this introduction by explaining to the reader with specific evidence that there was once a real King Midas.

TEACH

- Have students read the rest of the article independently. Remind students to note their responses to the side-column questions.
- Provide class time for students to practice fluency.

ASSESS

- To evaluate students' understanding of the structure of the text as well as their comprehension of the argument of the article, have them complete the Information Outline on *Interactive Reading* page 297.
- Evaluate students' mastery of "The Funeral Banquet of King Midas" by using the Vocabulary Check and the Comprehension Check on Teacher's Edition pages 92 and 93.

The Golden Touch

Greek Myth ▪ page 298

INTRODUCE

- Remind students of the times they have encountered the word *treasure* in this chapter: Lemon Brown's harmonica was a treasure; Yuè Shêng and Yuè Cang fought over a treasure; scientists analyzed an archaeological treasure. Point out that depending on a person's culture and circumstances, different things might be treasured.

- Tell students that the story of "The Golden Touch," which they're about to read, teaches the difference between true treasure and false treasure. Invite students to predict what its theme will be.

- Explain to students that myths reflect the heritage, traditions, attitudes, and beliefs of a group of people. Tell students that as they read, they should look for how this myth reflects the traditions, attitudes, and beliefs of the ancient Greeks.

MODEL

- Remind students that they will be using the "Think-Aloud" strategy for this story.

- Pause at the first sidenote. Lead students to identify the differences between King Midas and his daughter.

TEACH

- Have students read the rest of the myth independently, responding to the side-column questions and comments in their books.

- After students finish reading, encourage them to find passages in which the myth teller's attitudes can be inferred—attitudes toward wealth or toward Midas, for instance.

ASSESS AND EXTEND

- Assign the Project on *Interactive Reading* page 305 as an extension activity. Encourage students to use their retellings of the myth to explore questions of attitudes, values, and beliefs.

- Evaluate students' mastery of "The Golden Touch" by using the Vocabulary and Comprehension Checks on pages 96 and 97.

DIFFERENTIATING INSTRUCTION
The Golden Touch

- **Learners Having Difficulty** This selection is appropriate for these students. You may want to preview selection vocabulary with them before they read independently.

- **Benchmark Students** This selection will pose no difficulty for these students. You may wish to have these learners take turns reading dialogue aloud with expression.

- **Advanced Students** You might want to have these students extend the reading by doing a research project about other folk tales on the topic of greed.

TEACHER TO TEACHER
Different kinds of "Think-Aloud" comments might be raised at different points in the myth. For the first "Think-Aloud" sidenote, predictions and comments about the myth genre would be very appropriate. For the later notes, comments and questions on the meanings of characters' actions are more likely to arise.

It's About Time

■ *Interactive Reading,* page 262

Reading Standard 1.1 Analyze idioms to infer the literal and figurative meanings of phrases.

Reading Standard 1.3 Use words within the appropriate context, and show ability to verify those meanings by definition, restatement, comparison, or contrast.

A. Context Clues

Circle the context clues that help you figure out the meaning of each boldface word.

1. Mariano told me the house was built out of **adobe** bricks, which are made from clay.

2. Tomorrow morning you and I have something important to do to prepare for your **cumpleaños**—your birthday.

3. As you grow up, you will discover many other things that tie us, many other **similarities.**

4. My birthday **celebration** was a repeat of the first night's dinner, except that there were presents, even more food, and a big cake with candles.

B. Figurative Language

An **idiom** is an expression peculiar to a language that does not mean what it says literally. For example, the phrase "broke my heart" does not really mean that one's heart is broken in pieces; it means that someone has been extremely disappointed.

Underline the idiom in each of the following sentences about "It's About Time." Then, rewrite the phrase so that it means literally what it says.

1. Benny's heart sank when he realized he'd have to visit his relatives.

_____

2. Mariano, Benny's cousin, was pretty cool.

_____

3. Benny was all shaken up when he realized he and his *abuelo* looked so much alike.

_____

It's About Time

■ *Interactive Reading,* page 262

Reading Standard 3.7 Analyze a work of literature, showing how it reflects the heritage, traditions, attitudes, and beliefs of its author.

Academic Vocabulary

analyze	take apart a text to examine some aspect of it (for example, you can analyze plot, characters, theme, attitude)

A. Circle the letter of the best response to each item below.

1. Why does Benny dread the first day of June?
   A That's when school ends.
   B That's when his parents start bugging him about visiting his grandparents.
   C That's when he has to give his parents the list of birthday presents he wants.
   D That's the day he has to travel to New Mexico all by himself.

2. How does Benny's grandfather feel about the land?
   F He says it gives him strength.
   G He says it will be worth a lot of money in the future.
   H He says Ben should leave the city and live there.
   J He says the land has been hard on him.

3. When Benny arrives in Tierra Linda, what is his attitude toward the place?
   A He's delighted to explore it.
   B He thinks it's dull and boring.
   C He is eager to learn about his family history.
   D He is stunned by the beauty of its landscape.

4. How does Benny's attitude change by the end of the story?
   F By the end of the story he thinks Tierra Linda is beautiful.
   G By the end of the story he feels more strongly that it is dull.
   H He realizes at the end of the story that he loves cities.
   J He realizes at the end of the story that he does not share his grandparents' love of the land.

B. Analyzing Attitude

What evidence in the story suggests that the writer admires the culture and values of rural Mexican Americans?

_____

_____

The Buried Treasure

■ *Interactive Reading,* page 279

Reading Standard 1.3 Use words within the appropriate context, and show ability to verify those meanings by definition, restatement, comparison, or contrast.

Vocabulary Development

summoned, *verb*	called or sent for
tenants, *noun*	people who pay rent to use land or a building
bewildered, *adjective*	hopelessly confused

A. Words in Context

Use words from the word box to complete the paragraph below. Use each word only once.

One day, as he lay dying, Yuè Shêng's sick father (1) _____ him and his brother, Yuè Cang, to his bedside. He told them what possessions they would inherit from him. After his father passed away, Yuè Shêng went to work alongside the (2) _____ that rented land from Yuè Cang. While working, Yuè Shêng was (3)_____ to discover jars filled with gold that his father had buried in the ground. His father had left them for him, as his inheritance.

B. Restatement

Define the boldface word by restating the sentence in your own words.

1. Yuè Cang was **bewildered** to open the buried jars and discover snakes instead of gold.

   _____

   _____

2. Yuè Shêng and Yuè Cang were **summoned** by their father.

   _____

   _____

3. The **tenants** of the fields used the land for farming.

   _____

   _____

The Buried Treasure

■ *Interactive Reading,* page 279

Reading Standard 3.7 Analyze a work of literature, showing how it reflects the heritage, traditions, attitudes, and beliefs of its author.

Academic Vocabulary

basic situation	conditions that exist at the beginning of a story
resolution	end of the plot, when all loose ends are tied up

A. Circle the letter of the best response to each item below.

1. What is the **basic situation** of "The Buried Treasure"?
   - **A** A rich man has put his money into jars and buried them.
   - **B** Two greedy brothers decide to find the location of their father's gold.
   - **C** A rich man dies and leaves nothing to his sons.
   - **D** A man asks his sons for money.

2. According to his father, when will Yuè Shêng inherit the money?
   - **F** when he learns to relax and enjoy himself
   - **G** when he stops bullying his brother
   - **H** when he learns the value of hard work
   - **J** when he finds the buried treasure

3. How does Yuè Shêng learn the location of the treasure?
   - **A** He dreams about it.
   - **B** He overhears his father talking about it.
   - **C** He sees a map in his brother's desk.
   - **D** His wife spies on his father for him.

4. What happens in the story's **resolution**?
   - **F** The younger brother loses all of his father's treasure.
   - **G** The younger brother has the father's treasure and uses it wisely.
   - **H** The older brother is punished and all his money taken away.
   - **J** The older brother wins the father's treasure.

B. According to this folk tale, how should children treat their parents?

_____

_____

The Funeral Banquet of King Midas

■ *Interactive Reading,* page 287

Reading Standard 1.3 Use words within the appropriate context, and show ability to verify those meanings by definition, restatement, comparison, or contrast.

Vocabulary Development

archaeologists, *noun*	scientists who study the culture of the past
excavating, *verb*	uncovering or exposing by digging
avalanche, *noun*	mass of loosened snow, earth, rocks, and so on, suddenly and swiftly sliding down a mountain
interior, *noun*	place situated within; inside

A. Words in Context
Use words from the word box to complete the paragraph below. Use each word once.

Centuries ago a fierce mass of rock had slid down a mountain. It was a terrible (1) _____ that buried the small village. Now the site was visited by a team of (2) _____ who were studying the historic event. They couldn't wait to begin (3) _____ the village beneath the rock. Somewhere within the (4) _____ of that mound lay the crushed frames of ancient houses and other archaeological treasures.

B. Using Vocabulary Words in Sentences
Use each vocabulary word correctly in a sentence.

1. **archaeologists:** _____

_____

2. **excavating:** _____

_____

3. **avalanche:** _____

_____

4. **interior:** _____

_____

The Funeral Banquet of King Midas

■ *Interactive Reading,* page 287

Reading Standard 2.7 Evaluate the unity, coherence, logic, internal consistency, and structural patterns of text.

Academic Vocabulary

logical order	arrangement of text so that one detail is logically connected to the next
unity	arrangement of text in which all details support the main idea or topic
chronological order	order in which events happened

A. Circle the letter of the best response to each item below.

1. Which sentence below does *not* use **logical order**?

   A The archaeologists were surprised to find the blankets because cloth rots quickly.

   B Rodney Young was an archaeologist who discovered the tomb of Midas.

   C The real Midas lived in Turkey, and a goat was roasted at his funeral.

   D Lack of oxygen slowed the decay process, so the textiles were preserved.

2. Which of the following sentences destroys the **unity** of all these sentences as a whole?

   F Midas's tomb was very dry and airtight.

   G The lack of oxygen in the tomb slowed down the process of decay.

   H But how could anyone be sure it was really the tomb of King Midas?

   J Once the tomb was opened, air got in and rapid decay occurred.

3. Which part of the article uses **chronological order**?

   A the description of the banquet

   B the discovery of the tomb

   C the description of the sludge

   D the illustrations and captions

B. What is the most important fact you found in this article?

_____

_____

The Golden Touch

■ *Interactive Reading,* page 298

Reading Standard 1.3 Use words within the appropriate context, and show ability to verify those meanings by definition, restatement, comparison, or contrast.

Vocabulary Development

mortal, *noun*	human being who must one day die
strewn, *verb*	scattered; spread about
rigid, *adjective*	stiff and hard

A. Words in Context

Use words from the word box to complete the paragraph below. Use each word only once.

King Midas was a (1) _____, a human who dared defy the gods. He asked for the golden touch, and as a result his little daughter was turned to gold and stood (2) _____ like a statue, unable to move. All the furnishings of the palace were (3) _____ around him on the ground, also golden.

B. Words in Other Contexts

In "The Golden Touch" the vocabulary words are used in the context of an ancient Greek myth. Complete the following items, thinking of other contexts for these words.

1. How might a sportscaster use the word **mortal**?

   _____

2. Describe something that might be **strewn** about a house.

   _____

3. Name a circumstance in which someone becomes **rigid** with shock or surprise.

   _____

The Golden Touch

■ *Interactive Reading*, page 298

Reading Standard 3.7 Analyze a work of literature, showing how it reflects the heritage, traditions, attitudes, and beliefs of its author.

Academic Vocabulary

complication	event that adds to the conflict in a story
resolution	end of a plot, when the conflict is resolved and all loose ends are tied up

A. Circle the letter of the best response to each item below.

1. What does Midas like better than anything else?
   - **A** grapes
   - **B** gold
   - **C** beauty
   - **D** the gods

2. Why does the god Bacchus offer Midas a free wish?
   - **F** Midas was kind to Bacchus's old teacher.
   - **G** Bacchus has a habit of offering one mortal one wish each day.
   - **H** Bacchus wants to teach Midas a lesson about greed.
   - **J** Bacchus wants to teach Midas not to get mixed up with the gods.

3. What horrible **complication** occurs after Midas gets the Golden Touch?
   - **A** His furniture turns to gold.
   - **B** Bacchus turns to gold.
   - **C** Marigold turns to gold.
   - **D** Midas himself turns to gold.

4. What has Midas learned at the **resolution** of the story?
   - **F** He learns that gold is important.
   - **G** He learns to beware of the gods who offer wishes.
   - **H** He learns to love life more than gold.
   - **J** He learns to love his daughter more.

B. How did the tellers of this myth feel about gold versus nature? Support your analysis with details from the story.

_____

_____

_____

Reading for Life

CHAPTER OBJECTIVES

Students will—

- Develop confidence and skills through reading the Practice Read.

- Use the "Close Reading" strategy to understand informational documents.

- Follow technical directions, and solve problems using informational documents.

- Clarify word meanings and origins.

TEACHER TO TEACHER

You may want to review the basics of skimming and scanning because students may have to do both while using the "Close Reading" strategy. Remind them that *skimming* is a useful skill for close reading because it involves looking over a document to get the general idea of its content. *Scanning* involves looking for key words or phrases to help unlock meaning.

Reading Standard 2.1
Compare and contrast the features and elements of consumer materials to gain meaning from documents (e.g., warranties, contracts, product information, instruction manuals).

Reading Standard 2.5
Understand and explain the use of a complex mechanical device by following technical directions.

Reading Standard 2.6
Use information from a variety of consumer, workplace, and public documents to explain a situation or decision and to solve a problem.

Start with the Strategy and Practice Read

(Interactive Reading, pages 308–320*)*

About the Strategy: "Close Reading"

The "Close Reading" strategy involves identifying one's purpose for reading and then scanning the text for heads, subheads, and special features. The core of the strategy lies in students' close, careful reading to be sure they understand the material. Pictures, diagrams, illustrations, and footnotes—carefully checked—also promote comprehension. Because the strategy gives students just a few steps to follow, in a particular order, it works well for those who have problems focusing for long periods of time.

Introduce the Strategy

Explain to students that "Close Reading" involves the reading of useful, day-to-day materials such as directions for doing or making something, information on how something works, or a description of policies and procedures, such as those in local or regional government. "Close Reading" involves exploring all the characteristics of the text—heads, illustrations, lists, footnotes, and illustrations and photos—to completely understand the work. The "Close Reading" strategy involves—

- Identifying one's purpose for reading.
- Skimming and scanning the text.
- Reading slowly and carefully.
- Studying diagrams, illustrations, footnotes, and glossary entries.
- Rereading carefully any information that seems confusing.

Model the Strategy

- Place Transparency 8 on the overhead projector. Then, read each bulleted question to students, and allow time for them to respond.

- Remind students that the "Close Reading" strategy includes not only the text but also the titles, footnotes, illustrations, and other helpful features.

- Note that students will use the "Close Reading" strategy as they read "The Runaround."

Apply the Strategy with the Practice Read

- Have students read the Before You Read note on page 308. Discuss that although documents may change over the years, the practice of selling goods still favors the seller, and the expression *caveat emptor* (buyer beware) is still a buyer's best guide.

- Direct students to read "The Runaround," beginning on *Interactive Reading* pages 308–318, using the comments and questions in the side column to guide them.

- After students finish reading the selection, briefly elicit their initial responses. Ask: Will Mr. Merton be happy in his new pet situation? Has he been treated fairly? Would you buy a DigiPet from that manufacturer?

Assess

- Have students return to the text of "The Runaround," marking it up with their own notes and comments.

- Have students complete the Own the Text activities either individually or with partners.

- Both now and as the chapter continues, you may want to provide a few real-life examples of warranties and related informational materials. (Try to accumulate a mixture of "plain English" and "not-so-plain English" warranties.) Invite students to evaluate these materials as an informal assessment.

- Finally, use the Vocabulary Check on page 104 and the Comprehension Check on page 105 of the Teacher's Edition to evaluate students' mastery of "The Runaround."

TEACHER TO TEACHER

"Close Reading" is a strategy that works well when students read individually. Whenever possible, emphasize the usefulness of the strategy when reading documents that students encounter outside of school.

TEACHING RESOURCES

Graphic Organizers, Teacher's Edition, Section Three

Support the Selections in
Holt Literature and Language Arts

(Chapter 8, pages 528–559)

Interact with Informational Texts

- Before students begin to read each selection, remind them to use the "Close Reading" strategy, which involves carefully reading the basic text and taking note of features, footnotes, photos, or illustrations that may accompany the text.

- If students are using the "Close Reading" strategy throughout the course of their reading, then filling out graphic organizers may be optional.

Assess

- Use the graphic organizers in *Interactive Reading* as an alternative assessment.

- After students read each selection, you may want to pause and review some of the technical terms they've encountered. A quick informal assessment can be done by having students match the named features to details on the illustrations.

- Evaluate students' grasp of "Close Reading" by asking them to explain to classmates how the strategy works.

Selections in *Holt Literature and Language Arts*	Graphic Organizers in *Interactive Reading*
Skateboard Park Documents, p. 532	**Decision Tree,** p. 321
Leash-Free Dog Run Documents, p. 536	**Business Letter Template,** p. 322
WarpSpeedNet Documents, p. 541	**Quick-Reference Guide Jumble,** p. 323
SweetPlayer Documents, p. 546	**Consumer Feedback Form,** p. 324
Computers, p. 550	**Directions Check,** p. 325

Build Independence Through Interactive Selections

(*Interactive Reading*, pages 326–343)

Passports: Don't Leave Home Without One

Carolyn Liberatore Lavine ▪ page 326

INTRODUCE

- Invite a volunteer to read aloud the Before You Read note for this selection. Point out that this selection helps students in two different practical areas: first, the process of applying for a passport, and second, the process of reading an informational text.

- Ask how many students or members of their families have passports (from the United States or from another nation). Briefly discuss what passports are for: They make it legal to cross borders from one country to another. In many nations (but not in the United States), passports are also used internally as identity papers.

MODEL

- Model the "Close Reading" strategy by calling to students' attention the numbering and boldfacing of each step in the process of getting a passport. Have them also note the items written in italics, asking students why italics might have been used in each place.

TEACH

- Direct students to continue reading the selection, noting their responses to the side-column notes in their books.

- Help students as needed with titles and names of offices, such as "Bureau of Consular Affairs" and the abbreviation *ID*. If possible, bring in your own passport to show students what it looks like.

- Have students add the article to their Personal Reading Logs.

ASSESS AND EXTEND

- Have students complete the Practicing the Standards and Keeping Track activities.

- Use the Vocabulary Check on page 104 and the Comprehension Check on page 105 of the Teacher's Edition to evaluate students' mastery of "Passports: Don't Leave Home Without One."

- Assign the Passport Application project on *Interactive Reading* page 330 as an extension activity.

DIFFERENTIATING INSTRUCTION
Passports: Don't Leave
Home Without One

- **Learners Having Difficulty** This selection is suitable for learners having difficulty. Have these students preview the selection, underlining new or difficult words. Then, have them check the meanings of these words in a dictionary before reading.

- **Benchmark Students** On-level students should have no problems reading this article. The numbering of the various sections in this article makes it easy to assign for reading aloud, one numbered section per student. Treat the introductory and concluding passages as one section apiece.

- **Advanced Students** This article should pose no difficulties for advanced readers. These students may want to look up basic information on visa and inoculation requirements for countries they are interested in traveling to or working in someday.

- **Learners Having Difficulty**
This selection offers a perfect
opportunity for students to
grapple with a real-world
problem. The subheads, labels,
and callouts break the article
into chunks of manageable
length.

- **Benchmark Students** You
might read the three introductory paragraphs aloud. Then,
have students work with partners to read silently, pausing
at each section break and each
subheading to discuss the
material.

- **Advanced Students** Groups
of two or three might use a
computer to research and
report to the class on the
processes of decomposition
and recycling.

TEACHER TO TEACHER

This selection provides an excellent jumping-off point for discussions on ways in which
adults and young people alike
can help conserve the earth.

Earth-Friendly Products?

page 331

INTRODUCE

- Tell students that this article teaches how to become earth-friendly
consumers, with a focus on the recycling and biodegradability of
packaging.

- Have students read the Before You Read note. Ask how many students have heard the words *recyclable* or *biodegradable* before. Ask
what they think each term means. After a brief discussion, explain
that this article will help students to understand the subject better—
and perhaps make them more earth-aware than they had been.

MODEL

- Direct students' attention to the first side-column note. Call on a
volunteer to offer a prediction. Remind the class that paying attention to titles and subtitles is part of being a "close reader."

- Point out the vocabulary definitions on the first page of the article.
Tell students that in real life they should clarify unfamiliar words
by looking for context clues, by checking for footnotes or a glossary, or by looking in a dictionary.

TEACH

- Allow students time to read the article independently. Encourage
them to write their comments, questions, and responses in the
side-column.

- When students have finished reading, ask students which information they felt they needed to re-read to clarify. Remind students
that re-reading is an important reading skill, one that is especially
useful when reading documents.

- Finally, have students add this article to their Personal Reading
Logs.

ASSESS AND EXTEND

- Have students return to the text of "Earth-Friendly Products?" and
mark it up with their own notes and comments. Be sure they
complete the Practicing the Standards and Keeping Track activities.

- As an informal assessment, have students check their progress
using the Checklist for Standards Mastery.

- Use the Vocabulary Check on page 106 and the Comprehension
Check on page 107 of the Teacher's Edition to evaluate students'
mastery of the standards for this article.

- Assign the "Is It Recyclable?" project to pairs or small groups of
students as an extension activity. If you wish, more advanced students may be allowed to complete their projects independently.

Locks

Neil Ardley ▪ page 339

INTRODUCE

- Tell students that they will read a detailed description of how locks work. Discuss with students any background knowledge they may have about locks and keys.

MODEL

- Remind students to use the "Close Reading" strategy as they read this article.
- Have students preview the article, paying close attention to its section heads. Then, ask a volunteer to predict what two types of locks this article will focus on. Emphasize to students that when "close reading," they should pay attention to all the features of a work.

TEACH

- Allow classroom time for students to read independently, jotting down their comments in the sidenotes of the text.
- Elicit from students what they learned about combination locks, cylinder locks, and electronic locks. Ask them, in particular, how the illustrations of the insides of a cylinder lock helped them to understand how it works.
- Encourage students to enter their responses to this article in the Personal Reading Logs.

ASSESS AND EXTEND

- Have students return to the text of "Locks" and mark it up with their own notes and comments. Be sure they complete the Practicing the Standards and Keeping Track activities.
- Use the Vocabulary Check on page 108 and the Comprehension Check on page 109 of the Teacher's Edition to evaluate students' mastery of the standards.
- Assign the Diagramming a Mechanical Device project as an extension activity. Note that a number of reference books are available that show the workings of mechanical devices. Ask your school librarian to point your students toward these sources for their work on the projects.

DIFFERENTIATING INSTRUCTION
Locks ◄►

- **Learners Having Difficulty** Have these students preview the selection vocabulary and the illustrations before reading the text.
- **Benchmark Students** These students, who may have an interest in mechanical things (and this may or may not include your best readers), will have an advantage in confronting this text. Students who know a lot about "shop" may be able to help their more academically oriented peers.
- **Advanced Students** This group should have no problem reading the selection, although they may not be as mechanically oriented as other students. You may want to pair one of these students with one of your benchmark students for this selection.

TEACHER TO TEACHER

Once students have a good grasp of the "Close Reading" strategy and once they understand how it helps them concentrate on a text, they may be allowed to use it at their own pace and in their own ways.

The Runaround

■ *Interactive Reading,* page 308

Reading Standard 1.3 Use word meanings within the appropriate context, and show ability to verify those meanings by definition, restatement, example, comparison, or contrast.

Vocabulary Development

mode, *noun*	state of functioning or operation
promptly, *adverb*	on time; soon
alteration, *noun*	change; adjustment
excludes, *verb*	leaves out; refuses to consider or include
expired, *verb*	became inactive or invalid

A. Words in Context

Use the words above to complete this paragraph. Use each word only once.

Alert! Alert! You have placed this device in a dangerous state called Sudden Response (1) _____. Are you sure you want to do this? If not, press the De-Activate button (2) _____ before full Sudden Response takes effect. You have thirty seconds to de-activate the device. That (3) _____ the time you've already wasted while waiting to push the button. It is probably already too late to make any (4) _____ in the machine's state. Unfortunately, the time has just (5) _____. You slowpoke, what are you going to do now?

B. Questions of Context

Respond to each item below on the line provided.

1. Give an example of something you do not want to buy after the freshness date has **expired.**

   _____

2. Describe the difference between RECORD **mode** and PLAYBACK **mode.**

   _____

3. Describe a situation in which a piece of clothing would need **alteration.**

   _____

4. Compare and contrast a person who arrives **promptly** to class to a person who arrives late.

   _____

The Runaround

■ *Interactive Reading,* page 308

Reading Standard 2.1 Compare and contrast the features and elements of consumer materials to gain meaning from documents.

Academic Vocabulary

consumer	someone who buys and uses something
warranty	guarantee or assurance; a document that explains what rights the consumer has or what can be done if the product doesn't work
instruction manual	document that explains how to set up and use a product

---

A. Circle the letter of the best response to each item below.

1. Which type of consumer document is referred to in "The Runaround"?
   A a contract
   B a warranty
   C an instruction manual
   D technical directions

2. In "The Runaround," who is the **consumer**?
   F DigitPet™ Global
   G Mr. Merton Morton
   H Trudi Tranh
   J Fifi

3. What action does Merton take that violates the **warranty** and automatically makes his claim invalid?
   A He buys the product.
   B He sends in his registration card.
   C He performs an operation on his DigiPet.
   D He consults with the consumer relations department.

B. In "The Runaround," which did you enjoy reading more, the series of business letters or the warranty? Explain.

_____

_____

_____

_____

_____

Passports: Don't Leave Home Without One

■ *Interactive Reading,* page 326

Reading Standard 1.3 Use word meanings within the appropriate context, and show ability to verify those meanings by definition, restatement, example, comparison, or contrast.

Vocabulary Development

ambassador, *noun*	person who represents one nation while living in another nation
obtain, *verb*	get; acquire
official, *adjective*	having to do with a recognized authority such as a government office
affirm, *verb*	say that something is true; agree
embassy, *noun*	offices of an ambassador and the ambassador's staff
consulate, *noun*	office of the consul, the person appointed by a government to aid and serve its citizens

A. Words in Context
Use the words above to complete this paragraph. Use each word only once.

Our class went on a tour of the French (1) _____ here in Washington, D.C. The (2) _____ is located within the embassy. It is there to assist tourists. A person stopped to ask us if we were trying to (3) _____ visas. It turned out that he was our tour guide. He showed us the building, and then we came to a big door with the (4) _____ seal of France on it. "The (5) _____ is away today," our guide said, "so I cannot allow you to enter his office. However, I can (6) _____ that it has a lovely view."

B. Restatement
Write the appropriate vocabulary word for each underlined word or phrase.

1. We tried to <u>get our hands on</u> tickets for tonight's game, but none were left. _____

2. "That distinguished-looking man," she said, "was once the U.S. <u>top-level representative</u> to Mexico." _____

3. When I <u>declare positively</u> that something is true, you can believe me. _____

Passports: Don't Leave Home Without One

■ *Interactive Reading,* page 326

Reading Standard 2.6 Use information from a variety of consumer, workplace, and public documents to explain a situation or decision and to solve a problem.

Academic Vocabulary

workplace document	document circulated in a place of work
public document	document made available to the public by a government agency or a not-for-profit agency
consumer document	document supplied to the buyer of a product, giving information about the product or its use

A. Circle the letter of the best response to each item below.

1. Which of the following is *not* necessary in applying for a passport?
   A filling out a one-page form
   B writing a brief statement about your life
   C providing a photograph of yourself
   D showing an official copy of your birth certificate

2. How can you get a passport if you're under eighteen?
   F You can't. You have to wait till you're old enough.
   G A government official must testify that you are a good person.
   H You must show two forms of ID to the county clerk.
   J A parent or guardian, with identification, must accompany you.

3. In addition to a passport, some countries require that travelers obtain—
   A a railway pass   **C** traveler's checks
   B a credit card   **D** a visa

4. What kind of document is a passport application?
   F a public document   **H** a consumer document
   G a workplace document   **J** a memorandum

B. A friend has asked you how to apply for a passport. Explain the main points of the procedure to your friend.

_____

_____

Earth-Friendly Products?

■ *Interactive Reading,* page 331

Reading Standard 1.3 Use word meanings within the appropriate context, and show ability to verify those meanings by definition, restatement, example, comparison, or contrast.

Vocabulary Development

biodegradable, *adjective*	able to be broken down by the action of living organisms
skeptical, *adjective*	doubtful; having reservations about something
reclaimed, *verb*	rescued; recovered for use
decomposition, *noun*	decay; the breaking down of a substance into simple substances

A. Words in Context
Use the words above to complete this paragraph. Use each word only once.

When shopping for groceries, be (1)_____ of the claims you see on every product. Many companies announce boldly that their products are (2) _____, but often the claim is false. Other companies claim that purchasers can recycle the packaging, but often only one or two of its components can be (3) _____. In a landfill, only a small percentage of containers can be broken down by (4) _____.

B. Synonyms
Write the letter of the synonym or definition for each vocabulary word.

_____ 1. **reclaimed**   **A** decay

_____ 2. **decomposition**   **B** disbelieving

_____ 3. **biodegradable**   **C** rescued for reuse

_____ 4. **skeptical**   **D** able to be broken down

Earth-Friendly Products?

■ *Interactive Reading,* page 331

Reading Standard 2.1 Compare and contrast the features and elements of consumer materials to gain meaning from documents (for example, warranties, contracts, product information, instruction manuals).

Academic Vocabulary

workplace document	document circulated in a place of work such as an office
public document	document made available to the public by a government agency or a not-for-profit agency
consumer document	document supplied to the buyer of a product, giving information about the product or its use

A. Circle the letter of the best response to each item below.

1. The "Plastics Decoded" feature presents information—
   A in alphabetical order   **C** in chronological order
   B in a graph   **D** in a list

2. According to the article, why are juice boxes so difficult to recycle?
   F they contain six layers of material
   G there are too many to recycle
   H they contain a tough outer coating of plastic
   J they have a layer of insulating material

3. Where in the article can you find detailed information about recycling codes and what they mean?
   A in the first paragraph   **C** by scanning the subheads
   B in the table on the last page   **D** in the "Recyclable?" section

B. What information in "Earth-Friendly Products?" might be used in a workplace document? Explain.

_____

_____

_____

_____

Locks ■ *Interactive Reading*, page 339

Reading Standard 1.3 Use word meanings within the appropriate context, and show ability to verify those meanings by definition, restatement, example, comparison, or contrast.

Vocabulary Development

projections, *noun*	things that jut or stick out
altered, *verb*	changed in some way
serrated, *adjective*	having sawlike notches along the edge
ultrasonic, *adjective*	sound wave higher than the kind that people can hear

A. Words in Context
Use the words above to complete this paragraph. Use each word only once.

Judy had always used a cylinder lock on the tool chest she kept in the garage. However, she was afraid that her little brother would open it with the key she left in her room. It was a (1) _____ key with many (2) _____, and it was easy to see what kind of lock it would open. So Judy tried a combination lock, and (3) _____ the combination every week. Then she forgot the latest combination, so she bought a lock operated with an (4) _____ code signal.

B. Example
Give an example of each of the following vocabulary words.

1. something that is **serrated**

_____

2. something that can be **altered**

_____

3. something that is **ultrasonic**

_____

4. something that has **projections**

_____

Locks ■ *Interactive Reading,* page 339

Reading Standard 2.5 Understand and explain the use of a complex mechanical device by following technical directions.

Academic Vocabulary

figure	diagram or other illustration in an informational text
diagram	drawing, usually labeled, that shows how something is arranged
technical directions	instructions for how to do, make, or use something complicated or specialized
process	action that moves toward a goal and that is made up of a series of smaller actions or steps

A. Circle the letter of the best response to each question below.

1. How does a cylinder lock work?
   A It is operated by a metal key.
   B It uses wooden keys with large projections.
   C The pattern of projections in a key pushes up a set of pins in the lock.
   D It has a round cylinder that releases a bolt.

2. What does the **figure** of the key make clear?
   F the need for keys   **H** how a cylinder turns
   G the way the springs work   **J** how serration enables keys to work

3. What is the purpose of the pins in the cylinder lock?
   A They block the gap between the cylinder and the body of the lock.
   B They provide tension for the bolt and turn the cylinder.
   C They push the bolt in and release the key.
   D They withdraw the bolt and hold the key.

B. If you were writing instructions on how to operate an electronic lock, what would you tell your reader?

_____

_____

_____

_____

Chapter 1

Practice Read: Duncan, Junior

Vocabulary Check, page 8
- **A:** 1. responsibility
  2. apartment
  3. exercise
  4. humidity
  5. canine
- **B:** 1. humidity
  2. exercise
  3. canine
  4. responsibility
  5. apartment

Comprehension Check, page 9
- **A:** 1. C
  2. J
  3. C
- **B:** Responses will vary. Perhaps DJ saves Jeremy or another child when the river floods.

The No-Guitar Blues

Vocabulary Check, page 10
- **A:** 1. fidgeted
  2. perpetual
  3. reluctantly
  4. charity
  5. resounded
- **B:** 1. resounded; Sample answer: The church bells resounded throughout the town.
  2. reluctantly; Sample answer: Reluctantly the child returned her pacifier to her mother.
  3. fidgeted; Sample answer: I fidgeted in my seat because I was nervous.
  4. perpetual; Sample answer: The pendulum of the clock swung in perpetual motion.

Comprehension Check, page 11
- **A:** 1. A
  2. G
  3. B
- **B:** Responses will vary widely. Encourage creative responses that demonstrate an understanding of character and motivation as part of the plot. For example, the couple might be annoyed at Fausto's deception, but they would be glad that he didn't keep the money for himself.

Music from the Start

Vocabulary Check, page 12
- **A:** 1. archaeologists
  2. representation
  3. accompaniment
  4. transformed
  5. harmonious
- **B:** 1. B
  2. G
  3. B
  4. H

Comprehension Check, page 13
- **A:** 1. C
  2. H
  3. A
- **B:** Responses will vary. Emphasis should be placed upon the writer's ability to summarize the culture's contribution.

Orpheus and the Underworld

Vocabulary Check, page 14
- **A:** 1. lyre
  2. wicked
  3. shadow
  4. palace
  5. fierce
- **B:** 1. palace
  2. fierce
  3. shadow
  4. wicked
  5. lyre

Comprehension Check, page 15
- **A:** 1. A
  2. J
  3. A
  4. H
- **B:** Responses will vary. Encourage students to use their imaginations when it comes to characters and situations. For example, Orpheus might be a popular rock star and Eurydice the daughter of an important government official.

Chapter 2

Practice Read: John Adams: The Forgotten Man; Do the Right Thing: A Simple Plan

Vocabulary Check, page 22

A: 1. unanimous
   2. patriots
   3. tyrant
   4. nominated
B: Answers will vary. Possible related words: name; patriotic; unite; tyranny, tyrannical.

Comprehension Check, page 23

A: 1. C
   2. F
   3. A
B: Answers will vary. Students' paragraphs should show an understanding of why the school board's action was unfair, at least in the eyes of the team.

New Directions; Field Work

Vocabulary Check, page 24

A: 1. despondent
   2. ominous
   3. provisions
   4. stamina
   5. domestic
   6. insidious
B: 1. insidious
   2. despondent
   3. provisions
   4. domestic

Comprehension Check, page 25

A: 1. A
   2. G
   3. C
B: Answers will vary. Students' responses should show comprehension of Mrs. Johnson's character as depicted in the narrative and of valid comparisons and contrasts between 1903 and the present.

You Took the Words Right Out of My Mouth . . .

Vocabulary Check, page 26

A: 1. prosperity
   2. partisans
   3. debatable
   4. inconsequential
   5. simulating
B: 1. prosperity, Latin
   2. simulating, Latin
   3. partisan, Italian and Latin
   4. debatable, Latin

Comprehension Check, page 27

A: 1. D
   2. J
   3. B
   4. F
   5. B
B: Answers will vary. Most students will say that the column's alphabetical organization works well.

Prometheus Steals Fire from Heaven; Paul's Popcorn

Vocabulary Check, page 28

A: 1. forethought
   2. cunning
   3. considerable
   4. irrigated
   5. resources
   6. quick-witted
B: 1. cunning
   2. forethought
   3. resources

Comprehension Check, page 29

A: 1. B
   2. F
   3. D
B: Students' responses will vary. However, a valid response will describe someone who has either sacrificed for other people or brought the values of humor and hard work to the settlers of a large new territory.

Chapter 3

Practice Read: Lost and Found

Vocabulary Check, page 36
- **A:** 1. catapulted
  2. distressed
  3. ascended
- **B:** Sentences will vary; sample sentence: Christo4 was *dismayed and upset* when he found that his wallet was gone, but he also seemed *distressed* when it was returned.

Comprehension Check, page 37
- **A:** 1. B
  2. G
  3. A
- **B:** Students' paragraphs will vary, but they should explain how the setting influences "Lost and Found."

The Fog Horn

Vocabulary Check, page 38
- **A:** 1. subterranean
  2. immense
  3. primeval
  4. abruptly
  5. verify
- **B:** 1. verify
  2. primeval
  3. immense
  4. subterranean
  5. abruptly

Comprehension Check, page 39
- **A:** 1. A
  2. F
  3. C
- **B:** Possible answer: The fog horn, although not a person, plays the important role of interpreter for the monster. The monster sees it as kin.

The Birth of a Legend

Vocabulary Check, page 40
- **A:** 1. complied
  2. submerged
  3. nonchalant
- **B:** 1. nonchalant
  2. submerged
  3. complied

Comprehension Check, page 41
- **A:** 1. A
  2. H
  3. B
- **B:** Responses will vary. Some students could find the interviews with eyewitnesses to be essential. Others may like the brief history provided in the first part of the article.

Greyling

Vocabulary Check, page 42
- **A:** 1. kin
  2. roiling
  3. wallowed
  4. slough
- **B:** Answers will vary. Possible answers:
  1. Aunt Betty (and so on)
  2. the contents of one's stomach after eating too much
  3. a piece of flaky skin that had been sunburned
  4. a hippopotamus

Comprehension Check, page 43
- **A:** 1. B
  2. F
  3. C
  4. H
- **B:** Answers will vary. Sample answer: I'd tell them not to grieve because I am happy and have the best of two worlds, the sea and the land. Also, I'd tell them that I will always visit them once a year without fail.

Chapter 4

Practice Read: Wise Old Woman; Legacy II

Vocabulary Check, page 50

A: 1. decree
2. conquer
3. clustered
4. bewilderment

B: 1. another attack
2. only order left
3. wrong
4. ruled by force

Comprehension Check, page 51

A: 1. A
2. G
3. D

B: Students may restate the theme as "wisdom comes in all forms." Students' observations about the theme's importance will vary.

Out of the Ghetto

Vocabulary Check, page 52

A: 1. benediction
2. reluctantly
3. desperation
4. enclosure

B: 1. C
2. J
3. C
4. G

Comprehension Check, page 53

A: 1. B
2. G
3. A

B: Students may point out that the theme of "Out of the Ghetto" is echoed in *The Diary of Anne Frank*.

An Anne Frank Scrapbook

Vocabulary Check, page 54

A: 1. debilitated
2. haven
3. tolerance
4. in conjunction with

B: 1. haven: safe place
2. tolerance: understanding
3. in conjunction with: together with
4. debilitated: weakened

Comprehension Check, page 55

A: 1. D
2. J
3. A

B: Answers will vary. Students may mention encyclopedias, documentaries, and nonfiction books in the library.

A Family in Hiding

Vocabulary Check, page 56

A: 1. insatiable
2. allotted
3. enthusiasm
4. reverberated

B: 1. allotted
2. insatiable
3. enthusiasm
4. reverberated

Comprehension Check, page 57

A: 1. D
2. G
3. D

B: Answers will vary. Most students will recognize that the themes in this selection most probably recur in other works of literature dealing with war, loss, and survival.

Chapter 5

Practice Read: The Overhead Man

Vocabulary Check, page 64

A: 1. fuming
2. erupt
3. massive
4. consequences

B: Sample answers:
1. consequences
2. massive
3. fuming
4. erupt

Comprehension Check, page 65

A: 1. C
2. H
3. B

B: The story presents the theory that hatred causes violent physical effects in the outer world. The conclusion of the story is ambiguous about whether or not we should believe the story.

The Bells

Comprehension Check, page 66

A: 1. B
2. F
3. C
4. H

B: Students should identify the bells as sleigh or sledge bells, wedding bells, alarm bells, and iron church bells. Metaphors and similes will vary.

from Beyond the Grave

Vocabulary Check, page 67

A: 1. compelling
2. tangible
3. elusive
4. ritual

B: 1. compelling
2. ritual
3. tangible
4. elusive

Comprehension Check, page 68

A: 1. C
2. H
3. A

B: Answers will vary, but students should support their reasoning.

A Dream Within a Dream

Comprehension Check, page 69

A: 1. B
2. J
3. D

B: Answers will vary.

Chapter **6**

Practice Read: Skywriting

Comprehension Check, page 77

A: 1. B
2. G
3. C

B: Answers will vary. Possible answer: "He understood what words are for. They are/thoughts made visible." I like these lines because they express in a new and interesting way the purpose of words.

The Midnight Ride of Billy Dawes

Comprehension Check, page 78

A: 1. C
2. J
3. A

B: Answers will vary. Possible answer: Students should recognize that the poet wanted to retell a familiar story in a different way.

The Wreck of the Hesperus

Comprehension Check, page 79

A: 1. D
2. H
3. C
4. F

B: Paragraphs will vary. Sample paragraph: The wind and water swept the *Hesperus* ever closer to land. With no hand to guide her, the schooner plunged and tossed in the sea. Meanwhile, the snow blew furiously, and ice built up on the masts and sails. At this point, nothing could save the ship from wrecking on the rocky coast of Norman's Woe.

Schooners

Comprehension Check, page 80

A: 1. B
2. H
3. D

B: Possible answer: Schooners were used in the slave trade.

Lincoln Monument: Washington *and* Mr. Longfellow and His Boy

Comprehension Check, page 81

A: 1. C
2. F
3. B

B: Explanations will vary. His purpose seems to have been to urge people to be confident that right will prevail.

Chapter 7

Practice Read: It's About Time

Vocabulary Check, page 88

A: 1. mud and straw
   2. birthday
   3. things that tie us
   4. dinner, presents, a big cake with candles

B: Sample answers:
   1. heart sank; became disappointed
   2. pretty cool; friendly and up-to-date
   3. all shaken up; taken by surprise

Comprehension Check, page 89

A: 1. D
   2. F
   3. B
   4. F

B: Answers will vary. Sample response: See the grandfather's speech for supporting details. The boy changes and comes to see his grandfather's wisdom.

The Buried Treasure

Vocabulary Check, page 90

A: 1. summoned
   2. tenants
   3. bewildered

B: 1. Yuè Cang was stunned to find snakes instead of gold in the jars.
   2. Yuè Shêng and Yuè Cang were called to their father's bedside.
   3. The renters used the land for farming.

Comprehension Check, page 91

A: 1. A
   2. H
   3. A
   4. G

B: Answers will vary. Sample response: Parents should be obeyed and respected. The older brother obviously is disrespectful to his father, and we disapprove of his attitude.

The Funeral Banquet of King Midas

Vocabulary Check, page 92

A: 1. avalanche
   2. archaeologists
   3. excavating
   4. interior

B: Sample sentences:
   1. The **archaeologists** were astounded by the treasures they uncovered.
   2. Tools such as picks and shovels are often used when **excavating** sites.
   3. The skiers were swept over by a sudden **avalanche.**
   4. The **interior** was filled with blackness.

Comprehension Check, page 93

A: 1. C
   2. H
   3. B

B: Answers will vary. Sample answers: The artifacts found inside the tomb provide clues to life in Phrygia. Chemists used "sludges" to learn what items were in King Midas's funeral feast.

The Golden Touch

Vocabulary Check, page 94

A: 1. mortal
   2. rigid
   3. strewn

B: Sample answers:
   1. A sportscaster might say, "After all, these guys are only **mortal.** They can't perform miracles."
   2. The word **strewn** could describe clothes and other items on a bedroom floor.
   3. He became **rigid** with shock when elected class president.

Comprehension Check, page 95

A: 1. B
   2. F
   3. C
   4. H

B: Answers will vary. Sample answer: This myth teaches us that nature with all its beauties is worth more than hard, cold gold. For details see Marigold's feelings (lines 13–18), Bacchus's words (lines 42–51), and the end (lines 171–175).

Chapter 8

Practice Read: The Runaround

Vocabulary Check, page 102

A: 1. mode
2. promptly
3. excludes
4. alteration
5. expired

B: Possible answers:
1. milk, eggs, juice
2. A VCR would be in the RECORD mode if someone wanted to tape a television program so that he or she could see it later in the PLAYBACK mode.
3. A piece of clothing needs alteration if it is too long or is torn.
4. A person who arrives promptly to class will be better prepared than someone who comes late and misses what the teacher said.

Comprehension Check, page 103

A: 1. B
2. G
3. C

B: Answers will vary. Most students will prefer reading the letters that together form a narrative.

Passports: Don't Leave Home Without One

Vocabulary Check, page 104

A: 1. embassy   4. ambassador
2. obtain   5. affirm
3. official

B: 1. obtain   3. affirm
2. ambassador

Comprehension Check, page 105

A: 1. B
2. J
3. D
4. F

B: Wording will vary, but all major points should be covered as in the following sample: First, you have to get a passport application, which you can do by writing to the Passport Services office of the State Department in Washington or by going to a county office building or a main post office. You fill out the entire form and submit it with an official copy of your birth certificate, a pair of identical passport photos, and a check or money order payable to "Passport Office" for the fees involved in processing. If you're under eighteen, you also need a parent or guardian, with official ID of his or her own, to accompany you. You have to sign your application and affirm that everything on it is true.

Earth-Friendly Products?

Vocabulary Check, page 106

A: 1. skeptical
2. biodegradable
3. reclaimed
4. decomposition

B: 1. C
2. A
3. D
4. B

Comprehension Check, page 107

A: 1. D
2. F
3. B

B: Answers will vary, but most students will find the listing of recycling codes useful in a workplace document.

Locks

Vocabulary Check, page 108

A: 1. serrated
2. projections
3. altered
4. ultrasonic

B: Sample answers:
1. knives
2. a dress
3. a dog whistle
4. a rocky cliff

Comprehension Check, page 109

A: 1. C
2. J
3. A

B: Answers will vary. Sample answer: In order to activate an electronic lock using a card key, simply swipe the magnetic-strip side of the card through the slit in the lock. Other locks may require you to insert the card key into the lock.

Section Two

Answer Key to
Pupil's Edition of
Interactive Reading

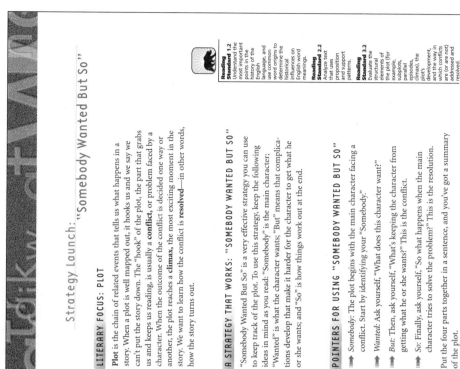

Chapter **1**

Structures

Patterns of Meaning

Chapter Preview In this chapter you will—

Read: Selections	**Interact with Text:** Graphic Organizers
Practice Read: Duncan, Junior by Heidi Schulman *Interactive Reading*, p. 2	"Somebody Wanted But So" Chart *Interactive Reading*, p. 10
Broken Chain by Gary Soto *Holt Literature and Language Arts*, p. 7	Plot Diagram • *Interactive Reading*, p. 11
Road Warriors, Listen Up by Madeline Travers Hovland *Holt Literature and Language Arts*, p. 20	Main-Idea Chart • *Interactive Reading*, p. 12
Flowers for Algernon by Daniel Keyes *Holt Literature and Language Arts*, p. 23	Story Map • *Interactive Reading*, p. 13
Memory a Matter of Brains and Brawn by Lauran Neergaard *Holt Literature and Language Arts*, p. 58	Evaluation Chart • *Interactive Reading*, p. 14
The Landlady by Roald Dahl *Holt Literature and Language Arts*, p. 62	Foreshadowing Chart • *Interactive Reading*, p. 5
The No-Guitar Blues by Gary Soto *Interactive Reading*, p. 17	Project: Author Study • *Interactive Reading*, p. 27
Music from the Start by Patricia Hunt-Jones *Interactive Reading*, p. 28	Project: Musical Time Line • *Interactive Reading*, p. 35
Orpheus and the Underworld by Mollie McLean and Anne Wiseman *Interactive Reading*, p. 36	Project: Storyboard • *Interactive Reading*, p. 43

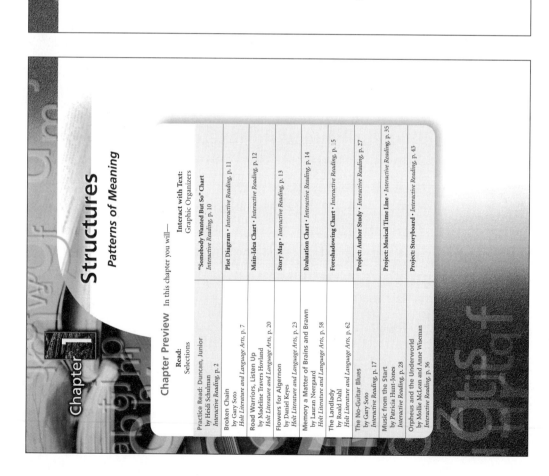

Strategy Launch: "Somebody Wanted But So"

LITERARY FOCUS: PLOT

Plot is the chain of related events that tells us what happens in a story. When a plot is well mapped out, it hooks us and we say we can't put the story down. The "hook" of the plot, the part that grabs us and keeps us reading, is usually a **conflict**, or problem faced by a character. When the outcome of the conflict is decided one way or another, the plot reaches a **climax**, the most exciting moment in the story. We want to learn how the conflict is **resolved**—in other words, how the story turns out.

A STRATEGY THAT WORKS: "SOMEBODY WANTED BUT SO"

"Somebody Wanted But So" is a very effective strategy you can use to keep track of the plot. To use this strategy, keep the following ideas in mind as you read: "Somebody" is the main character; "Wanted" is what the character wants; "But" means that complications develop that make it harder for the character to get what he or she wants; and "So" is how things work out at the end.

POINTERS FOR USING "SOMEBODY WANTED BUT SO"

➡ *Somebody:* The plot begins with the main character facing a conflict. Start by identifying your "Somebody."

➡ *Wanted:* Ask yourself, "What does this character want?"

➡ *But:* Then, ask yourself, "What's keeping the character from getting what he or she wants?" This is the conflict.

➡ *So:* Finally, ask yourself, "So what happens when the main character tries to solve the problem?" This is the resolution.

Put the four parts together in a sentence, and you've got a summary of the plot.

Reading Standard 1.2 Understand the most important points in the history of the English language, and use common word origins to determine the historical influences on English word meanings.

Reading Standard 2.2 Analyze text that uses proposition and support patterns.

Reading Standard 3.2 Evaluate the structural elements of the plot (for example, subplots, parallel episodes, climax), the plot's development, and the way in which conflicts are (or are not) addressed and resolved.

Strategy Launch **1**

Practice Read

BEFORE YOU READ

Here's a story that will probably be easy to identify with. It's about a teen who wants a dog. You've already gotten a head start, because now you know what the "somebody" (a teen) "wants" (a dog). Read on to find out the specifics.

Duncan, Junior

Heidi Schulman

I turned fourteen about two months ago, and that's when I decided it was time to get a dog. After all, my family and I live way out in the country, and the place is about as close to doggie heaven as anywhere on earth. For shade, we've got bushy pine trees that go up a hundred feet into the air. We've got a wide, muddy river to splash in, and in the spring and summer the meadows are filled with purple and yellow wildflowers and tall grasses so soft they'd tickle a pup's paws. It's quiet enough to hear a cat meow a quarter of a mile away, and between the beavers and birds and old jackrabbits that like to come close to the back door and never get bored. It's perfect.

10   I explained my decision to my parents. They had other ideas for me, though, and none of them had anything to do with the word **"canine."**

"Jeremy," said my father. That's my name, by the way—Jeremy.

SOMEBODY WANTED BUT SO

Pause at line 16. What's the "But" part of this plot, or the conflict?

Jeremy's parents don't want to get a dog.

VOCABULARY DEVELOPMENT

canine (kā´nīn´) adj.: of or like a dog.

Canine is from the Latin word canis for "dog."

2   Chapter 1   Structures: Patterns of Meaning

20 "Jeremy," dad said, "who's going to walk the dog in the middle of winter when it's five below zero and the sky is pitch black and the wind is howling and sleet is blowing into your face?"

I had a feeling dad would say that. I was prepared.

"I won't have to walk him," I answered. I'll just let him out and he can walk himself. This is the country, Dad. There's land everywhere."

30 My comeback was brilliant, if I do say so myself. And it was completely based on fact. Our house sits in the middle of a huge meadow that stretches, gosh, I don't know how far it really stretches, but trust me, this meadow is seriously huge. You can't even see any other houses from where we live. In fact, our closest neighbors are the birds that hang out in the pine trees.

My mother, of course, had her own strong opinion. You can always count on that with mom.

"Jeremy Gottlieb. Do you think I'm going to let an animal run around outside by himself, get filthy dirty, and then track mud and pine needles inside all over my clean carpet? I don't think so."

40 It was time for brilliant comeback number two. I'd really worked on this one.

"I'll make him dog boots, mom. Little rubber things with Velcro closings. That way he'll be clean when he comes in."

"Nice try," said my mom. "How about a fish instead?"

I couldn't blame my parents for being down on the dog idea. The last time we'd had a dog, we lived in New York City in a crowded two-bedroom **apartment** on the fifth floor of an old brick apartment building. If you tried

50 to compare the place we lived then to the place we live now,

EVALUATE

Underline Jeremy's replies to his parents' objections. How effectively does he reply to their reasons for not having a dog?

Students' responses may vary. He effectively refutes his dad's reason, but the reply he gives his mother seems a stretch.

VOCABULARY DEVELOPMENT

apartment (ə-pär´mənt) n.: room or group of rooms to live in.

In England, apartments are called flats, because they are usually on one floor.

Practice Read   3

Page 4

SOMEBODY WANTED BUT SO

Pause at line 58. What do you know about "Somebody" so far? **His name is Jeremy Gottlieb; he's 14; he used to live in a two-bedroom apartment in a six-story building in New York City, but now he and his parents live in the country.**

VOCABULARY DEVELOPMENT

exercise (ek′sər·sīz′) n.: activity for the purpose of training or developing the body or mind.

humidity (hyōō·mid′ə·tē) n.: moistness; dampness.

When you come to a long word, you can often find a shorter word inside it that you already know. Circle the smaller word inside *humidity*.

the only thing you could say was they were exact opposites. Here, we have nature, nature, and more nature. There, we had cement, cement, and more cement. Our street was just one six-story brick apartment building after another. There were no trees and there was no grass. The only things that grew were scrawny little weeds trying to bust out from the cracks in the sidewalks.

It wasn't exactly a good place for a pet who needs **exercise**. But my aunt was moving and couldn't take her 10-year-old dog Duncan with her. I remember the night I convinced my parents to take him. I begged. I promised to walk the dog every day. I did everything but have a tantrum, because I knew for sure that would backfire on me.

It was about 95 degrees that night. The (humidity) was high and we were all sweating like pigs. I think the reason my parents finally gave in and took the dog was that the heat had gone to their brains and they just wanted to go to sleep.

So Duncan came to live with us. He was a black poodle who'd never had a haircut and looked like a stringy mop that had come to life. He had a limp, and because of it, he'd trip sometimes and run into the couch or a table. But it never seemed to bother him.

Duncan and I became close pals. But I hardly ever walked him.

I can still remember the way my mother looked at me on freezing mornings as she put her woolly brown winter coat on over her pajamas to take Duncan for his walk. I got out of it by pretending to be asleep. I was never really sure why my parents let me get away with it, but I think it was probably because they came to love Duncan, too.

Page 5

INFER

What does the story about Duncan have to do with Jeremy's asking for a dog in the country? **The two episodes are parallel: In each, Jeremy wants a dog, faces the opposition of his parents, but gets the dog with their permission anyway. This flashback fills in background on Jeremy's family history concerning pets.**

WORD KNOWLEDGE

In line 106, Jeremy compares Duncan Junior to a tornado, which is a violent whirling column of air, with wind speeds up to three hundred miles per hour.

Tornado came into English from the Spanish word *tornar*, meaning "turn." Spanish, in turn, borrowed from a Latin word meaning "thunder."

Duncan lived a long life, by the way. We had my mom to thank for that. She refused to believe the vet when he said Duncan had a slipped disc and should be put down because he'd never be able to walk right. She just marched the dog out of the vet's office, borrowed a baby's playpen from neighbors, and made Duncan stay in there with a heating pad wrapped around his bad leg. Duncan got better, and lived to be fifteen. But me, I never got better about taking him out.

So, to be honest, my parents had a pretty good reason for saying no to me when I said I wanted another dog. I didn't exactly have a great track record. But that didn't mean I was going to take "no" for an answer. I knew my parents loved dogs, and I've got a strong will just like my mom. So I just kept bringing it up, and bringing it up until, well, you get the picture.

When they finally gave in, I named the dog Duncan Junior.

Every dog has his own personality. Which is my way of saying Duncan Junior turned out to be a lot different from Duncan Senior. He was a big guy, very muscular and strong. He had a short shiny coat and was all white, except for two black ears. DJ, which is what I called him for short, had more energy than a tornado, and his favorite thing in the whole entire world was running. We got him in the spring, and he and I would spend every afternoon and weekend running near the river. He'd run along the muddy river bank, leaping over the limbs of willow trees that had blown down in the spring winds. There was my big white dog, practically up to his little black ears in muddy water, following the current, trying to pick up every stick and tree branch that floated by, brown eyes shining, the happiest

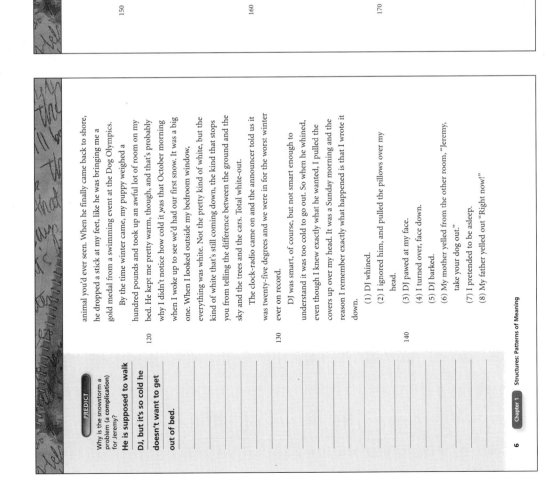

PREDICT

Why is the snowstorm a problem (a complication) for Jeremy?

He is supposed to walk

DJ, but it's so cold he

doesn't want to get

out of bed.

animal you'd ever seen. When he finally came back to shore, he dropped a stick at my feet, like he was bringing me a gold medal from a swimming event at the Dog Olympics.

By the time winter came, my puppy weighed a
120   hundred pounds and took up an awful lot of room on my bed. He kept me pretty warm, though, and that's probably why I didn't notice how cold it was that October morning when I woke up to see we'd had our first snow. It was a big one. When I looked outside my bedroom window, everything was white. Not the pretty kind of white, but the kind of white that's still coming down, the kind that stops you from telling the difference between the ground and the sky and the trees and the cars. Total white-out.

The clock-radio came on and the announcer told us it was twenty-five degrees and we were in for the worst winter ever on record.

DJ was smart, of course, but not smart enough to
130   understand it was too cold to go out. So when he whined, even though I knew exactly what he wanted, I pulled the covers up over my head. It was a Sunday morning and the reason I remember exactly what happened is that I wrote it down.

(1) DJ whined.

(2) I ignored him, and pulled the pillows over my head.

(3) DJ pawed at my face.

(4) I turned over, face down.

(5) DJ barked.

(6) My mother yelled from the other room, "Jeremy, take your dog out."

(7) I pretended to be asleep.

(8) My father yelled out "Right now!"

(9) I kept pretending. After all, it worked in New York City.

(10) My mother groaned and said to my father, "Here we go again, Sam."

(11) My father said, "Helen" (that's my mom) "don't do it."

(12) My mom said, "I'm doing it just this once, and never again."

(13) I thought: "Yes!"

What happened next wasn't very pretty.

I heard my mom's slippers on the floor and heard the back door open.

150   "Let's go, DJ," she said. Then her voice got louder. "DJ, let's go now!"

DJ whined. I heard my mother shuffle back into bed. DJ came back into my room and whined again.

My mother called out, "Jeremy, we know you're just pretending to be asleep. But you'd better get up. Your dog won't go outside with me."

You can only listen to a dog whine up to a certain point, and that point is exactly four minutes and 11
160   seconds. When DJ reached that mark, I faced the awful truth. My dog wouldn't go out of the house with anyone but me. Not only that, but he wouldn't even walk if I was at the back door waiting for him. I had to walk with him.

"You're carrying loyalty too far," I said to DJ the next morning. It was 6 A.M., and I was outside walking my dog. I was wearing at least three sweaters, and my teeth were chattering because the temperature was so low the snow had turned to ice.

170   But DJ just smiled and ran along, waiting for me at every turn. You practically couldn't see him in the snow.

SOMEBODY WANTED BUT SO

Pause at line 172. The plot develops to a climax. What does Jeremy cio?

He gets out of bed

to walk his dog.

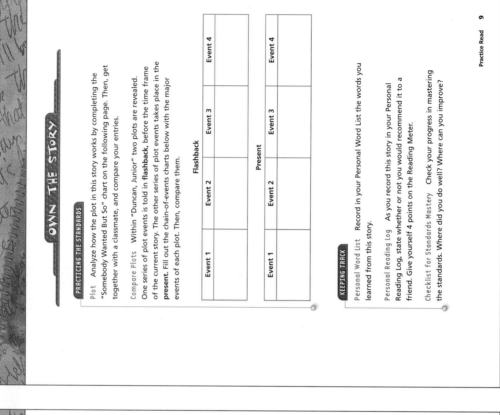

OWN THE STORY

PRACTICING THE STANDARDS

Plot Analyze how the plot in this story works by completing the "Somebody Wanted But So" chart on the following page. Then, get together with a classmate, and compare your entries.

Compare Plots Within "Duncan, Junior" two plots are revealed. One series of plot events is told in **flashback**, before the time frame of the current story. The other series of plot events takes place in the **present.** Fill out the chain-of-events charts below with the major events of each plot. Then, compare them.

Flashback			
Event 1	Event 2	Event 3	Event 4

Present			
Event 1	Event 2	Event 3	Event 4

KEEPING TRACK

Personal Word List Record in your Personal Word List the words you learned from this story.

Personal Reading Log As you record this story in your Personal Reading Log, state whether or not you would recommend it to a friend. Give yourself 4 points on the Reading Meter.

Checklist for Standards Mastery Check your progress in mastering the standards. Where did you do well? Where can you improve?

Practice Read   9

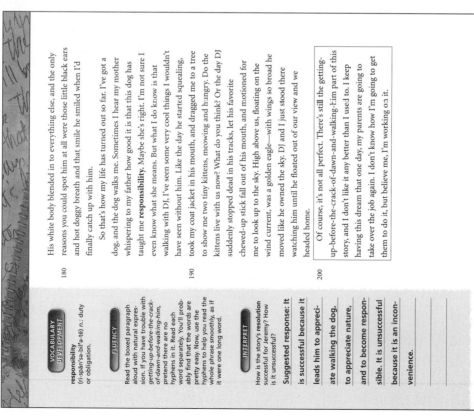

His white body blended in to everything else, and the only reasons you could spot him at all were those little black ears and hot doggy breath and that smile he smiled when I'd finally catch up with him.

So that's how my life has turned out so far. I've got a dog, and the dog walks me. Sometimes I hear my mother whispering to my father how good it is that this dog has taught me **responsibility.** Maybe she's right. I'm not sure I even know what she means. But what I do know is that walking with DJ, I've seen some very cool things I wouldn't have seen without him. Like the day he started squealing, took my coat jacket in his mouth, and dragged me to a tree to show me two tiny kittens, meowing and hungry. Do the kittens live with us now? What do you think? Or the day DJ suddenly stopped dead in his tracks, let his favorite chewed-up stick fall out of his mouth, and motioned for me to look up to the sky. High above us, floating on the wind current, was a golden eagle—with wings so broad he moved like he owned the sky. DJ and I just stood there watching him until he floated out of our view and we headed home.

Of course, it's not all perfect. There's still the getting-up-before-the-crack-of-dawn-and-walking-him part of this story, and I don't like it any better than I used to. I keep having this dream that one day, my parents are going to take over the job again. I don't know how I'm going to get them to do it, but believe me, I'm working on it.

VOCABULARY DEVELOPMENT

responsibility
(ri-spän′sə-bil′ə-tē) *n.:* duty or obligation.

FLUENCY

Read the boxed paragraph aloud with natural expression. If you have trouble with *getting-up-before-the-crack-of-dawn-and-walking-him,* pretend there are no hyphens in it. Read each word separately. You'll probably find that the words are pretty easy. Now, use the hyphens to help you read the whole phrase smoothly, as if it were one long word.

INTERPRET

How is the story's resolution successful for Jeremy? How is it unsuccessful?

Suggested response: It is successful because it leads him to appreciate nature, and to become responsible. It is unsuccessful because it is an inconvenience.

8   Chapter 1   Structures: Patterns of Meaning

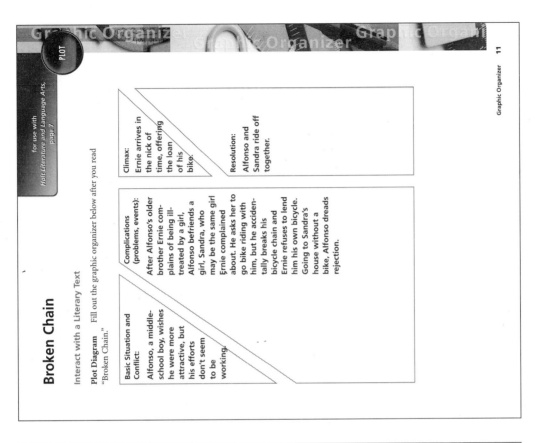

PLOT

for use with
Holt Literature and Language Arts,
page 7

Broken Chain

Interact with a Literary Text

Plot Diagram   Fill out the graphic organizer below after you read "Broken Chain."

Basic Situation and Conflict:	Complications (problems, events):	Climax:
Alfonso, a middle-school boy, wishes he were more attractive, but his efforts don't seem to be working.	After Alfonso's older brother Ernie complains of being ill-treated by a girl, Alfonso befriends a girl, Sandra, who may be the same girl Ernie complained about. He asks her to go bike riding with him, but he accidentally breaks his bicycle chain and Ernie refuses to lend him his own bicycle. Going to Sandra's house without a bike, Alfonso dreads rejection.	Ernie arrives in the nick of time, offering the loan of his bike.
		Resolution: Alfonso and Sandra ride off together.

Graphic Organizer   **11**

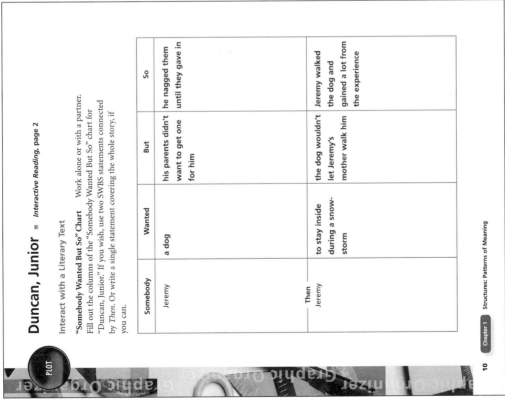

PLOT

Duncan, Junior ■ *Interactive Reading,* page 2

Interact with a Literary Text

"Somebody Wanted But So" Chart   Work alone or with a partner. Fill out the columns of the "Somebody Wanted But So" chart for "Duncan, Junior." If you wish, use two SWBS statements connected by *Then.* Or write a single statement covering the whole story, if you can.

Somebody	Wanted	But	So
Jeremy	a dog	his parents didn't want to get one for him	he nagged them until they gave in
Then Jeremy	to stay inside during a snowstorm	the dog wouldn't let Jeremy's mother walk him	Jeremy walked the dog and gained a lot from the experience

Road Warriors, Listen Up

ANALYZING TEXT

for use with
Holt Literature and Language Arts,
page 20

Interact with an Informational Text

Main-Idea Chart The **main idea** is the most important point the writer is making about a subject. In a well-written article the main idea is clearly supported by details.

After you read "Road Warriors, Listen Up," fill out this graphic organizer. First, write the subject of the article. Then, fill in the details the writer provides about the subject. Finally, think about those details, and decide what overall idea they express about the subject. Write the main idea in its box.

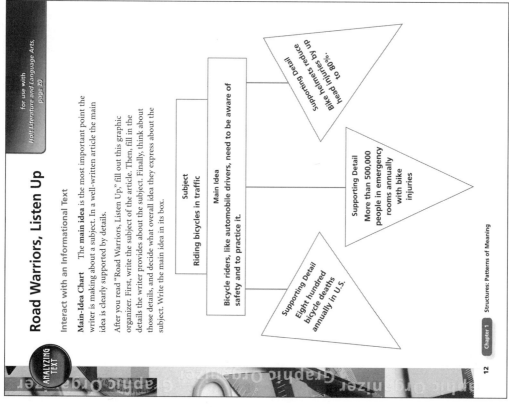

Subject
Riding bicycles in traffic

Main Idea
Bicycle riders, like automobile drivers, need to be aware of safety and to practice it.

Supporting Detail
Eight hundred bicycle deaths annually in U.S.

Supporting Detail
More than 500,000 people in emergency rooms annually with bike injuries

Supporting Detail
Bike helmets by up to 80% reduce head injuries

Chapter 1 | Structures: Patterns of Meaning

PLOT

Flowers for Algernon

for use with
Holt Literature and Language Arts,
page 23

Interact with a Literary Text

Story Map Long stories and novels are likely to have more plot complications than short stories. "Flowers for Algernon" certainly has a more complicated plot than the other stories you are reading in Chapter 1. Fill out the story map below as you read "Flowers for Algernon" to be sure you understand the plot events.

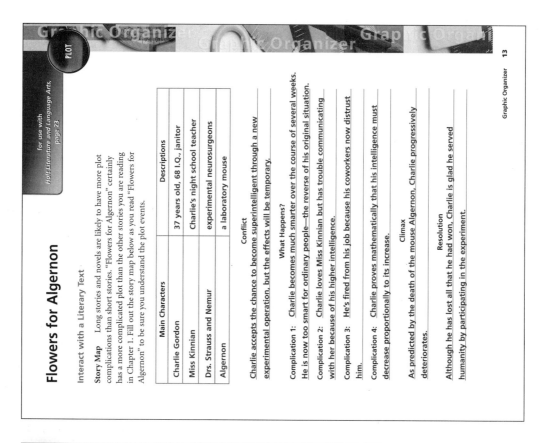

Main Characters	Descriptions
Charlie Gordon	37 years old, 68 I.Q., janitor
Miss Kinnian	Charlie's night school teacher
Drs. Strauss and Nemur	experimental neurosurgeons
Algernon	a laboratory mouse

Conflict
Charlie accepts the chance to become superintelligent through a new experimental operation, but the effects will be temporary.

What Happens?

Complication 1: Charlie becomes much smarter over the course of several weeks. He is now too smart for ordinary people—the reverse of his original situation.

Complication 2: Charlie loves Miss Kinnian but has trouble communicating with her because of his higher intelligence.

Complication 3: He's fired from his job because his coworkers now distrust him.

Complication 4: Charlie proves mathematically that his intelligence must decrease proportionally to its increase.

Climax
As predicted by the death of the mouse Algernon, Charlie progressively deteriorates.

Resolution
Although he has lost all that he had won, Charlie is glad he served humanity by participating in the experiment.

Graphic Organizer

13

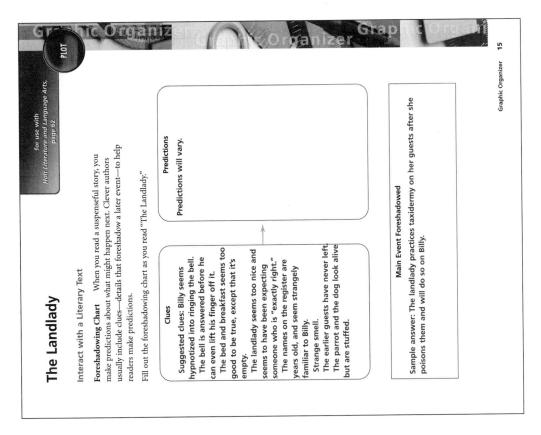

PLOT

for use with
Holt Literature and Language Arts,
page 62

The Landlady

Interact with a Literary Text

Foreshadowing Chart When you read a suspenseful story, you make predictions about what might happen next. Clever authors usually include clues—details that foreshadow a later event—to help readers make predictions.

Fill out the foreshadowing chart as you read "The Landlady."

Clues

Suggested clues: Billy seems hypnotized into ringing the bell. The bell is answered before he can even lift his finger off it. The bed and breakfast seems too good to be true, except that it's empty. The landlady seems too nice and seems to have been expecting someone who is "exactly right." The names on the register are years old, and seem strangely familiar to Billy. Strange smell. The earlier guests have never left. The parrot and the dog look alive but are stuffed.

Predictions

Predictions will vary.

Main Event Foreshadowed

Sample answer: The landlady practices taxidermy on her guests after she poisons them and will do so on Billy.

Graphic Organizer 15

ANALYZING TEXT

for use with
Holt Literature and Language Arts,
page 58

Memory a Matter of Brains and Brawn

Interact with an Informational Text

Evaluation Chart In an effective informational or persuasive text, the main idea is stated as a proposition at the beginning. The proposition is then supported by reasons. The first sentence of "Memory a Matter of Brains and Brawn" is the proposition: "The brain is like a muscle: Use it or lose it."

Below are the reasons that the writer of the article gives for believing that proposition. For each reason, decide whether it is a fact, a statistic, an anecdote, an example, a definition, or an expert opinion. Then, evaluate how effective you think each reason is. Rate the reasons on a scale of 1–4, with 4 the highest rating. If you think a reason could be made stronger, say how you would change it.

Reason	Type of Reason	Effectiveness	How I Would Change It
Mental exercise seems crucial to retaining brainpower.	expert opinion ("growing conclusion from research")	3	Make it more specific; add quotation from an expert.
Bad memory linked to lifestyle risks that people can change	fact	3	Give statistics for these links.
Alzheimer's patients can be helped by mental exercise.	expert opinion ("provocative new research suggests . . .")	3	Wait until research conclusions are more solid.
"Read, read, read. . . . Anything that stimulates the brain to think."	expert opinion	4	
The brain continually rewires and adapts itself, even growing some new neurons.	fact	4	Specify types of brain functions related to new neuron growth.
Alzheimer's linked to less education and poor reading habits	fact	4	

Chapter 1 Structures: Patterns of Meaning

14

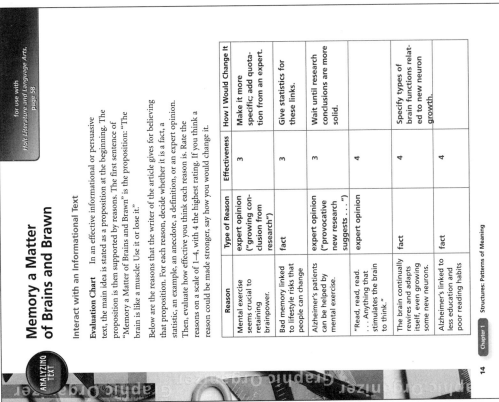

Literature

SHORT STORY

AUTHOR STUDY

Gary Soto was born and raised in Fresno, California. He has written many books of fiction and poetry about what it is like to grow up as a Mexican American. Many of Soto's stories and poems come from his own childhood experiences. In addition to writing, Soto teaches and produces short films for Spanish-speaking children.

BEFORE YOU READ

Think about something you've always wanted. What would you do if you finally had the chance to get it, but you weren't sure if the way you were able to get it was quite right? In this story, Fausto has the "no-guitar blues," but possibly not for long.

"The No-Guitar Blues" was made into a short film, called *The Pool Party*. Of all Soto's stories this is the only one that has been adapted for film.

Keep the following in mind as you read:

- Many Spanish words and phrases appear in this story. Use the footnotes to learn what they mean and how to pronounce them.
- Los Lobos (the Wolves) is a rock group.

Reading Standard 3.2 Evaluate the structural elements of the plot (for example, subplots, parallel episodes, climax), the plot's development, and the way in which conflicts are (or are not) addressed and resolved.

The No-Guitar Blues

Gary Soto

The moment Fausto saw the group Los Lobos on "American Bandstand," he knew exactly what he wanted to do with his life—play guitar. His eyes grew large with excitement as Los Lobos ground out a song while teenagers bounced off each other on the crowded dance floor.

He had watched "American Bandstand" for years and had heard Ray Camacho and the Teardrops at Romain Playground, but it had never occurred to him that he too might become a musician. That afternoon Fausto knew his mission in life: to play guitar in his own band; to sweat out his songs and prance around the stage; to make money and dress weird.

10

PREDICT

"The No-Guitar Blues"—what might that title mean? Figure it out, and you'll be able to predict the basic situation of this story. Then, keep reading, and find out what happens.

Students' responses will vary.

_____

_____

_____

_____

_____

_____

SOMEBODY WANTED BUT SO

The first sentence in the story tells you who the somebody is and what he wants. Circle the words or phrases that give you this information. Put an *S* above the word that identifies the "Somebody" and a *W* above the words that identify what he "Wants."

Gary Soto **17**

· · · · · · **Notes** · · · · · ·

Fausto turned off the television set and walked outside, wondering how he could get enough money to buy a guitar. He couldn't ask his parents because they would just say, "Money doesn't grow on trees" or "What do you think we are, bankers?" And besides, they hated rock music. They were into the *conjunto*[1] music of Lydia Mendoza, Flaco Jimenez, and Little Joe and La Familia. And, as Fausto recalled, the last album they bought was *The Chipmunks Sing Christmas Favorites.*

But what the heck, he'd give it a try. He returned inside and watched his mother make tortillas. He leaned against the kitchen counter, trying to work up the nerve to ask her for a guitar. Finally, he couldn't hold back any longer.

"Mom," he said, "I want a guitar for Christmas."

She looked up from rolling tortillas. "Honey, a guitar costs a lot of money."

"How 'bout for my birthday next year," he tried again.

"I can't promise," she said, turning back to her tortillas, "but we'll see."

Fausto walked back outside with a buttered tortilla. He knew his mother was right. His father was a warehouseman at Berven Rugs, where he made good money but not enough to buy everything his children wanted. Fausto decided to mow lawns to earn money, and was pushing the mower down the street before he realized it was winter and no one would hire him. He returned the mower and picked up a rake. He hopped onto his sister's bike (his had two flat tires) and rode north to the nicer section of Fresno in search of work. He went door-to-door, but after three hours he managed to get only one job, and not to rake

1. ***conjunto*** (kän-kho͞on'to): style of music popular near the U.S.-Mexico border.

leaves. He was asked to hurry down to the store to buy a loaf of bread, for which he received a grimy, dirt-caked quarter.

He also got an orange, which he ate sitting at the curb. While he was eating, a dog walked up and sniffed his leg. Fausto pushed him away and threw an orange peel skyward. The dog caught it and ate it in one gulp. The dog looked at Fausto and wagged his tail for more. Fausto tossed him a slice of orange, and the dog snapped it up and licked his lips.

"How come you like oranges, dog?"

The dog blinked a pair of sad eyes and whined.

"What's the matter? Cat got your tongue?" Fausto laughed at his joke and offered the dog another slice.

At that moment a dim light came on inside Fausto's head. He saw that it was sort of a fancy dog, a terrier or something, with dog tags and a shiny collar. And it looked well fed and healthy. In his neighborhood, the dogs were never licensed, and if they got sick they were placed near the water heater until they got well.

This dog looked like he belonged to rich people. Fausto cleaned his juice-sticky hands on his pants and got to his feet. The light in his head grew brighter. It just might work. He called the dog, patted its muscular back, and bent down to check the license.

"Great," he said. "There's an address."

The dog's name was Roger, which struck Fausto as weird because he'd never heard of a dog with a human name. Dogs should have names like Bomber, Freckles, Queenie, Killer, and Zero.

Gary Soto   **19**

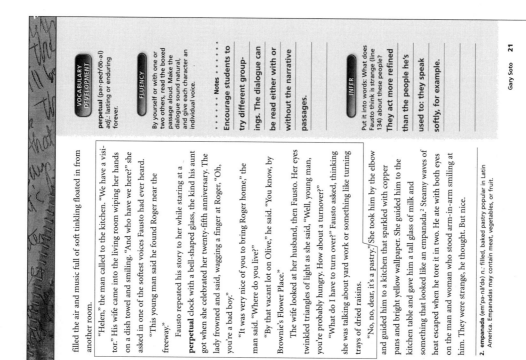

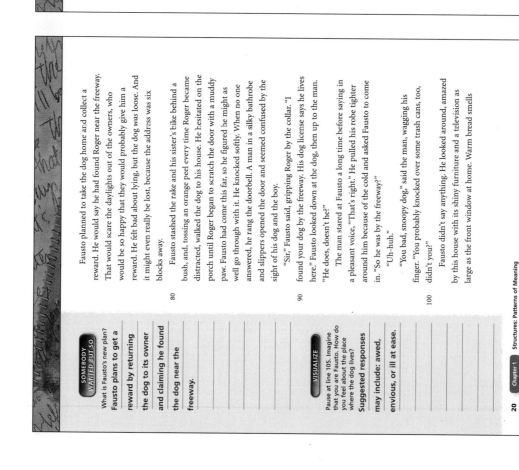

VOCABULARY DEVELOPMENT

perpetual (pər-pĕch'ōō-əl) *adj.*: lasting or enduring forever.

FLUENCY

By yourself or with one or two others, read the boxed passage aloud. Make the dialogue sound natural, and give each character an individual voice.

• • • • • Notes • • • • • •

Encourage students to try different groupings. The dialogue can be read either with or without the narrative passages.

INFER

Put it into words: What does Fausto think is strange (line 134) about these people? **They act more refined than the people he's used to: they speak softly, for example.**

filled the air and music full of soft tinkling floated in from another room.

"Helen," the man called to the kitchen. "We have a visitor." His wife came into the living room wiping her hands on a dish towel and smiling. "And who have we here?" she asked in one of the softest voices Fausto had ever heard.

"This young man said he found Roger near the freeway."

Fausto repeated his story to her while staring at a **perpetual** clock with a bell-shaped glass, the kind his aunt got when she celebrated her twenty-fifth anniversary. The lady frowned and said, wagging a finger at Roger, "Oh, you're a bad boy."

"It was very nice of you to bring Roger home," the man said. "Where do you live?"

"By that vacant lot on Olive," he said. "You know, by Brownie's Flower Place."

The wife looked at her husband, then Fausto. Her eyes twinkled triangles of light as she said, "Well, young man, you're probably hungry. How about a turnover?"

"What do I have to turn over?" Fausto asked, thinking she was talking about yard work or something like turning trays of dried raisins.

"No, no, dear, it's a pastry." She took him by the elbow and guided him to a kitchen that sparkled with copper pans and bright yellow wallpaper. She guided him to the kitchen table and gave him a tall glass of milk and something that looked like an empanada.² Steamy waves of heat escaped when he tore it in two. He ate with both eyes on the man and woman who stood arm-in-arm smiling at him. They were strange, he thought. But nice.

2. **empanada** (em'pə-nä'də) *n.*: filled, baked pastry popular in Latin America. Empanadas may contain meat, vegetables, or fruit.

Gary Soto **21**

SOMEBODY WANTED BUT SO

What is Fausto's new plan? **Fausto plans to get a reward by returning the dog to its owner and claiming he found the dog near the freeway.**

VISUALIZE

Pause at line 105. Imagine that you are Fausto. How do you feel about the place where the dog lives? **Suggested responses may include: awed, envious, or ill at ease.**

Fausto planned to take the dog home and collect a reward. He would say he had found Roger near the freeway. That would scare the daylights out of the owners, who would be so happy that they would probably give him a reward. He felt bad about lying, but the dog *was* loose. And it might even really be lost, because the address was six blocks away.

Fausto stashed the rake and his sister's bike behind a bush, and, tossing an orange peel every time Roger became distracted, walked the dog to his house. He hesitated on the porch until Roger began to scratch the door with a muddy paw. Fausto had come this far, so he figured he might as well go through with it. He knocked softly. When no one answered, he rang the doorbell. A man in a silky bathrobe and slippers opened the door and seemed confused by the sight of his dog and the boy.

"Sir," Fausto said, gripping Roger by the collar. "I found your dog by the freeway. His dog license says he lives here." Fausto looked down at the dog, then up to the man. "He does, doesn't he?"

The man stared at Fausto a long time before saying in a pleasant voice, "That's right." He pulled his robe tighter around him because of the cold and asked Fausto to come in. "So he was by the freeway?"

"Uh-huh."

"You bad, snoopy dog," said the man, wagging his finger. "You probably knocked over some trash cans, too, didn't you?"

Fausto didn't say anything. He looked around, amazed by this house with its shiny furniture and a television as large as the front window at home. Warm bread smells

Chapter 1 Structures: Patterns of Meaning

20

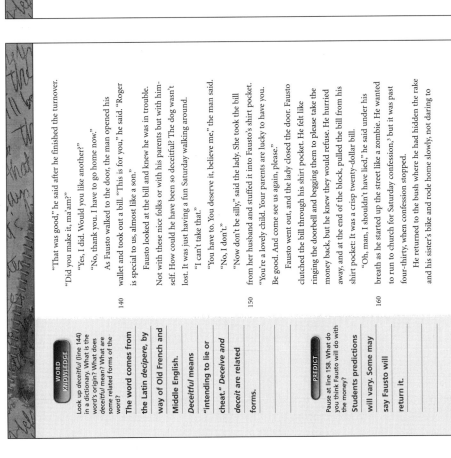

Page 22

WORD
KNOWLEDGE

Look up *deceitful* (line 144) in a dictionary. What is the word's origin? What does *deceitful* mean? What are some related forms of the word?

The word comes from the Latin *decipere*, by way of Old French and Middle English. *Deceitful* means "intending to lie or cheat." *Deceive* and *deceit* are related forms.

PREDICT

Pause at line 158. What do you think Fausto will do with the money? **Students predictions will vary. Some may say Fausto will return it.**

"That was good," he said after he finished the turnover. "Did you make it, ma'am?"

"Yes, I did. Would you like another?"

"No, thank you. I have to go home now."

140 As Fausto walked to the door, the man opened his wallet and took out a bill. "This is for you," he said. "Roger is special to us, almost like a son."

Fausto looked at the bill and knew he was in trouble. Not with these nice folks or with his parents but with himself. How could he have been so deceitful? The dog wasn't lost. It was just having a fun Saturday walking around.

"I can't take that."

"You have to. You deserve it, believe me," the man said.

"No, I don't."

150 "Now don't be silly," said the lady. She took the bill from her husband and stuffed it into Fausto's shirt pocket. "You're a lovely child. Your parents are lucky to have you. Be good. And come see us again, please."

Fausto went out, and the lady closed the door. Fausto clutched the bill through his shirt pocket. He felt like ringing the doorbell and begging them to please take the money back, but he knew they would refuse. He hurried away, and at the end of the block, pulled the bill from his shirt pocket: It was a crisp twenty-dollar bill.

160 "Oh, man, I shouldn't have lied," he said under his breath as he started up the street like a zombie. He wanted to run to church for Saturday confession,[3] but it was past four-thirty, when confession stopped.

He returned to the bush where he had hidden the rake and his sister's bike and rode home slowly, not daring to

3. In the Roman Catholic religion, a person seeks God's forgiveness by telling his or her sins to a priest. This is called **confession**.

22   **Chapter 1**   Structures: Patterns of Meaning

Page 23

· · · · · · Notes · · · · · ·

touch the money in his pocket. At home, in the privacy of his room, he examined the twenty-dollar bill. He had never had so much money. It was probably enough to buy a secondhand guitar. But he felt bad, like the time he stole a dollar from the secret fold inside his older brother's wallet.

Fausto went outside and sat on the fence. "Yeah," he said. "I can probably get a guitar for twenty. Maybe at a yard sale—things are cheaper."

His mother called him to dinner.

170 The next day he dressed for church without anyone telling him. He was going to go to eight o'clock mass.

"I'm going to church, Mom," he said. His mother was in the kitchen cooking *papas*[4] and *chorizo con huevos*.[5] A pile of tortillas lay warm under a dish towel.

"Oh, I'm so proud of you, Son." She beamed, turning over the crackling *papas*.

His older brother, Lawrence, who was at the table reading the funnies, mimicked, "Oh, I'm so proud of you, my son," under his breath.

180 At Saint Theresa's he sat near the front. When Father Jerry began by saying that we are all sinners, Fausto thought he looked right at him. Could he know? No, he thought. I only did it yesterday. But he couldn't forget the man and the lady, whose names he didn't even know, and the empanada they had given him. It had a strange name but tasted really good. He wondered how they got rich. And how that dome clock worked. He had asked his mother once how his aunt's clock worked. She said it just worked, the way the refrigerator works. It just did.

190

4. *papas* (pä'päs) n.: potatoes.
5. *chorizo con huevos* (chō-rē'zō-kōn wä'vōs): sausage with eggs.

VOCABULARY DEVELOPMENT

fidgeted (fij'it-id) v.: moved in a restless, a nervous, or an uneasy way.

Gary Soto   23

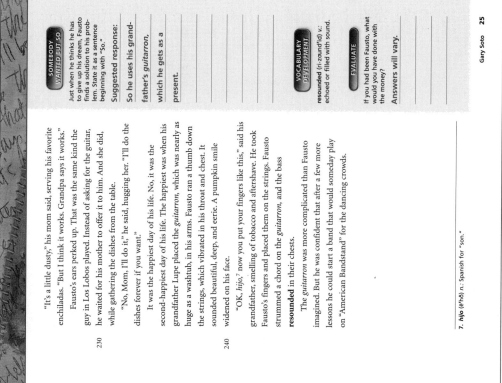

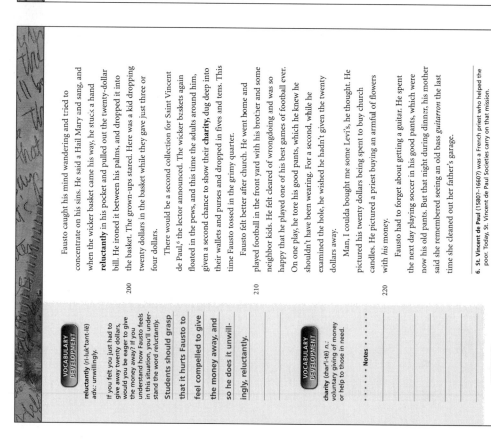

Left page (24)

VOCABULARY DEVELOPMENT

reluctantly (ri·luk'tant·lē) *adv.*: unwillingly.

If you felt you just had to give away twenty dollars, would you be eager to give the money away? If you understand how Fausto feels in this situation, you'll understand the word *reluctantly.*

Students should grasp that it hurts Fausto to feel compelled to give the money away, and so he does it unwillingly, reluctantly.

_____

VOCABULARY DEVELOPMENT

charity (char'i·tē) *n.*: voluntary giving of money or help to those in need.

• • • • • • **Notes** • • • • • •

_____
_____
_____
_____
_____

Fausto caught his mind wandering and tried to concentrate on his sins. He said a Hail Mary and sang, and when the wicker basket came his way, he stuck a hand **reluctantly** in his pocket and pulled out the twenty-dollar bill. He ironed it between his palms, and dropped it into
200 the basket. The grown-ups stared. Here was a kid dropping twenty dollars in the basket while they gave just three or four dollars.

There would be a second collection for Saint Vincent de Paul,[6] the lector announced. The wicker baskets again floated in the pews, and this time the adults around him, given a second chance to show their **charity,** dug deep into their wallets and purses and dropped in fives and tens. This time Fausto tossed in the grimy quarter.

Fausto felt better after church. He went home and
210 played football in the front yard with his brother and some neighbor kids. He felt cleared of wrongdoing and was so happy that he played one of his best games of football ever. On one play, he tore his good pants, which he knew he shouldn't have been wearing. For a second, while he examined the hole, he wished he hadn't given the twenty dollars away.

Man, I coulda bought me some Levi's, he thought. He pictured his twenty dollars being spent to buy church candles. He pictured a priest buying an armful of flowers
220 with *his* money.

Fausto had to forget about getting a guitar. He spent the next day playing soccer in his good pants, which were now his old pants. But that night during dinner, his mother said she remembered seeing an old bass *guitarron* the last time she cleaned out her father's garage.

6. **St. Vincent de Paul** (1580?–1660?) was a French priest who helped the poor. Today, St. Vincent de Paul Societies carry on that mission.

Right page (25)

"It's a little dusty," his mom said, serving his favorite enchiladas. "But I think it works. Grandpa says it works."

Fausto's ears perked up. That was the same kind the guy in Los Lobos played. Instead of asking for the guitar, he waited for his mother to offer it to him. And she did,
230 while gathering the dishes from the table.

"No, Mom, I'll do it," he said, hugging her. "I'll do the dishes forever if you want."

It was the happiest day of his life. No, it was the second-happiest day of his life. The happiest was when his grandfather Lupe placed the *guitarron,* which was nearly as huge as a washtub, in his arms. Fausto ran a thumb down the strings, which vibrated in his throat and chest. It sounded beautiful, deep, and eerie. A pumpkin smile widened on his face.
240 "OK, *hijo,*[7] now you put your fingers like this," said his grandfather, smelling of tobacco and aftershave. He took Fausto's fingers and placed them on the strings. Fausto strummed a chord on the *guitarron,* and the bass **resounded** in their chests.

The *guitarron* was more complicated than Fausto imagined. But he was confident that after a few more lessons he could start a band that would someday play on "American Bandstand" for the dancing crowds.

7. *hijo* (ē'hō) *n.*: Spanish for "son."

SOMEBODY WANTED BUT SO

Just when he thinks he has to give up his dream, Fausto finds a solution to his problem. State it as a sentence beginning with "So."

Suggested response:

So he uses his grandfather's *guitarron,* which he gets as a present.

_____
_____
_____

VOCABULARY DEVELOPMENT

resounded (ri·zound'id) *v.*: echoed or filled with sound.

EVALUATE

If you had been Fausto, what would you have done with the money?

Answers will vary.

_____
_____

Gary Soto   25

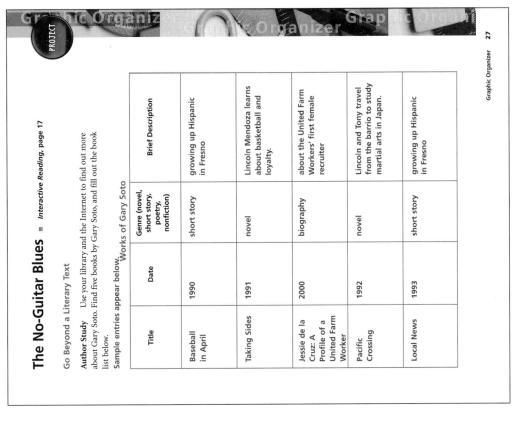

PROJECT

Graphic Organizer

The No-Guitar Blues ■ *Interactive Reading, page 17*

Go Beyond a Literary Text

Author Study Use your library and the Internet to find out more about Gary Soto. Find five books by Gary Soto, and fill out the book list below.
Sample entries appear below.

Works of Gary Soto

Title	Date	Genre (novel, short story, poetry, nonfiction)	Brief Description
Baseball in April	1990	short story	growing up Hispanic in Fresno
Taking Sides	1991	novel	Lincoln Mendoza learns about basketball and loyalty.
Jessie de la Cruz: A Profile of a United Farm Worker	2000	biography	about the United Farm Workers' first female recruiter
Pacific Crossing	1992	novel	Lincoln and Tony travel from the barrio to study martial arts in Japan.
Local News	1993	short story	growing up Hispanic in Fresno

27   Graphic Organizer

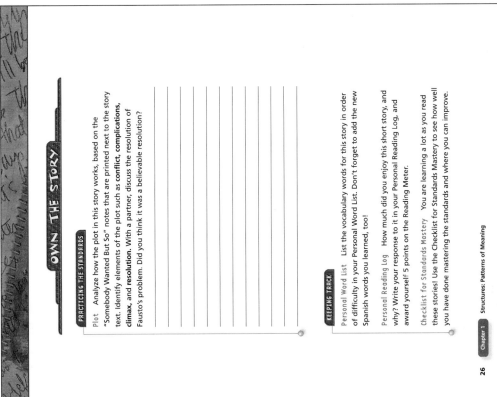

OWN THE STORY

PRACTICING THE STANDARDS

Plot Analyze how the plot in this story works, based on the "Somebody Wanted But So" notes that are printed next to the story text. Identify elements of the plot such as **conflict, complications, climax,** and **resolution**. With a partner, discuss the resolution of Fausto's problem. Did you think it was a believable resolution?

KEEPING TRACK

Personal Word List List the vocabulary words for this story in order of difficulty in your Personal Word List. Don't forget to add the new Spanish words you learned, too!

Personal Reading Log How much did you enjoy this short story, and why? Write your response to it in your Personal Reading Log, and award yourself 5 points on the Reading Meter.

Checklist for Standards Mastery You are learning a lot as you read these stories! Use the Checklist for Standards Mastery to see how well you have done mastering the standards and where you can improve.

26   Chapter 1   Structures: Patterns of Meaning

Information

ARTICLE

Reading Standard 2.2 Analyze text that uses proposition and support patterns.

from Archaeology's dig, June/July 2000

Music from the Start

Patricia Hunt-Jones

And I've often wondered how did it all start?
Who found out that nothing can capture a heart,
Like a melody can? Well, whoever it was, I'm a fan.

—from the song "Thank You for the Music"
by the 1970s rock-and-roll group ABBA

When you're hanging out in your room listening to the
sounds of 'N Sync, Britney Spears, or Fresh Prince, did you
ever wonder when people started making music? Well, hold
onto your headphones because, believe it or not, people

10   have been playing musical instruments for more than
10,000 years. In fact, **archaeologists** recently discovered
flutes in China that are around 9,000 years BMTV (Before
Music Television), making them among the oldest playable
multinote musical instruments ever found.

But the story of how people developed music is about
more than the discovery of old instruments. Through

"Music from the Start" by Patricia Hunt-Jones from *Archaeology's dig,* vol. 2, no. 3, June/July 2000. Copyright © 2000 by the Archaeological Institute of America. Reprinted by permission of *Archaeology's dig magazine.*

sculpture, paintings, writing on tablets and tombs, and
even Bible stories, archaeologists have learned how
people of ancient cultures created and improved the

20   music they loved.

Ancient Music Makers

The earliest **representation** of people playing musical
instruments appeared on Sumerian writing tablets in
Mesopotamia (now modern Iraq) around 3000 B.C.
Sumerian music was first played on drums and bird-bone
flutes (both of which archaeologists have found in the
area). The Sumerians later developed stringed instruments
such as lutes, harps, and lyres. As the centuries passed,
Sumerian kings paid musicians to write and play music for

30   festivals and religious holidays.

Assyrian musicians in a parade, about 7th century B.C.

VOCABULARY DEVELOPMENT

transformed (trans•fôrmd') v.: changed the form or appearance of.

The prefix *trans-* is from a Latin word meaning "over, on the other side of, through, or across." What is a *transformer?* a *transfusion? transportation?*

A *transformer* consists of two coils of wire that transfer energy from one coil to the other. A *transfusion* is a passage of blood from one person to another.

***Transportation* means carrying people or goods from one place to another.**

• • • • • • Notes • • • • • •

Appreciation for the sound of Sumerian stringed instruments carried over to ancient Egypt. During the next 1,000 years, Egyptian musicians **transformed** the harp, originally a three-string instrument, into a 20-string instrument.

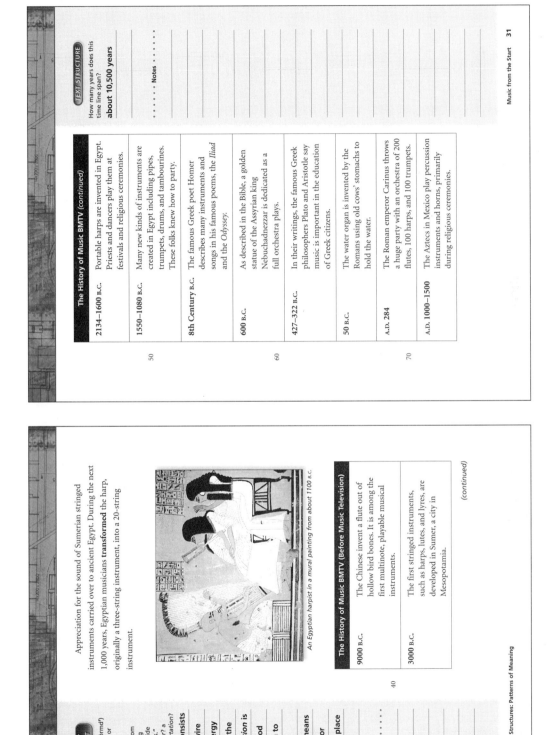

An Egyptian harpist in a mural painting from about 1100 B.C.

The History of Music BMTV (Before Music Television)	
9000 B.C.	The Chinese invent a flute out of hollow bird bones. It is among the first multinote, playable musical instruments.
3000 B.C.	The first stringed instruments, such as harps, lutes, and lyres, are developed in Sumer, a city in Mesopotamia.

(continued)

The History of Music BMTV *(continued)*	
2134–1600 B.C.	Portable harps are invented in Egypt. Priests and dancers play them at festivals and religious ceremonies.
1550–1080 B.C.	Many new kinds of instruments are created in Egypt including pipes, trumpets, drums, and tambourines. These folks knew how to party.
8th Century B.C.	The famous Greek poet Homer describes many instruments and songs in his famous poems, the *Iliad* and the *Odyssey*.
600 B.C.	As described in the Bible, a golden statue of the Assyrian king Nebuchadnezzar is dedicated as a full orchestra plays.
427–322 B.C.	In their writings, the famous Greek philosophers Plato and Aristotle say music is important in the education of Greek citizens.
50 B.C.	The water organ is invented by the Romans using old cows' stomachs to hold the water.
A.D. 284	The Roman emperor Carinus throws a huge party with an orchestra of 200 flutes, 100 harps, and 100 trumpets.
A.D. 1000–1500	The Aztecs in Mexico play percussion instruments and horns, primarily during religious ceremonies.

TEXT STRUCTURE

How many years does this time line span?

about 10,500 years

• • • • • • Notes • • • • • •

While we have a lot of information about Egyptian music, musicians, and instruments, we have no idea how their music sounded. We do know that the ancient Egyptians so enjoyed music that their cow-goddess, Hathor, ruled over love, joy, and—you guessed it—music. Paintings and reliefs in royal tombs show Egyptians—from the wives

80 of pharaohs to the lowliest slaves—playing music as far back as 2600 B.C. In Egypt, music was mostly played during religious ceremonies, great festivals, and large parades. Even divorcing Egyptian couples would fight over who owned the rights to instruments, written music, and musicians (who were slaves).

Besides stringed instruments, Egyptian musicians also played pipes and trumpets. In fact, two trumpets, one of bronze and gold, the other silver, were found in the tomb of the boy king, Tutankhamen. They are now in the Cairo

90 Museum, as is the mummified body of Harmosis, ancient Egypt's greatest musician.

The Greek Beat

The ancient Greeks weren't the first culture to develop *mousike* (their word for music) and instruments, but they made the biggest contribution to the art of Western music as we know it today. The instruments found in: Greece were similar to those in Sumer and Egypt. How do we know this? Herodotus, a 5th-century B.C. Greek historian, writes about Greeks traveling to Sumer and Egypt to study and

100 borrow their instrument-making skills and musicology (the science of writing and creating music). Pythagoras, the 6th-century mathematician, also went to Sumer to study the science of music. He would eventually develop the octave, the group of eight notes—do, re, mi, etc.—that became the foundation for modern Western music.

Scene from a Greek vase, about 5th century B.C.

Which instruments made the Greeks get up and boogie? Ancient writings tell of how audiences loved the *aulos*, which was a double-pipe flute. The two pipes were played at the same time, and archaeologists believe this

110 created a **harmonious** sound. We don't know which pipe carried the melody (main music line) and which carried the harmony (complementary music line), or even how they sounded together. We do know that the flute players had to wear a head harness (much like a retainer) to hold the pipes to their lips.

The ancient Greeks also developed the *phorminx*, a seven-string lyre, and the cithara, which was a popular instrument used in local concerts. They also created one of the first organs. The organ player would move a lever

120 which would drive air into a pipe using water pressure to create a sound.

In Greece, music was so popular that it was played as **accompaniment** to everyday chores and during battle training for soldiers. During concerts, audiences shoved and pushed each other for the best seats. Musicians

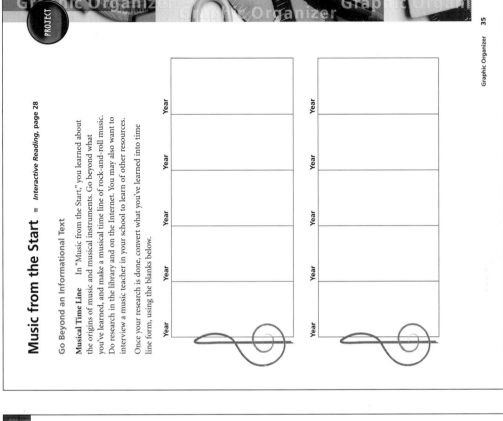

Music from the Start ■ *Interactive Reading, page 28*

Go Beyond an Informational Text

Musical Time Line In "Music from the Start," you learned about the origins of music and musical instruments. Go beyond what you've learned, and make a musical time line of rock-and-roll music. Do research in the library and on the Internet. You may also want to interview a music teacher in your school to learn of other resources. Once your research is done, convert what you've learned into time line form, using the blanks below.

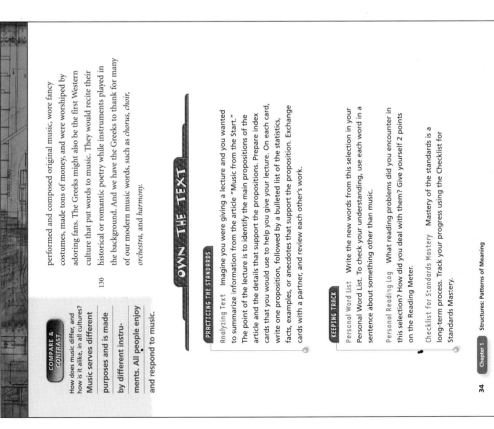

performed and composed original music, wore fancy costumes, made tons of money, and were worshiped by adoring fans. The Greeks might also be the first Western culture that put words to music. They would recite their historical or romantic poetry while instruments played in 130 the background. And we have the Greeks to thank for many of our modern music words, such as *chorus, choir, orchestra,* and *harmony.*

COMPARE & CONTRAST

How does music differ, and how is it alike, in all cultures? **Music serves different purposes and is made by different instruments. All people enjoy and respond to music.**

OWN THE TEXT

PRACTICING THE STANDARDS

Analyzing Text Imagine you were giving a lecture and you wanted to summarize information from the article "Music from the Start." The point of the lecture is to identify the main propositions of the article and the details that support the propositions. Prepare index cards that you would use to help you give your lecture. On each card, write one proposition, followed by a bulleted list of the statistics, facts, examples, or anecdotes that support the proposition. Exchange cards with a partner, and review each other's work.

KEEPING TRACK

Personal Word List Write the new words from this selection in your Personal Word List. To check your understanding, use each word in a sentence about something other than music.

Personal Reading Log What reading problems did you encounter in this selection? How did you deal with them? Give yourself 2 points on the Reading Meter.

Checklist for Standards Mastery Mastery of the standards is a long-term process. Track your progress using the Checklist for Standards Mastery.

Literature

MYTH

Reading Standard 3.2 Evaluate the structural elements of the plot, the plot's development, and the way in which conflicts are (or are not) addressed and resolved.

ORPHEUS AND THE UNDERWORLD

a Greek myth retold by Mollie McLean and Anne Wiseman

The Underworld

Many times the Greeks told of a dark kingdom called Hades (hā'dēz'). They said people went to this place when they died. No one was sure where Hades was. Some said it was at the edge of the world. Others said it was under the very ground upon which men walked. That is why some people called it the Underworld.

The kingdom of Hades had two parts—one beautiful, one ugly. The beautiful part was filled with sunlight and happiness. Here lived those who had been good on earth. The other part was dark and sad. Those who had been wicked lived here.

10 When a man died, Mercury came to take him to the Underworld. He led him down a dark road until they came to a great river. This river was called the Styx (stiks). Here Charon (ker'ən), an old boatman, was waiting. If the dead

IDENTIFY

Pause at line 6. Circle the two different names given for the place being described.

VOCABULARY DEVELOPMENT

wicked (wik'id) *adj.*: morally bad or wrong.

Wicked comes from the Old English *wicce*, meaning "witch."

WORD KNOWLEDGE

Mercury (line 12) is the name of a Roman god (this Greek name is Hermes).

Mercury is also the name of a planet and of a chemical element.

---

man had a penny in his mouth, Charon would take him across the river in his boat. He would not take him if the dead man's friends had forgotten the money.

Once across the river, they came to a dark **palace**. Here

20 lived Pluto, king of the Underworld, and his beautiful wife, Proserpina. Outside the gate sat Cerberus (sur'bər·əs), a fierce three-headed dog with a hissing snake for a tail. He would let everyone pass into the palace. He would let no one out.

Inside the palace, it was cold and dark. The king and queen sat quietly on black chairs. Their pale faces were sad. They were so still that they looked as if they were made of stone.

Into this room, Mercury would lead the man who had

30 died. Pluto would ask Mercury if the man with him had led a good life. If the messenger-god said yes, the king sent the man to the beautiful part of Hades. If Mercury said no, Pluto gave the man some terrible labor.

Pluto had given terrible labors to many wicked men. One man had to roll a giant rock up a hill. Just as he came to the top, a magic power pushed the rock away from him. Down it would go, and the man would have to try once more. He would push the rock to the top again and again. Each time it would roll back.

40 Tantalus had been a cruel man on earth. In Hades, he had to stand in water which came up to his shoulders. But when he tried to take a drink, the water would run away. He was always thirsty. Over his head grew apples and oranges. But when he put his hand out for them, they would fly away. He was always hungry.

Pluto had also given hard labors to cruel women. Three sisters who had been wicked and mean had to carry water from a well in a sieve.

IDENTIFY

If somebody wanted to get across the River Styx to the Underworld, what would he or she need?

A penny in his or her
mouth to pay the
boatman

VOCABULARY DEVELOPMENT

palace (pal'əs) *n.*: residence of a king, an emperor, a bishop, and so on.

Palace comes from the Latin *palatium*, after *Palatium*, one of the Seven Hills of Rome, where Augustus lived.

WORD KNOWLEDGE

Look up *tantalize* in a dictionary. Explain how its meaning is related to the mythic Tantalus (line 40).

The verb *tantalize*
describes what
Tantalus experienced
in Hades. It means
"tease or torment
someone by
withholding some-
thing desirable."

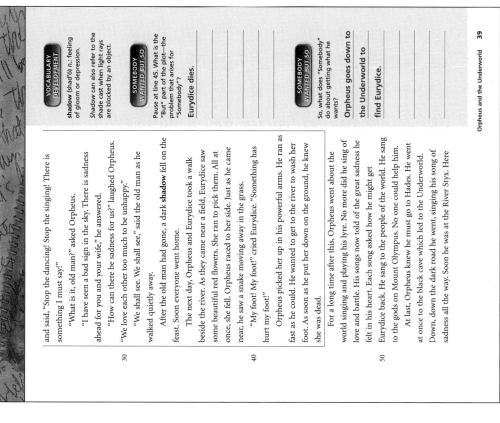

lyre (līr) *n.:* small stringed instrument of the harp family.

Pause at line 6. Who's the "Somebody" in this story?

Orpheus

Pause at line 19. What does Orpheus want?

Orpheus wants the

love of Eurydice.

Imagine you are an ancient storyteller telling this story to a crowd gathered around a campfire. Read the boxed passage aloud with expression.

Orpheus Goes to the Underworld

50 The people of the world were afraid of Hades. They did not want to go to this dark place until their time had come. Once in a long time a mighty hero had to go to the Underworld. The next story tells of one of these heroes.

In all of Greece there was no better singer than Orpheus (ôr′fē·əs). When he sang and played his **lyre**, people would stop their work and hurry to his side. Animals of the forest would come near. Fierce monsters would sit quietly at his feet. Even tall trees would bend their heads to hear his song.

Orpheus went from place to place singing his songs of love and battle. One day he saw a beautiful girl in the crowd. He fell in love with her at once. He stopped playing
10 and walked over to her.

"What is your name?" he asked.

"I am called Eurydice (yoō·rĭd′i·sē′)," she said quietly.

"I shall sing my next song for you," said Orpheus.

He picked up his lyre and sang a beautiful song. When Eurydice heard the song, she fell in love with the singer.

For many days, Orpheus stayed in this place. No longer did he wish to go about the world singing. He wanted only to please Eurydice. Every day he sang her a new song of
20 love.

Then one fine day, Orpheus and Eurydice were married. All their friends came to wish them happiness. There was a great feast. There was dancing and singing. Everyone was very happy until an old man stepped out of the crowd

---

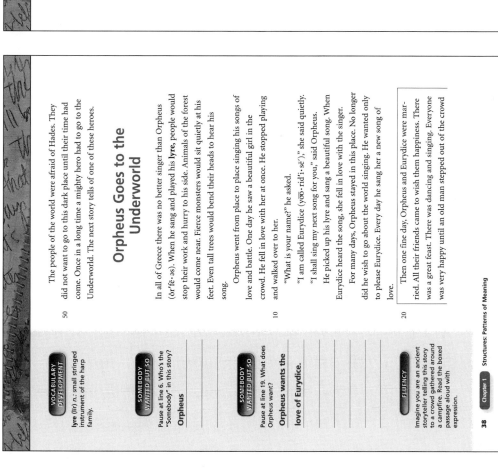

and said, "Stop the dancing! Stop the singing! There is something I must say!"

"What is it, old man?" asked Orpheus.

"I have seen a bad sign in the sky. There is sadness ahead for you and your wife," he answered.
30 "How can there be sadness for us?" laughed Orpheus. "We love each other too much to be unhappy."

"We shall see. We shall see," said the old man as he walked quietly away.

After the old man had gone, a dark **shadow** fell on the feast. Soon everyone went home.

The next day, Orpheus and Eurydice took a walk beside the river. As they came near a field, Eurydice saw some beautiful red flowers. She ran to pick them. All at once, she fell. Orpheus raced to her side. Just as he came
40 near, he saw a snake moving away in the grass.

"My foot! My foot!" cried Eurydice. "Something has hurt my foot!"

Orpheus picked her up in his powerful arms. He ran as fast as he could. He wanted to get to the river to wash her foot. As soon as he put her down on the ground, he knew she was dead.

For a long time after this, Orpheus went about the world singing and playing his lyre. No more did he sing of love and battle. His songs now told of the great sadness he
50 felt in his heart. Each song asked how he might get Eurydice back. He sang to the people of the world. He sang to the gods on Mount Olympus. No one could help him.

At last, Orpheus knew he must go to Hades. He went at once to the black cave which led to the Underworld. Down, down the dark road he went, singing his song of sadness all the way. Soon he was at the River Styx. Here

shadow (shad′ō) *n.:* feeling of gloom or depression.

Shadow can also refer to the shade cast when light rays are blocked by an object.

Pause at line 45. What is the "But" part of the plot—the problem that arises for "Somebody"?

Eurydice dies.

So, what does "Somebody" do about getting what he wants?

Orpheus goes down to

the Underworld to

find Eurydice.

fierce (firs) *adj.*: of a violently cruel nature; savage; wild.

Re-read lines 59–68. Circle the part that tells what Orpheus wants and his reason for wanting it.

Pause at line 78. What is the "But" that Pluto makes as a condition for Orpheus to get what he wants?
Pluto tells Orpheus that Eurydice will follow him out of Hades, but he must not look back at her until he sees the sun, or she will be lost to him.

Pause at line 78. What do you think is going to happen? **He will look back and lose her.**

stood the **fierce** old boatman. He had heard Orpheus coming. He, too, had felt the magic power of the hero's song. He took him across the river without a word.

On into the kingdom of Hades walked Orpheus. At the sound of his singing, Tantalus forgot how hungry and thirsty he was. The man pushing the rock stopped his hard labor. The three sisters put their sieves on the ground and listened to the beautiful music. Orpheus walked on. He passed the cruel three-headed dog and went into the palace of Pluto. Here he saw the king and queen. He fell on his knees before them. Looking up, he said, "I have come to ask you to give me back my beautiful Eurydice. I cannot live without her."

The king and queen had heard the young hero's song. Their hearts had been moved by its sadness. Pluto said, "No one has ever left Hades before. We will let Eurydice go because of your beautiful singing."

"You are very kind, Pluto," said Orpheus. "Where shall I look for her?"

"Do not look for her," said the king. "Go back the way you have come. She will follow you. Do not look back at her until you can see the light of the sun. If you once turn, she will be lost forever. Now, go! Remember my words!"

Orpheus started the long trip back. Out of the palace he went. He passed the three-headed dog. He went over the river. Soon he was on the dark road which led up to the world. As he walked, he listened for footsteps behind him. He heard nothing. He began to wonder if Pluto had played some terrible trick on him. He walked on. Still he could hear nothing. Orpheus could stand it no longer. Just as he reached the end of the road, he turned around.

"Eurydice!" he called.

There before him, he saw a gray shadow. It was his beautiful wife.

"Orpheus!" she cried. "You should not have turned so soon! We were almost free! Goodbye! Goodbye!"

With a sad smile, she went back to the Underworld. Orpheus followed her, but this time no one would listen to his song. He knew he was lost forever.

After a time, Orpheus went back to the world. Never again did he sing a song of love!

Orpheus and his lyre in a scene from a Greek vase, about 6th century B.C.

Complete a "Somebody Wanted But So" statement to summarize the plot.
Orpheus wanted the love of Eurydice, but she died, so he went to the Underworld to find her and bring her back to the world of the living. But Pluto told him he must not look back at Eurydice during their journey; so Orpheus began his journey back with her. But Orpheus grew worried and impatient, so he looked back and Eurydice had to return to the Underworld.

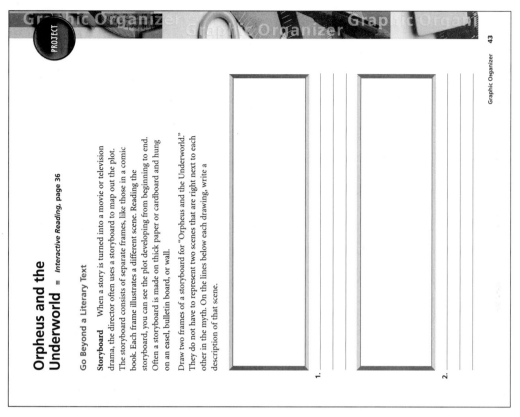

Orpheus and the Underworld ■ *Interactive Reading, page 36*

Go Beyond a Literary Text

Storyboard When a story is turned into a movie or television drama, the director often uses a storyboard to map out the plot. The storyboard consists of separate frames, like those in a comic book. Each frame illustrates a different scene. Reading the storyboard, you can see the plot developing from beginning to end. Often a storyboard is made on thick paper or cardboard and hung on an easel, bulletin board, or wall.

Draw two frames of a storyboard for "Orpheus and the Underworld." They do not have to represent two scenes that are right next to each other in the myth. On the lines below each drawing, write a description of that scene.

1.

2.

Graphic Organizer   43

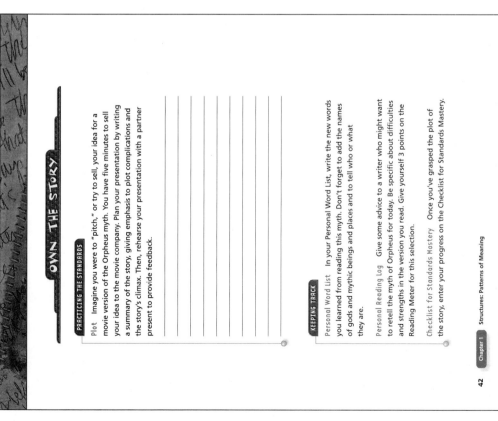

OWN THE STORY

PRACTICING THE STANDARDS

Plot Imagine you were to "pitch," or try to sell, your idea for a movie version of the Orpheus myth. You have five minutes to sell your idea to the movie company. Plan your presentation by writing a summary of the story, giving emphasis to plot complications and the story's climax. Then, rehearse your presentation with a partner present to provide feedback.

KEEPING TRACK

Personal Word List In your Personal Word List, write the new words you learned from reading this myth. Don't forget to add the names of gods and mythic beings and places and to tell who or what they are.

Personal Reading Log Give some advice to a writer who might want to retell the myth of Orpheus for today. Be specific about difficulties and strengths in the version you read. Give yourself 3 points on the Reading Meter for this selection.

Checklist for Standards Mastery Once you've grasped the plot of the story, enter your progress on the Checklist for Standards Mastery.

42   Chapter 1   Structures: Patterns of Meaning

Chapter 2

Characters
Doing the Right Thing

Chapter Preview In this chapter you will—

Read: Selections	Interact with Text: Graphic Organizers
Practice Reads: John Adams: The Forgotten Man by Mara Rockliff; Do the Right Thing: A Simple Plan by *Rosemont High Register* editorial staff • *Interactive Reading*, p. 46	Comparison Grid • *Interactive Reading*, p. 54
from Harriet Tubman: Conductor on the Underground Railroad by Ann Petry *Holt Literature and Language Arts*, p. 87	What If? Chart • *Interactive Reading*, p. 55
The Fugitive Slave Acts of 1793 and 1850 by Flo Ota De Lange *Holt Literature and Language Arts*, p. 101	Venn Diagram • *Interactive Reading*, p. 56
Barbara Frietchie by John Greenleaf Whittier *Holt Literature and Language Arts*, p. 107	Character-Traits Cluster • *Interactive Reading*, p. 57
Too Soon a Woman by Dorothy M. Johnson *Holt Literature and Language Arts*, p. 114	Motivations Web • *Interactive Reading*, p. 58
Union Pacific Railroad Poster; Home, Sweet Soddie by Flo Ota De Lange *Holt Literature and Language Arts*, p. 122	Comparison Chart • *Interactive Reading*, p. 59
Mrs. Flowers *from* I Know Why the Caged Bird Sings by Maya Angelou *Holt Literature and Language Arts*, p. 130	Problem-Resolution Chart • *Interactive Reading*, p. 60
Mrs. Flowers's Recipes *Holt Literature and Language Arts*, p. 137	Process Chart • *Interactive Reading*, p. 61
New Directions by Maya Angelou; Field Work by Rose Del Castillo Guilbault *Interactive Reading*, p. 63	Comparison Chart • *Interactive Reading*, p. 73
You Took the Words Right Out of My Mouth . . . by Evan Morris *Interactive Reading*, p. 74	Project: Glossary Templates • *Interactive Reading*, p. 78
Prometheus Steals Fire from Heaven retold by Anne Terry White; Paul's Popcorn by Walter Blair *Interactive Reading*, p. 79	Contrast Chart • *Interactive Reading*, p. 87

Strategy Launch: "Compare and Contrast"

LITERARY FOCUS: CHARACTER AND MOTIVATION

Good writers make their characters seem like real people. They do this through **characterization**. Characterization includes showing what the character looks like, what the character says, and how the character acts. Characterization also might include information about how other people feel about the character and what the character thinks. Well-drawn characters have believable **motivations:** They do things for reasons that are convincing.

One interesting way to analyze characters' motivations and actions is to compare characters from different time periods. Ask yourself: "Would these characters have acted differently in another setting or another time frame?"

A STRATEGY THAT WORKS: "COMPARE AND CONTRAST"

You compare and contrast things all the time in real life. You may, for example, note similarities between two new bands, or you may note differences in the quality of food at competing restaurants.

When you read, you also use your skills of comparing and contrasting. Here's how.

POINTERS FOR USING "COMPARE AND CONTRAST"

▸ Read both selections, and take notes on a comparison grid like the one that follows the Practice Reads.

▸ Identify the key actions taken by each character. Then, look for motives for each character's actions.

▸ Evaluate the characters' historical setting or the writer's historical period. Does the time frame affect the attitudes, motivations, and dreams of the characters in any way?

Reading Standard 1.2 Understand the most important points in the history of the English language, and use common word origins to determine the historical influences on English word meanings.

Reading Standard 2.3 Find similarities and differences between texts in the treatment, scope, or organization of ideas.

Reading Standard 3.3 Compare and contrast motivations and reactions of literary characters from different historical eras confronting similar situations or conflicts.

Strategy Launch **45**

Practice Read

Following this account of John Adams is an editorial from a student newspaper. You will compare and contrast the editorial with this account of John Adams.

Here are some facts you should know before you read "John Adams: The Forgotten Man."
- John Adams was born in 1735 in Braintree, Massachusetts. He died in Braintree on July 4, 1826.
- Adams was regarded by his contemporaries as one of the most important statesmen of the revolutionary era.
- His reputation faded in the nineteenth century, but a modern edition of the correspondence between Adams and his wife, Abigail, has helped bring both Adamses back into the spotlight.

John Adams:
The Forgotten Man

Mara Rockliff

VOCABULARY DEVELOPMENT

nominated (näm'a-nāt'ad) v.: named; here, specifically, named as a candidate for something.

Nominate is from the Latin word for "name." What is a *nominee*?
a person named or nominated

He **nominated** George Washington to head the Continental Army, and he persuaded Thomas Jefferson to draft the Declaration of Independence. He was our country's first vice president and second president. Few men contributed more to the formation of the United States, but Adams's face does not appear on any U.S. coin or bill. What was it about earnest, hardworking John Adams that people wanted to forget?

10   The problem was his personality. John Adams was so totally honest he sometimes seemed rude. He held

46   Chapter 2   Characters: Doing the Right Thing

passionate beliefs, and he flew into such tempers that Benjamin Franklin said he was "absolutely out of his senses." He was stubborn and conceited—and fiercely independent. He was driven only by his conscience and his sense of public duty.

Adams was not a people person. More than anything, he loved to read. "You'll never be alone with a poet in your pocket," he wrote his fourteen-year-old son.

20   As a boy in Massachusetts, though, John Adams never studied if he could avoid it. He liked to be outdoors, hunting and fishing, wrestling, swimming, and skating. He was a daydreamer, a prankster, a school-skipper. He hated Latin grammar, and he begged his father to let him work at something else instead. "Well," his father said, "my meadow yonder needs a ditch." After two days of digging ditches, John was happy to return to his Latin.

Doing the Right Thing

Adams went on to Harvard, where he found learning more exciting. Then he turned to a career in the law. This was
30   the mid-1700s. As a young Boston lawyer, Adams found himself in the thick of events that would lead to the Revolutionary War. He protested the British stamp tax and, like most Americans, objected to the regiments of British soldiers sent to America to enforce it.

In 1770, when panicked British Redcoats fired into an angry, rock-hurling mob in Boston, his fellow **patriots** seized the chance to whip up anti-British feeling. John's cousin Samuel Adams called the incident the "Boston Massacre." Silversmith Paul Revere engraved a picture
40   showing British soldiers killing peaceful citizens.

IDENTIFY

Underline the sentence in the first paragraph of the article that asks a question. Underline the sentence in the second paragraph that answers that question.

• • • • • Notes • • • • • • •

VOCABULARY DEVELOPMENT

patriots (pā'trē-ats) n.: those who love and support their own country.

Patriot is from the Greek word *pater*, meaning "father." How does the idea of father enter into the words *patron* and *patrimony*?

Practice Reads   47

And John Adams? He did what his principles told him was right. He lent his legal talents to the conflict—on the soldiers' side. He believed that everyone deserved a fair trial, and he knew the British soldiers would never get one without a good lawyer. Adams managed to convince a Boston jury that the British soldiers shot in self-defense. Radical newspapers called Adams a traitor. But in his own eyes, defending those soldiers did not make him less of a patriot.

A Love Story—and a Shared Sense of Public Duty

50 For ten years Adams lived in Paris and London, working for his country. He hardly ever saw his family. Abigail, his wife, called herself a widow. She ran the farm, managed his business affairs, and raised their four children on her own. She wrote often to her husband—sometimes three times a day. Abigail also had strong principles and a strong sense of public duty. During the debates about the Declaration of Independence, Abigail urged her husband to "remember 60 the ladies, and be more generous and favorable to them than your ancestors." If the colonists would not obey the unjust laws the British passed, she pointed out, why should women obey unjust laws that men passed without giving them a voice? Abigail said that she gave up the comfort of her husband's presence for all those years as a sacrifice for her country.

"The Most Insignificant Office"

When Adams came home in 1789, he found his reputation had improved in his absence—perhaps because he hadn't 70 been around to pick fights with people. When Washington,

IDENTIFY
Underline the line in this section that explains the heading "Doing the Right Thing" (line 27).

INTERPRET
What does Abigail Adams mean in lines 60–61 when she says that her husband should be more generous to the ladies "than your ancestors"?
She means that he should regard the rights of women more than his ancestors did. Women did not have the right to vote.

Restate Abigail Adams's reasoning in lines 61–64 in your own words.
If the colonists feel they should not obey unjust laws passed by the British, why should women obey unjust laws passed by men? She is referring to the vote.

the hero of the war, became the nation's first president, Adams was elected vice president.

Adams hated the vice presidency. He called it "the most insignificant office that ever the invention of man contrived or his imagination conceived."

By the beginning of their second term, Adams had lost some of his popularity and most of his teeth. President Washington, still universally admired but also toothless, wore ivory dentures set in wood and attached by a metal spring. To prevent his mouth from popping open, he had 80 to keep his jaw clenched all the time, which may have added to his image as a dignified and silent man. Adams refused to get false teeth. He would let nothing interfere with his talking, even if the missing teeth made him hard to understand.

Washington declined a third term. Who would take his place? In '89 and '92, the vote for Washington had been **unanimous.** So in a way, 1796 was the first real election— which meant the bugs weren't quite worked out.

90 The Federalists backed Adams for president and Thomas Pinckney for vice president. The Democratic-Republicans backed Jefferson for president and Aaron Burr for vice president. But all the candidates got lumped together in one vote. The man with the most votes would be president; the man with the second most votes would be vice president.

And whose job was it to count the votes? Why, the current vice president and presiding officer of the Senate. Whatever flaws Adams had, no one who knew him 100 ever doubted his honesty. He made his careful count and solemnly announced the result: the new president of the United States was . . . "John Adams." And the vice

INTERPRET
What does this detail about the teeth reveal about John Adams's character (lines 76–85)?
His appearance was not as important to him as his ability to speak easily. He did not want to keep his mouth shut!

VOCABULARY DEVELOPMENT
unanimous (yōō-nan'ə-məs) *adj.*: based on complete agreement.
Unanimous is built on the Latin words *unus*, meaning "one," and *animus*, meaning "mind." What other words can you think of that are based on these Latin words? unite, animate, and so on

IDENTIFY
How did the voting system in 1796 differ from the system we use today (lines 93–96)?
Voting today is by party. Voters vote for president and vice president together.

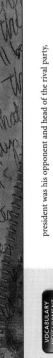

president was his opponent and head of the rival party, Thomas Jefferson.

Enemy Attacks

Adams hated party politics, but he could not escape them. Because he supported a strong central government, his rivals, who wanted to keep power with the states, said he was a **tyrant**.

It was a bizarre twist: Jefferson, the Virginia aristocrat, with his 5,000-acre estate at Monticello, his white-columned mansion, and his two hundred slaves, now stood for democracy and equality. And Adams, a plain Yankee farmer who split his own firewood and cut his own hay, said *set* for *sit* and *ain't* for *isn't*, and refused on moral grounds ever to own a slave, was seen as an elitist. (The irony wasn't lost on Adams. In later years, he called his modest Massachusetts farm Montezillo—"small mountain"—a joke on Jefferson's "big mountain," Monticello.)

Old Patriots, Old Rivals, Old Friends

Adams lost his battle for reelection in 1800. He turned the "splendid misery" (as Abigail called the White House) over to his old rival, Jefferson, which must have seemed a fair revenge. Adams stayed away from the inauguration, and the two men didn't speak for years. After Jefferson retired, though, they renewed their friendship, and a steady stream of letters moved between Montezillo and Monticello for the rest of their lives.

Adams died on July 4, 1826, the fiftieth birthday of the nation he helped found. His last words were "Thomas Jefferson survives." He didn't know his friend and rival had died that morning.

VOCABULARY DEVELOPMENT

tyrant (tī'rənt) *n.*: absolute ruler, especially one who is cruel.

Tyrant is from the Greek word *tyrannos.* Which dinosaur gets its name from the word *tyrant?*
Tyrannosaurus rex

COMPARE & CONTRAST

How does the writer compare and contrast Adams and Jefferson? Underline the points of comparison.

INFER

Why is it fitting that both Jefferson and Adams died on July 4?
They both worked so hard for independence, to build a new nation; it is fitting that they died on the nation's birthday.

Do the Right Thing: A Simple Plan

Rosemont High Register editorial staff

OCTOBER 2001

Here is a real-life drama. It happened right here at Rosemont High last month.

The girls' basketball team sat around the room looking glum. "You would think in the year 2001 things would be fair," muttered one player. "Yeah, right," replied another.

At Rosemont High, not everyone was happy. Because of budget cuts, the girls' basketball team would suffer. One coach was let go, the season was shortened, and the school bus would be unavailable for travel to games.

The boys' basketball team was not affected by cuts.

The girls' team got the news right after their first practice of the season. The next day they met to talk over the news.

"What I want to know is how come the boys' team isn't affected by all this?" The speaker was Raisa.

"Are you kidding? The boys are gods!" That was Thelma.

A small voice joined in the conversation. "What can we *do* about the situation? Is it too late to protest?"

The team looked in some surprise at Ana. She was the shortest, shyest person on the team. No one knew her well because she had recently moved to town.

Ana went on in her quiet voice. "I mean, *I* know it's unfair, and *you* know it's unfair, and I bet even the school

IDENTIFY

What unfair situation does the girls' basketball team face? Underline the results of the budget cut.
The cuts to the school budget have had a negative impact on their team, but the boys' team is unaffected.

Practice Reads **51**

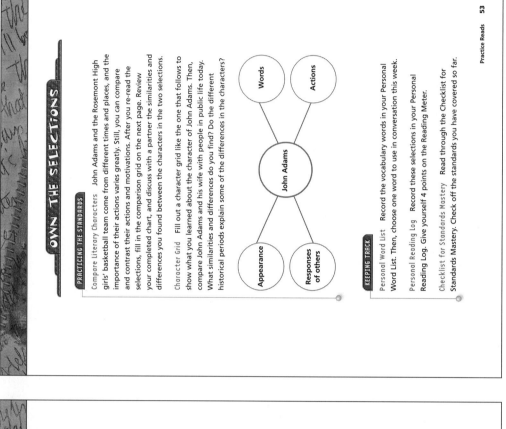

OWN THE SELECTIONS

PRACTICING THE STANDARDS

Compare Literary Characters   John Adams and the Rosemont High girls' basketball team come from different times and places, and the importance of their actions varies greatly. Still, you can compare and contrast their actions and motivations. After you re-read the selections, fill in the comparison grid on the next page. Review your completed chart, and discuss with a partner the similarities and differences you found between the characters in the two selections.

Character Grid   Fill out a character grid like the one that follows to show what you learned about the character of John Adams. Then, compare John Adams and his wife with people in public life today. What similarities and differences do you find? Do the different historical periods explain some of the differences in the characters?

Words

Actions

John Adams

Appearance

Responses of others

KEEPING TRACK

Personal Word List   Record the vocabulary words in your Personal Word List. Then, choose one word to use in conversation this week.

Personal Reading Log   Record these selections in your Personal Reading Log. Give yourself 4 points on the Reading Meter.

Checklist for Standards Mastery   Read through the Checklist for Standards Mastery. Check off the standards you have covered so far.

Practice Reads   53

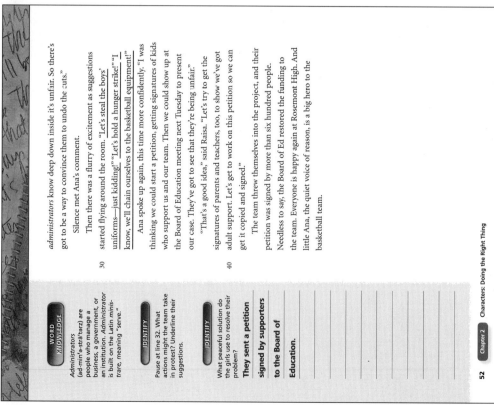

WORD KNOWLEDGE

Administrators (ad-min′ə-strā′tərz) are people who manage a business, a government, or an institution. *Administrator* is built on the Latin *minis-trare*, meaning "serve."

IDENTIFY

Pause at line 32. What actions might the team take in protest? Underline their suggestions.

IDENTIFY

What peaceful solution do the girls use to resolve their problem?

They sent a petition signed by supporters to the Board of Education.

administrators know deep down inside it's unfair. So there's got to be a way to convince them to undo the cuts."

Silence met Ana's comment.

Then there was a flurry of excitement as suggestions
30 started flying around the room. "Let's steal the boys' uniforms—just kidding!" "Let's hold a hunger strike!" "I know, we'll chain ourselves to the basketball equipment!"

Ana spoke up again, this time more confidently. "I was thinking we could start a petition, getting signatures of kids who support us and our team. Then we could show up at the Board of Education meeting next Tuesday to present our case. They've got to see that they're being unfair."

"That's a good idea," said Raisa. "Let's try to get the signatures of parents and teachers, too, to show we've got
40 adult support. Let's get to work on this petition so we can get it copied and signed."

The team threw themselves into the project, and their petition was signed by more than six hundred people. Needless to say, the Board of Ed restored the funding to the team. Everyone is happy again at Rosemont High. And little Ana, the quiet voice of reason, is a big hero to the basketball team.

52   Chapter 2   Characters: Doing the Right Thing

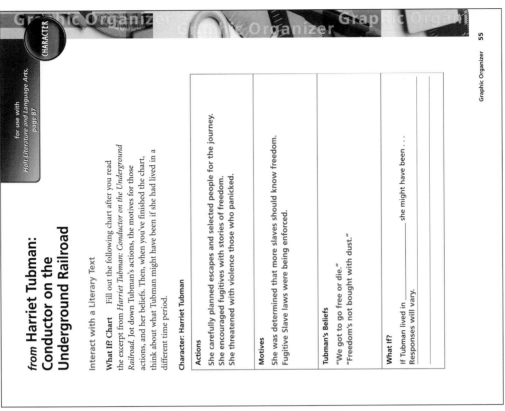

CHARACTER

for use with
Holt Literature and Language Arts,
page 87

from Harriet Tubman: Conductor on the Underground Railroad

Interact with a Literary Text

What If? Chart   Fill out the following chart after you read the excerpt from *Harriet Tubman: Conductor on the Underground Railroad*. Jot down Tubman's actions, the motives for those actions, and her beliefs. Then, when you've finished the chart, think about what Tubman might have been if she had lived in a different time period.

Character: Harriet Tubman

Actions
She carefully planned escapes and selected people for the journey. She encouraged fugitives with stories of freedom. She threatened with violence those who panicked.

Motives
She was determined that more slaves should know freedom. Fugitive Slave laws were being enforced.

Tubman's Beliefs
"We got to go free or die." "Freedom's not bought with dust."

What If?
If Tubman lived in _____ she might have been . . . Responses will vary.

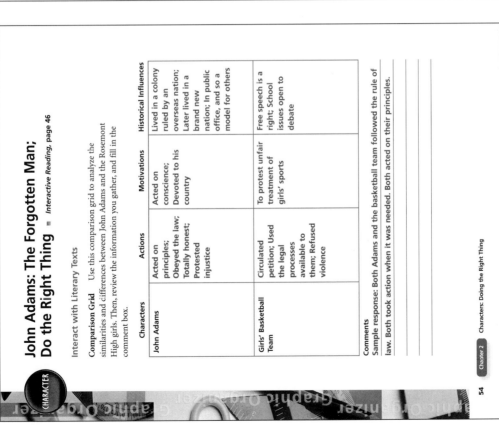

CHARACTER

John Adams: The Forgotten Man; Do the Right Thing ■ *Interactive Reading,* page 46

Interact with Literary Texts

Comparison Grid   Use this comparison grid to analyze the similarities and differences between John Adams and the Rosemont High girls. Then, review the information you gather, and fill in the comment box.

Characters	Actions	Motivations	Historical Influences
John Adams	Acted on principles; Obeyed the law; Totally honest; Protested injustice	Acted on conscience; Devoted to his country	Lived in a colony ruled by an overseas nation; Later lived in a brand new nation; In public office, and so a model for others
Girls' Basketball Team	Circulated petition; Used the legal processes available to them; Refused violence	To protest unfair treatment of girls' sports	Free speech is a right; School issues open to debate

Comments

Sample response: Both Adams and the basketball team followed the rule of law. Both took action when it was needed. Both acted on their principles.

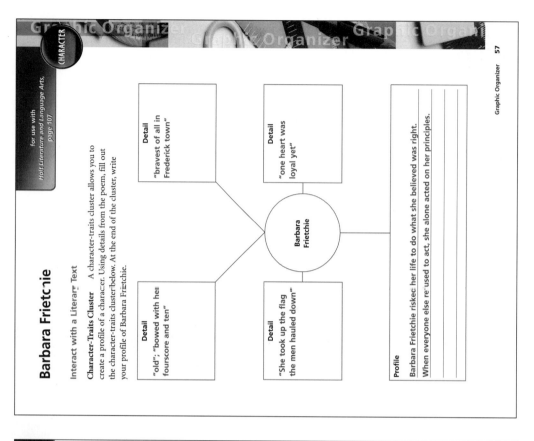

CHARACTER

for use with
Holt Literature and Language Arts,
page 107

Barbara Frietchie

Interact with a Literary Text

Character-Traits Cluster   A character-traits cluster allows you to create a profile of a character. Using details from the poem, fill out the character-traits cluster below. At the end of the cluster, write your profile of Barbara Frietchie.

Detail
"old"; "bowed with her fourscore and ten"

Detail
"bravest of all in Frederick town"

Barbara Frietchie

Detail
"She took up the flag the men hauled down"

Detail
"one heart was loyal yet"

Profile
Barbara Frietchie risked her life to do what she believed was right. When everyone else refused to act, she alone acted on her principles.

Graphic Organizer 57

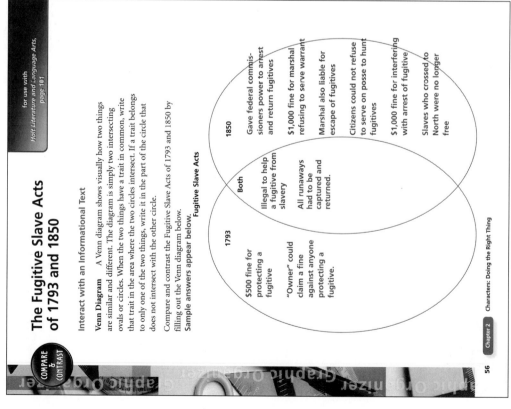

COMPARE & CONTRAST

for use with
Holt Literature and Language Arts,
page 101

The Fugitive Slave Acts of 1793 and 1850

Interact with an Informational Text

Venn Diagram   A Venn diagram shows visually how two things are similar and different. The diagram is simply two intersecting ovals or circles. When the two things have a trait in common, write that trait in the area where the two circles intersect. If a trait belongs to only one of the two things, write it in the part of the circle that does not intersect with the other circle.

Compare and contrast the Fugitive Slave Acts of 1793 and 1850 by filling out the Venn diagram below.
Sample answers appear below.

Fugitive Slave Acts

1793

$500 fine for protecting a fugitive

"Owner" could claim a fine against anyone protecting a fugitive.

Both

Illegal to help a fugitive from slavery

All runaways had to be captured and returned.

1850

Gave federal commissioners power to arrest and return fugitives

$1,000 fine for marshal refusing to serve warrant

Marshal also liable for escape of fugitives

Citizens could not refuse to serve on posse to hunt fugitives

$1,000 fine for interfering with arrest of fugitive.

Slaves who crossed to North were no longer free

Chapter 2   Characters: Doing the Right Thing   56

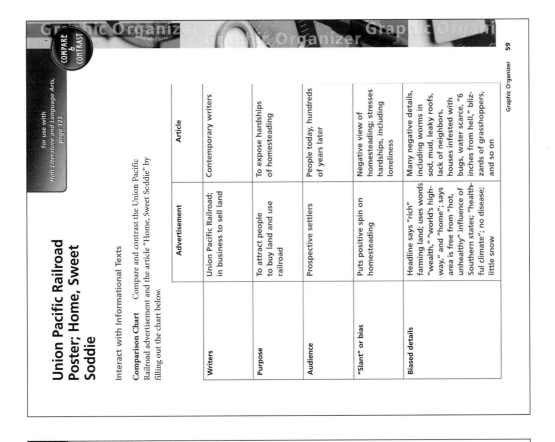

COMPARE & CONTRAST

for use with
Holt Literature and Language Arts,
page 123

Union Pacific Railroad Poster; Home, Sweet Soddie

Interact with Informational Texts

Comparison Chart   Compare and contrast the Union Pacific Railroad advertisement and the article "Home, Sweet Soddie" by filling out the chart below.

	Advertisement	Article
Writers	Union Pacific Railroad; in business to sell land	Contemporary writers
Purpose	To attract people to buy land and use railroad	To expose hardships of homesteading
Audience	Prospective settlers	People today, hundreds of years later
"Slant" or bias	Puts positive spin on homesteading	Negative view of homesteading; stresses hardships, including loneliness
Biased details	Headline says "rich" farming land; uses words "wealth," "world's highway," and "home"; says area is free from "hot, unhealthy" influence of Southern states; "healthful climate"; no disease; little snow	Many negative details, including worms in sod, mud, leaky roofs, lack of neighbors, houses infested with bugs, water scarce, "6 inches from hell," blizzards of grasshoppers, and so on

Graphic Organizer   **59**

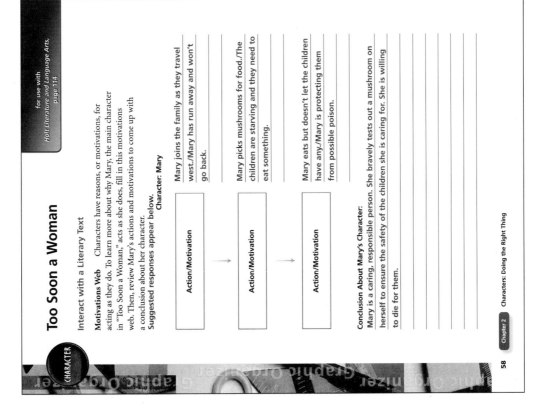

CHARACTER

for use with
Holt Literature and Language Arts,
page 114

Too Soon a Woman

Interact with a Literary Text

Motivations Web   Characters have reasons, or motivations, for acting as they do. To learn more about why Mary, the main character in "Too Soon a Woman," acts as she does, fill in this motivations web. Then, review Mary's actions and motivations to come up with a conclusion about her character.
Suggested responses appear below.
Character: Mary

Action/Motivation → Mary joins the family as they travel west./Mary has run away and won't go back.

Action/Motivation → Mary picks mushrooms for food./The children are starving and they need to eat something.

Action/Motivation → Mary eats but doesn't let the children have any./Mary is protecting them from possible poison.

Conclusion About Mary's Character:
Mary is a caring, responsible person. She bravely tests out a mushroom on herself to ensure the safety of the children she is caring for. She is willing to die for them.

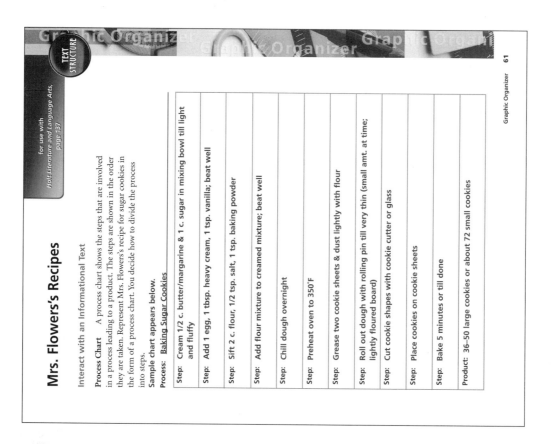

for use with
Holt Literature and Language Arts,
page 137

Mrs. Flowers's Recipes

Interact with an Informational Text

Process Chart   A process chart shows the steps that are involved in a process leading to a product. The steps are shown in the order they are taken. Represent Mrs. Flowers's recipe for sugar cookies in the form of a process chart. You decide how to divide the process into steps.

Sample chart appears below.

Process: Baking Sugar Cookies

Step: Cream 1/2 c. butter/margarine & 1 c. sugar in mixing bowl till light and fluffy

Step: Add 1 egg, 1 tbsp. heavy cream, 1 tsp. vanilla; beat well

Step: Sift 2 c. flour, 1/2 tsp. salt, 1 tsp. baking powder

Step: Add flour mixture to creamed mixture; beat well

Step: Chill dough overnight

Step: Preheat oven to 350°F

Step: Grease two cookie sheets & dust lightly with flour

Step: Roll out dough with rolling pin till very thin (small amt. at time; lightly floured board)

Step: Cut cookie shapes with cookie cutter or glass

Step: Place cookies on cookie sheets

Step: Bake 5 minutes or till done

Product: 36–50 large cookies or about 72 small cookies

Graphic Organizer   **61**

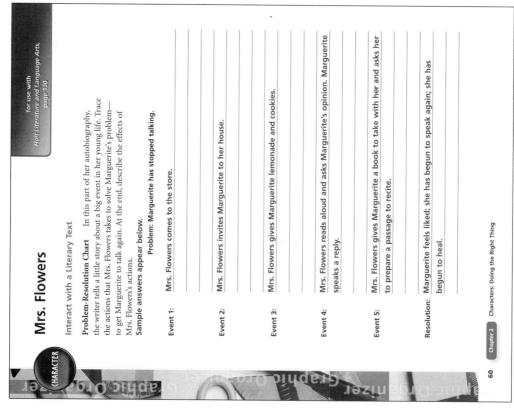

for use with
Holt Literature and Language Arts,
page 130

Mrs. Flowers

Interact with a Literary Text

Problem-Resolution Chart   In this part of her autobiography, the writer tells a little story about a big event in her young life. Trace the actions that Mrs. Flowers takes to solve Marguerite's problem—to get Marguerite to talk again. At the end, describe the effects of Mrs. Flowers's actions.

Sample answers appear below.

Problem: **Marguerite has stopped talking.**

Event 1:   Mrs. Flowers comes to the store.

Event 2:   Mrs. Flowers invites Marguerite to her house.

Event 3:   Mrs. Flowers gives Marguerite lemonade and cookies.

Event 4:   Mrs. Flowers reads aloud and asks Marguerite's opinion. Marguerite speaks a reply.

Event 5:   Mrs. Flowers gives Marguerite a book to take with her and asks her to prepare a passage to recite.

Resolution: Marguerite feels liked; she has begun to speak again; she has begun to heal.

Chapter 2   Characters: Doing the Right Thing

60

Literature

ESSAY

AUTHOR STUDY

The excerpt "Mrs. Flowers" from Maya Angelou's *I Know Why the Caged Bird Sings* creates a vivid picture of the young Marguerite and the woman who helped change her life. In Angelou's "New Directions," you will meet Mrs. Annie Johnson, Angelou's grandmother, who decided "to step off the road and cut me a new path."

Maya Angelou was born in St. Louis, Missouri, in 1928, and raised in Stamps, Arkansas, where she lived with her grandmother. After leaving Stamps, Angelou won a scholarship to the California Labor School, where she took evening classes in dance and drama. In 1954 and 1955, she toured Europe and Africa in a State Department–sponsored production of the opera *Porgy and Bess*. In addition to her many short stories, magazine articles, and poems, Angelou has written and produced a ten-part television series on Africanisms in American life. In 1992, she wrote and read a poem for the inauguration of President Bill Clinton.

BEFORE YOU READ

You are about to read about two characters living in different times and places. Despite their differences, both characters face hardships with courage and strength.

Here are some details about these selections:

- "New Directions" is an essay about Mrs. Annie Johnson, Maya Angelou's grandmother, who lived in Arkansas in the early twentieth century.
- "Field Work" is a true narrative that focuses on the field workers in the Salinas Valley in California in the later part of the twentieth century.
- Both texts are about people who are not afraid of hard work.

Reading Standard 3.3 Compare and contrast motivations and reactions of literary characters from different historical eras confronting similar situations or conflicts.

New Directions

Maya Angelou

In 1903 the late Mrs. Annie Johnson of Arkansas found herself with two toddling sons, very little money, a slight ability to read and add simple numbers. To this picture add a disastrous marriage and the burdensome fact that Mrs. Johnson was a Negro.

When she told her husband, Mr. William Johnson, of her dissatisfaction with their marriage, he conceded that he too found it to be less than he expected, and had been

10 secretly hoping to leave and study religion. He added that he thought God was calling him not only to preach but to do so in Enid, Oklahoma. He did not tell her that he knew a minister in Enid with whom he could study and who had a friendly, unmarried daughter. They parted amicably, Annie keeping the one-room house and William taking most of the cash to carry himself to Oklahoma.

Annie, over six feet tall, big-boned, decided that she would not go to work as a **domestic** and leave her "precious babes" to anyone else's care. There was no possibility

20 of being hired at the town's cotton gin or lumber mill, but maybe there was a way to make the two factories work for her. In her words, "I looked up the road I was going and back the way I come, and since I wasn't satisfied, I decided to step off the road and cut me a new path." She told herself that she wasn't a fancy cook but that she could "mix groceries well enough to scare hungry away and keep from starving a man."

"New Directions" from *Wouldn't Take Nothing for My Journey Now* by Maya Angelou. Copyright © 1993 by Maya Angelou. For online information about other Random House, Inc., books and authors, see the Internet Web site at http://www.randomhouse.com. Reprinted by permission of *Random House, Inc.*

IDENTIFY

What do you learn about the time and place Mrs. Johnson lived in?

She lived in Arkansas in the early part of the twentieth century.

WORD KNOWLEDGE

The word *amicably* (line 13) means "in a friendly way" and comes from the Latin word *amicus*, which means "friend."

The Spanish word *amigo* comes from the same Latin word.

VOCABULARY DEVELOPMENT

domestic (də·mes′tik) *n.*: servant for the home, such as a maid or cook.

In this context, *domestic* is a noun meaning "household servant." It comes from the Latin *domus*, meaning "house" or "home." More often *domestic* is used as an adjective, meaning "having to do with a home."

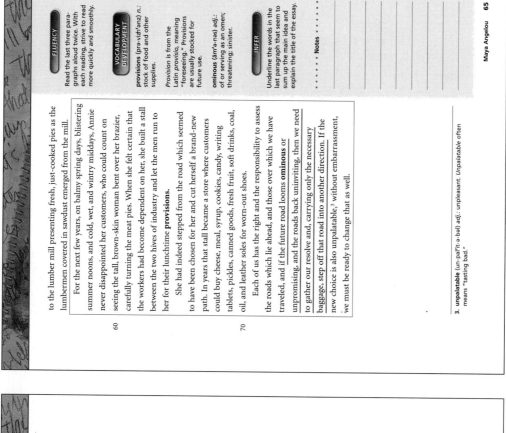

She made her plans meticulously[1] and in secret. One early evening to see if she was ready, she placed stones in two five-gallon pails and carried them three miles to the cotton gin. She rested a little, and then, discarding some rocks, she walked in the darkness to the sawmill five miles farther along the dirt road. On her way back to her little house and her babies, she dumped the remaining rocks along the path.

That same night she worked into the early hours boiling chicken and frying ham. She made dough and filled the rolled-out pastry with meat. At last she went to sleep.

The next morning she left her house carrying the meat pies, lard, an iron brazier,[2] and coals for a fire. Just before lunch she appeared in an empty lot behind the cotton gin. As the dinner noon bell rang, she dropped the savories into boiling fat and the aroma rose and floated over to the workers who spilled out of the gin, covered with white lint, looking like specters. Most workers had brought their lunches of pinto beans and biscuits or crackers, onions and cans of sardines, but they were tempted by the hot meat pies which Annie ladled out of the fat. She wrapped them in newspapers, which soaked up the grease, and offered them for sale at a nickel each. Although business was slow, those first days Annie was determined. She balanced her appearances between the two hours of activity.

So, on Monday if she offered hot, fresh pies at the cotton gin and sold the remaining cooled-down pies at the lumber mill for three cents, then on Tuesday she went first

---

1. **meticulously** (mə·tik′yoo·ləs·lē) *adv.*: extremely carefully; with great attention to detail.
2. **brazier** (brā′zhər) *n.*: metal container that holds burning coals or charcoal, used to warm a room or grill food.

INFER

Why do you think Mrs. Johnson walks with rocks in the pails?

She was testing her ability to walk the required distances carrying heavy pails of food.

WORD KNOWLEDGE

A *cotton gin* (line 40) was the building where the seeds were removed from the newly picked cotton. A gin was the device that removed the seeds.

WORD KNOWLEDGE

Savories (line 41) are tasty bits of food. The word is more commonly used in Canada and England.

Savor (sā′vər) is a verb meaning "enjoy with great delight."

INTERPRET

Pause at line 51. What do Mrs. Johnson's actions reveal about her personality?

Suggested response:

She is determined to succeed.

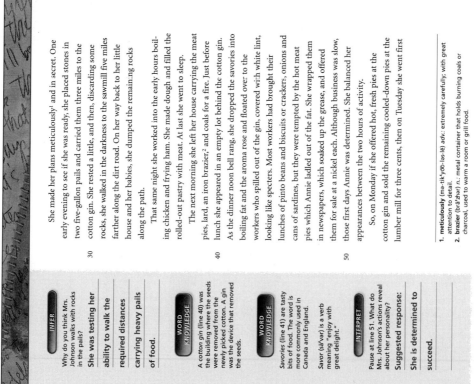

to the lumber mill presenting fresh, just-cooked pies as the lumbermen covered in sawdust emerged from the mill.

For the next few years, on balmy spring days, blistering summer noons, and cold, wet, and wintry middays, Annie never disappointed her customers, who could count on seeing the tall, brown-skin woman bent over her brazier, carefully turning the meat pies. When she felt certain that the workers had become dependent on her, she built a stall between the two hives of industry and let the men run to her for their lunchtime **provisions.**

She had indeed stepped from the road which seemed to have been chosen for her and cut herself a brand-new path. In years that stall became a store where customers could buy cheese, meal, syrup, cookies, candy, writing tablets, pickles, canned goods, fresh fruit, soft drinks, coal, oil, and leather soles for worn-out shoes.

Each of us has the right and the responsibility to assess the roads which lie ahead, and those over which we have traveled, and if the future road looms **ominous** or unpromising, and the roads back uninviting, then we need to gather our resolve and, carrying only the necessary baggage, step off that road into another direction. If the new choice is also unpalatable,[3] without embarrassment, we must be ready to change that as well.

---

3. **unpalatable** (un·pal′it·ə·bəl) *adj.*: unpleasant. *Unpalatable* often means "tasting bad."

FLUENCY

Read the last three paragraphs aloud twice. With each reading, strive to read more quickly and smoothly.

VOCABULARY DEVELOPMENT

provisions (prə·vizh′ənz) *n.*: stock of food and other supplies.

Provision is from the Latin *provisio,* meaning "foreseeing." *Provisions* are usually stocked for future use.

ominous (äm′ə·nəs) *adj.*: of or serving as an omen; threatening; sinister.

INFER

Underline the words in the last paragraph that seem to sum up the main idea and explain the title of the essay.

* * * * *   **Notes**   * * * * * *

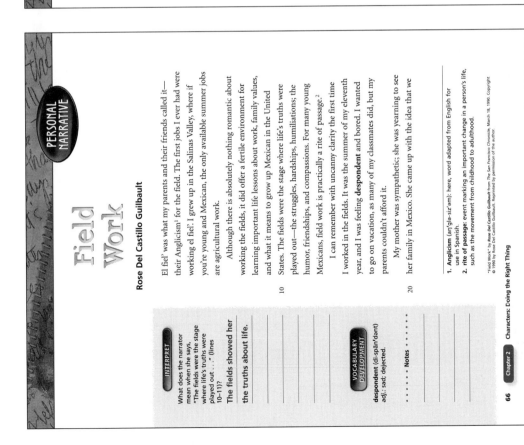

PERSONAL NARRATIVE

Field Work

Rose Del Castillo Guilbault

El fiel' was what my parents and their friends called it—their Anglicism[1] for the field. The first jobs I ever had were working el fiel'. I grew up in the Salinas Valley, where if you're young and Mexican, the only available summer jobs are agricultural work.

Although there is absolutely nothing romantic about working the fields, it did offer a fertile environment for learning important life lessons about work, family values, and what it means to grow up Mexican in the United States. The fields were the stage where life's truths were played out—the struggles, hardships, humiliations; the humor, friendships, and compassions. For many young Mexicans, field work is practically a rite of passage.[2]

I can remember with uncanny clarity the first time I worked in the fields. It was the summer of my eleventh year, and I was feeling despondent and bored. I wanted to go on vacation, as many of my classmates did, but my parents couldn't afford it.

My mother was sympathetic; she was yearning to see her family in Mexico. She came up with the idea that we

could earn the $50 we needed for Greyhound bus tickets to Mexicali[3] if we both worked the garlic harvest that was about to begin on the farm where we lived.

The first hurdle to earning the money was persuading my traditional Mexican father to let us do it. He had made it clear to my mother that he did not want her to work. To him, a working wife implied his inability to support his family.

To this day, I have no idea how she convinced him that it was all right. Maybe it was because the job was very short-term—five days—or maybe it was because we hadn't been to Mexico in more than a year. My father knew an annual visit to see relatives was my mother's lifeline. In any case, my father agreed to lobby his boss the next day to let us join the garlic-picking crew.

The boss was skeptical about employing us. Not because he was concerned about hiring a woman and a child; he worried more about our inexperience and stamina. After all, this was a man's job and he had a deadline. What if we slowed things down and he had to keep a worker for an extra day?

"Since when is picking garlic such an art?" my mother retorted when my father told her that night about the boss's reservations. But then he added that the boss had decided to take a chance on us.

We started immediately—at 6 A.M. the next day. The August morning was cold and gray, still shrouded in damp fog. We wore layers of clothes—a T-shirt, a sweat shirt, a windbreaker—to protect us from the early-morning chill and later discard when the afternoon sun got too hot. We

---

1. **Anglicism** (aŋ'glə-sĭz'əm): here, word adapted from English for use in Spanish.
2. **rite of passage**: event marking an important change in a person's life, such as the movement from childhood to adulthood.

3. **Mexicali** (meks'i-kä'lē): city in northwestern Mexico, near the California border.

INTERPRET

What does the narrator mean when she says, "The fields were the stage where life's truths were played out . . ." (lines 10–11)?

The fields showed her the truths about life.

VOCABULARY DEVELOPMENT

despondent (dĭ-spän'dənt) *adj.*: sad; dejected.

· · · · · · Notes · · · · · ·

IDENTIFY

What do the narrator and her mother decide to do? Why do they decide to do it?

They decide to go to work picking garlic; they want to earn money to visit relatives in Mexico.

IDENTIFY

Why does the narrator's father decide to get work for his wife and daughter? Underline his reasons.

VOCABULARY DEVELOPMENT

stamina (stăm'ə-nə) *n.*: endurance; resistance to fatigue, illness, hardship, and so on.

· · · · · · Notes · · · · · ·

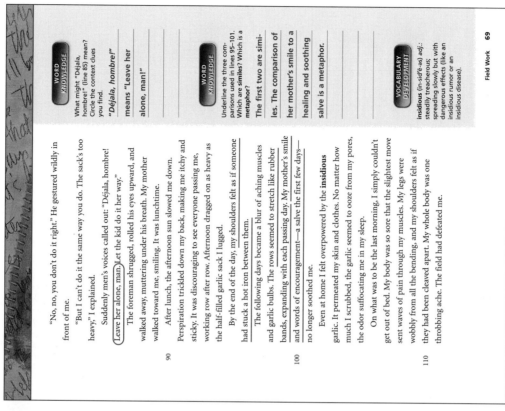

"No, no, you don't do it right." He gestured wildly in front of me.

"But I can't do it the same way you do. The sack's too heavy," I explained.

Suddenly men's voices called out: "Déjala, hombre! Leave her alone, man! Let the kid do it her way."

The foreman shrugged, rolled his eyes upward, and walked away, muttering under his breath. My mother walked toward me, smiling. It was lunchtime.

90 After lunch, the afternoon sun slowed me down. Perspiration trickled down my back, making me itchy and sticky. It was discouraging to see everyone passing me, working row after row. Afternoon dragged on as heavy as the half-filled garlic sack I lugged.

By the end of the day, my shoulders felt as if someone had stuck a hot iron between them.

The following days became a blur of aching muscles and garlic bulbs. The rows seemed to stretch like rubber bands, expanding with each passing day. My mother's smile and words of encouragement—a salve the first few days—
100 no longer soothed me.

Even at home I felt overpowered by the **insidious** garlic. It permeated my skin and clothes. No matter how much I scrubbed, the garlic seemed to ooze from my pores, the odor suffocating me in my sleep.

On what was to be the last morning, I simply couldn't get out of bed. My body was so sore that the slightest move sent waves of pain through my muscles. My legs were wobbly from all the bending, and my shoulders felt as if they had been cleaved apart. My whole body was one
110 throbbing ache. The field had defeated me.

WORD KNOWLEDGE

What might "Déjala, hombre!" (line 85) mean? Circle the context clues you find.

"Déjala, hombre!" means "Leave her alone, man!"

WORD KNOWLEDGE

Underline the three comparisons used in lines 95–101. Which are **similes**? Which is a **metaphor**?

The first two are similes. The comparison of her mother's smile to a healing and soothing salve is a metaphor.

VOCABULARY DEVELOPMENT

insidious (in-sĭd'ē-əs) adj.: steadily treacherous; spreading slowly but with dangerous effects (like an insidious rumor or an insidious disease.

Field Work 69

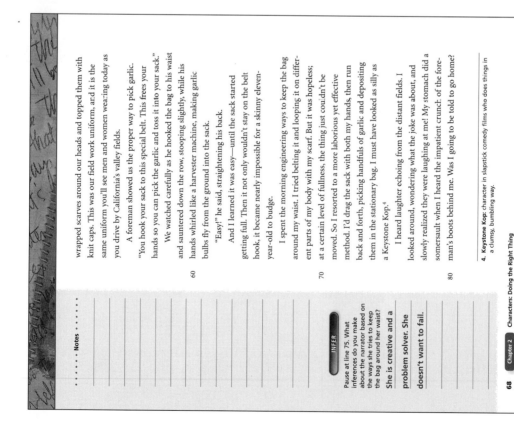

. . . . Notes . . . .

wrapped scarves around our heads and topped them with knit caps. This was our field work uniform, and it is the same uniform you'll see men and women wearing today as you drive by California's valley fields.

A foreman showed us the proper way to pick garlic. "You hook your sack to this special belt. This frees your hands so you can pick the garlic and toss it into your sack."

We watched carefully as he hooked the bag to his waist
60 and sauntered down the row, stooping slightly, while his hands whirled like a harvester machine, making garlic bulbs fly from the ground into the sack.

"Easy!" he said, straightening his back.

And I learned it was easy—until the sack started getting full. Then it not only wouldn't stay on the belt hook, it became nearly impossible for a skinny eleven-year-old to budge.

I spent the morning engineering ways to keep the bag around my waist. I tried belting it and looping it on differ-
70 ent parts of my body with my scarf. But it was hopeless; at a certain level of fullness, the thing just couldn't be moved. So I resorted to a more laborious yet effective method. I'd drag the sack with both my hands, then run back and forth, picking handfuls of garlic and depositing them in the stationary bag. I must have looked as silly as a Keystone Kop.[4]

I heard laughter echoing from the distant fields. I looked around, wondering what the joke was about, and slowly realized they were laughing at me! My stomach did a
80 somersault when I heard the impatient crunch of the foreman's boots behind me. Was I going to be told to go home?

4. **Keystone Kop:** character in slapstick comedy films who does things in a clumsy, bumbling way.

INFER

Pause at line 75. What inferences do you make about the ways she tries to keep the bag around her waist?

She is creative and a problem solver. She doesn't want to fail.

68 Chapter 2 Characters: Doing the Right Thing

Left page (70)

EVALUATE

Underline the mother's statement in line 114. How do you feel about what she says?

Responses will vary.

"I just can't do it," I sobbed to my mother, the tears tasting like garlic.

"Anything worth having is worth working for," she said gently.

"I don't care about the vacation. I'm too tired. It's not worth it," I cried.

120 "There are only a few rows left. Are you sure you can't finish?" my mother persisted.

But to me the few rows might as well have been hundreds. I felt bad about giving up after working so hard, but it just didn't seem fair to pay such a high price to go on vacation. After all, my friends didn't have to.

My mother was very quiet all day. I'd forgotten it was to have been her vacation, too. My father was surprised to see us sitting neatly dressed when he came home. He listened quietly to my mother's explanation, and after a thoughtful pause said, "Well, if we all pitch in, we can still finish up the rows tonight, right on schedule."

130 As I looked at my father's dust-rimmed, bloodshot eyes, his dusty hair and mud-stained overalls, I was over-whelmed with a strange mixture of pity and gratitude. I knew by the slope of his shoulders he was very tired from his own grueling field work. And finishing up our leftover work was nothing short of an act of love.

I was torn. The thought of doing battle with the field again filled me with dread. But I said nothing, swallowing my reluctance until it formed a lump in my throat.

140 That summer evening, the three of us worked side by side, teasing, talking, laughing, as we completed the task. It was dark, and we had grown silent by the time the last of the garlic sacks were lined up. The rosy glow from the

INFER

Why does the narrator go back to the fields? Circle the words that show the mixed emotions she feels toward her father.

She feels both pity and gratitude toward her father. She knows how hard he works, yet he is willing to work some more in the field to help her. Given how tired he is, she cannot give in to her own tiredness.

Right page (71)

setting sun made me feel as warm as the relief of knowing the work was finally over and done.

I worked every summer thereafter, some in the fields (never again picking garlic!) and later in the vegetable-packing sheds, always alongside my mother. Working together created an unusual bond between us. And through this relationship, and relationships with other Mexican families thrust into this agricultural society, I got an

150 education as solid and rich as the earth we worked.

IDENTIFY

Underline the passages that tell what the narrator gains by working in the fields.

• • • • • • Notes • • • • • •

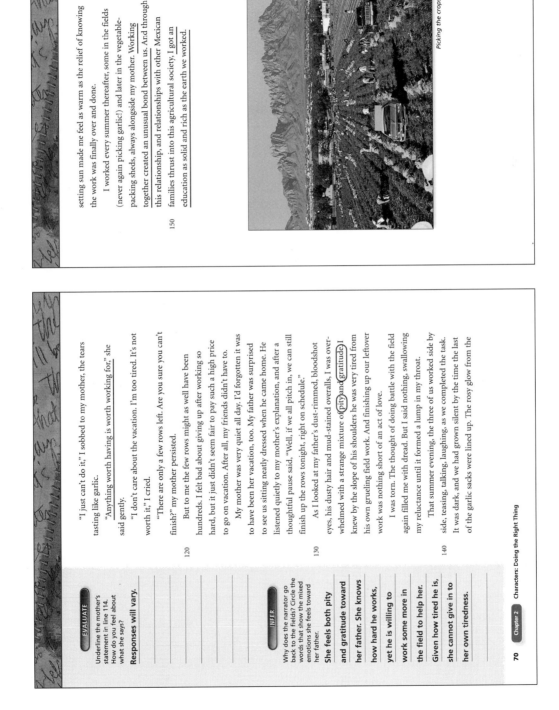

Picking the crops.

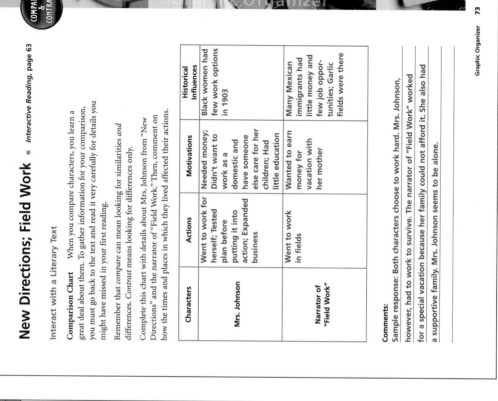

Graphic Organizer   COMPARE & CONTRAST   73

New Directions; Field Work ▪ *Interactive Reading*, page 63

Interact with a Literary Text

Comparison Chart   When you compare characters, you learn a great deal about them. To gather information for your comparison, you must go back to the text and read it very carefully for details you might have missed in your first reading.

Remember that *compare* can mean looking for similarities *and* differences. *Contrast* means looking for differences only.

Complete this chart with details about Mrs. Johnson from "New Directions" and the narrator of "Field Work." Then, comment on how the times and places in which they lived affected their actions.

Characters	Actions	Motivations	Historical Influences
Mrs. Johnson	Went to work for herself; Tested plan before putting it into action; Expanded business	Needed money; Didn't want to work as a domestic and have someone else care for her children; Had little education	Black women had few work options in 1903
Narrator of "Field Work"	Went to work in fields	Wanted to earn money for vacation with her mother	Many Mexican immigrants had little money and few job opportunities; Garlic fields were there

Comments:
Sample response: Both characters choose to work hard. Mrs. Johnson, however, had to work to survive. The narrator of "Field Work" worked for a special vacation because her family could not afford it. She also had a supportive family. Mrs. Johnson seems to be alone.

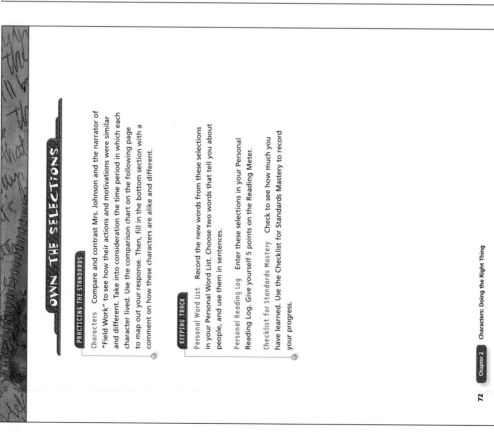

OWN THE SELECTIONS

PRACTICING THE STANDARDS

Characters   Compare and contrast Mrs. Johnson and the narrator of "Field Work" to see how their actions and motivations were similar and different. Take into consideration the time period in which each character lived. Use the comparison chart on the following page to map out your response. Then, fill in the bottom section with a comment on how these characters are alike and different.

KEEPING TRACK

Personal Word List   Record the new words from these selections in your Personal Word List. Choose two words that tell you about people, and use them in sentences.

Personal Reading Log   Enter these selections in your Personal Reading Log. Give yourself 5 points on the Reading Meter.

Checklist for Standards Mastery   Check to see how much you have learned. Use the Checklist for Standards Mastery to record your progress.

72   Chapter 2   Characters: Doing the Right Thing

Information

NEWS COLUMN

BEFORE YOU READ

Did reading about Mrs. Johnson's meat pies make your mouth water? Evan Morris has found a connection between food and our language. According to him, food is the source of hundreds of common English idioms. All right, chow down!

from The Word Detective

You Took the Words Right Out of My Mouth . . .

Evan Morris

Reading Standard 2.3 Find similarities and differences between texts in the treatment, scope, or organization of ideas.

Anyone who doubts that food occupies a place of honor in the human imagination need only open a dictionary of slang or common English idioms. Hundreds of our most commonly heard expressions are drawn from the chow line, and more are added every year. Here are a few choice tidbits (*tidbit* means "small tasty morsel," from the English dialect word *tid*, "tender," plus *bit*).

10 **a chicken in every pot:** "Economic prosperity." A very old metaphor, revived to take center stage as a campaign slogan in the 1928 U.S. presidential election (immediately preceding the Great Depression).

WORD KNOWLEDGE

The title of this news column is a common English idiom. What does it mean?

"You said what I was just about to say."

VOCABULARY DEVELOPMENT

prosperity (präs·per'ə·tē) *n.*: good fortune, success.

The word *prosperity* is built from the Latin stem *spes*, which means "hope." What connection do you see between *prosperity* and *hope?*

During times of prosperity, people feel hopeful.

"You Took the Words Right Out of My Mouth . . ." from *The Word Detective* by Evan Morris. Copyright © 2000 by Evan Morris. Reprinted by permission of *Algonquin Books of Chapel Hill, a division of Workman Publishing.*

---

easy as pie: "Very easy or simple," since the early twentieth century. Of **debatable** logic, since making a good pie is anything but easy. May be a mangling of *nice as pie*, "very nice," which makes much more sense.

20 **eat humble pie:** "To apologize and be forced to acknowledge one's errors," since about 1830. This phrase is actually a pun on *umble pie*, a lowly servants' dish made from the *umbles* ("innards," ultimately from the Latin *lumbus*, "loin") of deer, as opposed to the venison their masters ate.

milktoast: "An ineffectual or feeble man." Milktoast (toast soaked in milk, sometimes with added butter and sugar) has been fed to toothless infants for centuries and used as a metaphor for wimpiness just as long. Often spelled *milquetoast* in the United States, after Caspar Milquetoast, a popular old-time comic-strip character.

proof of the pudding is in the eating: "You can't judge a thing until you put it to its intended use," *proof* in this case meaning "test" or "trial." An old and oft-quoted proverb dating back at least to the seventeenth century.

30 **rhubarb:** "An uproar or ruckus." Thought to have come from the practice of having extras in theatrical crowd scenes say "rhubarb" over and over, **simulating** the sound of an angry mob.

VOCABULARY DEVELOPMENT

debatable (dē·bāt'ə·bəl) *adj.*: having strong points on both sides; worthy of debate.

The French word *debatre* means "fight; contend." What connection do you see between *debatable* and *debatre?*

People might fight over something that is debatable.

DECODING TIP

Not sure how to pronounce *milquetoast* (line 25)? It's pronounced exactly the same as *milk toast!*

VOCABULARY DEVELOPMENT

simulating (sim'yōō·lāt'iŋ) *v.*: taking on the external appearance of something; looking or acting like.

Simulating is built on the Latin *simul*, meaning "together with."

You Took the Words Right Out of My Mouth . . . **75**

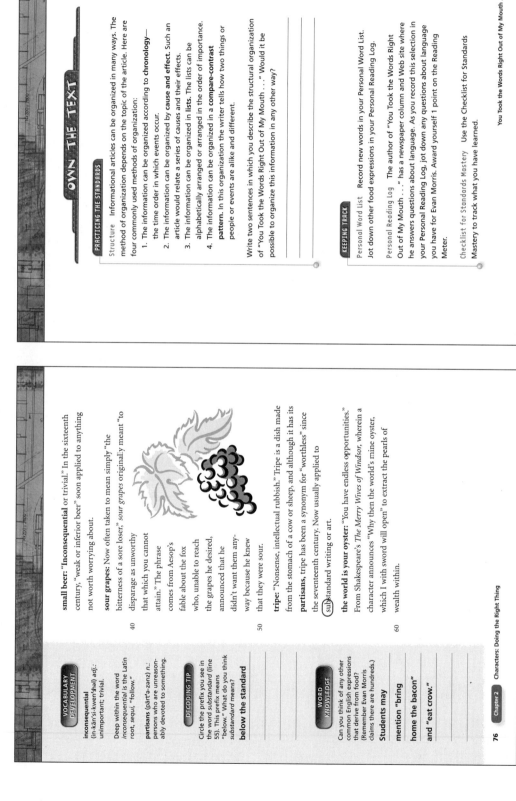

VOCABULARY DEVELOPMENT

inconsequential (in-kän'si-kwen'shal) *adj.*: unimportant; trivial.

Deep within the word *inconsequential* is the Latin root, *sequi,* "follow."

partisans (pärt'a-zanz) *n.*: persons who are unreasonably devoted to something.

DECODING TIP

Circle the prefix you see in the word *substandard* (line 55). This prefix means "below." What do you think *substandard* means?

below the standard

_____

WORD KNOWLEDGE

Can you think of any other common English expressions that derive from food? (Remember Evan Morris claims there are hundreds.)

Students may mention "bring home the bacon" and "eat crow."

_____

small beer: "Inconsequential or trivial." In the sixteenth century, "weak or inferior beer" soon applied to anything not worth worrying about.

40   **sour grapes:** Now often taken to mean simply "the bitterness of a sore loser," *sour grapes* originally meant "to disparage as unworthy that which you cannot attain." The phrase comes from Aesop's fable about the fox who, unable to reach the grapes he desired, announced that he didn't want them any- way because he knew 50   that they were sour.

tripe: "Nonsense, intellectual rubbish." Tripe is a dish made from the stomach of a cow or sheep, and although it has its **partisans,** tripe has been a synonym for "worthless" since the seventeenth century. Now usually applied to substandard writing or art.

the world is your oyster: "You have endless opportunities." From Shakespeare's *The Merry Wives of Windsor,* wherein a character announces "Why then the world's mine oyster, which I with sword will open" to extract the pearls of 60   wealth within.

OWN THE TEXT

PRACTICING THE STANDARDS

Structure Informational articles can be organized in many ways. The method of organization depends on the topic of the article. Here are four commonly used methods of organization:

1. The information can be organized according to **chronology**—the time order in which events occur.

2. The information can be organized by **cause and effect.** Such an article would relate a series of causes and their effects.

3. The information can be organized in **lists.** The lists can be alphabetically arranged or arranged in the order of importance.

4. The information can be organized in a **compare-contrast pattern.** In this organization the writer tells how two things or people or events are alike and different.

Write two sentences in which you describe the structural organization of "You Took the Words Right Out of My Mouth . . ." Would it be possible to organize this information in any other way?

_____

_____

_____

KEEPING TRACK

Personal Word List Record new words in your Personal Word List. Jot down other food expressions in your Personal Reading Log.

Personal Reading Log The author of "You Took the Words Right Out of My Mouth . . ." has a newspaper column and Web site where he answers questions about language. As you record this selection in your Personal Reading Log, jot down any questions about language you have for Evan Morris. Award yourself 1 point on the Reading Meter.

Checklist for Standards Mastery Use the Checklist for Standards Mastery to track what you have learned.

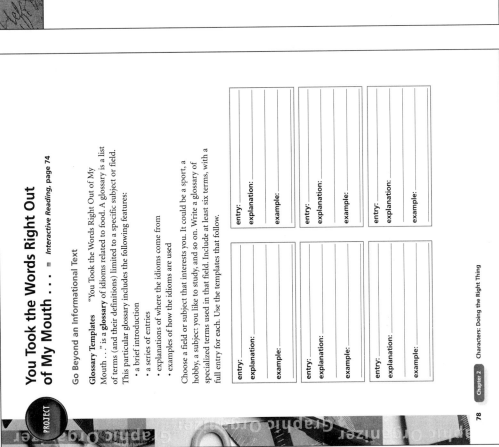

Literature

MYTH

BEFORE YOU READ

All cultures have stories telling how things came to be. The ancient Greeks and Romans told **myths** about how the world was created and how features of our earth came into being. Americans settling the West told **tall tales** about how land features were formed and how different inventions came about.

In the next two stories, you will meet two figures: Prometheus, who gives a great gift to humankind, and Paul Bunyan, who personifies the can-do spirit of the American West.

Reading Standard 3.3
Compare and contrast motivations and reactions of literary characters from different historical eras confronting similar situations or conflicts.

Prometheus Steals Fire from Heaven

a Greek myth, retold by Anne Terry White

There was a time when there were no gods. Heaven and Earth alone existed. They were the first parents, and from their union sprang the gigantic Titans. For ages the Titans ruled the world. But at last the gods, who were the children of the Titans, rebelled and overthrew them. Then it was that Zeus became supreme ruler of the universe and his wife and sister Hera became queen of heaven.

Now as yet there were no men on earth, and none of the animals seemed worthy to rule the rest. So the gods decided to make still another kind of creature. One of the Titans, Prometheus[1]—whose name means "**forethought**"—was chosen for the task.

10

IDENTIFY

Myths usually tell about the deeds of gods and heroes. Circle the names of gods and goddesses in the first paragraph. What famous ship was named after the Titans?

the *Titanic*

VOCABULARY DEVELOPMENT

forethought (fôr′thôt′) n.: planning beforehand.

Fore comes from the Old English *foran,* meaning "before."

1. **Prometheus** (prō-mē′thē-əs).

"Prometheus Steals Fire from Heaven" from Myths and Legends *by Anne Terry White. Copyright © 1959 and renewed © 1987 by* Golden Books, *a division of* Random House, Inc. *Reprinted by permission of the publisher.*

Prometheus Steals Fire from Heaven **79**

PROJECT

You Took the Words Right Out of My Mouth . . . ■ *Interactive Reading, page 74*

Go Beyond an Informational Text

Glossary Templates "You Took the Words Right Out of My Mouth . . ." is a **glossary** of idioms related to food. A glossary is a list of terms (and their definitions) limited to a specific subject or field. This particular glossary includes the following features:

- a brief introduction
- a series of entries
- explanations of where the idioms come from
- examples of how the idioms are used

Choose a field or subject that interests you. It could be a sport, a hobby, a subject you like to study, and so on. Write a glossary of specialized terms used in that field. Include at least six terms, with a full entry for each. Use the templates that follow.

entry:
explanation:
example:

entry:
explanation:
example:

entry:
explanation:
example:

entry:
explanation:
example:

entry:
explanation:
example:

entry:
explanation:
example:

78 Chapter 2 Characters: Doing the Right Thing

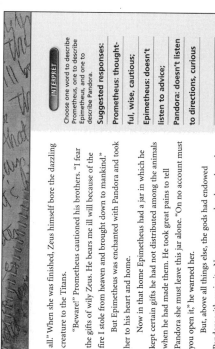

Down from heaven the Titan sped. He took clay and mixed it with water, kneaded it, and shaped it in the likeness of the gods. He made his creature stand upright, for he wanted man to look up at the stars and not down on the earth, like the animals. Then Prometheus thought:

"What gifts shall I give this work of my hands to make him superior to the rest of creation?"

Unfortunately, his brother Epimetheus²—which means "afterthought"—had already given all the great gifts to the animals. Strength and courage, **cunning** and speed—he had distributed them all. Wings, claws, horns, scales, shelly covering—nothing was left for man.

Then **quick-witted** Prometheus thought of fire. Oh, great and wonderful gift! "With fire," the Titan thought, "man can make weapons and subdue the beasts, forge tools, plow the earth, and master the arts. What matter that my creature has neither fur nor feathers, scales nor shell? Fire will warm his dwelling, and he need fear neither rain nor snow nor the wild north wind."

Back to heaven Prometheus sped, lit his torch at the chariot of the sun, brought down fire to man, and went away rejoicing.

But up on high Olympus, great Zeus frowned as he sat with the gods feasting on nectar and ambrosia. For Zeus was ever jealous of his power.

"This creature that looks to heaven is truly more than a match for the beasts," he thought. "Indeed, he is almost a match for the gods. But I will curb his ill-got power!"

Straightway Zeus made woman, lovely as a goddess. All the immortals bestowed gifts upon her to make her yet more captivating. And they called her Pandora—"Gift-of-

2. **Epimetheus** (ep'ə-mē'thē-əs).

IDENTIFY
According to the myth, why do we stand upright?
Prometheus wanted us to look at the stars, not down at the earth like the animals.

IDENTIFY
What gift does Prometheus give humans that will make up for their not having fur, feathers, scales, or a shell?
fire

VOCABULARY DEVELOPMENT
cunning (kun'ĭŋ) *n.:* skill in deception; slyness.
quick-witted (kwĭk'wĭt'ĭd) *adj.:* nimble of mind; alert.

IDENTIFY
Why does Zeus want to curb the power of humans?
He fears man will be a match for the gods.

Chapter 2   Characters: Doing the Right Thing   80

all." When she was finished, Zeus himself bore the dazzling creature to the Titans.

"Beware!" Prometheus cautioned his brothers. "I fear the gifts of wily Zeus. He bears me ill will because of the fire I stole from heaven and brought down to mankind."

But Epimetheus was enchanted with Pandora and took her to his heart and home.

Now in that home Epimetheus had a jar in which he kept certain gifts he had not distributed among the animals when he had made them. He took great pains to tell Pandora she must leave this jar alone. "On no account must you open it," he warned her.

But, above all things else, the gods had endowed Pandora with curiosity. No sooner was she alone than she sped to the forbidden jar.

"Surely it will do no harm if I just peek in and see what is there," thought she.

She slipped off the cover. And there flew out a host of evil plagues and all manner of disease, envy, spite, revenge—and scattered themselves far and wide. Pandora clapped on the lid. But it was too late. The jar was all but empty. Only hope had remained—hope which never leaves mankind.

There was no danger now that man would rival the gods—he had enemies far worse than wild beasts to contend with. But still Zeus could not forgive Prometheus.

"The thief who stole heaven's fire shall be punished as his love of man deserves!" Zeus declared. "He shall be chained to the highest rock of Mount Caucasus—where man can never climb. Scorched by the sun, he shall lie and groan. And I shall cause a vulture to prey upon his liver, which shall grow again as fast as it is devoured."

INTERPRET
Choose one word to describe Prometheus, one to describe Epimetheus, and one to describe Pandora.
Suggested responses:
Prometheus: thoughtful, wise, cautious;
Epimetheus: doesn't listen to advice;
Pandora: doesn't listen to directions, curious

INFER
Pause at line 66. How can hope make these plagues less devastating?
Hope lets people believe that things will be better. Hope is the opposite of despair.

IDENTIFY
Underline the horrible punishment Zeus gives to Prometheus.

Prometheus Steals Fire from Heaven   81

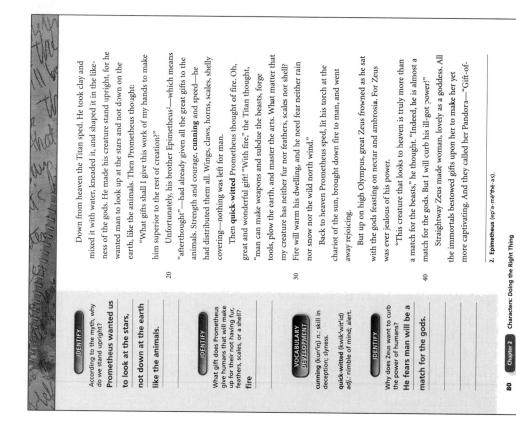

Right page (83)

TALL TALE

Paul Bunyan runs a lumber camp in the North Woods. Before this episode in Paul's adventures started, Paul had been tinkering with the Mississippi River. Ole (ō′le) in this story is one of Paul's workers. Babe is Paul's fabulous blue ox.

Paul's Popcorn

Walter Blair

Having got the water meandering around to make the soil moist, Paul figured he'd test the land out with popcorn. So he picked up a good healthy looking kernel, walked out to a likely looking place that had been **irrigated** lately, and dug a hole about a foot deep with his middle finger. He couldn't use his forefinger or thumb, naturally, because he was holding the corn between them.

10 Well, Paul had no more than started back to camp to get Ole to act as a witness, than there was a sort of sputtering up of brown dirt, and a cornstalk came skyhooting through in no time at all, the corn was up to Paul's knee. And by the time he got back with Ole, the cornstalk had grown so much that the top was buried in a cloud.

"Ole!" says Paul. "Climb up to the top of that baby and chop the top off so she won't grow any more!"

Ole started shinning up the stalk at a great rate. But the thing kept shooting up, and in a minute or so Ole, too,
20 was out of sight in that cloud. It was a handsome cloud with cottony bumps and scallopy edges, but Ole said afterwards that being inside of it wasn't different from being inside any old cloud. "Nothing but fog inside it," he said.

IDENTIFY

Tall tales are filled with exaggeration. In fact, the details are as oversized as the American West must have seemed to the settlers. As you read, circle the exaggerated details.

VOCABULARY DEVELOPMENT

irrigated (ir′ə-gāt′id) *v.:* supplied (land) with water by means of ditches or canals or sprinklers.

WORD KNOWLEDGE

The adjective *scallopy* (line 19) describes something that has curved edges like a scallop shell.

FLUENCY

Read the comic conversation in the box aloud. Use different, appropriate voices for the two characters and for the narration.

Paul's Popcorn 83

Left page (82)

INTERPRET

Prometheus has inspired many artists and writers. In what ways is he heroic?

He doesn't groan or
ask for pity; he doesn't
bend to the tyrant
(Zeus); he endures;
he doesn't display
his agony.

He summoned Hephaestus,[3] And high on the
mountain where eagles make their home, heaven's lame
smith—all unwilling—riveted the Titan to the rock. There
Prometheus hung in his chains. But he neither groaned nor
80 besought pity, neither regretted what he had done nor bent
his knee before the tyrant. The rock, the vulture, and the
chain—all that the proud can feel of pain—he endured,
and showed his agony to none.

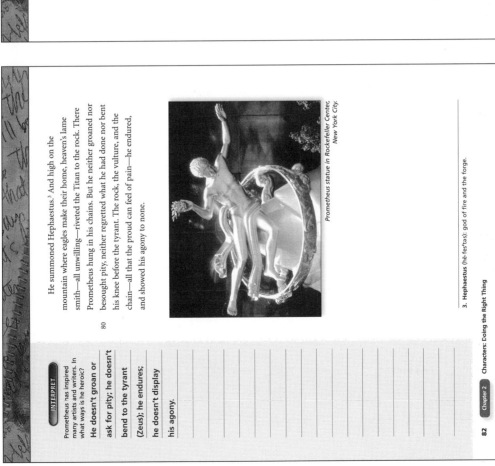

Prometheus statue in Rockefeller Center, New York City.

---

3. **Hephaestus** (hē-fes′təs): god of fire and the forge.

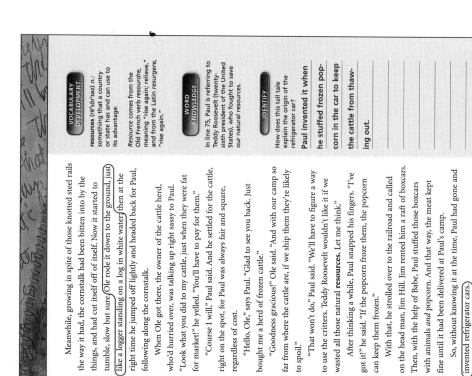

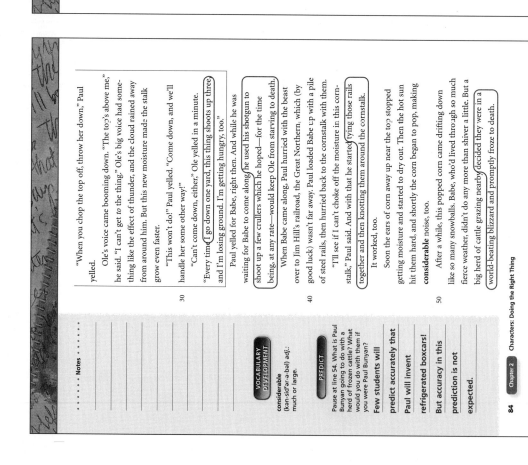

Page 85

Meanwhile, growing in spite of those knotted steel rails the way it had, the cornstalk had been bitten into by the things, and had cut itself off of itself. Now it started to tumble, slow but sure. Ole rode it down to the ground, just like a logger standing on a log in white water, then at the right time he jumped off lightly and headed back for Paul, following along the cornstalk.

When Ole got there, the owner of the cattle herd, who'd hurried over, was talking up right sassy to Paul. "Look what you did to my cattle, just when they were fat for market!" he yelled. "You'll have to pay for them."

"Course I will," Paul said. And he settled for the cattle, right on the spot, for Paul was always fair and square, regardless of cost.

"Hello, Ole," says Paul. "Glad to see you back. Just bought me a herd of frozen cattle."

"Goodness gracious!" Ole said. "And with our camp so far from where the cattle are, if we ship them they're likely to spoil."

"That won't do," Paul said. "We'll have to figure a way to use the critters. Teddy Roosevelt wouldn't like it if we wasted all those natural **resources**. Let me think."

After thinking a while, Paul snapped his fingers. "I've got it!" he said. "If the popcorn froze them, the popcorn can keep them frozen."

With that, he strolled over to the railroad and called on the head man, Jim Hill. Jim rented him a raft of boxcars. Then, with the help of Babe, Paul stuffed those boxcars with animals *and* popcorn. And that way, the meat kept fine until it had been delivered at Paul's camp.

So, without knowing it at the time, Paul had gone and invented refrigerator cars.

VOCABULARY DEVELOPMENT

resources (rē'sôr'saz) *n.*: something that a country or state has and can use to its advantage.

Resource comes from the Old French verb *resourdre,* meaning "rise again; relieve," and from the Latin *resurgere,* "rise again."

WORD KNOWLEDGE

In line 75, Paul is referring to Teddy Roosevelt (twenty-sixth president of the United States), who fought to save our natural resources.

IDENTIFY

How does this tall tale explain the origin of the refrigerator car? Paul invented it when he stuffed frozen popcorn in the car to keep the cattle from thawing out.

Paul's Popcorn   85

Page 84

Notes

"When you chop the top off, throw her down," Paul yelled.

Ole's voice came booming down. "The top's above me," he said. "I can't get *to* the thing." Ole's big voice had something like the effect of thunder, and the cloud rained away from around him. But this new moisture made the stalk grow even faster.

"This won't do!" Paul yelled. "Come down, and we'll handle her some other way!"

"Can't come down, either," Ole yelled in a minute. "Every time I go down one yard, this thing shoots up three and I'm losing ground. I'm getting hungry, too."

Paul yelled for Babe, right then. And while he was waiting for Babe to come along, he used his shotgun to shoot up a few crullers which he hoped—for the time being, at any rate—would keep Ole from starving to death.

When Babe came along, Paul hurried with the beast over to Jim Hill's railroad, the Great Northern, which (by good luck) wasn't far away. Paul loaded Babe up with a pile of steel rails, then hurried back to the cornstalk with them.

"I'll see if I can't choke off the moisture in this cornstalk," Paul said. And with that he started tying those rails together and then knotting them around the cornstalk.

It worked, too.

Soon the ears of corn away up near the top stopped getting moisture and started to dry out. Then the hot sun hit them hard, and shortly the corn began to pop, making **considerable** noise, too.

After a while, this popped corn came drifting down like so many snowballs. Babe, who'd lived through so much fierce weather, didn't do any more than shiver a little. But a big herd of cattle grazing nearby decided they were in a world-beating blizzard and promptly froze to death.

VOCABULARY DEVELOPMENT

considerable (kan-sid'ar-a-bal) *adj.*: much or large.

PREDICT

Pause at line 54. What is Paul Bunyan going to do with a herd of frozen cattle? What would you do with them if you were Paul Bunyan?

Few students will predict accurately that Paul will invent refrigerated boxcars! But accuracy in this prediction is not expected.

84   Chapter 2   Characters: Doing the Right Thing

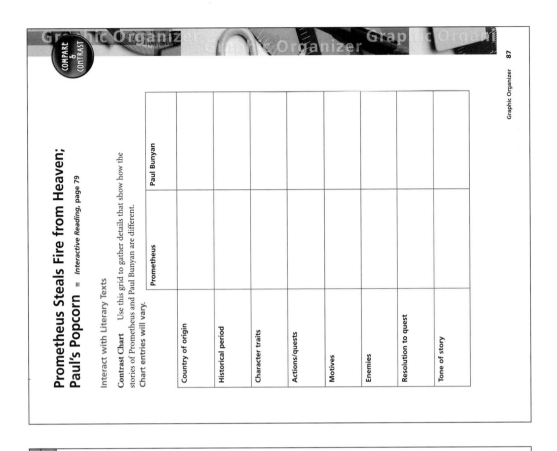

COMPARE & CONTRAST

Graphic Organizer   87

Prometheus Steals Fire from Heaven; Paul's Popcorn ■ *Interactive Reading,* page 79

Interact with Literary Texts

Contrast Chart   Use this grid to gather details that show how the stories of Prometheus and Paul Bunyan are different. Chart entries will vary.

	Prometheus	Paul Bunyan
Country of origin		
Historical period		
Character traits		
Actions/quests		
Motives		
Enemies		
Resolution to quest		
Tone of story		

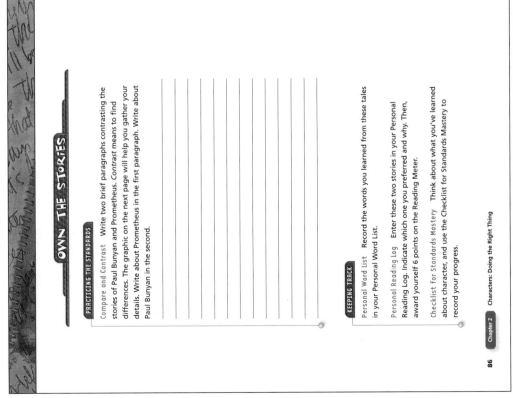

OWN THE STORIES

PRACTICING THE STANDARDS

Compare and Contrast   Write two brief paragraphs contrasting the stories of Paul Bunyan and Prometheus. *Contrast* means to find differences. The graphic on the next page will help you gather your details. Write about Prometheus in the first paragraph. Write about Paul Bunyan in the second.

_____

_____

_____

_____

_____

_____

_____

_____

KEEPING TRACK

Personal Word List   Record the words you learned from these tales in your Personal Word List.

Personal Reading Log   Enter these two stories in your Personal Reading Log. Indicate which one you preferred and why. Then, award yourself 6 points on the Reading Meter.

Checklist for Standards Mastery   Think about what you've learned about character, and use the Checklist for Standards Mastery to record your progress.

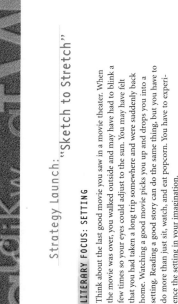

Chapter 3

Being There
Setting

Chapter Preview In this chapter you will—

Strategy Launch: "Sketch to Stretch"

LITERARY FOCUS: SETTING

Think about the last good movie you saw in a movie theater. When the movie was over, you walked outside and may have had to blink a few times so your eyes could adjust to the sun. You may have felt that you had taken a long trip somewhere and were suddenly back home. Watching a good movie picks you up and drops you into a setting. Reading a good story can do the same thing, but you have to do more than just sit, watch, and eat popcorn. You have to experience the setting in your imagination.

Setting is the time and place in which a story occurs. The setting of a story affects character and plot just as *your* setting affects the things you do and the kind of person you are.

A STRATEGY THAT WORKS: "SKETCH TO STRETCH"

The "Sketch to Stretch" strategy is a good way to express your feelings about a story, especially a story with a strong setting. In "Sketch to Stretch," you draw a picture of something (an object, an animal, a person) that expresses your general feeling about the story and its message.

POINTERS FOR USING "SKETCH TO STRETCH"

➤ After you read the story, ask yourself, "What is this story saying to me?" or "How does this story make me feel?"

➤ Capture your response in a sketch or drawing. You can draw symbols and objects that aren't in the story, if they help capture the story's essence for you.

➤ Remember: The point is not to illustrate the story. For example, let's say the story is about a couple who fall in love on a ship that later sinks into freezing-cold water. The sketch might be a simple heart shape that is broken by a wedge of ice. It's not an illustration of the ship. It is a symbol that suggests the meaning behind the story.

Reading Standard 1.3 Use word meanings within the appropriate context, and show ability to verify those meanings by definition, restatement, example, comparison, or contrast.

Reading Standard 2.1 (Grade 6 Review) Identify the structural features of popular media (for example, newspapers, magazines, online information).

Reading Standard 3.4 Analyze the relevance of the setting (for example, place, time, customs) to the mood, tone, and meaning of the text.

Strategy Launch **89**

Practice Read

One of the first questions that will probably pop into your mind as you read this story is "Where are we?" The questions and comments in the side columns will help you solve the puzzle presented by the setting. After you read the story, you will use the "Sketch to Stretch" strategy to suggest the meaning or feeling of the story—as you see it. So, as you read, think about what the setting is and how you would feel if you were in that place and time.

Lost and Found

Ed Combs

After lunch on the day before we arrived home Sander7 walked out of the public library and was nearly hit on the head by a wallet falling out of the sky.

Sander7 stared at the wallet lying on the ground. It was a perfectly normal-looking wallet of shiny green plastic, like the one his father tucked into his jacket pocket every morning as he got ready for work. Why did a wallet fall out of the sky as if it had been **catapulted** from another planet? Nothing ever fell out of the sky here. Nothing was even in the sky.

10   Looking around to see if anyone was watching, Sander7 quickly reached down and picked up the wallet. It fell open in his hands, revealing an identification card that read, "Christo4. Lookout. Crow's Nest Position. First shift. Contact number 4978." Well, nothing out of the ordinary, thought Sander7 as he heard the town's air circulation

PREDICT

Circle the name of the character in the first paragraph. What does this name tell you about the kind of story this will be?

The name followed by a number suggests this might be science fiction.

VOCABULARY DEVELOPMENT

catapulted (ca'ta-pult'ad) v.: shot or launched from.

Circle the context clues that help you define catapulted.

generator turn itself on. Why can't anything interesting ever happen around here? It's the same thing day after day—same temperature, same people, same routine. Even a wallet falling out of the sky turns out to be boring.

20   Sander7 wound through the neat sidewalks and streets until he got home. He slipped his cardkey into the door lock, waited for the beep that signaled the door to slide open, and stepped inside. The door slid shut after him, locking automatically like a prison cell. He headed to the kitchen and plucked a postage stamp–sized dry square out of a box. Even the food is boring, he thought as he tossed the square into the hydration machine. Seconds later the machine door popped open, and Sander7 reached in and pulled out a loaf of steaming bread.

30   Taking the bread over to the telephone, Sander7 dialed the contact number on the identification card of Christo4. After four rings, a shaky-sounding voice picked up. "Yes?"

"Hello, sir, my name is Sander7, and I think I just found your wallet. Christo4, right? Actually, it just fell in front of me out of nowhere." There was a long pause at the other end and the sound of things being shuffled around.

"Oh! Oh, I see. Yes, well, I guess that makes sense. I didn't even know my wallet was missing, but I can certainly guess how it might have happened."

40   Sander7 frowned. "Really? I'm glad you can, because I can't figure it out at all!"

Again, there was a long pause at the other end of the line. Finally, Christo4 said, "Um, look. My shift is over in about twenty minutes. Would you meet me at the USA Park near France Street? I'd like to buy you a snow cone for returning my wallet."

IDENTIFY

Re-read lines 9–20. Underline the words and phrases that give you clues about the setting.

INFER

Underline the words in the paragraph beginning on line 21 that suggest that the setting is a prison. Underline other clues in this paragraph that tell you something about the setting. Is it a pleasant place?

No, the setting is not pleasant. Even the food is predictable.

WORD KNOWLEDGE

Use clues in the story to figure out what a *hydration* (hī-drā'shan) *machine* (line 28) is.

It is a machine that adds water to dried out foods.

WORD KNOWLEDGE

Hydration is built on the Greek word *hydor*, meaning "water." What other English words are built on *hydor*?

hydroelectric,
hydrogen, hydrofoil,
hydroplane, and so on

Page 92

VOCABULARY DEVELOPMENT
distressed (di-strest') *adj.:* troubled; anxious.

IDENTIFY
Circle the context clues that help you figure out the meaning of *distressed*.

IDENTIFY
Although a park is usually a happy place, this one has a different mood. Underline the words and phrases that suggest something strange about this park. Can you guess what these statues are?
The statues show the past: people in a car, on an airplane, and on a Ferris wheel. Apparently these common things do not exist in this setting.

IDENTIFY
Underline the detail that tells you where Christo4 gets the snow cones from.

Sander7 frowned. Something seemed strange about this whole thing. Why did this guy sound so flustered? Why didn't he know his wallet was missing? And why was he offering to buy him a snow cone, the most expensive food on the planet? But anything would be better than hanging around here, so Sander7 said, "I'll be there."

50   When Sander7 arrived at USA Park, he saw a man sitting alone on a bench in front of the sculpture of a man and a woman riding something called an automobile. That must be Christo4, he thought. Christo4 looked **distressed**, his body hunched over, his head in his hands. The other sculptures in the park stood like silent ghosts: the one of men and women flying in some machine called an airplane, the one of a track that looped around and around with a cart with lots of wheels attached to it. The figures in the cart appeared to be smiling and screaming, some with their hands held up in the air.

60   But Christo4 wasn't smiling. Sander7 approached him.

"Hi," he said.

Christo4 finally spoke, as if to the air. "You know, I never thought I'd see the day. . . ."

"The day when what?" replied Sander7.

Christo4 looked him in the eye without saying anything for a moment. Then he said quietly, "Sander7, how old are you?"

70   "Almost twelve, sir."

"Well, I think 'almost twelve' will have to do in this case." Christo4 walked over to the snow cone vault and bought two snow cones. "Let's walk, shall we?" Sander7 followed as Christo4 began to wander among the statues.

"Sander7, tomorrow Mayor Ang4 will make a speech. He will tell everyone that we have arrived at the end of a

Page 93

80 very long trip—a trip across billions of miles and hundreds of years," Christo4 stopped and stared at the ground. "We've finally found a new home," he said.

Sander7 looked at him, not understanding. "What do you mean, 'a new home'? We all have homes already."

"Yes, but. . . ." Christo4 didn't know what to say. "Come with me." He began to walk quickly toward Switzerland Street. Sander7 almost had to run to keep up. When they got to the edge of the park, Christo4 pulled out a small metal wedge and put it into what looked like a tiny hole in 90 the wall of the nearest building.

"What's that?" Sander7 asked.

"It's an old-fashioned, earlier version of your cardkey," said Christo4. "It's just called a key."

Christo4 turned the key, and a part of the wall opened. Inside was a hidden stairway. They both entered. Sander7 jumped as the wall closed behind them. It made a squeaking sound he had never heard before. "That's just the sound of rusty metal scraping against metal," explained Christo4. 100 Sander7 had no idea what the word "rusty" meant, but he kept silent as he followed behind Christo4, stepping first quickly up the stairs, then slowing down as he **ascended** higher and higher. Finally, they reached the top. This time, Christo4 held his ID up to a small camera. The door slid open.

What Sander7 saw was anything but boring. It was a control room like the one he had seen at the town's power station. The center of the room was filled with lit-up computers that seemed as if they were people silently 110 thinking. Windows covered the walls, looking out like the eyes of the universe. Beyond those windows was the blackness of space.

IDENTIFY
What have you noticed about the street names? Check back through the story, and underline them. **The streets are named for countries on Earth.**

IDENTIFY
What do you think it means that Christo4 does not know what *rusty* means (line 99)? **It could mean that there is no iron or steel in this setting and no water to rust them. Maybe everything is plastic.**

VOCABULARY DEVELOPMENT
ascended (a-send'ad) v.: moved upward; climbed.
Sometimes the words in the sentence just go right ahead and tell you what a more difficult word means. Circle the words that define the word *ascended*.

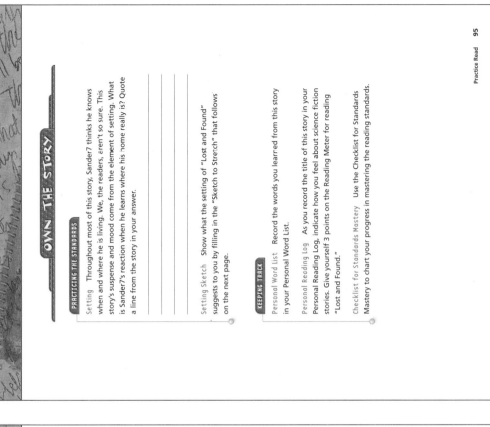

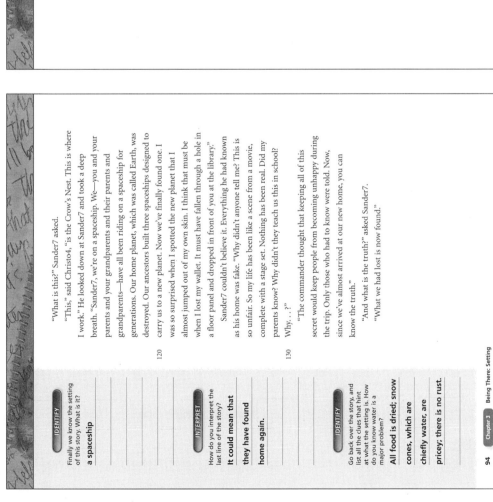

IDENTIFY

Finally we know the setting of this story. What is it?

a spaceship

"What is this?" Sander7 asked.

"This," said Christo4, "is the Crow's Nest. This is where I work." He looked down at Sander7 and took a deep breath. "Sander7, we're on a spaceship. We—you and your parents and your grandparents and their parents and grandparents—have all been riding on a spaceship for generations. Our home planet, which was called Earth, was destroyed. Our ancestors built three spaceships designed to

120 carry us to a new planet. Now we've finally found one. I was so surprised when I spotted the new planet that I almost jumped out of my own skin. I think that must be when I lost my wallet. It must have fallen through a hole in a floor panel and dropped in front of you at the library."

INTERPRET

How do you interpret the last line of the story?

It could mean that they have found home again.

Sander7 couldn't believe it. Everything he had known as his home was fake. "Why didn't anyone tell me? This is so unfair. So my life has been like a scene from a movie, complete with a stage set. Nothing has been real. Did my parents know? Why didn't they teach us this in school?

130 Why...?"

"The commander thought that keeping all of this secret would keep people from becoming unhappy during the trip. Only those who had to know were told. Now, since we've almost arrived at our new home, you can know the truth."

"And what is the truth?" asked Sander7.

"What we had lost is now found."

IDENTIFY

Go back over the story, and list all the clues that hint at what the setting is. How do you know water is a major problem?

All food is dried; snow cones, which are chiefly water, are pricey; there is no rust.

94 Chapter 3 Being There: Setting

OWN THE STORY

PRACTICING THE STANDARDS

Setting Throughout most of this story, Sander7 thinks he knows when and where he is living. We, the readers, aren't so sure. This story's suspense and mood come from the element of setting. What is Sander7's reaction when he learns where his home really is? Quote a line from the story in your answer.

Setting Sketch Show what the setting of "Lost and Found" suggests to you by filling in the "Sketch to Stretch" that follows on the next page.

KEEPING TRACK

Personal Word List Record the words you learned from this story in your Personal Word List.

Personal Reading Log As you record the title of this story in your Personal Reading Log, indicate how you feel about science fiction stories. Give yourself 3 points on the Reading Meter for reading "Lost and Found."

Checklist for Standards Mastery Use the Checklist for Standards Mastery to chart your progress in mastering the reading standards.

Practice Read 95

Graphic Organizer

SETTING & MOOD

for use with
Holt Literature and Language Arts,
page 153

In Trouble

Interact with a Literary Text

"Follow the Setting" Chart   Many stories have more than one setting. As the reader, you have to follow the story wherever it takes you. Remember that when the story takes you to different settings, the whole mood of the story can change. In this selection, Gary Paulsen takes you to four different settings, ranging from steel-breaking cold parts of Alaska to a toasty-warm cabin.

Use this chart to follow the setting. The first column is filled in for you. Fill in the rest of the chart, and you'll have a path to the story's settings.
Sample answers appear below.

Setting: Where	When story occurs	Setting words from the story	Mood the setting creates
a river in Alaska	probably winter	"whirlpool frozen into a cone," "water roaring through it at the bottom"	beautiful, but scary
the kennel area	a summer morning	"each dog with his own house," "on a chain that allows him to move in a circle"	humorous
a "trapping" run	the middle of January	"sharp-sided gully," fifty-foot drop, "frozen stream," "frozen waterfall"	cold and frightening
Paulsen's cabin	after the trapping run	"sitting in my cabin with the leg propped up on pillows by the woodstove"	warm, safe, comfortable, relieved

Graphic Organizer   **97**

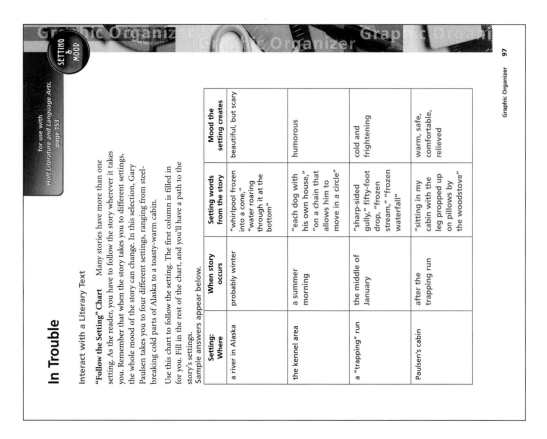

SETTING

Lost and Found ■ *Interactive Reading, page 90*

Interact with a Literary Text

"Sketch to Stretch"   Make a list of the words that describe the setting of "Lost and Found." Use specific details from the story.

Draw a sketch that represents how the story and its settings affected you. Think of symbols that represent the feeling you have about the story's setting. Before you draw, review the notes you made as you read the story. At the bottom of your sketch, explain briefly what you intended to show in your sketch.

Setting Words

Sample answers: nothing in the sky; town has air-circulation generator (therefore no air of its own); same temperature always; same routine; doors lock automatically as in prison; boring dried food; hydration machine used to make bread; snow cone most expensive food; no water; everything electronic

Sketch to Stretch

Write an explanation of your sketch.
Note to teacher: Accept any sketch that reflects a subjective response to the Practice Read. The picture should not be assessed for visual excellence. A completely literal illustration of the story's settings, with no indication of the story's impact on the student, indicates the student may not have fully understood the strategy. The sketch should be accompanied by a written explanation.

Chapter 3   **Being There: Setting**

96

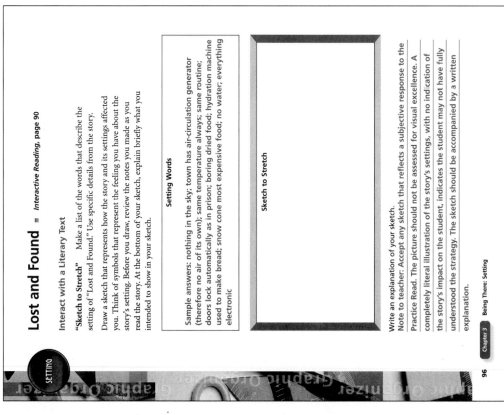

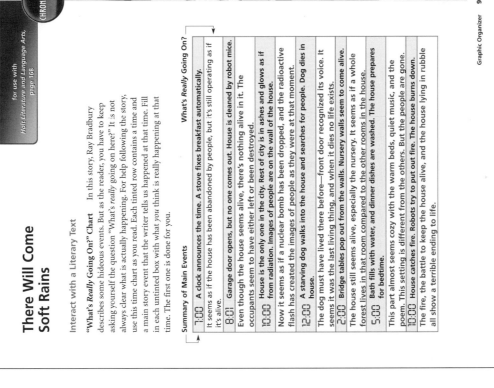

There Will Come Soft Rains

for use with
Holt Literature and Language Arts,
page 168

Interact with a Literary Text

"What's *Really* Going On?" Chart   In this story, Ray Bradbury describes some hideous events. But as the reader, you have to keep asking yourself the question "What's *really* going on here?" It is not always clear what is actually happening. For help following the story, use this time chart as you read. Each tinted row contains a time and a main story event that the writer tells us happened at that time. Fill in each untinted box with what *you* think is really happening at that time. The first one is done for you.

Summary of Main Events	What's *Really* Going On?
7:00 A clock announces the time. A stove fixes breakfast automatically.	It seems as if the house has been abandoned by people, but it's still operating as if it's alive.
8:01 Garage door opens, but no one comes out. House is cleaned by robot mice.	Even though the house seems alive, there's nothing alive in it. The occupants seem to have either left or been destroyed.
10:00 House is the only one in the city. Rest of city is in ashes and glows as if from radiation. Images of people are on the wall of the house.	Now it seems as if a nuclear bomb has been dropped, and the radioactive flash has created the images of people as they were at that moment.
12:00 A starving dog walks into the house and searches for people. Dog dies in house.	The dog must have lived there before—front door recognized its voice. It seems it was the last living thing, and when it dies no life exists.
2:00 Bridge tables pop out from the walls. Nursery walls seem to come alive.	The house still seems alive, especially the nursery. It seems as if a whole forest lives in that room compared to the other rooms in the house.
5:00 Bath fills with water, and dinner dishes are washed. The house prepares for bedtime.	This part almost seems cozy with the warm beds, quiet music, and the poem. This setting is different from the others. But the people are gone.
10:00 House catches fire. Robots try to put out fire. The house burns down.	The fire, the battle to keep the house alive, and the house lying in rubble all show a terrible ending to life.

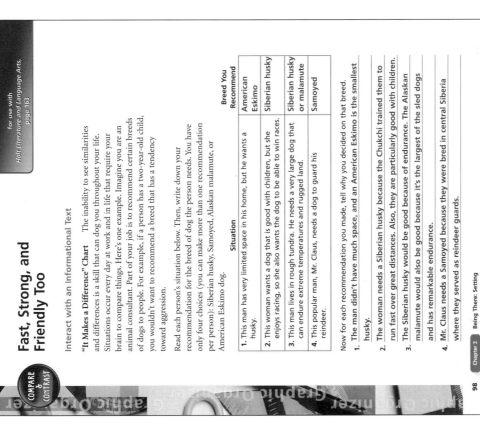

Fast, Strong, and Friendly Too

for use with
Holt Literature and Language Arts,
page 163

Interact with an Informational Text

"It Makes a Difference" Chart   The inability to see similarities and differences is a skill that can dog you throughout your life. Situations occur every day at work and in life that require your brain to compare things. Here's one example. Imagine you are an animal consultant. Part of your job is to recommend certain breeds of dogs to people. For example, if a person has a two-year-old child, you wouldn't want to recommend a breed that has a tendency toward aggression.

Read each person's situation below. Then, write down your recommendation for the breed of dog the person needs. You have only four choices (you can make more than one recommendation per person): Siberian husky, Samoyed, Alaskan malamute, or American Eskimo dog.

Situation	Breed You Recommend
1. This man has very limited space in his home, but he wants a husky.	American Eskimo
2. This woman wants a dog that is good with children, but she enjoys racing, so she also wants the dog to be able to win races.	Siberian husky
3. This man lives in rough tundra. He needs a very large dog that can endure extreme temperatures and rugged land.	Siberian husky or malamute
4. This popular man, Mr. Claus, needs a dog to guard his reindeer.	Samoyed

Now for each recommendation you made, tell why you decided on that breed.
1. The man didn't have much space, and an American Eskimo is the smallest husky.
2. The woman needs a Siberian husky because the Chukchi trained them to run fast over great distances. Also, they are particularly good with children.
3. The Siberian husky would be good because of endurance. The Alaskan malamute would also be good because it's the largest of the sled dogs and has remarkable endurance.
4. Mr. Claus needs a Samoyed because they were bred in central Siberia where they served as reindeer guards.

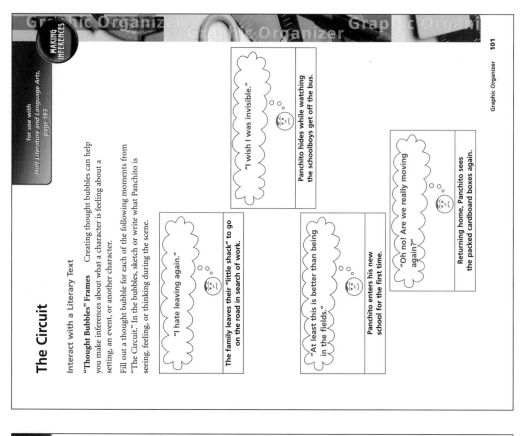

MAKING INFERENCES

for use with
Holt Literature and Language Arts,
page 183

The Circuit

Interact with a Literary Text

"Thought Bubbles" Frames   Creating thought bubbles can help you make inferences about what a character is feeling about a setting, an event, or another character.

Fill out a thought bubble for each of the following moments from "The Circuit." In the bubbles, sketch or write what Panchito is seeing, feeling, or thinking during the scene.

"I hate leaving again."

The family leaves their "little shack" to go on the road in search of work.

"I wish I was invisible."

Panchito hides while watching the schoolboys get off the bus.

"At least this is better than being in the fields."

Panchito enters his new school for the first time.

"Oh no! Are we really moving again?"

Returning home, Panchito sees the packed cardboard boxes again.

Graphic Organizer   **101**

TEXT STRUCTURE

for use with
Holt Literature and Language Arts,
page 173

Destination: Mars

Interact with an Informational Text

Matching Chart   Magazines are built around design features that make it easy for the reader to see the highlights quickly. If done well by the publisher, those same design features can increase sales of the magazine.

Read the following definitions of design features. Then, match the design feature to its use in "Destination: Mars." Write the letter of the example from the right column next to the correct label in the left column.

Design

c **Decorative typefaces** have elaborately designed characters that convey a distinct mood. They are often used in titles.

a **Contrast** refers to the visual effect of using different typefaces in an article. There might be one kind of typeface in the body of the article and another typeface with more emphasis in the beginning.

b **Symbols** help draw the eye to special features like charts or drawings.

d **Rule lines** draw your eye to something on the page. Rule lines can be thick or thin, plain or fancy, vertical or horizontal.

e Another kind of graphic is a **table** that provides information in an organized way.

Design Examples from "Destination: Mars"

a. **SO FAR** only robots have visited Mars.

b. ▲ **Inside the "can," the nickname for the simulated capsule, the crew**

c. *Destination: MARS*

d. **The Earthlings are coming! The Earthlings are coming!**

e. **EARTH**
Nickname: the Blue Planet
Length of day: 23 hours, 56 minutes
Length of year: 365 days
Moons: one
Planet surface: mostly wet and warm
Atmosphere: 98 percent oxygen and nitrogen mix

Chapter 3   Being There: Setting   **100**

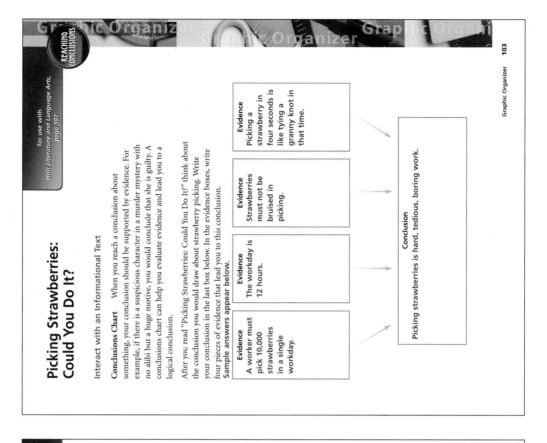

REACHING CONCLUSIONS

Graphic Organizer

for use with
Holt Literature and Language Arts,
page 197

Picking Strawberries: Could You Do It?

Interact with an Informational Text

Conclusions Chart When you reach a conclusion about something, your conclusion should be supported by evidence. For example, if there is a suspicious character in a murder mystery with no alibi but a huge motive, you would conclude that she is guilty. A conclusions chart can help you evaluate evidence and lead you to a logical conclusion.

After you read "Picking Strawberries: Could You Do It?" think about the conclusion you would draw about strawberry picking. Write your conclusion in the last box below. In the evidence boxes, write four pieces of evidence that lead you to this conclusion. **Sample answers appear below.**

| Evidence A worker must pick 10,000 strawberries in a single workday. | Evidence The workday is 12 hours. | Evidence Strawberries must not be bruised in picking. | Evidence Picking a strawberry in four seconds is like tying a granny knot in that time. |

Conclusion Picking strawberries is hard, tedious, boring work.

Graphic Organizer **103**

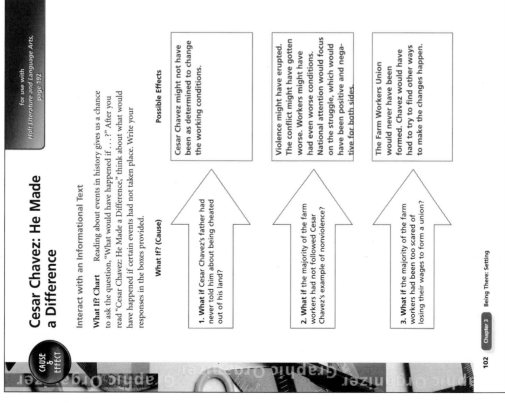

CAUSE & EFFECT

for use with
Holt Literature and Language Arts,
page 192

Cesar Chavez: He Made a Difference

Interact with an Informational Text

What If? Chart Reading about events in history gives us a chance to ask the question, "What would have happened if . . . ?" After you read "Cesar Chavez: He Made a Difference," think about what would have happened if certain events had not taken place. Write your responses in the boxes provided.

What If? (Cause) → **Possible Effects**

1. **What if** Cesar Chavez's father had never told him about being cheated out of his land?

Cesar Chavez might not have been as determined to change the working conditions.

2. **What if** the majority of the farm workers had not followed Cesar Chavez's example of nonviolence?

Violence might have erupted. The conflict might have gotten worse. Workers might have had even worse conditions. National attention would focus on the struggle, which would have been positive and negative for both sides.

3. **What if** the majority of the farm workers had been too scared of losing their wages to form a union?

The Farm Workers Union would never have been formed. Chavez would have had to try to find other ways to make the changes happen.

Chapter 3 Being There: Setting

102

Literature

SHORT STORY

AUTHOR STUDY

If you've read the science fiction story by **Ray Bradbury** called "There Will Come Soft Rains" (*Holt Literature and Language Arts*, page 168), you have an idea of the kind of writer Ray Bradbury is. You also have a glimmer of why he's such a popular writer. Sitting in his office surrounded by interesting toys, Bradbury creates science fiction and fantasy stories that keep us reading. But his stories do more than entertain. After you've read a Bradbury story, you might find yourself wondering if there is more to the story than an exciting plot.

BEFORE YOU READ

You can look up "fog horn" on the Internet and actually hear one. But it's not the same as being there. If you've ever heard a fog horn blast in the dead of a dark, foggy night, you may agree that it's the sound of loneliness. The following facts about fog horns and lighthouses may help you understand Bradbury's mysterious story. But don't be surprised if you have more questions at the end of the story than you do at the beginning.

Lighthouse Facts

- Lighthouses were built to save lives. They were built along coastlines that pose hazards to ships. With intense light beams, lighthouses warn ships of dangers, such as rocky ledges. Before lighthouses were built, many seamen went to their deaths because their ships crashed into land.
- The fog horn helps to guide ships in foggy weather. The sound is made by quickly releasing compressed air.
- Most lighthouses range in height from 33 feet to 208 feet and are built from wood, stone, brick, reinforced concrete, iron, or steel. They are not easy to destroy.
- Until recently, lighthouse keepers lived and worked at lighthouses to operate the signals. Now most lighthouses are automated.

Reading Standard 3.4
Analyze the relevance of the setting (for example, place, time, customs) to the mood, tone, and meaning of the text.

The Fog Horn

Ray Bradbury

Out there in the cold water, far from land, we waited every night for the coming of the fog, and it came, and we oiled the brass machinery and lit the fog light up in the stone tower. Feeling like two birds in the gray sky, McDunn and I sent the light touching out, red, then white, then red again, to eye the lonely ships. And if they did not see our light, then there was always our Voice, the great deep cry of our Fog Horn shuddering through the rags of mist to startle the gulls away like decks of scattered cards and make the waves turn high and foam.

"It's a lonely life, but you're used to it now, aren't you?" asked McDunn.

"Yes," I said. "You're a good talker, thank the Lord."

"Well, it's your turn on land tomorrow," he said, smiling, "to dance the ladies and drink gin."

"What do you think, McDunn, when I leave you out here alone?"

"On the mysteries of the sea." McDunn lit his pipe. It was a quarter past seven of a cold November evening, the heat on, the light switching its tail in two hundred directions, the Fog Horn bumbling in the high throat of the tower. There wasn't a town for a hundred miles down the coast, just a road which came lonely through dead country to the sea, with few cars on it, a stretch of two miles of cold water out to our rock, and rare few ships.

"The mysteries of the sea," said McDunn thoughtfully.

"You know, the ocean's the most confounded big snowflake

10

20

"The Fog Horn" from *The Golden Apples of the Sun* by Ray Bradbury. Copyright 1953 by Ray Bradbury. Reprinted by permission of *Don Congdon Associates, Inc.*

IDENTIFY

The box about lighthouses and fog horns in the Before You Read section gave you factual information. As you read this first page, you get more of a feel for what this particular lighthouse setting is like. Underline phrases and words that create the mood for this setting.

Examples might include: "cold water,"

"far from land," and

"the deep cry of our

Fog Horn shuddering

through the rags

of mist."

_____

_____

_____

_____

_____

Ray Bradbury   105

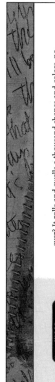

Left page (106)

Bradbury is known for his descriptive language. In line 34, underline the simile (a comparison using *like* or *as*) that helps you picture the fishes' eyes.

McDunn is good at telling a story. He makes the tower seem like a person. Underline the parts of his story that make us feel that the tower has a life of its own.

Underline the words that tell how McDunn's story of the fish affects the narrator.

Writers use foreshadowing to hint at events that might happen later. What could be foreshadowed in the paragraph beginning "Oh, the sea's full"?
Perhaps something from the bottom of the sea might appear in the story. Note that McDunn is nervous.

ever? It rolls and swells a thousand shapes and colors, no two alike. Strange. One night, years ago, I was here alone, when all of the fish of the sea surfaced out there.

Something made them swim in and lie in the bay, sort of trembling and staring up at the tower light going red, white, red, white across them so I could see their funny eyes. I turned cold. They were like a big peacock's tail, moving out there until midnight. Then, without so much as a sound, they slipped away, the million of them was gone. I kind of think maybe, in some sort of way, they came all those miles to worship. Strange. But think how the tower must look to them, standing seventy feet above the water, the God-light flashing out from it, and the tower declaring itself with a monster voice. They never came back, those fish, but don't you think for a while they thought they were in the Presence?"

I shivered. I looked out at the long gray lawn of the sea stretching away into nothing and nowhere.

"Oh, the sea's full." McDunn puffed his pipe nervously, blinking. He had been nervous all day and hadn't said why.

"For all our engines and so-called submarines, it'll be ten thousand centuries before we set foot on the real bottom of the sunken lands, in the fairy kingdoms there, and know *real* terror. Think of it, it's still the year 300,000 Before Christ down under there. While we've paraded around with trumpets, lopping off each other's countries and heads, they have been living beneath the sea twelve miles deep and cold in a time as old as the beard of a comet."

"Yes, it's an old world."

"Come on. I got something special I been saving up to tell you."

Right page (107)

• • • • • Notes • • • • • •

We ascended the eighty steps, talking and taking our time. At the top, McDunn switched off the room lights so there'd be no reflection in the plate glass. The great eye of the light was humming, turning easily in its oiled socket. The Fog Horn was blowing steadily, once every fifteen seconds.

Underline McDunn's line in the second paragraph that tells what the problem in the story will probably be.

"Sounds like an animal, don't it?" McDunn nodded to himself. "A big lonely animal crying in the night. Sitting here on the edge of ten billion years called out to the Deeps. I'm here, I'm here, I'm here. And the Deeps do answer, yes, they do. You been here now for three months, Johnny, so I better prepare you. About this time of year," he said, studying the murk and fog, "something comes to visit the lighthouse."

"The swarms of fish like you said?"

"No, this is something else. I've put off telling you because you might think I'm daft. But tonight's the latest I can put it off, for if my calendar's marked right from last year, tonight's the night it comes. I won't go into detail, you'll have to see it yourself. Just sit down there. If you want, tomorrow you can pack your duffel and take the motorboat in to land and get your car parked there at the dinghy pier on the cape and drive on back to some little inland town and keep your lights burning nights. I won't question or blame you. It's happened three years now, and this is the only time anyone's been here with me to **verify** it. You wait and watch."

A *dinghy* (dĭn'ē) (line 81) is a small rowboat.

Don't confuse the noun *dinghy*, a boat, with the adjective *dingy* (dĭn'jē), which means "shabby; not clean; grimy."

Half an hour passed with only a few whispers between us. When we grew tired of waiting, McDunn began describing some of his ideas to me. He had some theories about the Fog Horn itself.

verify (vĕr'ə-fī) *v:* confirm; prove to be true.

What do you predict will happen tonight?
Predictions will vary, but should include Something will come to visit the lighthouse.

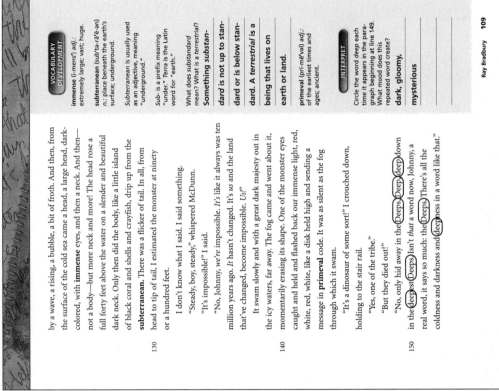

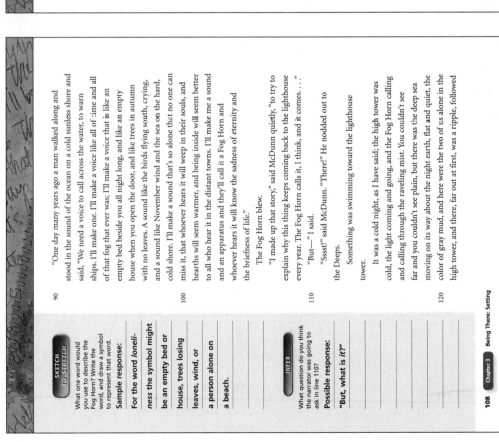

SKETCH TO STRETCH

What one word would you use to describe the Fog Horn? Write the word, and draw a symbol to represent that word.

Sample response:

For the word *loneli-ness* the symbol might be an empty bed or house, trees losing leaves, wind, or a person alone on a beach.

INFER

What question do you think the narrator was going to ask in line 110?

Possible response:

"But, what is it?"

90   "One day many years ago a man walked along and stood in the sound of the ocean on a cold sunless shore and said, "We need a voice to call across the water, to warn ships. I'll make one. I'll make a voice like all of time and all of that fog that ever was; I'll make a voice that is like an empty bed beside you all night long, and like an empty house when you open the door, and like trees in autumn with no leaves. A sound like the birds flying south, crying, and a sound like November wind and the sea on the hard,

100   cold shore. I'll make a sound that's so alone that no one can miss it, that whoever hears it will weep in their souls, and hearths will seem warmer, and being inside will seem better to all who hear it in the distant towns. I'll make me a sound and an apparatus and they'll call it a Fog Horn and whoever hears it will know the sadness of eternity and the briefness of life."

The Fog Horn blew.

"I made up that story," said McDunn quietly, "to try to explain why this thing keeps coming back to the lighthouse

110   every year. The Fog Horn calls it, I think, and it comes. . . ."

"But—" I said.

"Sssst!" said McDunn. "There!" He nodded out to the Deeps.

Something was swimming toward the lighthouse tower.

It was a cold night, as I have said; the high tower was cold, the light coming and going, and the Fog Horn calling and calling through the raveling mist. You couldn't see far and you couldn't see plain, but there was the deep sea moving on its way about the night earth, flat and quiet, the

120   color of gray mud, and here were the two of us alone in the high tower, and there, far out at first, was a ripple, followed

Chapter 3   Being There: Setting

---

by a wave, a rising, a bubble, a bit of froth. And then, from the surface of the cold sea came a head, a large head, dark-colored, with **immense** eyes, and then a neck. And then—not a body—but more neck and more! The head rose a full forty feet above the water on a slender and beautiful dark neck. Only then did the body, like a little island of black coral and shells and crayfish, drip up from the **subterranean**. There was a flicker of tail. In all, from

130   head to tip of tail, I estimated the monster at ninety or a hundred feet.

I don't know what I said. I said something.

"Steady, boy, steady," whispered McDunn.

"It's impossible!" I said.

"No, Johnny, *we're* impossible. *It's* like it always was ten million years ago. *It* hasn't changed. It's *us* and the land that've changed, become impossible. *Us?*"

It swam slowly and with a great dark majesty out in the icy waters, far away. The fog came and went about it,

140   momentarily erasing its shape. One of the monster eyes caught and held and flashed back our immense light, red, white, red, white, like a disk held high and sending a message in **primeval** code. It was as silent as the fog through which it swam.

"It's a dinosaur of some sort!" I crouched down, holding to the stair rail.

"Yes, one of the tribe."

"But they died out!"

"No, only hid away in the Deeps. Deep, deep down

150   in the deepest Deeps. Isn't *that* a word now, Johnny, a real word, it says so much: the Deeps. There's all the coldness and darkness and deepness in a word like that."

VOCABULARY DEVELOPMENT

immense (i-mens′) *adj.:* extremely large; vast; huge.

subterranean (sub′tə-rā′ē-ən) *n.:* place beneath the earth's surface; underground.

Subterranean is usually used as an adjective, meaning "underground."

Sub- is a prefix meaning "under." *Terra* is the Latin word for "earth."

What does *substandard* mean? What is a *terrestrial?* **Something *substandard* is not up to standard or is below standard. A *terrestrial* is a being that lives on earth or land.**

primeval (prī-mē′val) *adj.:* of the earliest times and ages; ancient.

INTERPRET

Circle the word *deep* each time it appears in the paragraph beginning at line 149. What mood does this repeated word create? **dark, gloomy,**

mysterious

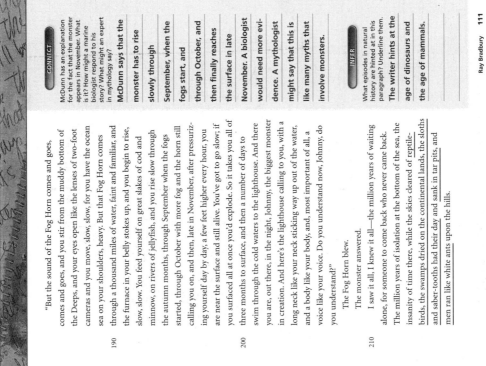

Notes

"What'll we do?"

"Do? We got our job, we can't leave. Besides, we're safer here than in any boat trying to get to land. That thing's as big as a destroyer and almost as swift."

"But here, why does it come *here*?"

The next moment I had my answer.

160 The Fog Horn blew.

And the monster answered.

A cry came across a million years of water and mist. A cry so anguished and alone that it shuddered in my head and my body. The monster cried out at the tower. The Fog Horn blew. The monster roared again. The Fog Horn blew. The monster opened its great toothed mouth and the sound that came from it was the sound of the Fog Horn itself. Lonely and vast and far away. The sound of isolation, a viewless sea, a cold night, apartness. That was the sound.

170 "Now," whispered McDunn, "do you know why it comes here?"

I nodded.

"All year long, Johnny, that poor monster there lying far out, a thousand miles at sea, and twenty miles deep maybe, biding its time, perhaps it's a million years old, this one creature. Think of it, waiting a million years; could *you* wait that long? Maybe it's the last of its kind. I sort of think that's true. Anyway, here come men on land and build this

180 lighthouse, five years ago. And set up their Fog Horn and sound it and sound it out toward the place where you bury yourself in sleep and sea memories of a world where there were thousands like yourself, but now you're alone, all alone in a world not made for you, a world where you have to hide.

COMPARE & CONTRAST

The monster and the Fog Horn seem as if they're speaking the same language. Underline the words in the paragraph beginning on line 162 that show the similarities between the sounds they make.

IDENTIFY

McDunn asks a question in lines 170–171. How does he go on to answer it?
The monster has been waiting maybe millions of years to find one of its kind.

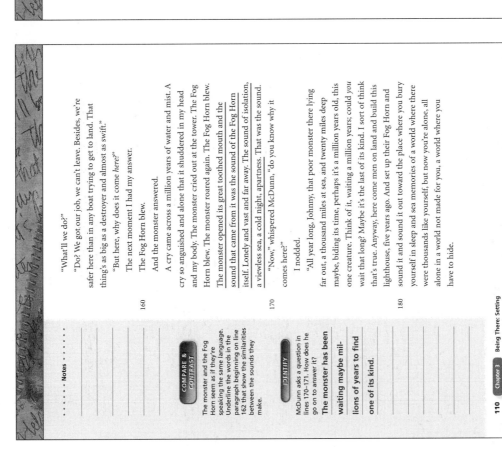

"But the sound of the Fog Horn comes and goes, comes and goes, and you stir from the muddy bottom of the Deeps, and your eyes open like the lenses of two-foot cameras and you move, slow, slow, for you have the ocean sea on your shoulders, heavy. But that Fog Horn comes

190 through a thousand miles of water, faint and familiar, and the furnace in your belly stokes up, and you begin to rise, slow, slow. You feed yourself on great slakes of cod and minnow, on rivers of jellyfish, and you rise slow through the autumn months, through September when the fogs started, through October with more fog and the horn still calling you on, and then, late in November, after pressurizing yourself day by day, a few feet higher every hour, you are near the surface and still alive. You've got to go slow; if you surfaced all at once you'd explode. So it takes you all of

200 three months to surface, and then a number of days to swim through the cold waters to the lighthouse. And there you are, out there, in the night, Johnny, the biggest monster in creation. And here's the lighthouse calling to you, with a long neck like your neck sticking way up out of the water, and a body like your body, and, most important of all, a voice like your voice. Do you understand now, Johnny, do you understand?"

The Fog Horn blew.

The monster answered.

210 I saw it all, I knew it all—the million years of waiting alone, for someone to come back who never came back. The million years of isolation at the bottom of the sea, the insanity of time there, while the skies cleared of reptilebirds, the swamps dried on the continental lands, the sloths and saber-tooths had their day and sank in tar pits, and men ran like white ants upon the hills.

CONNECT

McDunn has an explanation for the fact that the monster appears in November. What is it? How might a marine biologist respond to his story? What might an expert in mythology say?
McDunn says that the monster has to rise slowly through September, when the fogs start, and through October, and then finally reaches the surface in late November. A biologist would need more evidence. A mythologist might say that this is like many myths that involve monsters.

INFER

What episodes in natural history are hinted at in this paragraph? Underline them.
The writer hints at the age of dinosaurs and the age of mammals.

Ray Bradbury 111

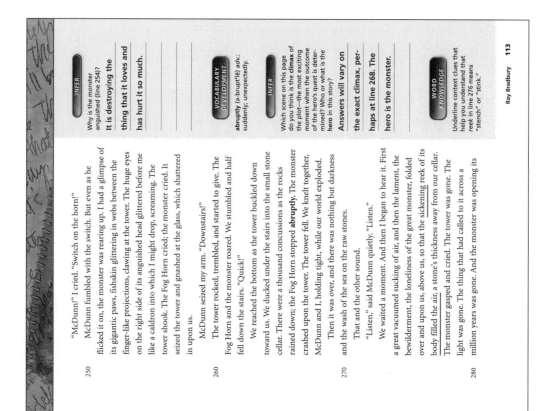

"McDunn!" I cried. "Switch on the horn!"

McDunn fumbled with the switch. But even as he flicked it on, the monster was rearing up. I had a glimpse of its gigantic paws, fishskin glittering in webs between the finger-like projections, clawing at the tower. The huge eyes on the right side of its anguished head glittered before me like a caldron into which I might drop, screaming. The tower shook. The Fog Horn cried; the monster cried. It seized the tower and gnashed at the glass, which shattered in upon us.

250

McDunn seized my arm. "Downstairs!"

The tower rocked, trembled, and started to give. The Fog Horn and the monster roared. We stumbled and half fell down the stairs. "Quick!"

260

We reached the bottom as the tower buckled down toward us. We ducked under the stairs into the small stone cellar. There were a thousand concussions as the rocks rained down; the Fog Horn stopped **abruptly**. The monster crashed upon the tower. The tower fell. We knelt together, McDunn and I, holding tight, while our world exploded.

Then it was over, and there was nothing but darkness and the wash of the sea on the raw stones.

That and the other sound.

270

"Listen," said McDunn quietly. "Listen."

We waited a moment. And then I began to hear it. First a great vacuumed sucking of air, and then the lament, the bewilderment, the loneliness of the great monster, folded over and upon us, above us, so that the sickening reek of its body filled the air, a stone's thickness away from our cellar. The monster gasped and cried. The tower was gone. The light was gone. The thing that had called to it across a million years was gone. And the monster was opening its

280

INFER

Why is the monster anguished (line 254)?

It is destroying the thing that it loves and has hurt it so much.

VOCABULARY DEVELOPMENT

abruptly (ə-brupt'lē) *adv.*: suddenly; unexpectedly.

INFER

Which scene on this page do you think is the climax of the plot—the most exciting moment when the outcome of the hero's quest is determined? Who or what is the hero in this story?

Answers will vary on the exact climax, perhaps at line 268. The hero is the monster.

WORD KNOWLEDGE

Underline context clues that help you understand that *reek* in line 276 means "stench" or "stink."

Ray Bradbury   113

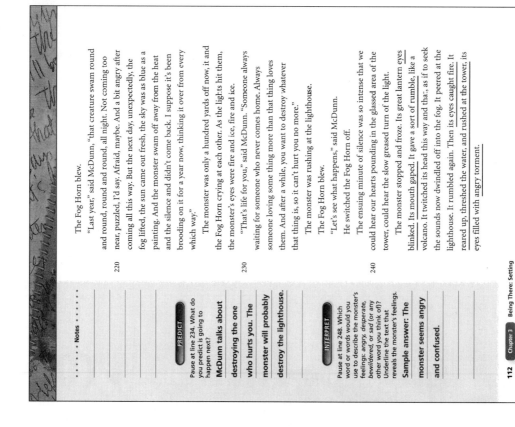

• • • • • • Notes • • • • • •

The Fog Horn blew.

"Last year," said McDunn, "that creature swam round and round, round and round, all night. Not coming too near, puzzled, I'd say. Afraid, maybe. And a bit angry after coming all this way. But the next day, unexpectedly, the fog lifted, the sun came out fresh, the sky was as blue as a painting. And the monster swam off away from the heat and the silence and didn't come back. I suppose it's been brooding on it for a year now, thinking it over from every which way."

220

The monster was only a hundred yards off now, it and the Fog Horn crying at each other. As the lights hit them, the monster's eyes were fire and ice, fire and ice.

"That's life for you," said McDunn. "Someone always waiting for someone who never comes home. Always someone loving some thing more than that thing loves them. And after a while, you want to destroy whatever that thing is, so it can't hurt you no more."

230

The monster was rushing at the lighthouse.

The Fog Horn blew.

"Let's see what happens," said McDunn.

He switched the Fog Horn off.

The ensuing minute of silence was so intense that we could hear our hearts pounding in the glassed area of the tower, could hear the slow greased turn of the light.

240

The monster stopped and froze. Its great lantern eyes blinked. Its mouth gaped. It gave a sort of rumble, like a volcano. It twitched its head this way and that, as if to seek the sounds now dwindled off into the fog. It peered at the lighthouse. It rumbled again. Then its eyes caught fire. It reared up, threshed the water, and rushed at the tower, its eyes filled with angry torment.

PREDICT

Pause at line 234. What do you predict is going to happen next?

McDunn talks about destroying the one who hurts you. The monster will probably destroy the lighthouse.

INTERPRET

Pause at line 248. Which word or words would you use to describe the monster's feelings: *angry, desperate, bewildered,* or *sad* (or any other word you think of)? Underline the text that reveals the monster's feelings.

Sample answer: The monster seems angry and confused.

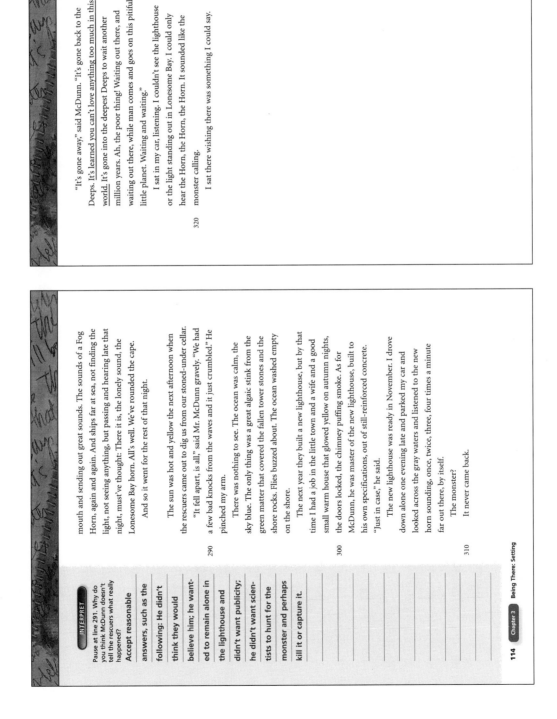

INTERPRET

Pause at line 291. Why do you think McDunn doesn't tell the rescuers what really happened?

Accept reasonable answers, such as the following: He didn't think they would believe him; he wanted to remain alone in the lighthouse and didn't want publicity; he didn't want scientists to hunt for the monster and perhaps kill it or capture it.

mouth and sending out great sounds. The sounds of a Fog Horn, again and again. And ships far at sea, not finding the light, not seeing anything, but passing and hearing late that night, must've thought: There it is, the lonely sound, the Lonesome Bay horn. All's well. We've rounded the cape.

And so it went for the rest of that night.

The sun was hot and yellow the next afternoon when the rescuers came out to dig us from our stoned-under cellar.

290 "It fell apart, is all," said Mr. McDunn gravely. "We had a few bad knocks from the waves and it just crumbled." He pinched my arm.

There was nothing to see. The ocean was calm, the sky blue. The only thing was a great algaic stink from the green matter that covered the fallen tower stones and the shore rocks. Flies buzzed about. The ocean washed empty on the shore.

The next year they built a new lighthouse, but by that time I had a job in the little town and a wife and a good small warm house that glowed yellow on autumn nights,

300 the doors locked, the chimney puffing smoke. As for McDunn, he was master of the new lighthouse, built to his own specifications, out of still-reinforced concrete.

"Just in case," he said.

The new lighthouse was ready in November. I drove down alone one evening late and parked my car and looked across the gray waters and listened to the new horn sounding, once, twice, three, four times a minute

310 far out there, by itself.

The monster?

It never came back.

"It's gone away," said McDunn. "It's learned you can't love anything too much in this world. It's gone into the deepest Deeps to wait another million years. Ah, the poor thing! Waiting out there, and waiting out there, while man comes and goes on this pitiful little planet. Waiting and waiting."

I sat in my car, listening. I couldn't see the lighthouse or the light standing out in Lonesome Bay. I could only hear the Horn, the Horn, the Horn. It sounded like the monster calling.

320 I sat there wishing there was something I could say.

EVALUATE

Underline the part of McDunn's remarks that seems to suggest the message of the story. Do you agree with it?

Students' responses will vary.

SKETCH TO STRETCH

Sketch a symbol of how you see the monster living out in the Deeps, "waiting and waiting."

Sketches might include a broken heart, a giant tear, or a monster with a thought bubble.

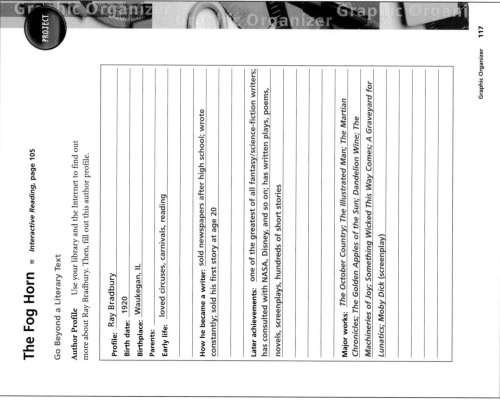

PROJECT

Graphic Organizer

The Fog Horn ■ *Interactive Reading, page 105*

Go Beyond a Literary Text

Author Profile Use your library and the Internet to find out more about Ray Bradbury. Then, fill out this author profile.

Profile: Ray Bradbury

Birth date: 1920

Birthplace: Waukegan, IL

Parents:

Early life: loved circuses, carnivals, reading

How he became a writer: sold newspapers after high school; wrote constantly; sold his first story at age 20

Later achievements: one of the greatest of all fantasy/science-fiction writers; has consulted with NASA, Disney, and so on; has written plays, poems, novels, screenplays, hundreds of short stories

Major works: *The October Country; The Illustrated Man; The Martian Chronicles; The Golden Apples of the Sun; Dandelion Wine; The Machineries of Joy; Something Wicked This Way Comes; A Graveyard for Lunatics; Moby Dick (screenplay)*

Graphic Organizer **117**

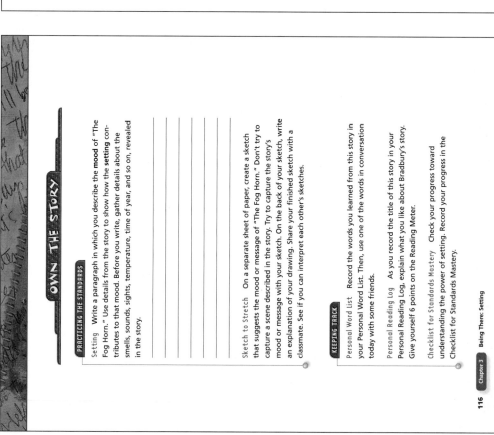

OWN THE STORY

PRACTICING THE STANDARDS

Setting Write a paragraph in which you describe the **mood** of "The Fog Horn." Use details from the story to show how the **setting** contributes to that mood. Before you write, gather details about the smells, sounds, sights, temperature, time of year, and so on, revealed in the story.

Sketch to Stretch On a separate sheet of paper, create a sketch that suggests the mood or message of "The Fog Horn." Don't try to capture a scene described in the story. Try to capture the story's mood or message with your sketch. On the back of your sketch, write an explanation of your drawing. Share your finished sketch with a classmate. See if you can interpret each other's sketches.

KEEPING TRACK

Personal Word List Record the words you learned from this story in your Personal Word List. Then, use one of the words in conversation today with some friends.

Personal Reading Log As you record the title of this story in your Personal Reading Log, explain what you like about Bradbury's story. Give yourself 6 points on the Reading Meter.

Checklist for Standards Mastery Check your progress toward understanding the power of setting. Record your progress in the Checklist for Standards Mastery.

Information

ARTICLE

Reading Standard 2.1 (Grade 6 Review) Identify the structural features of popular media (for example, newspapers, magazines, online information).

BEFORE YOU READ

This article about the world's most famous monster is from a Web site called *NOVA Online*. In Scotland and Ireland a lough, or loch (läkh), is a lake. Loch Ness is a lake in Scotland that has earned fame from a monster that might not really live there at all. The search for the monster has gone on for years. As you read, see if Nessie reminds you of Bradbury's lonely monster.

from NOVA Online

Birth of a Legend

Stephen Lyons

"Many a man has been hanged on less evidence than there is for the Loch Ness Monster."
—G. K. Chesterton

Residents at the coast of Loch Ness.

"The Beast of Loch Ness" by Stephen Lyons from *NOVA Online*, accessed January 2, 2001, at http://www.pbs.org/wgbh/nova/lochness/legend.html. Copyright © 2000 by WGBH Boston. Reprinted by permission of WGBH Educational Foundation.

TEXT STRUCTURE

Circle the quotation of G. K. Chesterton. A clever quotation at the beginning of an article can grab our attention and focus our thinking on the article's topic.

Does Chesterton believe in the monster? Explain.

Answers will vary, but students may suspect he does believe in it.

When the Romans first came to northern Scotland in the first century A.D., they found the Highlands occupied by fierce, tattoo-covered tribes they called the Picts, or painted people. From the carved, standing stones still found in the region around Loch Ness, it is clear the Picts were fascinated by animals and careful to render them with great fidelity. All the animals depicted on the Pictish stones are lifelike and

10　easily recognizable—all but one. The exception is a strange beast with an elongated beak or muzzle, a head locket or spout, and flippers instead of feet. Described by some scholars as a swimming elephant, the Pictish beast is the earliest known evidence for an idea that has held sway in the Scottish Highlands for at least 1,500 years—that Loch Ness is home to a mysterious aquatic animal.

In Scottish folklore, large animals have been associated with many bodies of water, from small streams to the largest lakes, often labeled Loch-na-Beistie on old maps.

20　These water-horses, or water-kelpies, are said to have magical powers and malevolent intentions. According to one version of the legend, the water-horse lures small children into the water by offering them rides on its back. Once the children are aboard, their hands become stuck to the beast and they are dragged to a watery death, their livers washing ashore the following day.

The earliest written reference linking such creatures to Loch Ness is in the biography of Saint Columba, the man credited with introducing Christianity to Scotland. In A.D.

30　565, according to this account, Columba was on his way to visit a Pictish king when he stopped along the shore of Loch Ness. Seeing a large beast about to attack a man who was swimming in the lake, Columba raised his hand, invoking the name of God and commanding the monster

• • • • • • Notes • • • • • •

WORD KNOWLEDGE

The words *beak* and *locket* (line 12) are defined in context by restatement. Underline the two restatements.

INFER

To be *malevolent* (ma-lev′a-lant) means "wishing someone harm" (line 22). Even if you didn't know the definition of *malevolent*, the context would give you a clue about the word's meaning. The description of what the water horse does to children should tell you that whatever *malevolent* means, it isn't very good.

The Latin prefix *mal-* means "wrong or bad." What does *maladjusted* mean?

"not well adjusted,
not well balanced."

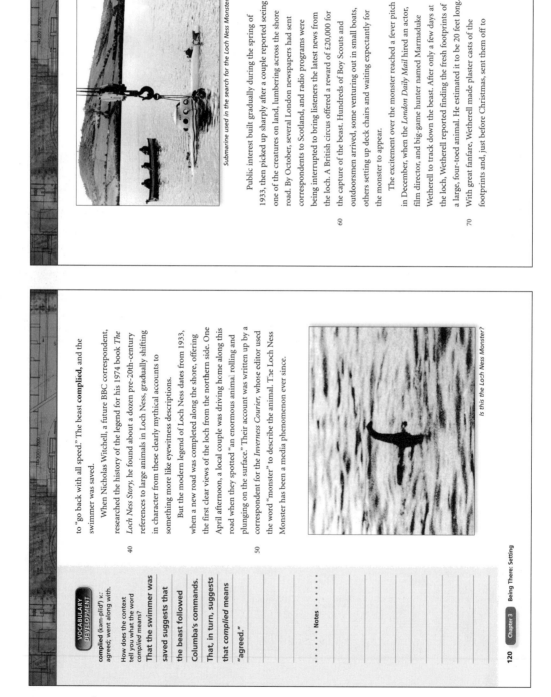

Submarine used in the search for the Loch Ness Monster.

Public interest built gradually during the spring of 1933, then picked up sharply after a couple reported seeing one of the creatures on land, lumbering across the shore road. By October, several London newspapers had sent correspondents to Scotland, and radio programs were being interrupted to bring listeners the latest news from the loch. A British circus offered a reward of £20,000 for the capture of the beast. Hundreds of Boy Scouts and outdoorsmen arrived, some venturing out in small boats, others setting up deck chairs and waiting expectantly for the monster to appear.

The excitement over the monster reached a fever pitch in December, when the *London Daily Mail* hired an actor, film director, and big-game hunter named Marmaduke Wetherell to track down the beast. After only a few days at the loch, Wetherell reported finding the fresh footprints of a large, four-toed animal. He estimated it to be 20 feet long. With great fanfare, Wetherell made plaster casts of the footprints and, just before Christmas, sent them off to

---

VOCABULARY DEVELOPMENT

complied (kəm-plīd') v.: agreed; went along with.

How does the context tell you what the word *complied* means?

That the swimmer was saved suggests that the beast followed Columba's commands. That, in turn, suggests that *complied* means "agreed."

to "go back with all speed." The beast complied, and the swimmer was saved.

When Nicholas Witchell, a future BBC correspondent, researched the history of the legend for his 1974 book *The Loch Ness Story,* he found about a dozen pre-20th-century references to large animals in Loch Ness, gradually shifting in character from these clearly mythical accounts to something more like eyewitness descriptions.

But the modern legend of Loch Ness dates from 1933, when a new road was completed along the shore, offering the first clear views of the loch from the northern side. One April afternoon, a local couple was driving home along this road when they spotted "an enormous animal rolling and plunging on the surface." Their account was written up by a correspondent for the *Inverness Courier,* whose editor used the word "monster" to describe the animal. The Loch Ness Monster has been a media phenomenon ever since.

Is this the Loch Ness Monster?

the Natural History Museum in London for analysis. While the world waited for the museum zoologists to return from holiday, legions of monster hunters descended on Loch Ness, filling the local hotels. Inverness was floodlit for the occasion, and traffic jammed the shoreline roads in both directions.

The bubble burst in early January, when museum zoologists announced that the footprints were those of a hippopotamus. They had been made with a stuffed hippo foot—the base of an umbrella stand or ashtray. It wasn't clear whether Wetherell was the perpetrator of the hoax or its gullible victim. Either way, the incident tainted the image of the Loch Ness Monster and discouraged serious investigation of the phenomenon. For the next three decades, most scientists scornfully dismissed reports of strange animals in the loch. Those sightings that weren't outright hoaxes, they said, were the result of optical illusions caused by boat wakes, wind slicks, floating logs, otters, ducks, or swimming deer.

Saw Something, They Did

Nevertheless, eyewitnesses continued to come forward with accounts of their sightings—more than 4,000 of them, according to Witchell's estimate. Most of the witnesses described a large creature with one or more humps protruding above the surface like the hull of an upturned boat. Others reported seeing a long neck or flippers. What was most remarkable, however, was that many of the eyewitnesses were sober, level-headed people: lawyers and priests, scientists and schoolteachers, policemen and fishermen—even a Nobel Prize winner.

WORD KNOWLEDGE
The word *perpetrator* (pur'pə-trā'tər) in line 82 means "one who commits something or originates something (something evil or offensive)." What is the "perpetrator of a hoax"?
originator of a trick

WORD KNOWLEDGE
Optical (ŏp'tĭ-kal) in line 88 is related to the words *optician* and *myopic*. They share the Greek root word *ops*, meaning "eye." What does *optical* mean?
Optical means "visual."

TEXT STRUCTURE
How would you sum up the main point of the first part of this article, lines 1–90?
Many people over the centuries have claimed to see the Loch Ness Monster.

WORD KNOWLEDGE
You can get an idea of what *protruding* (line 96) means by looking at the way it is used in the sentence. The "humps" were "protruding above the surface."

Wide view of Loch Ness.

Eyewitness Accounts

While no hard evidence for the existence of the Loch Ness Monster has yet turned up, heaps of anecdotal evidence exist. Although such eyewitness accounts are of little value scientifically, they can be compelling nevertheless. Below, lend an ear to several native Scots who swear they saw something in the loch. These tales were collected by the producers of the NOVA film *The Beast of Loch Ness*.

110   "I saw it, and nothing can take that away."

Well, we're talking about an incident that happened approximately 32 years ago, almost to the very day—mid-summer, June 1965. I, along with a friend, was on the south shore of Loch Ness, fishing for brown trout, looking almost directly into Urquhart Bay, when I saw something break the surface of the water. I glanced there, and I saw it, and then it wasn't there, it had disappeared.

WORD KNOWLEDGE
An *anecdote* (ăn'ĭk-dōt) is a short, entertaining story used to make a point. Anecdotes are often personal. What would you say *anecdotal evidence* is (line 104)?
evidence based on stories, not on facts

TEXT STRUCTURE
Circle the subheading for the first eyewitness account. What purpose does this heading have?
The heading contains an interesting quotation meant to draw readers' attention.

TEXT STRUCTURE
Who is speaking now? Turn to the next page to find out.
Ian Cameron, retired police superintendent

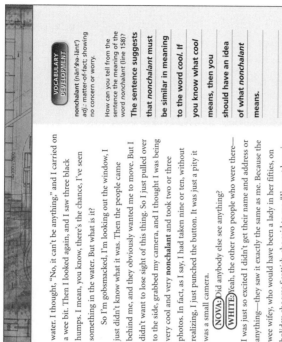

VOCABULARY DEVELOPMENT
submerged (sab-mûrjd') v.: plunged into water; sank.

TEXT STRUCTURE
Why do you think a description of the eyewitness is included at the end of this anecdote? (See line 140.)
It helps "prove" that the witness is reliable.

TEXT STRUCTURE
Who is talking now (line 145)? Where can you find out?
See line 177 on the next page.

WORD KNOWLEDGE
Gobsmacked (line 145) is British slang. What do you guess it means?
shocked, surprised, knocked over with a gob of something

But while watching, keeping an eye, and fishing gently, I saw an object surface. It was a large, black object—a whale-like object, going from infinity up, and came round onto a block end—and it **submerged**, to reappear a matter of seconds later. But on this occasion, the block end, which had been on my right, was now on my left, so I realized immediately that while in the process of surfacing, as it may, it had rotated. And with the predominant wind, the south-west wind, it appeared to be, I would say, at that stage drifting easily across.

So I called to my friend Willie Frazer, who incidentally had a sighting of an object on the loch almost a year ago to the very day. I called him, and he come up and joined me. We realized that it was drifting towards us, and, in fact, it came to within I would say about 250, 300 yards.

In no way am I even attempting to convert anybody to the religion of the object of Loch Ness. I mean, they can believe it, but it doesn't upset me if they don't believe it. Because I would question very much if I hadn't the extraordinary experience of seeing this object. If I hadn't seen it I would have without question given a lot of skepticism to what it was. But I saw it, and nothing can take that away.

—Ian Cameron, a retired superintendent of the Northern Police Force, lives with his wife Jessie in Inverness, Scotland, at the head of the loch. A keen angler, he is an authority on the Atlantic salmon.

"I'm gobsmacked, I just didn't know what it was."

Right, I'm driving along the loch side, glancing out of the window. You can see the rock formation, I was just down on the road there, it just rises. I saw this boiling in the water. I thought, "No, it can't be anything," and I carried on a wee bit. Then I looked again, and I saw three black humps. I mean, you know, there's the chance, I've seen something in the water. But what is it?

So I'm gobsmacked, I'm looking out the window, I just didn't know what it was. Then the people came behind me, and they obviously wanted me to move. But I didn't want to lose sight of this thing. So I just pulled over to the side, grabbed my camera, and I thought I was being very cool and very **nonchalant** and took two or three photos. In fact, as I say, I had taken nine or ten, without realizing, I just punched the button. It was just a pity it was a small camera.

NOVA: Did anybody else see anything?

WHITE: Yeah, the other two people who were there—I was just so excited I didn't get their name and address or anything—they saw it exactly the same as me. Because the wee wifey, who would have been a lady in her fifties, on holiday, she was Scottish, she said to me, "I've not been in the bar this morning!" And her husband said, "Ach, it's an eel! It's an eel!" And I said, "There's no eels that big!" And he said, "Ach, it's otters!" And I said, "You don't get otters swimming out like that!"

I saw what I saw, and I'm not going to be dissuaded. It wasn't just an imagination. I'm a sane guy, and I've got no ax to grind. As I say I sell pet food! What use to me is the Loch Ness Monster? Unless I can invent a food called, I don't know, Monster Munchies perhaps?

—Richard White lives in the village of Muir of Ord, north of Inverness. He runs his own business selling pet food.

VOCABULARY DEVELOPMENT
nonchalant (nän'shə-länt') adj.: matter-of-fact; showing no concern or worry.

How can you tell from the sentence the meaning of the word *nonchalant* (line 158)?
The sentence suggests that *nonchalant* must be similar in meaning to the word cool. If you know what cool means, then you should have an idea of what *nonchalant* means.

TEXT STRUCTURE
Circle the words *NOVA* and *WHITE* in lines 162 and 163. What does this text format indicate?
The format shows that an interviewer questioned White to get his story.

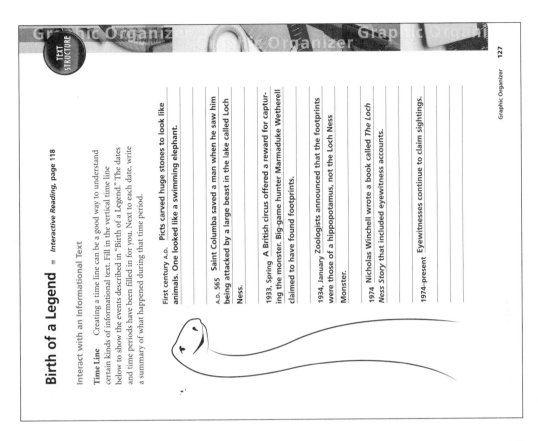

Birth of a Legend ■ *Interactive Reading,* page 118

Interact with an Informational Text

Time Line Creating a time line can be a good way to understand certain kinds of informational text. Fill in the vertical time line below to show the events described in "Birth of a Legend." The dates and time periods have been filled in for you. Next to each date, write a summary of what happened during that time period.

First century A.D. **Picts carved huge stones to look like animals. One looked like a swimming elephant.**

A.D. 565 **Saint Columba saved a man when he saw him being attacked by a large beast in the lake called Loch Ness.**

1933, Spring **A British circus offered a reward for capturing the monster. Big-game hunter Marmaduke Wetherell claimed to have found footprints.**

1934, January **Zoologists announced that the footprints were those of a hippopotamus, not the Loch Ness Monster.**

1974 **Nicholas Winchell wrote a book called *The Loch Ness Story* that included eyewitness accounts.**

1974–present **Eyewitnesses continue to claim sightings.**

Graphic Organizer **127**

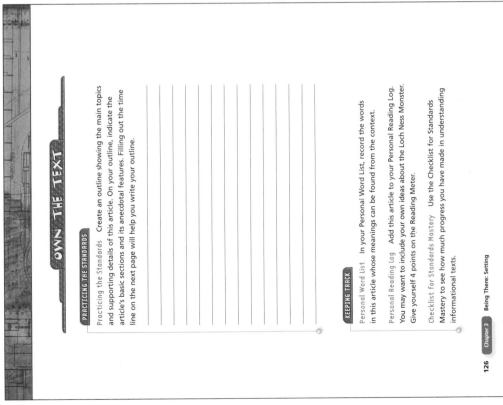

OWN THE TEXT

PRACTICING THE STANDARDS

Practicing the Standards Create an outline showing the main topics and supporting details of this article. On your outline, indicate the article's basic sections and its anecdotal features. Filling out the time line on the next page will help you write your outline.

KEEPING TRACK

Personal Word List In your Personal Word List, record the words in this article whose meanings can be found from the context.

Personal Reading Log Add this article to your Personal Reading Log. You may want to include your own ideas about the Loch Ness Monster. Give yourself 4 points on the Reading Meter.

Checklist for Standards Mastery Use the Checklist for Standards Mastery to see how much progress you have made in understanding informational texts.

Literature

LEGEND

BEFORE YOU READ

"Greyling," a story based on an old legend, has something in common with the many other tales passed down through the ages. First, a **metamorphosis**, or transformation, takes place, as in the story of the frog who turns into a handsome prince. Second, things are counted in threes, like the three stepsisters in "Cinderella" or the three little pigs.

Before you read, you might want to know that according to legend, *selchies* (sel'kēz) are seals who rise from the waves, change into humans, and come ashore. Selchies are great friends of the mermaids. Legend has it that a mermaid once died to save a seal's life and that ever since then, selchies have done all they could to help mermaids.

Reading Standard 3.4 Analyze the relevance of the setting (for example, place, time, customs) to the mood, tone, and meaning of the text.

Greyling

Jane Yolen

Once on a time when wishes were aplenty, a fisherman and his wife lived by the side of the sea. All that they ate came out of the sea. Their hut was covered with the finest mosses that kept them cool in the summer and warm in the winter. And there was nothing they needed or wanted except a child.

Each morning, when the moon touched down behind the water and the sun rose up behind the plains, the wife would say to the fisherman, "You have your boat and your nets and your lines. But I have no baby to hold in my arms." And again, in the evening, it was the same. She would weep and wail and rock the cradle that stood by the hearth. But year in and year out the cradle stayed empty.

10

VISUALIZE
Pause at line 13. Describe the setting of this story.

Like most folk tales, this one takes place "once upon a time."

The couple lives by the sea in a hut covered with mosses.

IDENTIFY
What does the couple want?

a child

"Greyling" by Jane Yolen. Copyright © 1968 by Jane Yolen. Reprinted by permission of Philomel Books, an imprint of Penguin Putnam Books for Young Readers, a division of Penguin Putnam Inc.

Now the fisherman was also sad that they had no child. But he kept his sorrow to himself so that his wife would not leave his grief and thus double her own. Indeed, he would not leave the hut each morning with a breath of song and return each night with a whistle on his lips. His nets were full but his heart was empty, yet he never told his wife.

20 One sunny day, when the beach was a tan thread spun between sea and plain, the fisherman as usual went down to his boat. But this day he found a small grey seal stranded on the sandbar, crying for its own.

The fisherman looked up the beach and down. He looked in front of him and behind. And he looked to the town on the great grey cliffs that sheared off into the sea. But there were no other seals in sight.

So he shrugged his shoulders and took off his shirt. Then he dipped it into the water and wrapped the seal pup carefully in its folds.

30 "You have no father and you have no mother," he said. "And I have no child. So you shall come home with me."

And the fisherman did no fishing that day but brought the seal pup, wrapped in his shirt, straight home to his wife.

When she saw him coming home early with no shirt on, the fisherman's wife ran out of the hut, fear riding in her heart. Then she looked wonderingly at the bundle which he held in his arms.

40 "It's nothing," he said, "but a seal pup I found stranded in the shallows and longing for its own. I thought we could give it love and care until it is old enough to seek its **kin.**"

The fisherman's wife nodded and took the bundle. Then she uncovered the wrapping and gave a loud cry. "Nothing!" she said. "You call this nothing?"

PREDICT
Pause at line 35. What do you think will happen when the fisherman brings the seal pup home?
Suggested response:
The seal pup will turn into a human baby.

VOCABULARY DEVELOPMENT

kin (kin) *n.:* relatives.

How can you figure out the meaning of *kin* (line 42)? Look in the previous sentence to find a context clue.

The words "its own" refer to relatives.

128 **Chapter 3** Being There: Setting

Greyling **129**

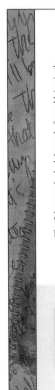

The fisherman looked. Instead of a seal lying in the folds, there was a strange child with great grey eyes and silvery grey hair, smiling up at him.

The fisherman wrung his hands. "It is a selchie," he cried. "I have heard of them. They are men upon the land and seals in the sea. I thought it was but a tale."

"Then he shall remain a man upon the land," said the fisherman's wife, clasping the child in her arms, "for I shall 50 never let him return to the sea."

"Never," agreed the fisherman, for he knew how his wife had wanted a child. And in his secret heart, he wanted one, too. Yet he felt, somehow, it was wrong.

"We shall call him Greyling," said the fisherman's wife, "for his eyes and hair are the color of a storm-coming sky. Greyling, though he has brought sunlight into our home."

And though they still lived by the side of the water in a 60 hut covered with mosses that kept them warm in the winter and cool in the summer, the boy Greyling was never allowed into the sea.

He grew from a child to a lad. He grew from a lad to a young man. He gathered driftwood for his mother's hearth and searched the tide pools for shells for her mantel. He mended his father's nets and tended his father's boat. But though he often stood by the shore or high in the town on 70 the great grey cliffs, looking and longing and grieving his heart for what he did not really know, he never went into the sea.

Then one wind-wailing morning just fifteen years from the day that Greyling had been found, a great storm blew up suddenly in the North. It was such a storm as had never been seen before: The sky turned nearly black and even the fish had trouble swimming. The wind pushed

IDENTIFY

What has the seal turned into?

a child

PREDICT

What do the wife's words foreshadow (lines 52–54)?

The wife's words

foreshadow that the

child will inevitably

have to return to

the sea.

WORD KNOWLEDGE

A *mantel* (line 67) is the shelf above a fireplace.

A *mantle* can also be a cloak or a shawl. The words are pronounced the same.

FLUENCY

This boxed paragraph reflects a dramatic shift in mood and contains strong images. Read this paragraph aloud several times. With each reading, try to improve the speed and smoothness of your delivery.

130 **Chapter 3** Being There: Setting

---

huge waves onto the shore. The waters gobbled up the little hut on the beach. And Greyling and the fisherman's wife were forced to flee to the town high on the great grey cliffs. There they looked down at the **roiling**, boiling sea. 80 Far from shore they spied the fisherman's boat, its sails flapping like the wings of a wounded gull. And clinging to the broken mast was the fisherman himself, sinking deeper with every wave.

The fisherman's wife gave a terrible cry. "Will no one save him?" she called to the people of the town who had gathered on the edge of the cliff. "Will no one save my own dear husband who is all of life to me?"

But the townsmen looked away. There was no man there who dared risk his life in that sea, even to save a 90 drowning soul.

"Will no one at all save him?" she cried out again.

"Let the boy go," said one old man, pointing at Greyling with his stick. "He looks strong enough."

But the fisherman's wife clasped Greyling in her arms and held his ears with her hands. She did not want him to go into the sea. She was afraid he would never return.

"Will no one save my own dear heart?" cried the fisherman's wife for a third and last time.

But shaking their heads, the people of the town 100 edged to their houses and shut their doors and locked their windows and set their backs to the ocean and their faces to the fires that glowed in every hearth.

"I will save him, Mother," cried Greyling, "or die as I try."

And before she could tell him no, he broke from her grasp and dived from the top of the great cliffs, down, down, down into the tumbling sea.

VOCABULARY DEVELOPMENT

roiling (roil'ĭn) *adj.*: stirred up; agitated.

Imaginative writers choose words for their sounds as well as for their meanings. What words in this passage rhyme?

roiling/boiling

PREDICT

What do you predict will happen when Greyling returns to the sea?

Answers will vary

but may include the

prediction that

Greyling will rejoin

his own kind.

Greyling 131

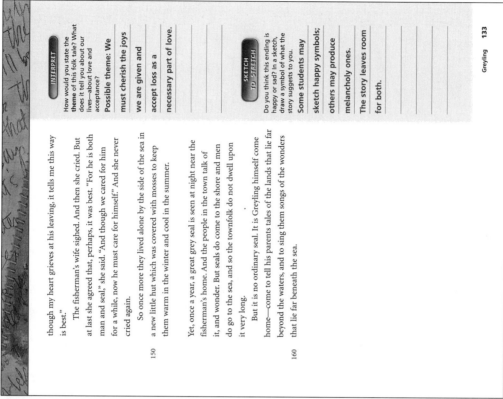

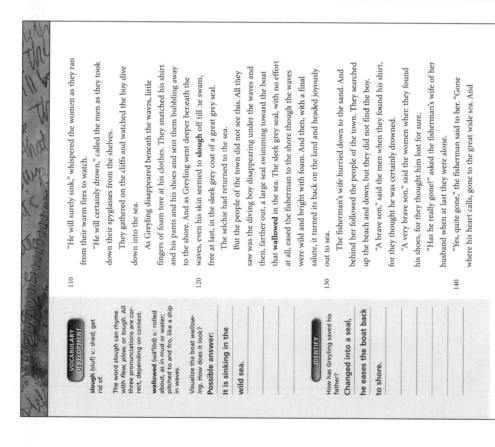

slough (sluf) *v*: shed; get rid of.

The word *slough* can rhyme with *flew*, *plow*, or *tough*. All three pronunciations are correct, depending on context.

wallowed (wä'lōd) *v*: rolled about, as in mud or water; pitched to and fro, like a ship in waves.

Visualize the boat *wallowing*. How does it look?

Possible answer:

It is sinking in the

wild sea.

IDENTIFY

How has Greyling saved his father?

Changed into a seal,

he eases the boat back

to shore.

"He will surely sink," whispered the women as they ran from their warm fires to watch.

"He will certainly drown," called the men as they took down their spyglasses from the shelves.

110 They gathered on the cliffs and watched the boy dive down into the sea.

As Greyling disappeared beneath the waves, little fingers of foam tore at his clothes. They snatched his shirt and his pants and his shoes and sent them bubbling away to the shore. And as Greyling went deeper beneath the waves, even his skin seemed to **slough** off till he swam,

120 free at last, in the sleek grey coat of a great grey seal.

The selchie had returned to the sea.

But the people of the town did not see this. All they saw was the diving boy disappearing under the waves and then, farther out, a large seal swimming toward the boat that **wallowed** in the sea. The sleek grey seal, with no effort at all, eased the fisherman to the shore though the waves were wild and bright with foam. And then, with a final salute, it turned its back on the land and headed joyously out to sea.

130 The fisherman's wife hurried down to the sand. And behind her followed the people of the town. They searched up the beach and down, but they did not find the boy.

"A brave son," said the men when they found his shirt, for they thought he was certainly drowned.

"A very brave son," said the women when they found his shoes, for they thought him lost for sure.

"Has he really gone?" asked the fisherman's wife of her husband when at last they were alone.

140 "Yes, quite gone," the fisherman said to her. "Gone where his heart calls, gone to the great wide sea. And

INTERPRET

How would you state the theme of this folk tale? What does it tell you about our lives—about love and acceptance?

Possible theme: We

must cherish the joys

we are given and

accept loss as a

necessary part of love.

though my heart grieves at his leaving, it tells me this way is best."

The fisherman's wife sighed. And then she cried. But at last she agreed that, perhaps, it was best. "For he is both man and seal," she said. "And though we cared for him for a while, now he must care for himself." And she never cried again.

150 So once more they lived alone by the side of the sea in a new little hut which was covered with mosses to keep them warm in the winter and cool in the summer.

Yet, once a year, a great grey seal is seen at night near the fisherman's home. And the people in the town talk of it, and wonder. But seals do come to the shore and men do go to the sea, and so the townfolk do not dwell upon it very long.

But it is no ordinary seal. It is Greyling himself come home—come to tell his parents tales of the lands that lie far beyond the waters, and to sing them songs of the wonders

160 that lie far beneath the sea.

SKETCH TO STRETCH

Do you think this ending is happy or sad? In a sketch, draw a symbol of what the story suggests to you.

Some students may

sketch happy symbols;

others may produce

melancholy ones.

The story leaves room

for both.

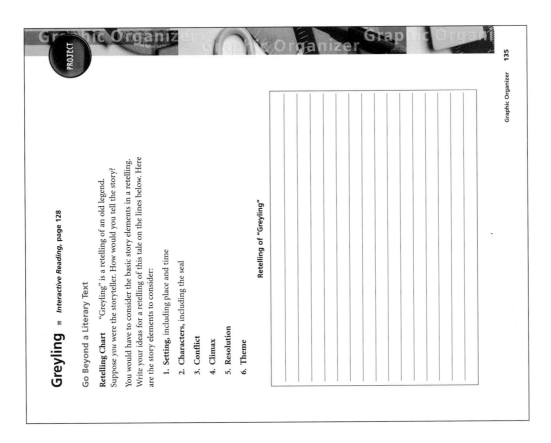

PROJECT

Graphic Organizer   Graphic Organizer   Graphic Organizer

Greyling ■ *Interactive Reading*, page 128

Go Beyond a Literary Text

Retelling Chart "Greyling" is a retelling of an old legend.
Suppose *you* were the storyteller. How would you tell the story?
You would have to consider the basic story elements in a retelling.
Write your ideas for a retelling of this tale on the lines below. Here
are the story elements to consider:

1. **Setting**, including place and time
2. **Characters**, including the seal
3. **Conflict**
4. **Climax**
5. **Resolution**
6. **Theme**

Retelling of "Greyling"

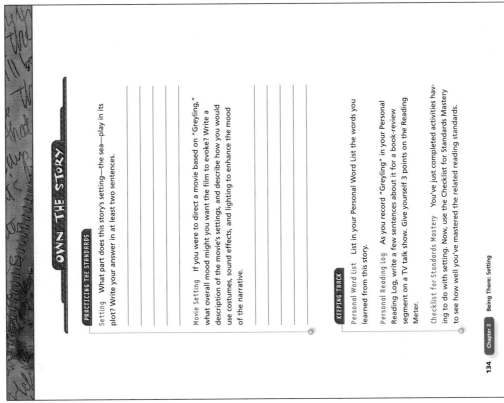

OWN THE STORY

PRACTICING THE STANDARDS

Setting What part does this story's setting—the sea—play in its
plot? Write your answer in at least two sentences.

Movie Setting If you were to direct a movie based on "Greyling,"
what overall mood might you want the film to evoke? Write a
description of the movie's settings, and describe how you would
use costumes, sound effects, and lighting to enhance the mood
of the narrative.

KEEPING TRACK

Personal Word List List in your Personal Word List the words you
learned from this story.

Personal Reading Log As you record "Greyling" in your Personal
Reading Log, write a few sentences about it for a book-review
segment on a TV talk show. Give yourself 3 points on the Reading
Meter.

Checklist for Standards Mastery You've just completed activities having to do with setting. Now, use the Checklist for Standards Mastery
to see how well you've mastered the related reading standards.

Chapter **4**
We Still Believe

Chapter Preview In this chapter you will—

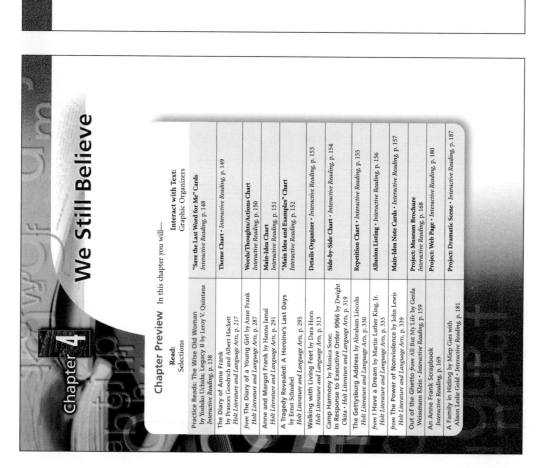

Strategy Launch:
"Save the Last Word for Me"

LITERARY FOCUS: THEME

The **theme** of a work of literature is its revelation or observation about life. A story's or poem's theme is not the same as its subject. Theme is what the story or poem or play *says about* the subject. For example, a story may be about a person who struggles to win a contest. The story's theme may be "Winning isn't everything."

Most themes are not stated directly. We must use key details in the story to arrive at a statement of theme. To do this, we make inferences. There is no one correct theme in a work of literature: Different readers may come up with different themes.

A STRATEGY THAT WORKS: "SAVE THE LAST WORD FOR ME"

Everyone's got something to say about what they read. But since no two people read a story in exactly the same way, you may feel unsure about your conclusions. One way to feel more confident about your ideas is to relate them to a very specific passage in what you've read. To do this, use the "Save the Last Word for Me" strategy.

POINTERS FOR USING "SAVE THE LAST WORD FOR ME"

➤ Read the text; mark passages you find interesting or important.

➤ When you're finished reading, re-read and identify what you think is the most important passage. Write it down.

➤ Then, write why you chose that passage. Include at least two reasons for your choice.

➤ Read the passage you selected to a small group, and let the group discuss it. Then, read to the group the reasons you chose that passage. If you wish, after your discussion, rewrite your reasons, or add to them. This is your last word! No one can disagree, add to, or change what you finally write.

Reading Standard 1.3
Use word meanings within the appropriate context, and show ability to verify those meanings by definition, restatement, example, comparison, or contrast.

Reading Standard 2.3 (Grade 6 Review)
Connect and clarify main ideas by identifying their relationships to other sources and related topics.

Reading Standard 3.5
Identify and analyze recurring themes (e.g., good versus evil) across traditional and contemporary works.

Strategy Launch **137**

Practice Read

BEFORE YOU READ

Times change: What we wear, where we live, how we travel, the language we use—all change. At heart, though, humanity seems to change very little. Ideas about right and wrong, cowardice and courage, and hope and despair, occupy much of our thoughts, just as they occupied the thoughts of people living hundreds and even thousands of years ago.

The essence of humanity is reflected in literature. You can read a love poem by Petrarch, an Italian poet who lived hundreds of years ago, and be struck by how similar its message is to the message of a poem written just last year.

After you read this folk tale, "The Wise Old Woman" by Yoshiko Uchida, you'll read a contemporary poem, "Legacy II" by Leroy V. Quintana. You'll see how the two selections reflect similar **themes**.

IDENTIFY

Where and when does this story take place? Underline the passages revealing this information.

VOCABULARY DEVELOPMENT

decree (dē-krē′) *v:* order; rule.

The Wise Old Woman

Yoshiko Uchida

Many long years ago, there lived an arrogant and cruel young lord who ruled over a small village in the western hills of Japan.

"I have no use for old people in my village," he said haughtily. "They are neither useful nor able to work for a living. I therefore **decree** that anyone over seventy-one must be banished from the village and left in the mountains to die."

10 "What a dreadful decree! What a cruel and unreasonable lord we have," the people of the village murmured. But the lord fearfully punished anyone who disobeyed him, and

Text from "The Wise Old Woman" from The Sea of Gold and Other Tales from Japan, adapted by Yoshiko Uchida. Copyright © 1965 by Yoshiko Uchida. Reprinted by permission of The Bancroft Library.

---

so villagers who turned seventy-one were tearfully carried into the mountains, never to return.

Gradually there were fewer and fewer old people in the village and soon they disappeared altogether. Then the young lord was pleased.

"What a fine village of young, healthy, and hard-working people I have," he bragged. "Soon it will be the finest village in all of Japan."

20 Now, there lived in this village a kind young farmer and his aged mother. They were poor, but the farmer was good to his mother, and the two of them lived happily together. However, as the years went by, the mother grew older, and before long she reached the terrible age of seventy-one.

"If only I could somehow deceive the cruel lord," the farmer thought. But there were records in the village books and everyone knew that his mother had turned seventy-one.

30 Each day the son put off telling his mother that he must take her into the mountains to die, but the people of the village knew that if he did not take his mother away soon, the lord would send his soldiers and throw them both into a dark dungeon to die a terrible death.

"Mother—" he would begin, as he tried to tell her what he must do, but he could not go on.

Then one day the mother herself spoke of the lord's dread decree. "Well, my son," she said, "the time has come 40 for you to take me to the mountains. We must hurry before the lord sends his soldiers for you." And she did not seem worried at all that she must go to the mountains to die.

IDENTIFY

Pause at line 13. What do the villagers and the young lord disagree about?

The young lord thinks old people are useless; the villagers do not agree.

INTERPRET

Pause at line 29. What conflict does the young farmer face?

If he obeys the young lord, his mother will die in the mountains alone; if he disobeys the young lord, both the farmer and his mother will be sent to a dungeon to die a terrible death.

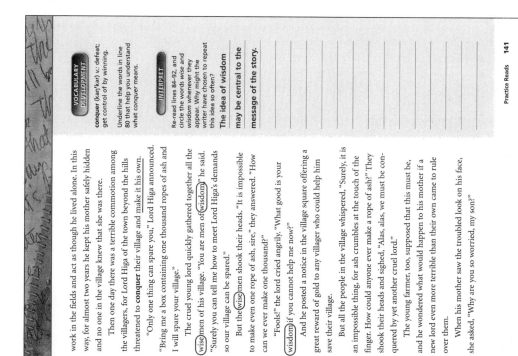

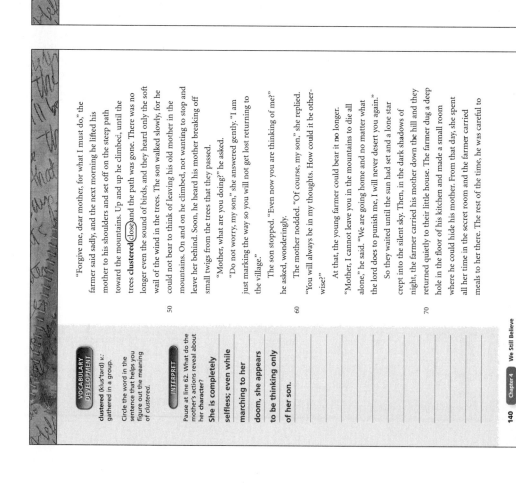

VOCABULARY DEVELOPMENT

clustered (klus'tərd) *v.*: gathered in a group.

Circle the word in the sentence that helps you figure out the meaning of *clustered*.

INTERPRET

Pause at line 62. What do the mother's actions reveal about her character?

She is completely selfless; even while marching to her doom, she appears to be thinking only of her son.

"Forgive me, dear mother, for what I must do," the farmer said sadly, and the next morning he lifted his mother to his shoulders and set off on the steep path toward the mountains. Up and up he climbed, until the trees clustered close and the path was gone. There was no longer even the sound of birds, and they heard only the soft wail of the wind in the trees. The son walked slowly, for he could not bear to think of leaving his old mother in the mountains. On and on he climbed, not wanting to stop and leave her behind. Soon, he heard his mother breaking off small twigs from the trees that they passed.

"Mother, what are you doing?" he asked.

"Do not worry, my son," she answered gently. "I am just marking the way so you will not get lost returning to the village."

The son stopped. "Even now you are thinking of me?" he asked, wonderingly.

The mother nodded. "Of course, my son," she replied. "You will always be in my thoughts. How could it be otherwise?"

At that, the young farmer could bear it no longer.

"Mother, I cannot leave you in the mountains to die all alone," he said. "We are going home and no matter what the lord does to punish me, I will never desert you again."

So they waited until the sun had set and a lone star crept into the silent sky. Then, in the dark shadows of night, the farmer carried his mother down the hill and they returned quietly to their little house. The farmer dug a deep hole in the floor of his kitchen and made a small room where he could hide his mother. From that day, she spent all her time in the secret room and the farmer carried meals to her there. The rest of the time, he was careful to

work in the fields and act as though he lived alone. In this way, for almost two years he kept his mother safely hidden and no one in the village knew that she was there.

Then one day there was a terrible commotion among the villagers, for Lord Higa of the town beyond the hills threatened to **conquer** their village and make it his own.

"Only one thing can spare you," Lord Higa announced. "Bring me a box containing one thousand ropes of ash and I will spare your village."

The cruel young lord quickly gathered together all the wisemen of his village. "You are men of wisdom," he said. "Surely you can tell me how to meet Lord Higa's demands so our village can be spared."

But the wisemen shook their heads. "It is impossible to make even one rope of ash, sire," they answered. "How can we ever make one thousand?"

"Fools!" the lord cried angrily. "What good is your wisdom if you cannot help me now?"

And he posted a notice in the village square offering a great reward of gold to any villager who could help him save their village.

But all the people in the village whispered, "Surely, it is an impossible thing, for ash crumbles at the touch of the finger. How could anyone ever make a rope of ash?" They shook their heads and sighed, "Alas, alas, we must be conquered by yet another cruel lord."

The young farmer, too, supposed that this must be, and he wondered what would happen to his mother if a new lord even more terrible than their own came to rule over them.

When his mother saw the troubled look on his face, she asked, "Why are you so worried, my son?"

VOCABULARY DEVELOPMENT

conquer (kän'kər) *v.*: defeat; get control of by winning.

Underline the words in line 80 that help you understand what *conquer* means.

INTERPRET

Re-read lines 84–92, and circle the words *wise* and *wisdom* whenever they appear. Why might the writer have chosen to repeat this idea so often?

The idea of wisdom may be central to the message of the story.

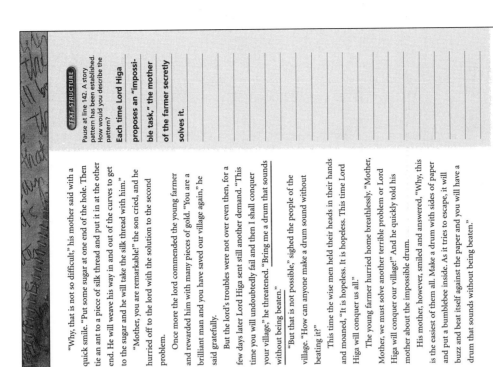

How does the mother's response to the problem (lines 110–114) reveal her worth?

The mother is not useless; she is able to solve problems quickly and effectively.

So the farmer told her of the impossible demand made by Lord Higa if the village was to be spared, but his mother did not seem troubled at all. Instead she laughed softly and said, "Why, that is not such an impossible task. All one has to do is soak ordinary rope in salt water and dry it well.
110 When it is burned, it will hold its shape and there is your rope of ash! Tell the villagers to hurry and find one thousand pieces of rope."

The farmer shook his head in amazement. "Mother, you are wonderfully wise," he said, and he rushed to tell the young lord what he must do.

"You are wiser than all the wise men of the village," the lord said when he heard the farmer's solution, and he rewarded him with many pieces of gold. The thousand ropes of ash were quickly made and the village was spared.

120 In a few days, however, there was another great commotion in the village as Lord Higa sent another threat. This time he sent a log with a small hole that curved and bent seven times through its length, and he demanded that a single piece of silk thread be threaded through the hole. "If you cannot perform this task," the lord threatened, "I shall come to conquer your village."

The young lord hurried once more to his wise men, but they all shook their heads in **bewilderment**. "A needle cannot bend its way through such curves," they moaned.

"Again we are faced with an impossible demand."

130 "And again you are stupid fools!" the lord said, stamping his foot impatiently. He then posted a second notice in the village square asking the villagers for their help.

Once more the young farmer hurried with the problem to his mother in her secret room.

Underline the second impossible task (lines 124–126).

bewilderment (bə-wǐl′dər-mənt) *n.*: state of confusion; puzzlement.

Which words in line 130 help you figure out the meaning of *bewilderment*? Underline those words.

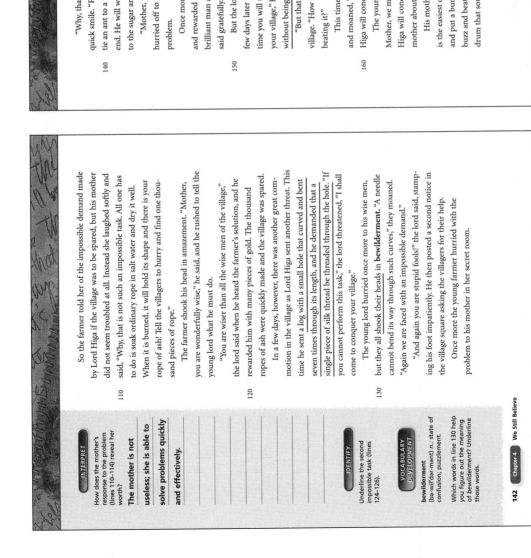

"Why, that is not so difficult," his mother said with a quick smile. "Put some sugar at one end of the hole. Then
140 tie an ant to a piece of silk thread and put it in at the other end. He will weave his way in and out of the curves to get to the sugar and he will take the silk thread with him."

"Mother, you are remarkable!" the son cried, and he hurried off to the lord with the solution to the second problem.

Once more the lord commended the young farmer and rewarded him with many pieces of gold. "You are a brilliant man and you have saved our village again," he said gratefully.

150 But the lord's troubles were not over even then, for a few days later Lord Higa sent still another demand. "This time you will undoubtedly fail and then I shall conquer your village," he threatened. "Bring me a drum that sounds without being beaten."

"But that is not possible," sighed the people of the village. "How can anyone make a drum sound without beating it?"

This time the wise men held their heads in their hands and moaned, "It is hopeless. It is hopeless. This time Lord
160 Higa will conquer us all."

The young farmer hurried home breathlessly. "Mother, Mother, we must solve another terrible problem or Lord Higa will conquer our village!" And he quickly told his mother about the impossible drum.

His mother, however, smiled and answered, "Why, this is the easiest of them all. Make a drum with sides of paper and put a bumblebee inside. As it tries to escape, it will buzz and beat itself against the paper and you will have a drum that sounds without being beaten."

Pause at line 142. A story pattern has been established. How would you describe the pattern?

Each time Lord Higa proposes an "impossible task," the mother of the farmer secretly solves it.

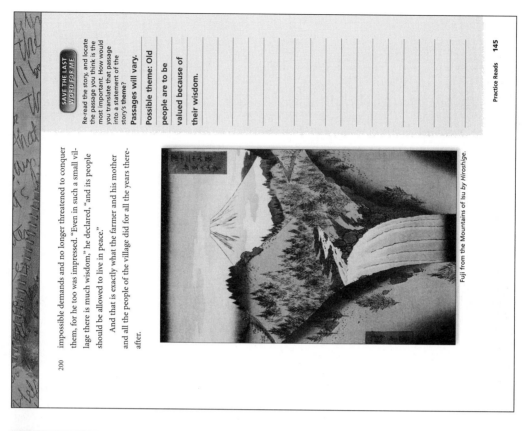

170   The young farmer was amazed at his mother's wisdom.
"You are far wiser than any of the wise men of the village,"
he said, and he hurried to tell the young lord how to meet
Lord Higa's third demand.

When the lord heard the answer, he was greatly
impressed. "Surely a young man like you cannot be wiser
than all my wise men," he said. "Tell me honestly, who has
helped you solve all these difficult problems?"

The young farmer could not lie. "My lord," he began
180   slowly, "for the past two years I have broken the law of the
land. I have kept my aged mother hidden beneath the floor
of my house, and it is she who solved each of your problems and saved the village from Lord Higa."

He trembled as he spoke, for he feared the lord's dis-
pleasure and rage. Surely now the soldiers would be summoned to throw him into the dark dungeon. But when he
glanced fearfully at the lord, he saw that the young ruler
was not angry at all. Instead, he was silent and thoughtful,
for at last he realized how much wisdom and knowledge
old people possess.

190   "I have been very wrong," he said finally. "And I must
ask the forgiveness of your mother and of all my people.
Never again will I demand that the old people of our village be sent to the mountains to die. Rather, they will be
treated with the respect and honor they deserve and share
with us the wisdom of their years."

And so it was. From that day, the villagers were no
longer forced to abandon their parents in the mountains,
and the village became once more a happy, cheerful place
in which to live. The terrible Lord Higa stopped sending his

PREDICT

Pause at line 177. Will the
young farmer tell the young
lord about his mother, or will
he lie?

Predictions will vary.

_____

_____

IDENTIFY

Circle the phrase in the
paragraph beginning at line
183 that you feel is most
important.

• • • • • • Notes • • • • • • •

INTERPRET

What does the change in the
young lord's behavior reveal
about the theme of the
story?

The young lord comes

to value wisdom; the

theme of the story

may be "wisdom is to

be valued."

200   impossible demands and no longer threatened to conquer
them, for he too was impressed. "Even in such a small village there is much wisdom," he declared, "and its people
should be allowed to live in peace."

And that is exactly what the farmer and his mother
and all the people of the village did for all the years thereafter.

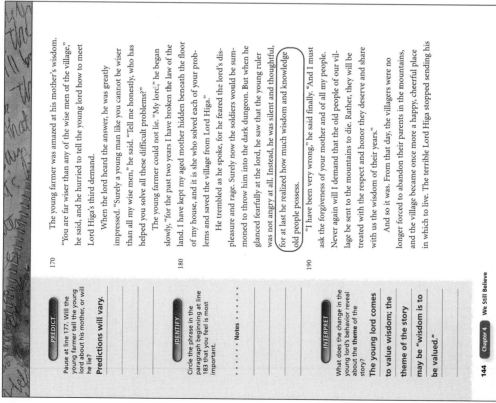

Fuji from the Mountains of Isu *by Hiroshige.*

**SAVE THE LAST
WORD FOR ME**

Re-read the story, and locate
the passage you think is the
most important. How would
you translate that passage
into a statement of the
story's theme?

Passages will vary.

Possible theme: Old

people are to be

valued because of

their wisdom.

_____

_____

_____

_____

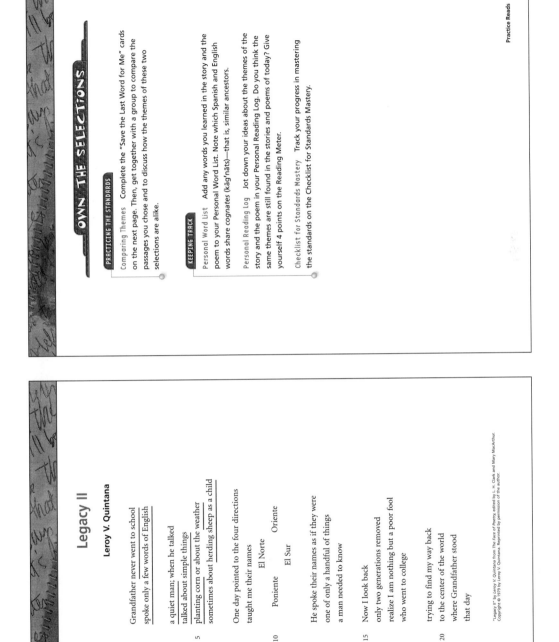

Legacy II

Leroy V. Quintana

IDENTIFY

Re-read lines 1–6, and underline the words that describe the speaker's grandfather.

TEXT STRUCTURE

The Spanish words for *north*, *south*, *east*, and *west* are laid out on the page like a compass so the reader can tell what each word means. How do the directions translate into English?

norte = north;

oriente = east;

sur = south;

poniente = west

Grandfather never went to school
spoke only a few words of English

a quiet man; when he talked
talked about simple things
5 planting corn or about the weather
sometimes about herding sheep as a child

One day pointed to the four directions
taught me their names

El Norte

10 Poniente   Oriente

El Sur

He spoke their names as if they were
one of only a handful of things
a man needed to know

15 Now I look back
only two generations removed
realize I am nothing but a poor fool
who went to college

trying to find my way back
20 to the center of the world
where Grandfather stood
that day

SAVE THE LAST WORD FOR ME

Which lines of the poem hold the most meaning for you? How would you state the poem's **theme,** based on those lines?

Lines will vary.

Possible theme:

Education does not

equal wisdom.

OWN THE SELECTIONS

PRACTICING THE STANDARDS

Comparing Themes   Complete the "Save the Last Word for Me" cards on the next page. Then, get together with a group to compare the passages you chose and to discuss how the themes of these two selections are alike.

KEEPING TRACK

Personal Word List   Add any words you learned in the story and the poem to your Personal Word List. Note which Spanish and English words share *cognates* (kăg′nāts)—that is, similar ancestors.

Personal Reading Log   Jot down your ideas about the themes of the story and the poem in your Personal Reading Log. Do you think the same themes are still found in the stories and poems of today? Give yourself **4 points** on the Reading Meter.

Checklist for Standards Mastery   Track your progress in mastering the standards on the Checklist for Standards Mastery.

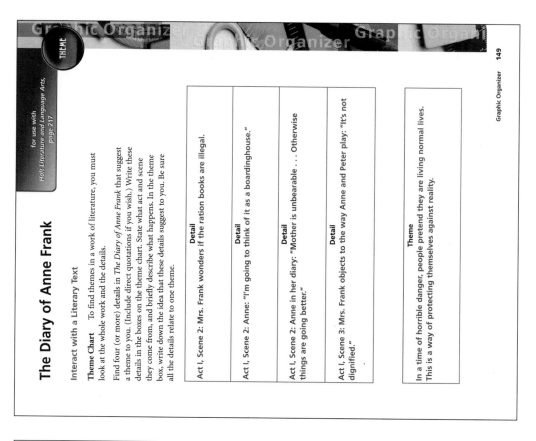

THEME

for use with
Holt Literature and Language Arts, page 217

The Diary of Anne Frank

Interact with a Literary Text

Theme Chart To find themes in a work of literature, you must look at the whole work and the details.

Find four (or more) details in *The Diary of Anne Frank* that suggest a theme to you. (Include direct quotations if you wish.) Write these details in the boxes on the theme chart. State what act and scene they come from, and briefly describe what happens. In the theme box, write down the idea that these details suggest to you. Be sure all the details relate to one theme.

Detail
Act I, Scene 2: Mrs. Frank wonders if the ration books are illegal.

Detail
Act I, Scene 2: Anne: "I'm going to think of it as a boardinghouse."

Detail
Act I, Scene 2: Anne in her diary: "Mother is unbearable . . . Otherwise things are going better."

Detail
Act I, Scene 3: Mrs. Frank objects to the way Anne and Peter play: "It's not dignified."

Theme
In a time of horrible danger, people pretend they are living normal lives. This is a way of protecting themselves against reality.

Graphic Organizer 149

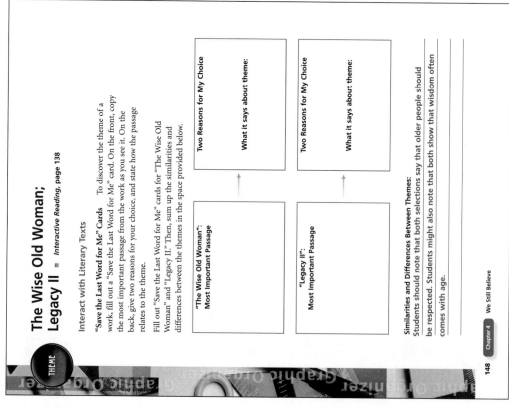

THEME

The Wise Old Woman; Legacy II ■ *Interactive Reading,* page 138

Interact with Literary Texts

"Save the Last Word for Me" Cards To discover the theme of a work, fill out a "Save the Last Word for Me" card. On the front, copy the most important passage from the work as you see it. On the back, give two reasons for your choice, and state how the passage relates to the theme.

Fill out "Save the Last Word for Me" cards for "The Wise Old Woman" and "Legacy II." Then, sum up the similarities and differences between the themes in the space provided below.

"The Wise Old Woman": Most Important Passage → **Two Reasons for My Choice**
What it says about theme:

"Legacy II": Most Important Passage → **Two Reasons for My Choice**
What it says about theme:

Similarities and Differences Between Themes:
Students should note that both selections say that older people should be respected. Students might also note that both show that wisdom often comes with age.

Chapter 4 We Still Believe 148

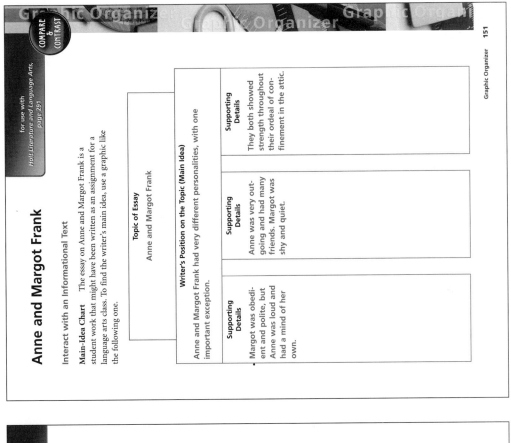

COMPARE & CONTRAST

for use with
Holt Literature and Language Arts,
page 291

Anne and Margot Frank

Interact with an Informational Text

Main-Idea Chart The essay on Anne and Margot Frank is a student work that might have been written as an assignment for a language arts class. To find the writer's main idea, use a graphic like the following one.

Topic of Essay
Anne and Margot Frank

Writer's Position on the Topic (Main Idea)
Anne and Margot Frank had very different personalities, with one important exception.

Supporting Details	Supporting Details	Supporting Details
Margot was obedient and polite, but Anne was loud and had a mind of her own.	Anne was very outgoing and had many friends. Margot was shy and quiet.	They both showed strength throughout their ordeal of confinement in the attic.

Graphic Organizer **151**

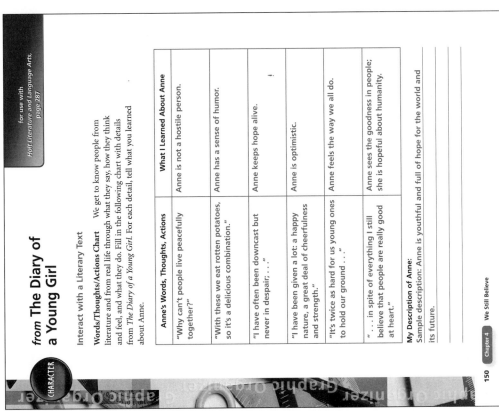

CHARACTER

for use with
Holt Literature and Language Arts,
page 287

from The Diary of a Young Girl

Interact with a Literary Text

Words/Thoughts/Actions Chart We get to know people from literature and from real life through what they say, how they think and feel, and what they do. In the following chart with details from *The Diary of a Young Girl.* For each detail, tell what you learned about Anne.

Anne's Words, Thoughts, Actions	What I Learned About Anne
"Why can't people live peacefully together?"	Anne is not a hostile person.
"With these we eat rotten potatoes, so it's a delicious combination."	Anne has a sense of humor.
"I have often been downcast but never in despair; . . ."	Anne keeps hope alive.
"I have been given a lot: a happy nature, a great deal of cheerfulness and strength."	Anne is optimistic.
"It's twice as hard for us young ones to hold our ground . . ."	Anne feels the way we all do.
". . . in spite of everything I still believe that people are really good at heart."	Anne sees the goodness in people; she is hopeful about humanity.

My Description of Anne:
Sample description: Anne is youthful and full of hope for the world and its future.

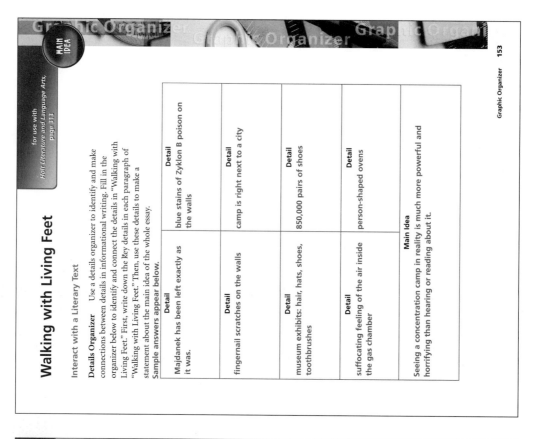

MAIN IDEA

for use with
Holt Literature and Language Arts,
page 313

Walking with Living Feet

Interact with a Literary Text

Details Organizer   Use a details organizer to identify and make connections between details in informational writing. Fill in the organizer below to identify and connect the details in "Walking with Living Feet." First, write down the key details in each paragraph of "Walking with Living Feet." Then, use these details to make a statement about the main idea of the whole essay. Sample answers appear below.

Detail	Detail
Majdanek has been left exactly as it was.	blue stains of Zyklon B poison on the walls

Detail	Detail
fingernail scratches on the walls	camp is right next to a city

Detail	Detail
museum exhibits: hair, hats, shoes, toothbrushes	850,000 pairs of shoes

Detail	Detail
suffocating feeling of the air inside the gas chamber	person-shaped ovens

Main Idea
Seeing a concentration camp in reality is much more powerful and horrifying than hearing or reading about it.

Graphic Organizer **153**

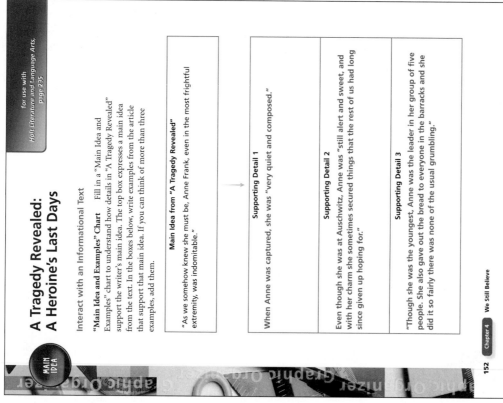

MAIN IDEA

for use with
Holt Literature and Language Arts,
page 225

A Tragedy Revealed: A Heroine's Last Days

Interact with an Informational Text

"Main Idea and Examples" Chart   Fill in a "Main Idea and Examples" chart to understand how details in "A Tragedy Revealed" support the writer's main idea. The top box expresses a main idea from the text. In the boxes below, write examples from the article that support that main idea. If you can think of more than three examples, add them.

Main Idea from "A Tragedy Revealed"

"As we somehow knew she must be, Anne Frank, even in the most frightful extremity, was indomitable."

Supporting Detail 1

When Anne was captured, she was "very quiet and composed."

Supporting Detail 2

Even though she was at Auschwitz, Anne was "still alert and sweet, and with her charm she sometimes secured things that the rest of us had long since given up hoping for."

Supporting Detail 3

"Though she was the youngest, Anne was the leader in her group of five people. She also gave out the bread to everyone in the barracks and she did it so fairly there was none of the usual grumbling."

Chapter 4   **We Still Believe**

152

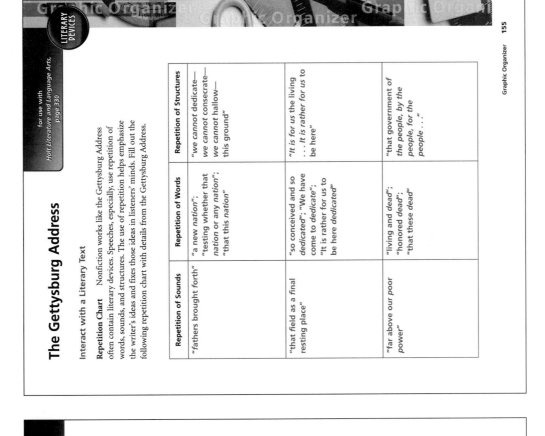

for use with
Holt Literature and Language Arts,
page 330

The Gettysburg Address

Interact with a Literary Text

Repetition Chart Nonfiction works like the Gettysburg Address often contain literary devices. Speeches, especially, use repetition of words, sounds, and structures. The use of repetition helps emphasize the writer's ideas and fixes those ideas in listeners' minds. Fill out the following repetition chart with details about the Gettysburg Address.

Repetition of Sounds	Repetition of Words	Repetition of Structures
"fathers brought forth"	*"a new nation"*; *"testing whether that nation or any nation"*; *"that this nation"*	*"we cannot dedicate— we cannot consecrate— we cannot hallow— this ground"*
"that field as a final resting place"	*"so conceived and so dedicated"*; *"We have come to dedicate"*; *"It is rather for us to be here dedicated"*	*"It is for us the living . . . It is rather for us to be here"*
"far above our poor power"	*"living and dead"*; *"honored dead"*; *"that these dead"*	*"that government of the people, by the people, for the people . . ."*

Graphic Organizer **155**

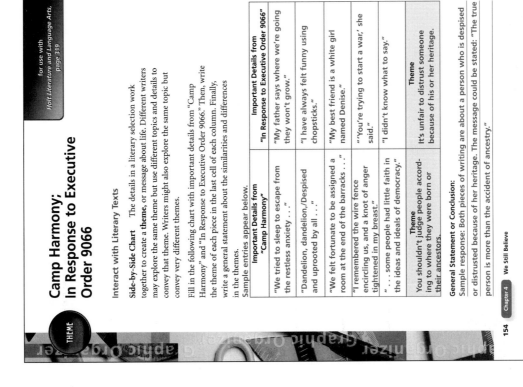

for use with
Holt Literature and Language Arts,
page 319

Camp Harmony;
In Response to Executive Order 9066

Interact with Literary Texts

Side-by-Side Chart The details in a literary selection work together to create a **theme**, or message about life. Different writers may explore the same theme but use different topics and details to convey that theme. Writers might also explore the same topic but convey very different themes.

Fill in the following chart with important details from "Camp Harmony" and "In Response to Executive Order 9066." Then, write the theme of each piece in the last cell of each column. Finally, write a general statement about the similarities and differences in the themes.

Sample entries appear below.

Important Details from "Camp Harmony"	Important Details from "In Response to Executive Order 9066"
"We tried to sleep to escape from the restless anxiety . . ."	"My father says where we're going they won't grow."
"Dandelion, dandelion,/Despised and uprooted by all . . ."	"I have always felt funny using chopsticks."
"We felt fortunate to be assigned a room at the end of the barracks . . ."	"My best friend is a white girl named Denise."
"I remembered the wire fence encircling us, and a knot of anger tightened in my breast."	"'You're trying to start a war,' she said."
" . . . some people had little faith in the ideas and ideals of democracy."	"I didn't know what to say."
Theme You shouldn't judge people according to where they were born or their ancestors.	**Theme** It's unfair to distrust someone because of his or her heritage.

General Statement or Conclusion:

Sample response: Both pieces of writing are about a person who is despised or distrusted because of her heritage. The message could be stated: "The true person is more than the accident of ancestry."

154 Chapter 4 **We Still Believe**

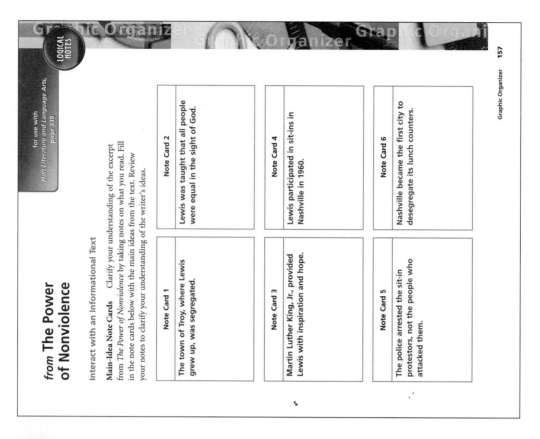

Graphic Organizer

LOGICAL NOTES

for use with
Holt Literature and Language Arts,
page 339

from The Power of Nonviolence

Interact with an Informational Text

Main-Idea Note Cards   Clarify your understanding of the excerpt from *The Power of Nonviolence* by taking notes on what you read. Fill in the note cards below with the main ideas from the text. Review your notes to clarify your understanding of the writer's ideas.

Note Card 1	Note Card 2
The town of Troy, where Lewis grew up, was segregated.	Lewis was taught that all people were equal in the sight of God.

Note Card 3	Note Card 4
Martin Luther King, Jr., provided Lewis with inspiration and hope.	Lewis participated in sit-ins in Nashville in 1960.

Note Card 5	Note Card 6
The police arrested the sit-in protestors, not the people who attacked them.	Nashville became the first city to desegregate its lunch counters.

Graphic Organizer   **157**

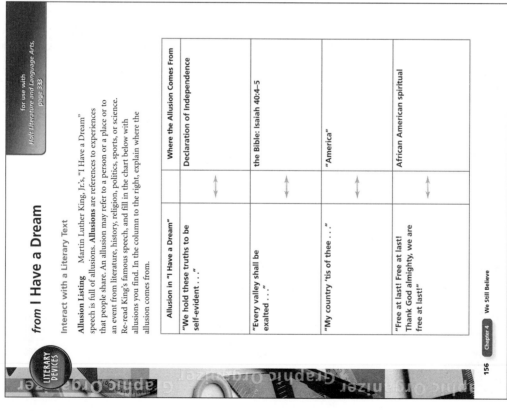

Graphic Organizer

LITERARY DEVICES

for use with
Holt Literature and Language Arts,
page 333

from I Have a Dream

Interact with a Literary Text

Allusion Listing   Martin Luther King, Jr.'s, "I Have a Dream" speech is full of allusions. **Allusions** are references to experiences that people share. An allusion may refer to a person or a place or to an event from literature, history, religion, politics, sports, or science. Re-read King's famous speech, and fill in the chart below with the allusions you find. In the column to the right, explain where the allusion comes from.

Allusion in "I Have a Dream"		Where the Allusion Comes From
"We hold these truths to be self-evident . . ."	↕	Declaration of Independence
"Every valley shall be exalted . . ."	↕	the Bible: Isaiah 40:4–5
"My country 'tis of thee . . ."	↕	"America"
"Free at last! Free at last! Thank God almighty, we are free at last!"	↕	African American spiritual

Chapter 4   We Still Believe

156

Literature

MEMOIR

AUTHOR STUDY

Gerda Weissmann was a fifteen-year-old schoolgirl when Germany invaded Poland in 1939. Gradually, during the German occupation of Poland, the Weissmanns lost all their freedoms; each member of the family was eventually arrested by the Nazis. Gerda was the only member of her family who survived. Gerda spent three years in slave-labor camps. She survived a brutal "death march" from Germany to Czechoslovakia, through snow and freezing temperatures. When the Allies liberated Czechoslovakia, Gerda weighed only sixty-eight pounds. Among the American soldiers who saved her was her future husband, Kurt Klein. Gerda Weissmann Klein eventually settled in the United States, where she and her husband raised two daughters—who never had to experience the horrors that their mother miraculously survived.

BEFORE YOU READ

This excerpt from Gerda Weissmann Klein's book *All But My Life* opens when the Nazis are about to take her father to a slave-labor camp in Sucha. Her beloved brother Arthur has already been taken away. Gerda and her mother have orders to go to a slave-labor camp in Wadowitz the following Monday.

Here is what you need to know before you begin Gerda's story:

- World War II lasted from 1939 to 1945. Germany invaded Poland in 1939.
- The Nazis targeted Jews, Gypsies, and many other groups of people for extinction. Many victims of the Nazis were used for slave labor during the war. Millions of them died from disease, starvation, and freezing temperatures. Millions of others were killed in the death camps, which were designed to kill large numbers of people quickly and efficiently.
- SS troops were the main enforcers of Nazi policy. SS troopers were known for their brutality.

Reading Standard 3.5 Identify and analyze recurring themes (e.g., good versus evil) across traditional and contemporary works.

---

from All But My Life

Out of the Ghetto

Gerda Weissmann Klein

In the morning we did not talk about the train that was to leave a few hours hence. Silently we sat at the table. Then Papa picked up his Bible and started to read. Mama and I just sat looking at him. Then all of a sudden Papa looked up and asked Mama where my skiing shoes were.

"Why?" I asked, baffled.

"I want you to wear them tomorrow when you go to Wadowitz."

"But Papa, skiing shoes in June?"

10   He said steadily: "I want you to wear them tomorrow."

"Yes, Papa, I will," I said in a small voice.

I wonder why Papa insisted; how could he possibly have known? Those shoes played a vital part in saving my life. They were sturdy and strong, and when three years later they were taken off my frozen feet they were good still. . . .

When it came time to leave, Papa and Mama embraced. Then Papa put his hands on my head in **benediction**, as he had done for Arthur. His hands trem-

20   bled. He held me a while, then lifted my chin up and looked into my eyes. We were both weeping.

"My child," he managed. It was a question and a promise. I understood. I threw myself wildly into his embrace, clinging to him in **desperation** for the last time. I gave him my most sacred vow: "Yes, Papa." We had always understood each other, but never better than in that last hour.

INFER

Pause at line 10. Why does the father insist that Gerda wear skiing shoes?

Suggested response:

Shoes would protect her feet in freezing weather.

VOCABULARY DEVELOPMENT

benediction (ben′ə·dik′shən) *n.:* blessing.

desperation (des′pər·ā′shən) *n.:* state of hopelessness or despair.

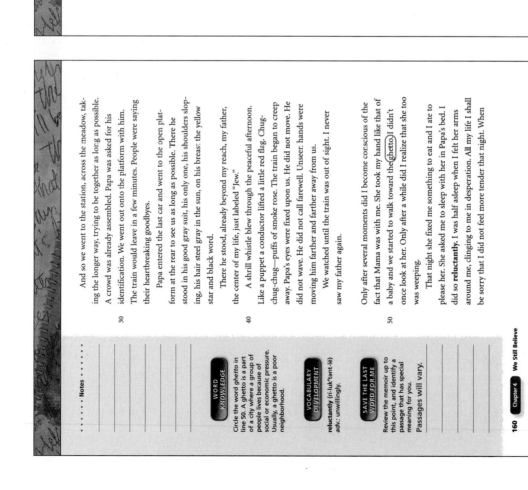

· · · · · · Notes · · · · · · ·

WORD KNOWLEDGE

Circle the word *ghetto* in line 50. A ghetto is a part of a city where a group of people lives because of social or economic pressure. Usually, a ghetto is a poor neighborhood.

VOCABULARY DEVELOPMENT

reluctantly (ri·luk'tant·le) *adv*: unwillingly.

SAVE THE LAST WORD FOR ME

Review the memoir up to this point, and identify a passage that has special meaning for you. Passages will vary.

And so we went to the station, across the meadow, taking the longer way, trying to be together as long as possible. A crowd was already assembled. Papa was asked for his identification. We went out onto the platform with him. The train would leave in a few minutes. People were saying their heartbreaking goodbyes.

Papa entered the last car and went to the open platform at the rear to see us as long as possible. There he stood in his good gray suit, his only one, his shoulders sloping, his hair steel gray in the sun, on his breast: the yellow star and black word.

There he stood, already beyond my reach, my father, the center of my life, just labeled "Jew."

A shrill whistle blew through the peaceful afternoon. Like a puppet a conductor lifted a little red flag. Chug-chug-chug—puffs of smoke rose. The train began to creep away. Papa's eyes were fixed upon us. He did not move. He did not wave. He did not call farewell. Unseen hands were moving him farther and farther away from us.

We watched until the train was out of sight. I never saw my father again.

Only after several moments did I become conscious of the fact that Mama was with me. She took my hand like that of a baby and we started to walk toward the ghetto. I didn't once look at her. Only after a while did I realize that she too was weeping.

That night she fixed me something to eat and I ate to please her. She asked me to sleep with her in Papa's bed. I did so **reluctantly.** I was half asleep when I felt her arms around me, clinging to me in desperation. All my life I shall be sorry that I did not feel more tender that night. When

INFER

Pause at line 74. What do Gerda's mother's actions reveal about her character? Students should recognize that the mother is religious, calm, and practical.

Mama needed me most, I wanted to be alone. I pulled away like a wounded animal that wants to lick its wounds in peace. Finally I fell asleep—on a pillow soaked with my mother's tears.

We rose early. While I put on my skiing boots, Mama made me a cup of cocoa—the precious cocoa which she had saved for almost three years for a special occasion.

"Aren't you eating, Mama?" I asked.

"It's Monday," she answered. Mama had fasted every Monday for half a day since Arthur had left.

"But today," I said, "you should eat something."

"Today especially not," she answered from the window, holding the ivory-bound prayer book she had carried as a bride. She prayed and watched me—and I watched her. The chives were uprooted on the windowsill. Yesterday we had taken out the few remaining jewels, sewed some into Papa's jacket, Mama's corset, my coat.

A shrill whistle blew through the ghetto. It was time to leave.

When we had made our way downstairs, we saw the woman with the lovely complexion, Miss Pilzer, screaming and begging to be allowed to go with her mother. The dying old woman was thrown on a truck meant for the aged and ill. Here the SS man kicked her and she screamed. He kicked her again.

On the same truck were Mr. Kollander, the man with paralyzed legs, and the mother with her little girls. The twins were smiling; unaware of what was happening, they were busy catching the raindrops. An epileptic woman was put on the truck; her dog jumped after her. The SS man kicked him away, but the dog kept on trying to get in the truck. To our horror, the SS man pulled his gun and shot

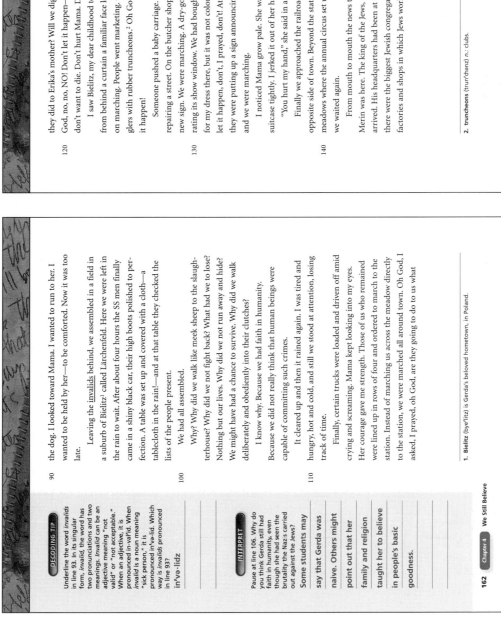

162 Chapter 4 We Still Believe

DECODING TIP

Underline the word *invalids* in line 93. In its singular form, *invalid*, the word has two pronunciations and two meanings. *Invalid* can be an adjective meaning "not valid" or "not acceptable." When an adjective, it is pronounced in·val′id. When *invalid* is a noun meaning "sick person," it is pronounced in′va·lid. Which way is *invalids* pronounced in line 93?

in′va·lidz

INTERPRET

Pause at line 106. Why do you think Gerda still had faith in humanity, even though she had seen the brutality the Nazis carried out against the Jews?

Some students may say that Gerda was naive. Others might point out that her family and religion taught her to believe in people's basic goodness.

---

90 the dog. I looked toward Mama. I wanted to run to her. I wanted to be held by her—to be comforted. Now it was too late.

Leaving the invalids behind, we assembled in a field in a suburb of Bielitz[1] called Larchenfeld. Here we were left in the rain to wait. After about four hours the SS men finally came in a shiny black car, their high boots polished to perfection. A table was set up and covered with a cloth—a tablecloth in the rain!—and at that table they checked the lists of the people present.

100 We had all assembled.

Why? Why did we walk like meek sheep to the slaughterhouse? Why did we not fight back? What had we to lose? Nothing but our lives. Why did we not run away and hide? We might have had a chance to survive. Why did we walk deliberately and obediently into their clutches?

I know why. Because we had faith in humanity. Because we did not really think that human beings were capable of committing such crimes.

It cleared up and then it rained again. I was tired and

110 hungry, hot and cold, and still we stood at attention, losing track of time.

Finally, certain trucks were loaded and driven off amid crying and screaming. Mama kept looking into my eyes. Her courage gave me strength. Those of us who remained were lined up in rows of four and ordered to march to the station. Instead of marching us across the meadow directly to the station, we were marched all around town. Oh God, I asked, I prayed, oh God, are they going to do to us what

---

1. **Bielitz** (bye′litz) is Gerda's beloved hometown, in Poland.

---

they did to Erika's mother? Will we dig our own grave? Oh

120 God, no, NO! Don't let it happen—don't! I am afraid. I don't want to die. Don't hurt Mama. Don't—

I saw Bielitz, my dear childhood town. Here and there from behind a curtain a familiar face looked out. We kept on marching. People went marketing. Guards beat stragglers with rubber truncheons.[2] Oh God, I prayed, don't let it happen!

Someone pushed a baby carriage. Workmen were repairing a street. On the butcher shop they were painting a new sign. We were marching. A dry-goods store was deco-

130 rating its show window. We had bought the flowered fabric for my dress there, but it was not colorfast. Oh God, don't let it happen, don't, I prayed, don't! At the movie theater they were putting up a sign announcing a new feature— and we were marching.

I noticed Mama grow pale. She was gripping her suitcase tightly. I jerked it out of her hand.

"You hurt my hand," she said in a whisper.

Finally we approached the railroad station on the opposite side of town. Beyond the station were open

140 meadows where the annual circus set up its tents. There we waited again.

From mouth to mouth the news traveled: "Merin!" Merin was here. The king of the Jews, as he was called, had arrived. His headquarters had been at Sosnowitz where there were the biggest Jewish congregation, the largest factories and shops in which Jews worked.

---

2. **truncheons** (trun′chənz) n.: clubs.

INFER

Pause at line 134. What do you imagine the people going through their everyday activities were thinking while their neighbors were being forced to march?

Answers will vary.

Gerda Weissmann Klein   163

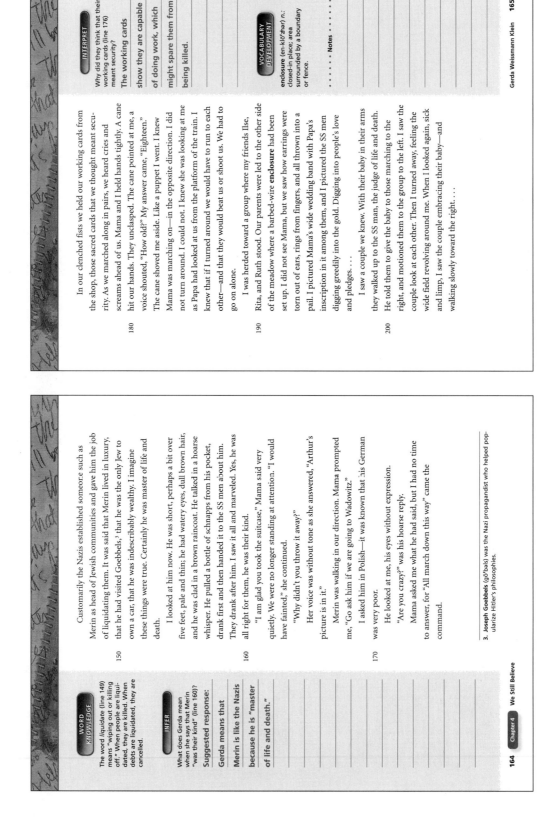

Page 164

WORD KNOWLEDGE

The word *liquidate* (line 149) means "wiping out or killing off." When people are liquidated, they are killed. When debts are liquidated, they are cancelled.

INFER

What does Gerda mean when she says that Merin "was their kind" (line 160)?

Suggested response:

Gerda means that Merin is like the Nazis because he is "master of life and death."

Customarily the Nazis established someone such as Merin as head of Jewish communities and gave him the job of liquidating them. It was said that Merin lived in luxury, that he had visited Goebbels,[3] that he was the only Jew to own a car, that he was indescribably wealthy. I imagine these things were true. Certainly he was master of life and death.

150 I looked at him now. He was short, perhaps a bit over five feet, pale and thin; he had watery eyes, dull brown hair, and he was clad in a brown raincoat. He talked in a hoarse whisper. He pulled a bottle of schnapps from his pocket, drank first and then handed it to the SS men about him. They drank after him. I saw it all and marveled. Yes, he was all right for them, he was their kind.

160 "I am glad you took the suitcase," Mama said very quietly. We were no longer standing at attention. "I would have fainted," she continued.

"Why didn't you throw it away?"

Her voice was without tone as she answered, "Arthur's picture is in it."

Merin was walking in our direction. Mama prompted me, "Go ask him if we are going to Wadowitz."

I asked him in Polish—it was known that his German

170 was very poor.

He looked at me, his eyes without expression.

"Are you crazy?" was his hoarse reply.

Mama asked me what he had said, but I had no time to answer, for "All march down this way" came the command.

3. **Joseph Goebbels** (gö'bəls) was the Nazi propagandist who helped popularize Hitler's philosophies.

Page 165

In our clenched fists we held our working cards from the shop, those sacred cards that we thought meant security. As we marched along in pairs, we heard cries and screams ahead of us. Mama and I held hands tightly. A cane 180 hit our hands. They unclasped. The cane pointed at me, a voice shouted, "How old?" My answer came, "Eighteen." The cane shoved me aside. Like a puppet I went. I knew Mama was marching on—in the opposite direction. I did not turn around. I could not. I knew she was looking at me as Papa had looked at us from the platform of the train. I knew that if I turned around we would have to run to each other—and that they would beat us or shoot us. We had to go on alone.

I was herded toward a group where my friends Ilse, 190 Rita, and Ruth stood. Our parents were led to the other side of the meadow where a barbed-wire **enclosure** had been set up. I did not see Mama, but we saw how earrings were torn out of ears, rings from fingers, and all thrown into a pail. I pictured Mama's wide wedding band with Papa's inscription in it among them, and I pictured the SS men digging greedily into the gold. Digging into people's love and pledges....

I saw a couple we knew. With their baby in their arms they walked up to the SS man, the judge of life and death. 200 He told them to give the baby to those marching to the right, and motioned them to the group to the left. I saw the couple look at each other. Then I turned away, feeling the wide field revolving around me. When I looked again, sick and limp, I saw the couple embracing their baby—and walking slowly toward the right....

INTERPRET

Why did they think that their working cards (line 176) meant security?

The working cards

show they are capable

of doing work, which

might spare them from

being killed.

VOCABULARY DEVELOPMENT

enclosure (en·klō'zhər) *n.*: closed-in place; area surrounded by a boundary or fence.

• • • • • • **Notes** • • • • • • •

Gerda Weissmann Klein **165**

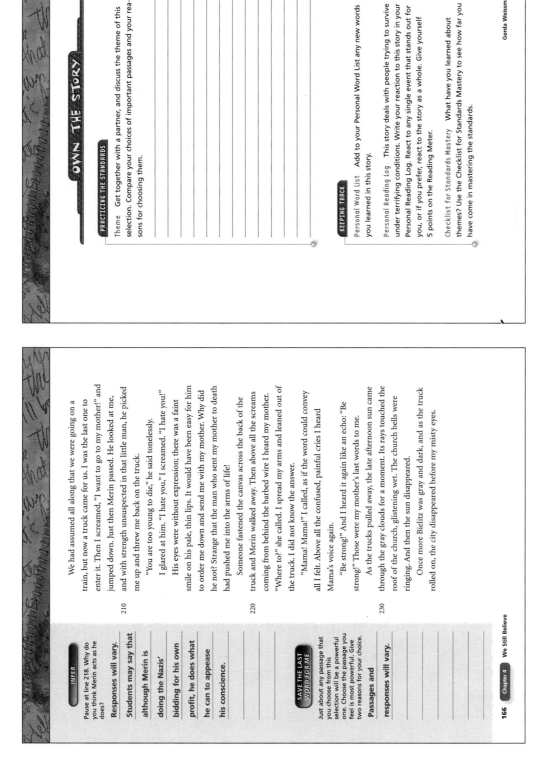

INFER

Pause at line 218. Why do you think Merin acts as he does?

Responses will vary.
Students may say that
although Merin is
doing the Nazis'
bidding for his own
profit, he does what
he can to appease
his conscience.

SAVE THE LAST
WORD FOR ME

Just about any passage that you choose from this selection will be a powerful one. Choose the passage you feel is most powerful. Give two reasons for your choice.

Passages and
responses will vary.

We had assumed all along that we were going on a train, but now a truck came for us. I was the last one to enter it. Then I screamed, "I want to go to my mother!" and jumped down. Just then Merin passed. He looked at me,

210 and with strength unsuspected in that little man, he picked me up and threw me back on the truck.

"You are too young to die," he said tonelessly.

I glared at him. "I hate you," I screamed. "I hate you!"

His eyes were without expression; there was a faint smile on his pale, thin lips. It would have been easy for him to order me down and send me with my mother. Why did he not? Strange that the man who sent my mother to death had pushed me into the arms of life!

Someone fastened the canvas across the back of the

220 truck and Merin walked away. Then above all the screams coming from behind the barbed wire I heard my mother. "Where to?" she called. I spread my arms and leaned out of the truck. I did not know the answer.

"Mama! Mama!" I called, as if the word could convey all I felt. Above all the confused, painful cries I heard Mama's voice again.

"Be strong!" And I heard it again like an echo: "Be strong!" Those were my mother's last words to me.

As the trucks pulled away, the late afternoon sun came

230 through the gray clouds for a moment. Its rays touched the roof of the church, glistening wet. The church bells were ringing. And then the sun disappeared.

Once more Bielitz was gray and dark, and as the truck rolled on, the city disappeared before my misty eyes.

OWN THE STORY

PRACTICING THE STANDARDS

Theme Get together with a partner, and discuss the theme of this selection. Compare your choices of important passages and your reasons for choosing them.

_____

_____

_____

_____

_____

_____

KEEPING TRACK

Personal Word List Add to your Personal Word List any new words you learned in this story.

Personal Reading Log This story deals with people trying to survive under terrifying conditions. Write your reaction to this story in your Personal Reading Log. React to any single event that stands out for you, or if you prefer, react to the story as a whole. Give yourself 5 points on the Reading Meter.

Checklist for Standards Mastery What have you learned about themes? Use the Checklist for Standards Mastery to see how far you have come in mastering the standards.

Information

PUBLIC DOCUMENT

BEFORE YOU READ

The following text is taken from parts of a Web site dedicated to the memory of Anne Frank and her family. When online, users can navigate the site by clicking buttons. Here, you'll turn the pages to learn about the Franks.

An Anne Frank Scrapbook

Frankfurt, Germany ■ 1929–1933

Anne Frank, born on June 12, 1929, was the second daughter of Otto and Edith Frank, both from respected German-Jewish families.

Anneliese Frank sleeping in a crib shortly after her birth.

From *Anne Frank: Her Life and Times*, accessed May 23, 2001, at http://www.annefrank.com/site/af_life/af_scrpbk/af_scrpbk01/history01.html.
Copyright © 2001 by *Anne Frank Center USA Inc.* Reprinted by permission of the publisher.

Reading Standard 2.3 (Grade 6 Review) Connect and clarify main ideas by identifying their relationships to other sources and related topics.

TEXT STRUCTURE

Skim through this selection, paying close attention to the headings. How is this selection organized? Students should realize that it is organized chronologically.

_____
_____
_____
_____
_____
_____
_____
_____

PROJECT

Out of the Ghetto ■ *Interactive Reading, page 159*

Go Beyond a Literary Text

Museum Brochure   The U.S. Holocaust Memorial Museum was chartered by Congress in 1980. It is dedicated to educating the public about the Holocaust and to providing a memorial to all those who suffered and died at the hands of the Nazi regime. Research this museum, and create a brochure for visitors. Use the template that follows to help guide your research.

The Museum and Its Mission: _____

Museum Location: _____

Hours/Tours: _____

Collections and Archives: _____

Online Exhibits: _____

Other: _____

Graphic Organizer

Page 170

DECODING TIP

This selection contains many European names. Languages such as German and Dutch pronounce many letters differently from English. For example, in *Aachen* (line 7), the *ch* is not pronounced as in *church*. It is pronounced as in *Bach*.

VOCABULARY DEVELOPMENT

tolerance (tal'ər-əns) *n.*: respect for views different from your own.

INTERPRET

What is ironic about Otto Frank's having served in the German army?

He fought for the people who would later kill his family.

Otto Frank could trace his family heritage in Frankfurt back to the seventeenth century, and Edith Hollander Frank came from a prominent Aachen family.

Anne and her older sister, Margot, were raised in Germany in an atmosphere of **tolerance**; the Franks had friends of many faiths and nationalities. Otto Frank served honorably as an officer in the German army during World War I.

Anne and her sister, Margot, with their father before their move to Amsterdam.

The Move to Amsterdam ■ 1933–1940

However, the circumstances of the early 1930s dramatically altered the situation for the Frank family. In the summer of 1933, Otto Frank left Frankfurt for Amsterdam to set up a branch of his brother's company called the Dutch Opekta Company.

Page 171

· · · · · · Notes · · · · · ·

Anne, her mother, and Margot hold hands in Frankfurt before their move.

Less than a year later, Edith, Margot, and Anne (four years old) joined Otto in Amsterdam.

A portrait (right) of Anne taken in a photo booth. The date and her weight are printed on the border.

SEPT 11 1934

By the mid-1930s, the Franks were settling into a normal routine in their apartment at 37 Merwedeplein: The girls were attending school, the family took vacations at the beach, and their circle of Jewish and non-Jewish friends grew.

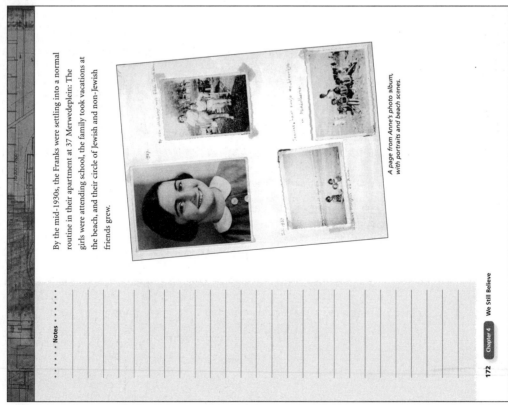

A page from Anne's photo album, with portraits and beach scenes.

Chapter 4 We Still Believe   172

In 1938, Otto expanded his business, going into partnership with a merchant, Hermann van Pels, also a Jewish refugee from Nazi Germany.

Living Under Nazi Rule ■ 1940–1942

30 Unfortunately, the Frank's belief that Amsterdam offered them a safe **haven** from Nazism was shattered when, in May 1940, Germany invaded the Netherlands and the Franks were once again forced to live under Nazi rule.

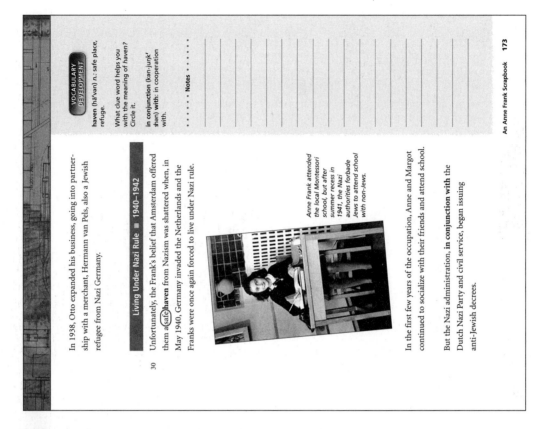

Anne Frank attended the local Montessori school, but after summer recess in 1941, the Nazi authorities forbade Jews to attend school with non-Jews.

In the first few years of the occupation, Anne and Margot continued to socialize with their friends and attend school.

But the Nazi administration, **in conjunction with** the Dutch Nazi Party and civil service, began issuing anti-Jewish decrees.

VOCABULARY DEVELOPMENT

haven (hā'ven) *n.:* safe place, refuge.

What clue word helps you with the meaning of *haven*? Circle it.

in conjunction (kən-junk' shən) **with:** in cooperation with.

· · · · · · · **Notes**

An Anne Frank Scrapbook   173

Page 174

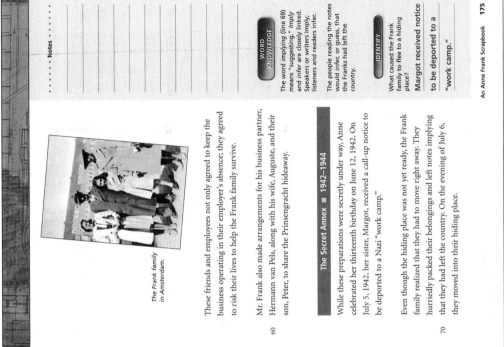

In May 1942, all Jews aged six and older were required to wear a yellow Star of David on their clothes. This was to set them apart from non-Jews.

All Jews had to register their businesses and, later, surrender them to non-Jews. Fortunately, Otto Frank, in anticipation of this decree, had already turned his business over to his non-Jewish colleagues Victor Kugler and Johannes Kleiman.

The Franks Plan to Go into Hiding ■ 1942

By 1942, mass arrests of Jews and mandatory service in German "work camps" were becoming routine. Fearful for their lives, the Frank family began to prepare to go into hiding.

They already had a place in mind—an annex of rooms above Otto Frank's office at 263 Prinsengracht in Amsterdam.

In addition, people on the office staff in the Dutch Opekta Company had agreed to help them. Besides Kugler and Kleiman, there were Miep and Jan Gies, Bep Voskuijl, and Bep's father—all considered to be trustworthy.

40

50

The word *mandatory,* in the first line under the heading, means "forced." It means that the Jews were handed over to authorities and forced to work in the camps.

The word is based on *manus,* Latin for "hand." How is *manus* used in *manufacture, manual,* and *mandate*? **Both** *manufacture* **and** *manual* **refer to making things with one's hands. A** *mandate* **is an order or command that is usually written (by hand).**

Page 175

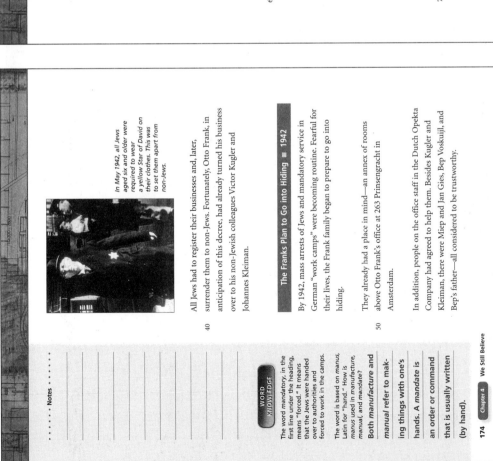

The Frank family in Amsterdam.

These friends and employees not only agreed to keep the business operating in their employer's absence; they agreed to risk their lives to help the Frank family survive.

Mr. Frank also made arrangements for his business partner, Hermann van Pels, along with his wife, Auguste, and their son, Peter, to share the Prinsengracht hideaway.

The Secret Annex ■ 1942–1944

While these preparations were secretly under way, Anne celebrated her thirteenth birthday on June 12, 1942. On July 5, 1942, her sister, Margot, received a call-up notice to be deported to a Nazi "work camp."

Even though the hiding place was not yet ready, the Frank family realized that they had to move right away. They hurriedly packed their belongings and left notes implying that they had left the country. On the evening of July 6, they moved into their hiding place.

60

70

The word *implying* (line 69) means "suggesting." *Imply* and *infer* are closely linked. Speakers or writers imply; listeners and readers infer.

The people reading the notes would *infer,* or guess, that the Franks had left the country.

What caused the Frank family to flee to a hiding place?

Margot received notice to be deported to a "work camp."

Less than two months after this photo was taken, Anne and her family went into hiding.

A week later, on July 13, the van Pels family joined the Franks. On November 16, 1942, the Secret Annex were joined by its eighth and final resident, Fritz Pfeffer.

For two years the Franks were part of an extended family in the Annex, sharing a confined space and living under constant dread of detection and arrest by the Nazis and

80   their Dutch sympathizers.

Arrest and Deportation ■ 1944

At approximately 10 A.M., August 4, 1944, the Frank family's greatest fear came true. A Nazi policeman and several Dutch collaborators appeared at 263 Prinsengracht, having received an anonymous phone call about Jews hiding there. They charged straight for the bookcase leading to the Secret Annex.

WORD KNOWLEDGE

A *collaborator* (kə-lab′ə-rā′tər) in this context (line 83) is someone who works with the enemy. Collaborators can also be people who work together on projects.

Karl Joseph Silberbauer, an Austrian Nazi, forced the residents to turn over all valuables. When he found out that Otto Frank had been a lieutenant in the German

90   army during World War I, he was a little less hostile. The residents were taken from the house, forced into a covered truck, taken to the Central Office for Jewish Emigration, and then to Weteringschans Prison.

Two of the helpers, Victor Kugler and Johannes Kleiman, were also imprisoned for their role in hiding the family. Miep Gies and Bep Voskuijl were not arrested, although Miep was brought in for questioning by the police.

A hinged bookcase at the rear of the office wall was all that separated the Secret Annex from the outside world.

On August 8, 1944, after a brief stay in Weteringschans

100   Prison, the residents of the Secret Annex were moved to Westerbork transit camp. They remained there for nearly a month, until September 3, when they were transported to the Auschwitz death camp in Poland. It was the last Auschwitz-bound transport ever to leave Westerbork.

INTERPRET

Re-read the last sentence on this page. What powerful irony does this sentence convey—that is, a sense that we know something that the people involved do not know?

We know now that if the Franks had been able to hold out for a month, they may have survived. They of course did not know this.

In October 1944, Anne and Margot were transported from Auschwitz to the Bergen-Belsen concentration camp in Germany. Thousands died from planned starvation and epidemics at Bergen-Belsen, which was without food, heat, medicine, or elementary sanitary conditions.

Hundreds of women and children were packed into one room at the Bergen-Belsen concentration camp. Bergen-Belsen became overcrowded with prisoners as the Nazis retreated from the Eastern Front.

Anne and Margot, already **debilitated** (contracted typhus and grew even sicker) Margot, nineteen years old, and Anne, fifteen years old, died in February and March, 1945.

After the War

Otto Frank was the only resident of the Annex to survive the Holocaust. He found it difficult to settle permanently in Amsterdam with its constant reminders of his lost family.

He and his second wife, Elfried Geiringer, also an Auschwitz survivor, moved to Basel, Switzerland, in 1953. Otto Frank died on August 19, 1980; he was ninety-one.

110

· · · · · · Notes · · · · · ·

VOCABULARY DEVELOPMENT

debilitated (dĕ-bĭl'ə-tāt'ad) *adj.:* weakened; made feeble.

Circle the words that help you figure out the meaning of *debilitated*.

CONNECT

This Web site reveals what one family—the Franks—experienced during World War II. Where might you look to find other sources on the topic of World War II? The library and Internet contain a wealth of information on the war.

OWN THE TEXT

PRACTICING THE STANDARDS

Main Ideas What ideas about the human condition can you draw from this collection of photographs and text?

Work with a partner to write a paragraph about the main ideas you can infer from "An Anne Frank Scrapbook" and from Gerda Weissmann Klein's account of her experiences.

_____

_____

A Poem from a Photograph Take one of the photographs in this scrapbook that you find especially interesting. Write a poem about the picture and the people in it. You do not have to find rhymes; you should find strong images to describe what you see in the picture and how it makes you feel. Give your poem a title.

_____

_____

_____

KEEPING TRACK

Personal Word List Add the new words you encountered to your Personal Word List. Look and listen for new words about history in newspapers, in magazines, and on television.

Personal Reading Log As you add this selection to your Personal Reading Log, write about the part that most interested you. Give yourself 2 points on the Reading Meter.

Checklist for Standards Mastery Use the Checklist for Standards Mastery to see how far you have come in mastering the standards.

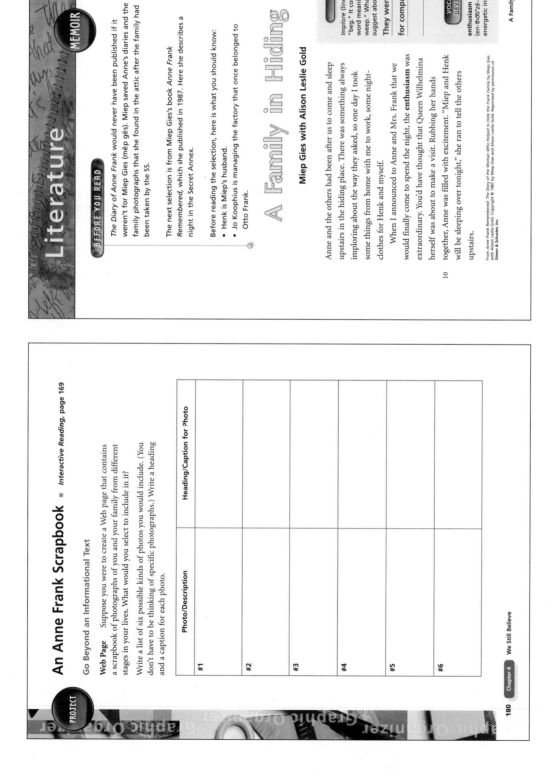

PROJECT

An Anne Frank Scrapbook ■ *Interactive Reading, page 169*

Go Beyond an Informational Text

Web Page Suppose you were to create a Web page that contains a scrapbook of photographs of you and your family from different stages in your lives. What would you select to include in it?

Write a list of six possible kinds of photos you would include. (You don't have to be thinking of specific photographs.) Write a heading and a caption for each photo.

	Photo/Description	Heading/Caption for Photo
#1		
#2		
#3		
#4		
#5		
#6		

180 Chapter 4 We Still Believe

Literature

BEFORE YOU READ

MEMOIR

The Diary of Anne Frank would never have been published if it weren't for Miep Gies (mēp gēs). Miep saved Anne's diaries and the family photographs that she found in the attic after the family had been taken by the SS.

The next selection is from Miep Gies's book *Anne Frank Remembered,* which she published in 1987. Here she describes a night in the Secret Annex.

Before reading the selection, here is what you should know:
- Henk is Miep's husband.
- Jo Koophius is managing the factory that once belonged to Otto Frank.

A Family in Hiding

Miep Gies with Alison Leslie Gold

Anne and the others had been after us to come and sleep upstairs in the hiding place. There was something always imploring about the way they asked, so one day I took some things from home with me to work, some night-clothes for Henk and myself.

When I announced to Anne and Mrs. Frank that we would finally come to spend the night, the **enthusiasm** was extraordinary. You'd have thought that Queen Wilhelmina herself was about to make a visit. Rubbing her hands together, Anne was filled with excitement. "Miep and Henk will be sleeping over tonight," she ran to tell the others upstairs.

10

From *Anne Frank Remembered: The Story of the Woman Who Helped to Hide the Frank Family* by Miep Gies with Alison Leslie Gold. Copyright © 1987 by Miep Gies and Alison Leslie Gold. Reprinted by permission of *Simon & Schuster, Inc.*

INFER

Implore (line 3) means "beg." It comes from a Latin word meaning "cry out, weep." What does this word suggest about the family?

They were desperate

for company.

VOCABULARY DEVELOPMENT

enthusiasm
(en-thō̅ō′zē-az′əm) *n.:* energetic interest.

A Family in Hiding **181**

Reading Standard 3.5 Identify and analyze recurring themes (e.g., good versus evil) across traditional and contemporary works.

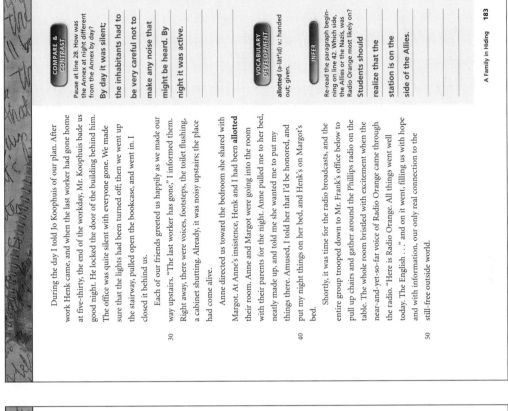

During the day I told Jo Koophuis of our plan. After work Henk came, and when the last worker had gone home at five-thirty, the end of the workday, Mr. Koophuis bade us good night. He locked the door of the building behind him. The office was quite silent with everyone gone. We made sure that the lights had been turned off; then we went up the stairway, pulled open the bookcase, and went in. I closed it behind us.

30 Each of our friends greeted us happily as we made our way upstairs. "The last worker has gone," I informed them. Right away, there were voices, footsteps, the toilet flushing, a cabinet shutting. Already, it was noisy upstairs; the place had come alive.

Anne directed us toward the bedroom she shared with Margot. At Anne's insistence, Henk and I had been **allotted** their room. Anne and Margot were going into the room with their parents for the night. Anne pulled me to her bed, neatly made up, and told me she wanted me to put my things there. Amused, I told her that I'd be honored, and 40 put my night things on her bed, and Henk's on Margot's bed.

Shortly, it was time for the radio broadcasts, and the entire group trooped down to Mr. Frank's office below to pull up chairs and gather around the Phillips radio on the table. The whole room bristled with excitement when the near-and-yet-so-far voice of Radio Orange came through the radio. "Here is Radio Orange. All things went well today. The English . . ." and on it went, filling us with hope and with information, our only real connection to the 50 still-free outside world.

COMPARE & CONTRAST

Pause at line 28. How was the Annex at night different from the Annex by day?

By day it was silent; the inhabitants had to be very careful not to make any noise that might be heard. By night it was active.

VOCABULARY DEVELOPMENT

allotted (ə-lät'ĭd) v.: handed out; given.

INFER

Re-read the paragraph beginning on line 42. Which side, the Allies or the Nazis, was Radio Orange most likely on?

Students should realize that the station is on the side of the Allies.

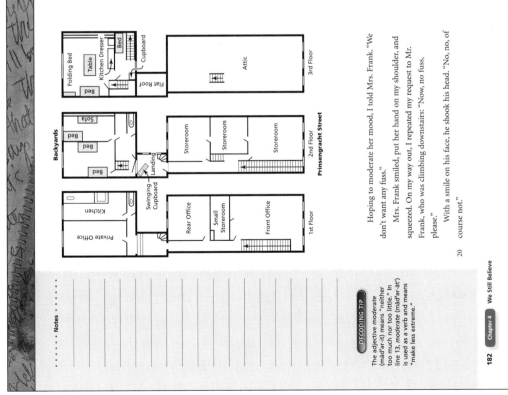

Backyards
Prinsengracht Street

Folding Bed | Table | Kitchen Dresser | Bed | Cupboard
Bed | Bed | Sofa | Bed
Swinging Cupboard | Landing
Kitchen | Private Office | Rear Office | Small Storeroom | Front Office
Storeroom | Storeroom | Storeroom
Flat Roof | Attic
1st Floor | 2nd Floor | 3rd Floor

DECODING TIP

The adjective *moderate* (mŏd'ər-ĭt) means "neither too much nor too little." In line 13, *moderate* (mŏd'ə-rāt') is used as a verb and means "make less extreme."

Hoping to moderate her mood, I told Mrs. Frank, "We don't want any fuss."

Mrs. Frank smiled, put her hand on my shoulder, and squeezed. On my way out, I repeated my request to Mr. Frank, who was climbing downstairs: "Now, no fuss, please."

20 With a smile on his face, he shook his head. "No, no, of course not."

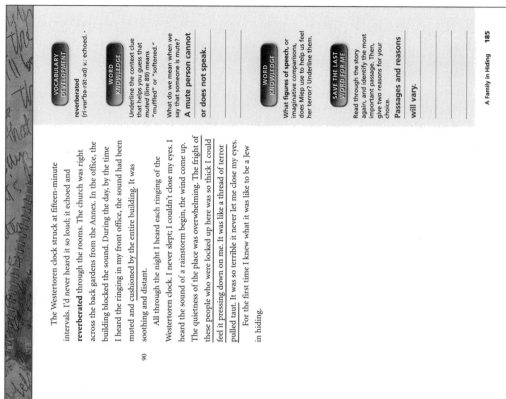

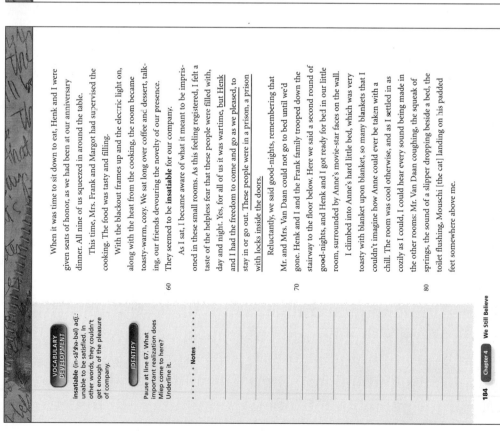

VOCABULARY DEVELOPMENT

insatiable (in-sā′sha-bal) *adj.:* unable to be satisfied. In other words, they couldn't get enough of the pleasure of company.

IDENTIFY

Pause at line 67. What important realization does Miep come to here? Underline it.

•••••• Notes ••••••

When it was time to sit down to eat, Henk and I were given seats of honor, as we had been at our anniversary dinner. All nine of us squeezed in around the table.

This time, Mrs. Frank and Margot had supervised the cooking. The food was tasty and filling.

With the blackout frames up and the electric light on, along with the heat from the cooking, the room became toasty-warm, cozy. We sat long over coffee and dessert, talk-
60 ing, our friends devouring the novelty of our presence. They seemed to be **insatiable** for our company.

As I sat, I became aware of what it meant to be impris-oned in these small rooms. As this feeling registered, I felt a taste of the helpless fear that these people were filled with, day and night. Yes, for all of us it was wartime, but Henk and I had the freedom to come and go as we pleased, to stay in or go out. These people were in a prison, a prison with locks inside the doors.

Reluctantly, we said good-nights, remembering that Mr. and Mrs. Van Daan could not go to bed until we'd
70 gone. Henk and I and the Frank family trooped down the stairway to the floor below. Here we said a second round of good-nights, and Henk and I got ready for bed in our little room, surrounded by Anne's movie-star faces on the wall.

I climbed into Anne's hard little bed, which was very toasty with blanket upon blanket, so many blankets that I couldn't imagine how Anne could ever be taken with a chill. The room was cool otherwise, and as I settled in as cozily as I could, I could hear every sound being made in the other rooms: Mr. Van Daan coughing, the squeak of
80 springs, the sound of a slipper dropping beside a bed, the toilet flushing, Mouschi [the cat] landing on his padded feet somewhere above me.

The Westertoren clock struck at fifteen-minute intervals. I'd never heard it so loud; it echoed and **reverberated** through the rooms. The church was right across the back gardens from the Annex. In the office, the building blocked the sound. During the day, by the time I heard the ringing in my front office, the sound had been muted and cushioned by the entire building. It was
90 soothing and distant.

All through the night I heard each ringing of the Westertoren clock. I never slept; I couldn't close my eyes. I heard the sound of a rainstorm begin, the wind come up. The quietness of the place was overwhelming. The fright of these people who were locked up here was so thick I could feel it pressing down on me. It was like a thread of terror pulled taut. It was so terrible it never let me close my eyes. For the first time I knew what it was like to be a Jew in hiding.

VOCABULARY DEVELOPMENT

reverberated (ri-vur′ba-rāt-ad) *v.:* echoed.

WORD KNOWLEDGE

Underline the context clue that helps you guess that *muted* (line 89) means "muffled" or "softened."

What do we mean when we say that someone is mute? **A mute person cannot or does not speak.**

WORD KNOWLEDGE

What figures of speech, or imaginative comparisons, does Miep use to help us feel her terror? Underline them.

SAVE THE LAST WORD FOR ME

Read through the story again, and identify the most important passage. Then, give two reasons for your choice. **Passages and reasons will vary.**

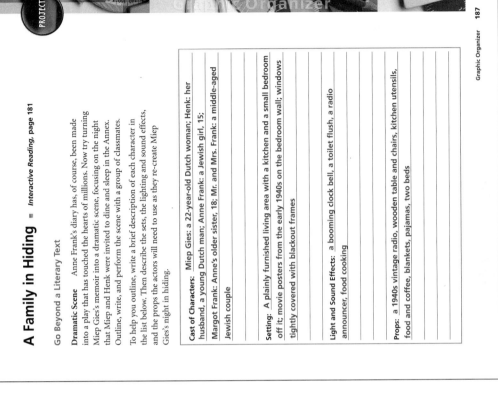

PROJECT — Graphic Organizer

A Family in Hiding ■ *Interactive Reading*, page 181

Go Beyond a Literary Text

Dramatic Scene   Anne Frank's diary has, of course, been made into a play that has touched the hearts of millions. Now try turning Miep Gies's memoir into a dramatic scene, focusing on the night that Miep and Henk were invited to dine and sleep in the Annex. Outline, write, and perform the scene with a group of classmates.

To help you outline, write a brief description of each character in the list below. Then describe the sets, the lighting and sound effects, and the props the actors will need to use as they re-create Miep Gies's night in hiding.

Cast of Characters: Miep Gies: a 22-year-old Dutch woman; Henk: her husband, a young Dutch man; Anne Frank: a Jewish girl, 15; Margot Frank: Anne's older sister, 18; Mr. and Mrs. Frank: a middle-aged Jewish couple

Setting: A plainly furnished living area with a kitchen and a small bedroom off it; movie posters from the early 1940s on the bedroom wall; windows tightly covered with blackout frames

Light and Sound Effects: a booming clock bell, a toilet flush, a radio announcer, food cooking

Props: a 1940s vintage radio, wooden table and chairs, kitchen utensils, food and coffee, blankets, pajamas, two beds

Graphic Organizer   **187**

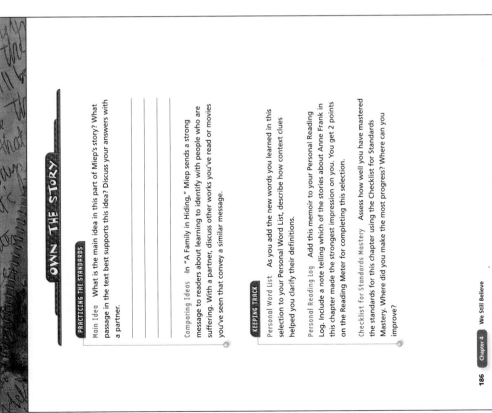

OWN THE STORY

PRACTICING THE STANDARDS

Main Idea   What is the main idea in this part of Miep's story? What passage in the text best supports this idea? Discuss your answers with a partner.

Comparing Ideas   In "A Family in Hiding," Miep sends a strong message to readers about learning to identify with people who are suffering. With a partner, discuss other works you've read or movies you've seen that convey a similar message.

KEEPING TRACK

Personal Word List   As you add the new words you learned in this selection to your Personal Word List, describe how context clues helped you clarify their definitions.

Personal Reading Log   Add this memoir to your Personal Reading Log. Include a note telling which of the stories about Anne Frank in this chapter made the strongest impression on you. You get 2 points on the Reading Meter for completing this selection.

Checklist for Standards Mastery   Assess how well you have mastered the standards for this chapter using the Checklist for Standards Mastery. Where did you make the most progress? Where can you improve?

186   Chapter 4   We Still Believe

Chapter 5

Imagine That!

Literary Devices

Chapter Preview In this chapter you will—

Strategy Launch: "Charting Literary Devices"

LITERARY FOCUS: LITERARY DEVICES

When you interpret a work of literature, you look for **literary devices.** Writers use many literary devices to tell a story or write a poem. Some writers use a great deal of description. They use **similes** to compare unlike things, using a word such as *like* or *as.* They use **metaphors** to compare unlike things without a specific word of comparison. They use **personification** to make a nonhuman thing come alive. They use **irony** to make us sense the gap between what seems appropriate and what actually happens in life. They use **dialect** to help us hear how people talk. Writers also experiment with **sentence length.** Some use long complex sentences. Others prefer short punchy sentences. All of these devices make up a writer's special **style.**

A STRATEGY THAT WORKS: "CHARTING LITERARY DEVICES"

The following strategy will help you examine a text for certain literary devices. Once you have combed the text for these devices, ask yourself: "How do these devices help me interpret a plot, a character, or a theme?"

POINTERS FOR "CHARTING LITERARY DEVICES"

➤ First, read the text for enjoyment. Put sticky notes on passages that stand out for you. You'll return to them later. (In this book you can mark up the story, so you might put a star next to passages you think are significant.)

➤ Next, re-read the passages you marked up. Mark passages that use devices such as repetition, figures of speech, irony, or dialect.

➤ Finally, ask yourself: "What do those passages contribute to the text's plot, characterization, or theme?"

Reading Standard 1.1 Analyze idioms, analogies, metaphors, and similes to infer the literal and figurative meanings of phrases.

Reading Standard 2.8 (Grade 6 Review) Note instances of fallacious reasoning in text.

Reading Standard 3.6 Identify significant literary devices (e.g., metaphor, symbolism, dialect, irony) that define a writer's style, and use those elements to interpret the work.

Strategy Launch **189**

Practice Read

BEFORE YOU READ

Your roof leaks. You hire someone to fix it, and he turns out to be very strange and a little scary. Not only does he fail to fix the roof, but he keeps asking for more money and threatens you for not paying. You begin to hate him. Hate is a powerful feeling, but can it actually make things happen?

The Overhead Man

Dan Greenberg

CHARTING LITERARY DEVICES

Pause at line 11. Underline words that are repeated so far. What effect does the repetition have on you? **"Drip, drip, drip" helps me *hear* the leak. It also creates tension.**

WORD KNOWLEDGE

An idiom is an expression peculiar to a particular language. An idiom does not mean what it literally says. Underline the idiom in line 15. What does it say literally? What does it mean figuratively? **Literally: Cats and dogs fell from the sky. Figuratively: It rained very hard.**

Drip, drip, drip.

That was how it started. With drips. The roof in my parlor was leaking.

Drip, drip, drip.

The drips were constant, never-ending. Morning, noon, night.

Drip, drip, drip.

10 What could I do? I thought of trying to fix it, but I couldn't climb up there. When it was built back a hundred years ago, my house had been a barn. Now it's a house with ceilings almost forty feet high.

"You'll need to wait until the rainy season ends," Felton, my next-door neighbor, told me.

Wonderful, I thought. The previous year, 1905, it rained cats and dogs for two and a half months straight here in San Francisco.

Drip, drip, drip.

I didn't know what I was going to do. Then, by pure chance, a notice on a wall jumped at me out of the blue.

20 "MAGGS & SON," it read. "Will fix anything. Chimneys, coal stoves, roofs, leaks. Satisfaction Guaranteed."

Perfect, I thought.

Maggs & Son turned out to be Maggs only. The first of Maggs's lies.

Maggs spat tobacco juice, missing my shoe by a mere inch and a half.

Maggs was a rough and raw sort with wild red-gray hair, a big red mustache, and bulging eyes. His teeth were stained brown with tobacco juice. His face was so red and sore it looked as if he'd scrubbed it with a metal brush.

30 "What can I do for ye, Mizz—"

"Derby," I said. "Lucy Derby. I have a leak, Mr. Maggs, in my roof."

I showed him the leak. He told me he'd fix it for five dollars. That sounded fine to me, so we shook hands on it. Maggs went about his business, and I went about mine.

Maggs brought over his tools and ladders. Then he climbed up on the roof, tying himself in with ropes for safety. For about an hour, I heard him banging around up there. When he came down (he was even redder in the face) if that were possible.

40 "She's all done," he told me.

"*She?*" I said.

"Your roof," he said. "Won't be givin' ye problems no more."

I paid him the five dollars, relieved to have the roof fixed. Or so I thought. The leak did stop, at least until midnight that night. Then it started again.

Drip, drip, drip.

WORD KNOWLEDGE

Underline "out of the blue" in line 19. What does this idiom mean literally? What does it mean figuratively? **Literally, it means that something fell from the blue sky. Figuratively, it means something appeared very suddenly and unexpectedly.**

PREDICT

What do you expect to happen later in the story, based on lines 23–24? **Maggs will lie about something.**

PREDICT

Why do you suppose the writer mentions these ropes (line 38)? **The ropes may play a part later in the story.**

CHARTING LITERARY DEVICES

Circle the words that describe Maggs on this page. What kind of character do you think he is? **Answers will vary.**

VOCABULARY DEVELOPMENT

erupt (ē-rupt') v.: burst forth.

EVALUATE

Pause at line 59. Do you believe Maggs's explanation? Explain.

Most students will not believe the explanation, because it is illogical. Maggs is a con man.

PREDICT

Pause at line 74. What do you think is going to happen to the red brick house?

Most students will predict that it will burn down or be destroyed in some way.

WORD KNOWLEDGE

Underline the idiom "hit the road" in line 76. What does it mean literally? What does it mean figuratively?

Literally it means Maggs smacked the road with his hand.

Figuratively, it means he took off, he left.

---

50   I went and got Maggs the next morning. He went through the same routine. He climbed up on the roof, banged around a while, then came down and told me it was all fixed. Only this time, the fee was ten dollars.

"Ten dollars!" I cried.

He explained. It was a new leak, a bigger one this time. Sometimes, he said, fixing one leak caused a new leak to erupt. This explanation didn't make much sense to me, but I let it go. I had work to do. I paid him the money, and all was fine—for two days.

60   Drip, drip, drip.

The leak came back. Maggs came back, too, and he did pretty much the same thing. Only this time he asked for fifty dollars.

"Fifty dollars!" I protested. I told I would not pay him fifty dollars, not for fixing the same leak he was supposed to have "fixed" earlier. In fact, I told him that I wasn't going to pay him anything at all.

"Well that's a shame," he said, wiping his grizzled chin.

"Why is that a shame?" I asked.

70   "Because things seem to happen to people who don't pay me my money."

I blinked. "Things?"

"There's a red brick house on Nob Hill, near the hotel," he said. "You watch that house."

Watch that house? Whatever did he mean by that? Maggs wouldn't explain. He hit the road without his money. Two days later, on page 4 of the *Chronicle*, I saw it. A red brick house on Nob Hill had burned to the ground.

A chill went down my spine.

80   Had Maggs been threatening me? Fortunately, my roof was holding up fine. There were no more leaks. I hoped

---

that was the end of my dealings with Maggs, but I was not so lucky.

Two days after I read about the fire, he showed up.

"Mizz Derby," he said with an oily smile.

"Mr. Maggs," I said. "My roof is fine. The drips haven't returned. I don't believe I called for your services."

He spat some tobacco juice which again nearly hit my feet. "I come for me money," he said.

90   I explained that I didn't intend to pay him any more money.

"Well," he said. "Ain't that a shame. Did ye hear about the red brick house, Mizz Derby?"

"Are you threatening me?" I asked.

He smiled an evil, tobacco-brown smile. It was clear: The price had gone up, too, to one hundred dollars.

"This is outrageous!" I said.

Maggs flashed another evil smile, then spat. "Ye do what ye like, Mizz Derby," he said.

100   The rest is a blur to me. I remember going inside and trying to forget the whole situation. Then the dripping started again.

Drip, drip, drip.

No, it was not my imagination. But how was it possible? Had Maggs climbed up there and poked a new hole in the roof? How could he have? I would have heard him.

I couldn't sleep that night. The dripping had gotten to me. In the morning I was going to pieces. I had to do something, so I spoke to Felton, my neighbor.

110   He said he could help. His brother-in-law knew someone. He'd get the word out.

CHARTING LITERARY DEVICES

Circle the words on this page that describe Maggs's appearance and actions. What do these descriptions tell you about the character of Maggs?

His smile is oily, evil, tobacco-brown. He spits close to Lucy's shoes. He asks for more money. He hints that he will burn her house down. He is not trustworthy.

WORD KNOWLEDGE

Underline the idiom "going to pieces" in line 109. What does it mean literally? What does it mean figuratively?

Literally it means she broke into many pieces. Figuratively it means she is very nervous and losing control.

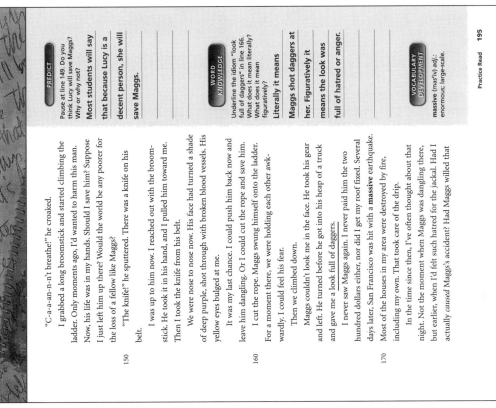

Pause at line 149. Do you think Lucy will save Maggs? Why or why not?

Most students will say that because Lucy is a decent person, she will save Maggs.

"C-a-a-n-n-n't breathe!" he croaked.

I grabbed a long broomstick and started climbing the ladder. Only moments ago, I'd wanted to harm this man. Now, his life was in my hands. Should I save him? Suppose I just left him up there? Would the world be any poorer for the loss of a fellow like Maggs?

150 "The knife!" he sputtered. There was a knife on his belt.

I was up to him now. I reached out with the broomstick. He took it in his hand, and I pulled him toward me. Then I took the knife from his belt.

We were nose to nose now. His face had turned a shade of deep purple, shot through with broken blood vessels. His yellow eyes bulged at me.

It was my last chance. I could push him back now and leave him dangling. Or I could cut the rope and save him.

160 I cut the rope. Maggs swung himself onto the ladder. For a moment there, we were holding each other awkwardly. I could feel his fear.

Then we climbed down.

Maggs couldn't look me in the face. He took his gear and left. He turned before he got into his heap of a truck and gave me a look full of daggers.

I never saw Maggs again. I never paid him the two hundred dollars either, nor did I get my roof fixed. Several days later, San Francisco was hit with a **massive** earthquake. Most of the houses in my area were destroyed by fire, including my own. That took care of the drip.

170 In the time since then, I've often thought about that night. Not the moment when Maggs was dangling there, but earlier, when I'd felt such hatred for the jackal. Had I actually *caused* Maggs's accident? Had Maggs willed that

Underline the idiom "look full of daggers" in line 166. What does it mean literally? What does it mean figuratively?

Literally it means

Maggs shot daggers at her. Figuratively it means the look was full of hatred or anger.

massive (măs'ĭv) *adj.*: enormous; large-scale.

Practice Read **195**

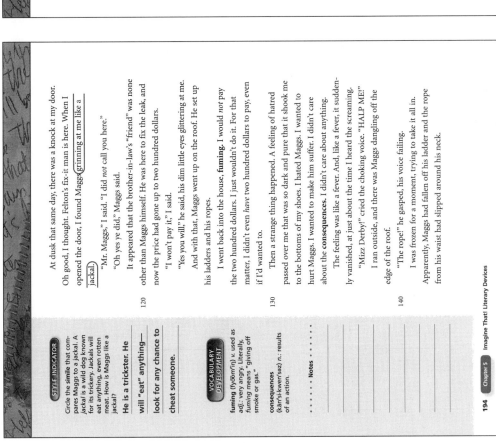

Circle the **simile** that compares Maggs to a jackal. A *jackal* is a wild dog known for its trickery. Jackals will eat anything, even rotten meat. How is Maggs like a jackal?

He is a trickster. He will "eat" anything— look for any chance to cheat someone.

fuming (fyōom'ĭn) *v.* used as *adj.*; very angry. Literally, *fuming* means "giving off smoke or gas."

consequences (kän'sĭ-kwen'săz) *n.*: results of an action.

. . . . . . **Notes** . . . . . .

At dusk that same day, there was a knock at my door. Oh good, I thought. Felton's fix-it man is here. When I opened the door, I found Maggs grinning at me like a jackal.

"Mr. Maggs," I said. "I did *not* call you here."

"Oh yes ye did," Maggs said.

It appeared that the brother-in-law's "friend" was none other than Maggs himself. He was here to fix the leak, and now the price had gone up to two hundred dollars.

120 "I won't pay it," I said.

"Yes you will," he said, his dim little eyes glittering at me. And with that, Maggs went up on the roof. He set up his ladders and his ropes.

I went back into the house, **fuming**. I would *not* pay the two hundred dollars. I just wouldn't do it. For that matter, I didn't even *have* two hundred dollars to pay, even if I'd wanted to.

130 Then a strange thing happened. A feeling of hatred passed over me that was so dark and pure that it shook me to the bottoms of my shoes. I hated Maggs. I wanted to hurt Maggs. I wanted to make him suffer. I didn't care about the **consequences**. I didn't care about anything.

The feeling was like a fever. And, like a fever, it suddenly vanished, at just about the time I heard the screaming. "Mizz Derby!" cried the choking voice. "HALP ME!" I ran outside, and there was Maggs dangling off the edge of the roof.

140 "The rope!" he gasped, his voice failing.

I was frozen for a moment, trying to take it all in. Apparently, Maggs had fallen off his ladder and the rope from his waist had slipped around his neck.

194 Chapter 5 Imagine That! Literary Devices

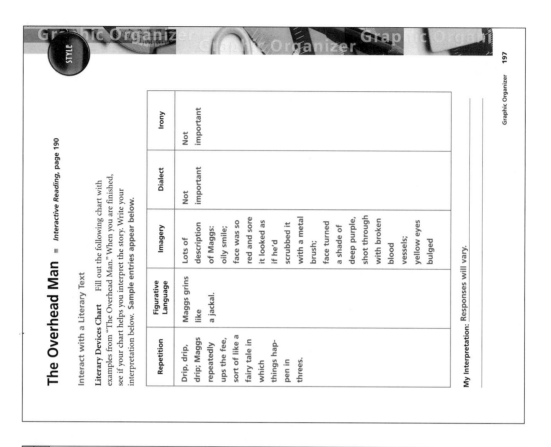

STYLE

The Overhead Man ■ *Interactive Reading, page 190*

Interact with a Literary Text

Literary Devices Chart Fill out the following chart with examples from "The Overhead Man." When you are finished, see if your chart helps you interpret the story. Write your interpretation below. **Sample entries appear below.**

Repetition	Figurative Language	Imagery	Dialect	Irony
Drip, drip, drip; Maggs repeatedly ups the fee, sort of like a fairy tale in which things happen in threes.	Maggs grins like a jackal.	Lots of description of Maggs: oily smile; face was so red and sore it looked as if he'd scrubbed it with a metal brush; face turned a shade of deep purple, shot through with broken blood vessels; yellow eyes bulged	Not important	Not important

My Interpretation: Responses will vary.

Graphic Organizer **197**

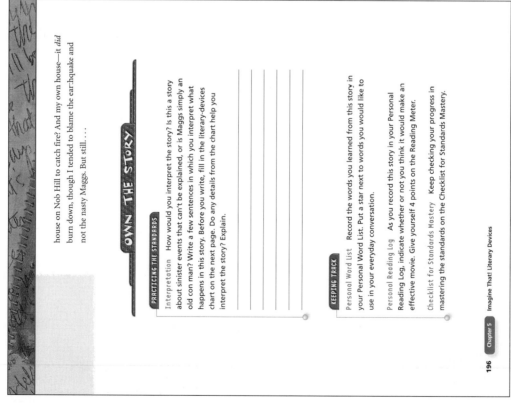

house on Nob Hill to catch fire? And my own house—it *did* burn down, though I tended to blame the earthquake and not the nasty Maggs. But still. . . .

OWN THE STORY

PRACTICING THE STANDARDS

Interpretation How would you interpret the story? Is this a story about sinister events that can't be explained, or is Maggs simply an old con man? Write a few sentences in which you interpret what happens in this story. Before you write, fill in the literary-devices chart on the next page. Do any details from the chart help you interpret the story? Explain.

_____

_____

_____

_____

KEEPING TRACK

Personal Word List Record the words you learned from this story in your Personal Word List. Put a star next to words you would like to use in your everyday conversation.

Personal Reading Log As you record this story in your Personal Reading Log, indicate whether or not you think it would make an effective movie. Give yourself 4 points on the Reading Meter.

Checklist for Standards Mastery Keep checking your progress in mastering the standards on the Checklist for Standards Mastery.

196 Chapter 5 Imagine That! Literary Devices

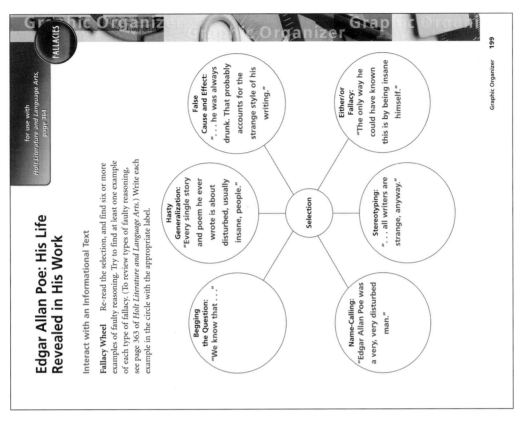

Edgar Allan Poe: His Life Revealed in His Work

for use with
Holt Literature and Language Arts,
page 364

FALLACIES

Interact with an Informational Text

Fallacy Wheel Re-read the selection, and find six or more examples of faulty reasoning. Try to find at least one example of each type of fallacy. (To review types of faulty reasoning, see page 363 of *Holt Literature and Language Arts*.) Write each example in the circle with the appropriate label.

Hasty Generalization: "Every single story and poem he ever wrote is about disturbed, usually insane, people."

False Cause and Effect: ". . . he was always drunk. That probably accounts for the strange style of his writing."

Either/or Fallacy: "The only way he could have known this is by being insane himself."

Stereotyping: ". . . all writers are strange, anyway."

Name-Calling: "Edgar Allan Poe was a very, very disturbed man."

Begging the Question: "We know that . . . "

Selection

Graphic Organizer   **199**

The Tell-Tale Heart

for use with
Holt Literature and Language Arts,
page 354

LITERARY DEVICES

Interact with a Literary Text

Irony Chart In **verbal irony** a person says one thing but means the opposite. In **situational irony** something happens that is the opposite of what we thought would happen or of what we think is the appropriate thing to happen. In **dramatic irony** the reader (or audience, in drama) knows something that a character in a story or play does not know.

Fill in this irony chart with examples of irony from "The Tell-Tale Heart." Be sure to compare your charts in class. **Sample answers appear below.**

Verbal Irony	Situational Irony	Dramatic Irony
"I loved the old man." "I pitied him."	The narrator claims he loves the old man, but he kills him.	The narrator claims to be sane, but readers suspect he is not.
	The officers sit smiling while the narrator rants and raves.	"I smiled—for what had I to fear?"
	"I smiled gaily to find the deed so far done." (People aren't usually cheerful when committing murder.)	"The officers were satisfied."

Olympic Games *and* The Old Olympic Games: A Report

INFERENCES

for use with
Holt Literature and Language Arts,
page 379

Interact with Informational Texts

Inference Chart   In the chart below, factual statements from the encyclopedia article "Olympic Games" are listed in the left column. In the middle column, next to each fact, is an unsupported inference made by the writer of "The Old Olympic Games: A Report" using that fact. The right column has been left blank for you to fill in with a supported inference based on each factual statement.

The Olympics

Factual Statement from "Olympic Games"	Unsupported Inference from "The Old Olympic Games: A Report"	Supported Inference
The first recorded Olympic contest took place in 776 B.C.	The Olympic games began a long time ago, before anyone knew how to write.	Ancient Greeks kept records of athletic events.
The only event in the first thirteen games was a running race of 210 yards.	The only thing the old Greeks could do was race. They weren't very strong, so they could run only 210 yards.	The ancient Greeks considered racing to be an important sport.
In 708 B.C., wrestling and pentathlon (jumping, running, discus throw, javelin throw, and wrestling) were added.	Then they learned how to wrestle, jump, and throw things.	Many sports performed in the ancient Olympics are still performed today in the modern Olympics.
In 648 B.C., the pancratium was added, a combination of boxing, wrestling, and kicking.	They didn't play fair, though, and kicked each other when they were boxing and wrestling.	Some sports performed in the ancient Olympics are no longer performed in the modern Olympics.
The Romans conquered Greece during the 140s B.C. . . . In A.D. 393, Emperor Theodosius I banned the games.	Some of them raced chariots using mules! If they were that silly, it's no wonder the Romans conquered them.	The Olympic Games lasted in Greece for over a thousand years before being banned by the Romans.

Raymond's Run

LITERARY DEVICES

for use with
Holt Literature and Language Arts,
page 565

Interact with a Literary Text

Literary Device Pie Chart   In "Raymond's Run," Toni Cade Bambara gives readers a rich feast of literary devices. **Literary devices** include allusion, dialect, and figures of speech such as similes, metaphors, and analogies. Find examples in the story of each type of device, and write them in the chart below.

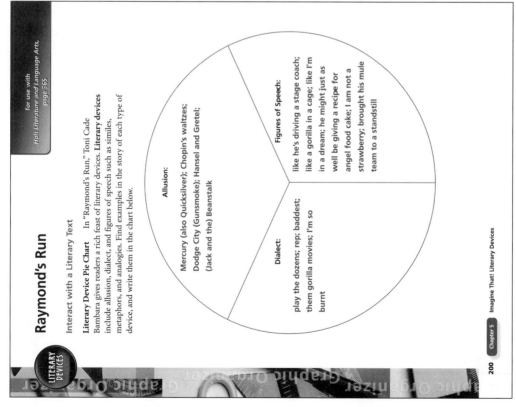

Allusion:
Mercury (also Quicksilver); Chopin's waltzes; Dodge City (Gunsmoke); Hansel and Gretel; (Jack and the) Beanstalk

Dialect:
play the dozens; rep; baddest; them gorilla movies; I'm so burnt

Figures of Speech:
like he's driving a stage coach; like I'm in a dream; he might just as well be giving a recipe for angel food cake; I am not a strawberry; brought his mule team to a standstill

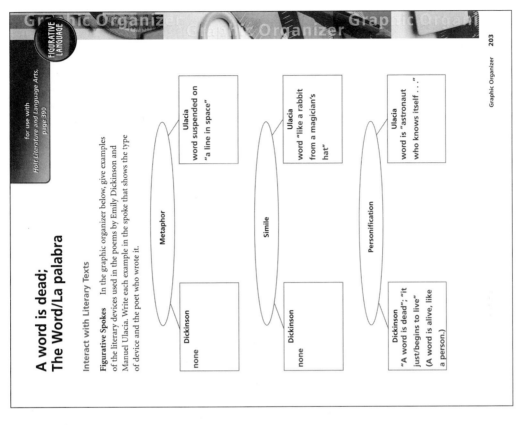

A word is dead; The Word/La palabra

FIGURATIVE LANGUAGE

for use with
Holt Literature and Language Arts,
page 390

Interact with Literary Texts

Figurative Spokes In the graphic organizer below, give examples of the literary devices used in the poems by Emily Dickinson and Manuel Ulacia. Write each example in the spoke that shows the type of device and the poet who wrote it.

Metaphor

Dickinson
none

Ulacia
word "suspended on "a line in space"

Simile

Dickinson
none

Ulacia
word "like a rabbit from a magician's hat"

Personification

Dickinson
"A word is dead"; "it just/begins to live" (A word is alive, like a person.)

Ulacia
word is "astronaut who knows itself . . ."

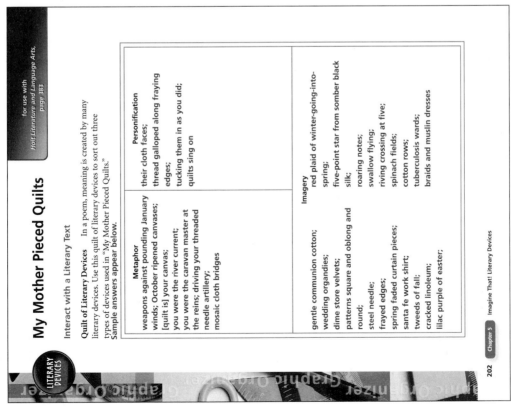

My Mother Pieced Quilts

LITERARY DEVICES

for use with
Holt Literature and Language Arts,
page 383

Interact with a Literary Text

Quilt of Literary Devices In a poem, meaning is created by many literary devices. Use this quilt of literary devices to sort out three types of devices used in "My Mother Pieced Quilts." Sample answers appear below.

Metaphor	Personification
weapons against pounding January winds; October ripened canvases; [quilt is] your canvas; you were the river current; you were the caravan master at the reins; driving your threaded needle artillery; mosaic cloth bridges	their cloth faces; thread galloped along fraying edges; tucking them in as you did; quilts sing on

Imagery	
gentle communion cotton; wedding organdies; dime store velvets; patterns square and oblong and round; steel needle; frayed edges; spring faded curtain pieces; santa fe work shirt; tweeds of fall; cracked linoleum; lilac purple of easter;	red plaid of winter-going-into-spring; five-point star from somber black silk; roaring notes; swallow flying; riving crossing at five; spinach fields; cotton rows; tuberculosis wards; braids and muslin dresses

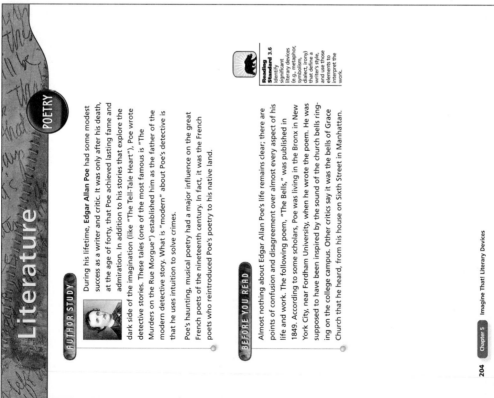

Literature

POETRY

AUTHOR STUDY

During his lifetime, **Edgar Allan Poe** had some modest success as a writer and critic. It was only after his death, at the age of forty, that Poe achieved lasting fame and admiration. In addition to his stories that explore the dark side of the imagination (like "The Tell-Tale Heart"), Poe wrote detective stories. These tales (one of the most famous is "The Murders on the Rue Morgue") established him as the father of the modern detective story. What is "modern" about Poe's detective is that he uses intuition to solve crimes.

Poe's haunting, musical poetry had a major influence on the great French poets of the nineteenth century. In fact, it was the French poets who reintroduced Poe's poetry to his native land.

BEFORE YOU READ

Almost nothing about Edgar Allan Poe's life remains clear; there are points of confusion and disagreement over almost every aspect of his life and work. The following poem, "The Bells," was published in 1849. According to some scholars, Poe was living in the Bronx in New York City, near Fordham University, when he wrote the poem. He was supposed to have been inspired by the sound of the church bells ringing on the college campus. Other critics say it was the bells of Grace Church that he heard, from his house on Sixth Street in Manhattan.

Reading Standard 3.6 Identify significant literary devices (e.g., metaphor, symbolism, dialect, irony) that define a writer's style, and use those elements to interpret the work.

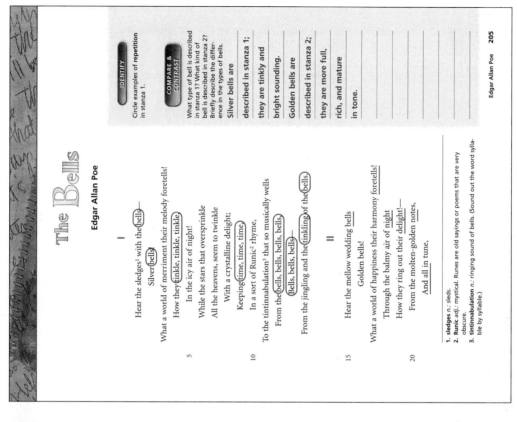

The Bells

Edgar Allan Poe

I

Hear the sledges[1] with the bells—
    Silver bells!
What a world of merriment their melody foretells!
    How they tinkle, tinkle, tinkle,
5   In the icy air of night!
While the stars that oversprinkle
All the heavens, seem to twinkle
    With a crystalline delight;
    Keeping time, time, time,
10   In a sort of Runic[2] rhyme,
To the tintinnabulation[3] that so musically wells
    From the bells, bells, bells, bells,
      Bells, bells, bells—
From the jingling and the tinkling of the bells.

II

15   Hear the mellow wedding bells
      Golden bells!
What a world of happiness their harmony foretells!
    Through the balmy air of night
    How they ring out their delight!—
20   From the molten-golden notes,
      And all in tune,

---

1. **sledges** *n.:* sleds.
2. **Runic** *adj.:* mystical. Runes are old sayings or poems that are very obscure.
3. **tintinnabulation** *n.:* ringing sound of bells. (Sound out the word syllable by syllable.)

IDENTIFY

Circle examples of repetition in stanza 1.

COMPARE & CONTRAST

What type of bell is described in stanza 1? What kind of bell is described in stanza 2? Briefly describe the difference in the types of bells.

Silver bells are

described in stanza 1;

they are tinkly and

bright sounding.

Golden bells are

described in stanza 2;

they are more full,

rich, and mature

in tone.

Edgar Allan Poe   **205**

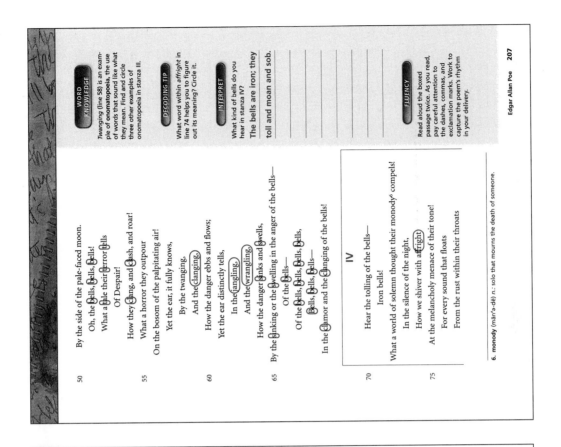

WORD KNOWLEDGE

Twanging (line 58) is an example of **onomatopoeia**, the use of words that sound like what they mean. Find and circle three other examples of onomatopoeia in stanza III.

DECODING TIP

What word within *affright* in line 74 helps you to figure out its meaning? Circle it.

INTERPRET

What kind of bells do you hear in stanza IV? **The bells are iron; they toll and moan and sob.**

FLUENCY

Read aloud the boxed passage twice. As you read, pay careful attention to the dashes, commas, and exclamation marks. Work to capture the poem's rhythm in your delivery.

50 By the side of the pale-faced moon.
Oh, the bells, bells, bells!
What a tale their terror tells
Of Despair!
How they clang, and clash, and roar!
What a horror they outpour
55 On the bosom of the palpitating air!
Yet the ear, it fully knows,
By the twanging,
And the clanging,
How the danger ebbs and flows;
60 Yet the ear distinctly tells,
In the jangling,
And the wrangling,
How the danger sinks and swells,
By the sinking or the swelling in the anger of the bells—
65 Of the bells—
Of the bells, bells, bells, bells,
Bells, bells, bells—
In the clamor and the clangor of the bells!

IV

Hear the tolling of the bells—
70 Iron bells!
What a world of solemn thought their monody⁶ compels!
In the silence of the night,
How we shiver with affright
At the melancholy menace of their tone!
75 For every sound that floats
From the rust within their throats

6. **monody** (mŏn′ə-dē) *n.*: solo that mourns the death of someone.

Edgar Allan Poe   **207**

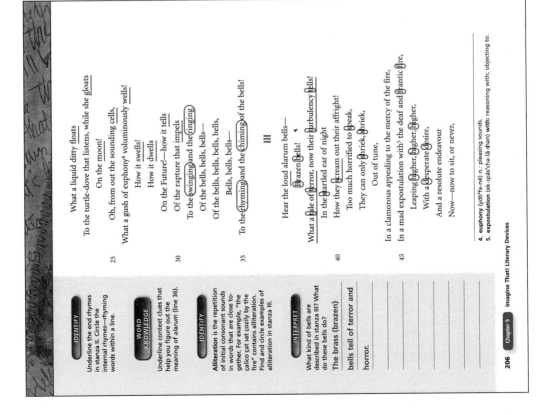

IDENTIFY

Underline the end rhymes in stanza II. Circle the internal rhymes—rhyming words within a line.

WORD KNOWLEDGE

Underline context clues that help you figure out the meaning of *alarum* (line 36).

IDENTIFY

Alliteration is the repetition of initial consonant sounds in words that are close together. For example, "the calico cat sat cozily by the fire" contains alliteration. Find and circle examples of alliteration in stanza III.

INTERPRET

What kind of bells are described in stanza III? What do these bells do? **The brass (brazen) bells tell of terror and horror.**

What a liquid ditty floats
To the turtle-dove that listens, while she gloats
25 On the moon!
Oh, from out the sounding cells,
What a gush of euphony⁴ voluminously wells!
How it swells!
How it dwells
30 On the Future!—how it tells
Of the rapture that impels
To the swinging and the ringing
Of the bells, bells, bells—
Of the bells, bells, bells, bells,
Bells, bells, bells—
35 To the rhyming and the chiming of the bells!

III

Hear the loud alarum bells—
Brazen bells!
What a tale of terror, now their turbulency tells!
In the startled ear of night
40 How they scream out their affright!
Too much horrified to speak,
They can only shriek, shriek,
Out of tune,
In a clamorous appealing to the mercy of the fire,
45 In a mad expostulation with⁵ the deaf and frantic fire,
Leaping higher, higher, higher,
With a desperate desire,
And a resolute endeavour
Now—now to sit, or never,

4. **euphony** (yōō′fə-nē) *n.*: pleasing sounds.
5. **expostulation** (ĕk-spŏs′chə-lā-shən) **with**: reasoning with; objecting to.

206 Chapter 5   Imagine That! Literary Devices

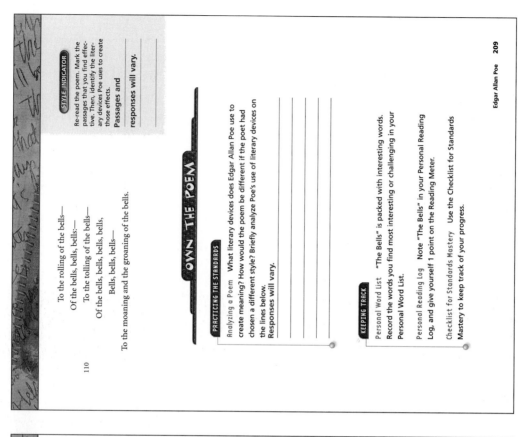

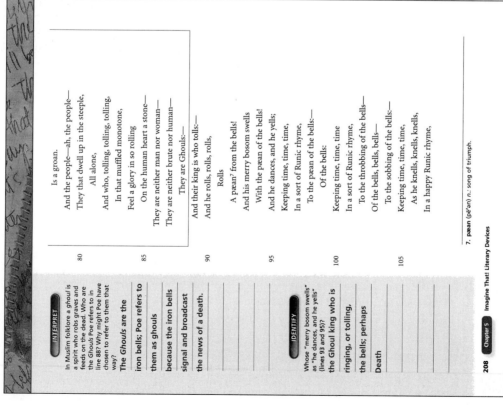

Left page (208)

INTERPRET

In Muslim folklore a *ghoul* is a spirit who robs graves and feeds on the dead. Who are the *Ghouls* Poe refers to in line 88? Why might Poe have chosen to refer to them that way?

The Ghouls are the

iron bells; Poe refers to

them as ghouls

because the iron bells

signal and broadcast

the news of a death.

```
           Is a groan.
       And the people—ah, the people—
       They that dwell up in the steeple,
           All alone,
       And who, tolling, tolling, tolling,
           In that muffled monotone,
       Feel a glory in so rolling
 80      On the human heart a stone—
       They are neither man nor woman—
       They are neither brute nor human—
           They are Ghouls:—
       And their king is who tolls:—
 85    And he rolls, rolls, rolls,
           Rolls
       A pæan⁷ from the bells!
       And his merry bosom swells
           With the pæan of the bells!
       And he dances, and he yells;
 90    Keeping time, time, time,
       In a sort of Runic rhyme,
       To the pæan of the bells:—
           Of the bells:
       Keeping time, time, time
 95    In a sort of Runic rhyme,
       To the throbbing of the bells—
       Of the bells, bells, bells—
       To the sobbing of the bells:—
       Keeping time, time, time,
100    As he knells, knells, knells,
       In a happy Runic rhyme,
```

IDENTIFY

Whose "merry bosom swells" as "he dances, and he yells" (lines 93 and 95)?

the Ghoul king who is

ringing, or tolling,

the bells; perhaps

Death

7. **pæan** (pē'ən) *n.*: song of triumph.

Right page (209)

```
       To the rolling of the bells—
       Of the bells, bells, bells:—
       To the tolling of the bells—
       Of the bells, bells, bells, bells—
           Bells, bells, bells—
110    To the moaning and the groaning of the bells.
```

OWN THE POEM

PRACTICING THE STANDARDS

Analyzing a Poem   What literary devices does Edgar Allan Poe use to create meaning? How would the poem be different if the poet had chosen a different style? Briefly analyze Poe's use of literary devices on the lines below.
Responses will vary.

KEEPING TRACK

Personal Word List   "The Bells" is packed with interesting words. Record the words you find most interesting or challenging in your Personal Word List.

Personal Reading Log   Note "The Bells" in your Personal Reading Log, and give yourself 1 point on the Reading Meter.

Checklist for Standards Mastery   Use the Checklist for Standards Mastery to keep track of your progress.

PROJECT

The Bells ■ *Interactive Reading,* page 204

Go Beyond a Literary Text

Annotated List of Works Find out more about Edgar Allan Poe's works by researching and naming at least three of his most famous stories and three of his most famous poems. Provide a one-sentence description of what each is about. Ask a librarian to help you find Poe's works and identify their subjects.
Sample entries appear below.

Story Title	Is About . . .
The Pit and the Pendulum	a prisoner being tortured by the Spanish Inquisition
The Cask of Amontillado	a man who sealed up an enemy behind a brick wall
The Murders on the Rue Morgue	a brilliant detective who solves a baffling series of murders in France

Poem Title	Is About . . .
The Raven	a strange, talking raven who haunts the speaker
Annabel Lee	a young woman, beloved of the speaker, who died "many and many a year ago in a kingdom by the sea"
Ulalume	a magical kingdom invented by the speaker

Information

NONFICTION

BEFORE YOU READ

Just about everything about Edgar Allan Poe's life is a mystery. Scholars often disagree about when and where he wrote his great works. Even more people disagree about what caused Poe's death in Baltimore, Maryland, in 1849. Was it drink? murder? rabies? Read on to find out about a modern mystery connected with Poe's death.

from Beyond the Grave

Troy Taylor

One of the most **compelling** cemeteries on the east coast is located in Baltimore, although many people are unaware that a portion of it even exists. It is called the Old Western Burial Ground, and it holds the remains of people such as Edgar Allan Poe, the son of Francis Scott Key, the grand-father of President James Buchanan, five former mayors of Baltimore, and fifteen generals from the Revolutionary War and the War of 1812.

Not all of the cemetery is easy to find, for the Westminster Presbyterian Church (now Westminster Hall)
10 was built over a large portion of the cemetery. These graves and tombs date back to a century before the church was built. Much of the cemetery, where Poe is buried, is still accessible above ground in the churchyard, but a large portion of the graveyard can only be reached by way of the catacombs underneath the building. It is here where the ghosts of this eerie graveyard are said to walk. Strangely

Reading Standard 2.8 (Grade 6 Review) Note instances of fallacious reasoning in text.

VOCABULARY DEVELOPMENT

compelling (kəm-pĕl'ĭn) *adj.:* irresistibly interesting; captivating.

WORD KNOWLEDGE

Catacombs (line 16) are a series of vaults or galleries in an underground burial place.

· · · · · · Notes · · · · · · ·

Beyond the Grave **211**

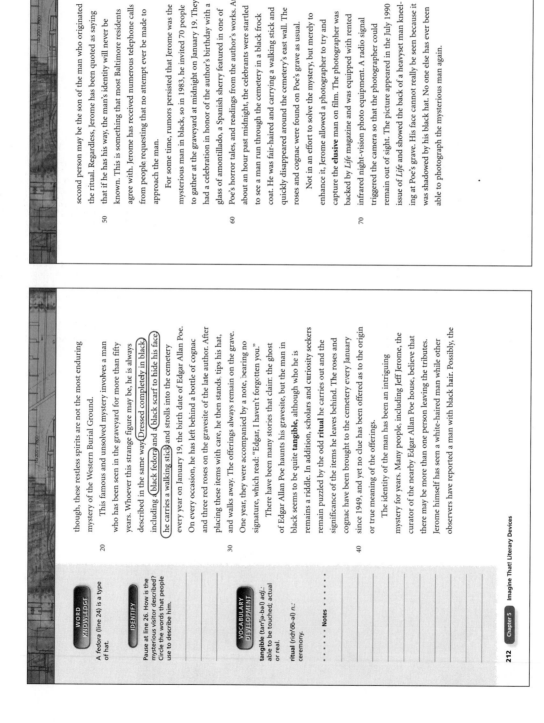

· · · · · · Notes · · · · · ·

though, these restless spirits are not the most enduring mystery of the Western Burial Ground.

This famous and unsolved mystery involves a man who has been seen in the graveyard for more than fifty years. Whoever this strange figure may be, he is always described in the same way. Dressed completely in black, including a black fedora and a black scarf to hide his face, he carries a walking stick and strolls into the cemetery every year on January 19, the birth date of Edgar Allan Poe. On every occasion, he has left behind a bottle of cognac and three red roses on the gravesite of the late author. After placing these items with care, he then stands, tips his hat, and walks away. The offerings always remain on the grave. One year, they were accompanied by a note, bearing no signature, which read: "Edgar, I haven't forgotten you."

There have been many stories that claim: the ghost of Edgar Allan Poe haunts his gravesite, but the man in black seems to be quite **tangible**, although who he is remains a riddle. In addition, scholars and curiosity seekers remain puzzled by the odd **ritual** he carries out and the significance of the items he leaves behind. The roses and cognac have been brought to the cemetery every January since 1949, and yet no clue has been offered as to the origin or true meaning of the offerings.

The identity of the man has been an intriguing mystery for years. Many people, including Jeff Jerome, the curator of the nearby Edgar Allan Poe house, believe that there may be more than one person leaving the tributes. Jerome himself has seen a white-haired man while other observers have reported a man with black hair. Possibly, the

second person may be the son of the man who originated the ritual. Regardless, Jerome has been quoted as saying that if he has his way, the man's identity will never be known. This is something that most Baltimore residents agree with. Jerome has received numerous telephone calls from people requesting that no attempt ever be made to approach the man.

For some time, rumors persisted that Jerome was the mysterious man in black, so in 1983, he invited 70 people to gather at the graveyard at midnight on January 19. They had a celebration in honor of the author's birthday with a glass of amontillado, a Spanish sherry featured in one of Poe's horror tales, and readings from the author's works. At about an hour past midnight, the celebrants were startled to see a man run through the cemetery in a black frock coat. He was fair-haired and carrying a walking stick and quickly disappeared around the cemetery's east wall. The roses and cognac were found on Poe's grave as usual.

Not in an effort to solve the mystery, but merely to enhance it, Jerome allowed a photographer to try and capture the **elusive** man on film. The photographer was backed by *Life* magazine and was equipped with rented infrared night-vision photo equipment. A radio signal triggered the camera so that the photographer could remain out of sight. The picture appeared in the July 1990 issue of *Life* and showed the back of a heavyset man kneeling at Poe's grave. His face cannot really be seen because it was shadowed by his black hat. No one else has ever been able to photograph the mysterious man again.

· · · · · · Notes · · · · · ·

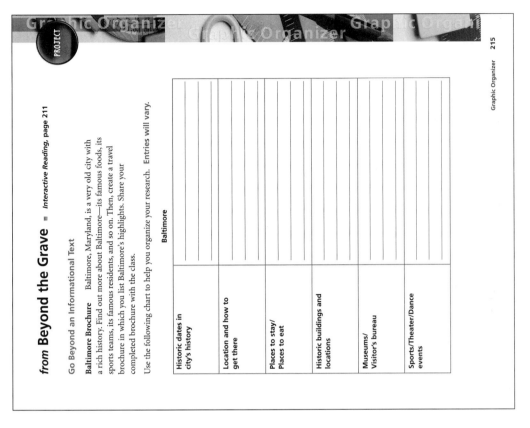

PROJECT

Graphic Organizer

from **Beyond the Grave** ■ *Interactive Reading,* page 211

Go Beyond an Informational Text

Baltimore Brochure   Baltimore, Maryland, is a very old city with a rich history. Find out more about Baltimore—its famous foods, its sports teams, its famous residents, and so on. Then, create a travel brochure in which you list Baltimore's highlights. Share your completed brochure with the class.

Use the following chart to help you organize your research. Entries will vary.

Baltimore

Historic dates in city's history	
Location and how to get there	
Places to stay/ Places to eat	
Historic buildings and locations	
Museums/ Visitor's bureau	
Sports/Theater/Dance events	

Graphic Organizer   **215**

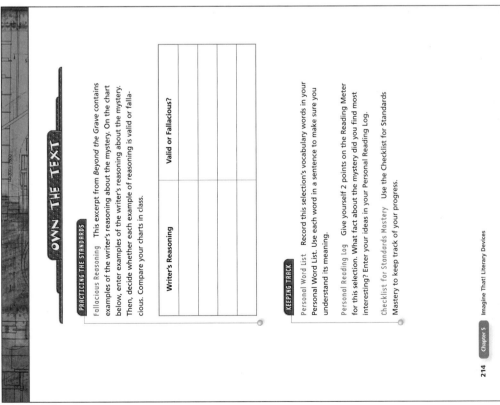

OWN THE TEXT

PRACTICING THE STANDARDS

Fallacious Reasoning   This excerpt from *Beyond the Grave* contains examples of the writer's reasoning about the mystery. On the chart below, enter examples of the writer's reasoning about the mystery. Then, decide whether each example of reasoning is valid or fallacious. Compare your charts in class.

Writer's Reasoning	Valid or Fallacious?

KEEPING TRACK

Personal Word List   Record this selection's vocabulary words in your Personal Word List. Use each word in a sentence to make sure you understand its meaning.

Personal Reading Log   Give yourself 2 points on the Reading Meter for this selection. What fact about the mystery did you find most interesting? Enter your ideas in your Personal Reading Log.

Checklist for Standards Mastery   Use the Checklist for Standards Mastery to keep track of your progress.

214   Chapter 5   Imagine That! Literary Devices

Literature — POETRY

Writers use the same basic tools to communicate—words. What makes some writing memorable and effective is the writer's *use* of the words. The following poems are about life. Each poet has something different to say about life, and each poet uses language differently, in his or her own style. Read on to see how each poet's style affects you, the reader.

Reading Standard 3.6 Identify significant literary devices (e.g., metaphor, symbolism, dialect, irony) that define a writer's style, and use those elements to interpret the work.

A Dream Within a Dream

Edgar Allan Poe

Take this kiss upon the brow!
And, in parting from you now,
Thus much let me avow—
You are not wrong, who deem
5   That my days have been a dream;*
Yet if hope has flown away*
In a night, or in a day,
In a vision, or in none,
Is it therefore the less gone?
10   All that we see or seem
Is but a dream within a dream.

I stand amid the roar
Of a surf-tormented shore,*
And I hold within my hand
15   Grains of the golden sand—

IDENTIFY
What is the poem's speaker doing in lines 1 and 2?
He kisses his love and prepares to leave.

INTERPRET
What might the speaker refer to when he says "my days" (line 5)?
He is talking about his life.

INTERPRET
What might the grains of sand symbolize (line 15)?
They symbolize life or the lives of people.

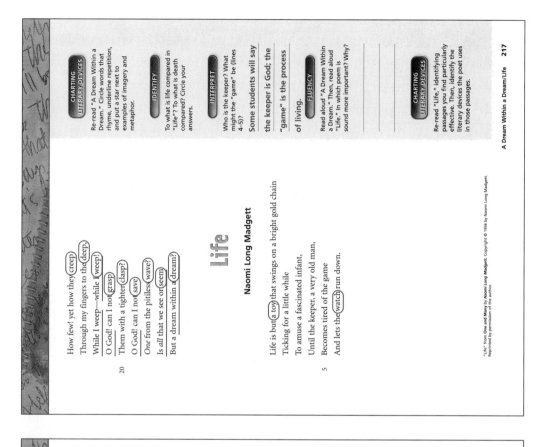

How few! yet how they creep
Through my fingers to the deep,
While I weep—while I weep!
O God! can I not grasp
Them with a tighter clasp?
20   O God! can I not save
One from the pitiless wave?
Is *all* that we see or seem
But a dream within a dream?

CHARTING LITERARY DEVICES
Re-read "A Dream Within a Dream." Circle words that rhyme, underline repetition, and put a star next to examples of imagery and metaphor.

IDENTIFY
To what is life compared in "Life"? To what is death compared? Circle your answers.

Life

Naomi Long Madgett

Life is but a toy that swings on a bright gold chain
Ticking for a little while
To amuse a fascinated infant,
Until the keeper, a very old man,
5   Becomes tired of the game
And lets the watch run down.

INTERPRET
Who is the keeper? What might the "game" be (lines 4–5)?
Some students will say the keeper is God; the "game" is the process of living.

FLUENCY
Read aloud "A Dream Within a Dream." Then, read aloud "Life." In which poem is sound more important? Why?

CHARTING LITERARY DEVICES
Re-read "Life," identifying passages you find particularly effective. Then, identify the literary devices the poet uses in those passages.

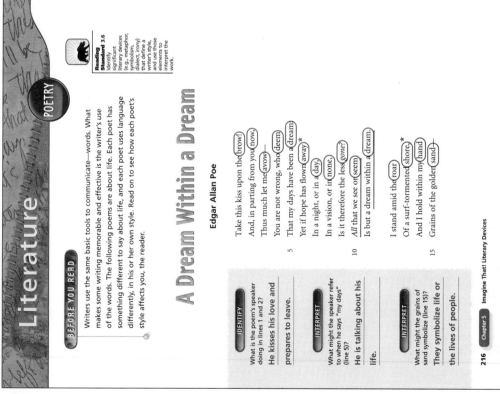

"Life" from *One and Many* by *Naomi Long Madgett*. Copyright © 1956 by Naomi Long Madgett. Reprinted by permission of the author.

A Dream Within a Dream/Life   **217**

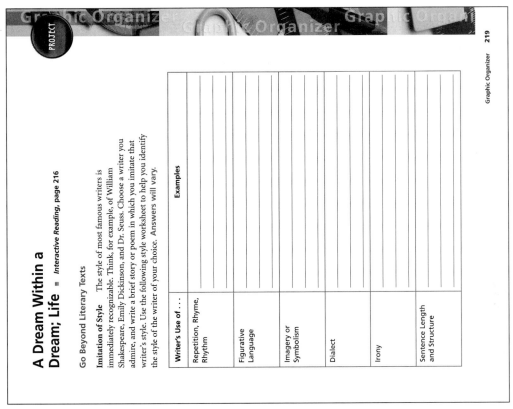

PROJECT

A Dream Within a Dream; Life ■ *Interactive Reading, page 216*

Go Beyond Literary Texts

Imitation of Style The style of most famous writers is immediately recognizable. Think, for example, of William Shakespeare, Emily Dickinson, and Dr. Seuss. Choose a writer you admire, and write a brief story or poem in which you imitate that writer's style. Use the following style worksheet to help you identify the style of the writer of your choice. Answers will vary.

Writer's Use of . . .	Examples
Repetition, Rhyme, Rhythm	
Figurative Language	
Imagery or Symbolism	
Dialect	
Irony	
Sentence Length and Structure	

Graphic Organizer **219**

OWN THE POEMS

PRACTICING THE STANDARDS

Compare Literary Devices One of these poems is over a hundred years old. The other poem is fairly recent. Compare and contrast the way each speaker sees life. What **metaphor** or metaphors does each speaker use to describe what life is like? What is the **tone** of each poem—that is, what attitude toward life does each speaker express? In your answer, be sure to quote lines from the poems.

Compare Style Write a brief description of the sounds you hear in Edgar Allan Poe's poem and in Naomi Long Madgett's poem. Use examples from the poems to support your analysis.

KEEPING TRACK

Personal Word List Write the words you learned from these poems in your Personal Word List. Practice at least two of the words in everyday conversation.

Personal Reading Log Enter your ideas about author's style in your Personal Reading Log. Then, give yourself 1 point on the Reading Meter.

Checklist for Standards Mastery Update the Checklist for Standards Mastery to indicate your understanding of author's style.

218 Chapter 5 Imagine That! Literary Devices

Strategy Launch: "Text Reformulation"

LITERARY FOCUS: POETRY

Poems take many different forms and have many purposes. Some poems, like **sonnets**, follow strict patterns of rhyme and meter. Other poems are written in **free verse**. Some, like **lyric poems**, express a feeling or an idea; others, like **narrative poems, ballads,** and **epic poems** tell stories. Ballads sing simple stories about love, betrayal, or death, and epics tell complex stories of heroic quests. **Odes** are written in praise of a person, place, or thing; **elegies** usually praise someone who has died. Emily Dickinson, a very great poet, said that she knew she was reading poetry when she felt the top of her head lift off. Not every poem makes readers feel that way. But every serious poem tries to.

A STRATEGY THAT WORKS: "TEXT REFORMULATION"

Sometimes poems can be hard to understand. To help make a poem's meaning clear, you can use a strategy called "Text Reformulation," in which you put the content of the poem into a different form.

POINTERS FOR USING "TEXT REFORMULATION"

➤ Rewrite a **lyric poem** as a journal entry or a letter.

➤ Rewrite a **narrative poem** as a news story.

➤ Rewrite a **ballad** as a hip-hop song.

➤ Rewrite an **epic poem** as a script for a feature film.

Reading Standard 2.4 Compare the original text to a summary to determine whether the summary accurately captures the main ideas, includes critical details, and conveys the underlying meaning.

Reading Standard 3.1 Determine and articulate the relationship between the purposes and characteristics of different forms of poetry (for example, ballad, lyric, couplet, epic, elegy, ode, sonnet).

Strategy Launch **221**

Chapter 6

Sound and Sense

Forms of Poetry

Chapter Preview In this chapter you will—

Read: Selections	Interact with Text: Graphic Organizers
Practice Read: Skywriting by Michael Ellis • *Interactive Reading,* p. 222	Text Reformulation: Personal Letter *Interactive Reading,* p. 224
Practice Read: The Midnight Ride of Billy Dawes by Dan Greenberg • *Interactive Reading,* p. 225	Text Reformulation: Comic Book *Interactive Reading,* p. 230
Valentine for Ernest Mann by Naomi Shihab Nye *Holt Literature and Language Arts,* p. 406	"Most Important Word" Graph *Interactive Reading,* p. 231
Paul Revere's Ride by Henry Wadsworth Longfellow *Holt Literature and Language Arts,* p. 410	Cause-and-Effect Chart • *Interactive Reading,* p. 232
The Cremation of Sam McGee by Robert W. Service; The Dying Cowboy; Maiden-Savin' Sam by Jenny Ellison *Holt Literature and Language Arts,* p. 417	Story Map • *Interactive Reading,* p. 233
from Beowulf; Casey at the Bat by Ernest Lawrence Thayer • *Holt Literature and Language Arts,* p. 428	Epic-Comparison Chart • *Interactive Reading,* p. 234
Summaries of "Casey at the Bat" *Holt Literature and Language Arts,* p. 435	Summary-Event List • *Interactive Reading,* p. 235
Oda a las gracias/Ode to Thanks by Pablo Neruda; Birdfoot's Grampa by Joseph Bruchac; Ode to a Toad by Anne-Marie Wulfsberg *Holt Literature and Language Arts,* p. 437	Cluster Map • *Interactive Reading,* p. 236
On the Grasshopper and the Cricket by John Keats • *Holt Literature and Language Arts,* p. 443	Line-by-Line Paraphrase • *Interactive Reading,* p. 237
O Captain! My Captain! by Walt Whitman *Holt Literature and Language Arts,* p. 447	Extended-Metaphor Chart *Interactive Reading,* p. 238
I Hear America Singing by Walt Whitman; I, Too by Langston Hughes *Holt Literature and Language Arts,* p. 451	Venn Diagram • *Interactive Reading,* p. 239
Langston Hughes: A Biography and a Summary *Holt Literature and Language Arts,* p. 455	Summary-Notes Chart • *Interactive Reading,* p. 240
The Wreck of the Hesperus by Henry Wadsworth Longfellow • *Interactive Reading,* p. 242	Project: Author Profile • *Interactive Reading,* p. 248
Schooners by Edwin Tunis • *Interactive Reading,* p. 249	Text Reformulation • *Interactive Reading,* p. 253
Lincoln Monument: Washington by Langston Hughes; Mr. Longfellow and His Boy by Carl Sandburg • *Interactive Reading,* p. 254	Project: Poetry Dartboard *Interactive Reading,* p. 259

Practice Read

BEFORE YOU READ

Suppose you could build your own rocket ship—a tiny rocket ship, actually, because it would have to fit in a small basement. In this lyric poem, written in free verse, one poet imagines building such a rocket ship. Then he turns the rocket ship into a poem.

Reading Standard 3.1 Determine and articulate the relationship between the purposes and characteristics of different forms of poetry.

SKYWRITING

Michael Ellis

Just suppose you could build your own
rocket ship. A little one, most likely,
unless your basement is a whole lot bigger
than mine.

5   You won't be going into space yourself. I guess
you could send a cat in your place. But what
would a cat find
to do way up there, in the infinite twinkling dark?
Chase space mice? Don't kid yourself. That rocket
10   isn't even big enough for a cat.
All it can lift is a piece of paper. You could write a poem
on the paper. Words don't weigh much.

But words can carry lots of weight. A friend of mine
once wrote a short poem to the world. He published it
15   in massive type, on billboards over streets
in towns where thousands could read it:
"War is over if you want it."

He understood what words are for. They are
thoughts made visible.

20   The sky is vast and fills our eyes, a giant
billboard everyone can see. Maybe the stars
spell out a poem written in a voice
we all forgot a long time past. Maybe the sky
whispers the lines, so quietly we can't quite hear.
25   There's room up there for your words too.
Write something that explains just who you are and
where you've been, or what you want and
how you see it. Write what you like—it's your rocket.

Launch a poem, and watch it make its way
30   across the universe.

IDENTIFY

To whom is the poet speaking?

to the reader

WORD KNOWLEDGE

Infinite (ĭn′fə-nĭt) is an adjective meaning "without end." There are three *i*'s in *infinite,* and all three are short. The final *e* is silent. A closely related word that has a long *e* sound at the end is *infinity.* Another closely related word, *finite,* has two long *i* sounds.

INTERPRET

How can words "carry lots of weight," even though they "don't weigh much" (lines 12–13)?

Responses will vary.

INTERPRET

How would you state lines 17–19 in your own words?

Possible response:

Words express our

thoughts to others.

INTERPRET

What is the speaker comparing a poem to in lines 29–30?

a ship or rocket

OWN THE POEM

PRACTICING THE STANDARDS

Text Reformulation   Reformulate this poem as a letter to a young poet. Use the graphic organizer on the next page for help with the personal letter format.

KEEPING TRACK

Personal Word List   Record the new words you learned from this poem in your Personal Word List.

Personal Reading Log   Record this poem in your Personal Reading Log, and give yourself 1 point on the Reading Meter.

Checklist for Standards Mastery   Check your progress in mastering the standards on the Checklist for Standards Mastery.

222   Chapter 6   Sound and Sense: Forms of Poetry

223   Practice Read

Practice Read

BEFORE YOU READ

"The Midnight Ride of Billy Dawes" is a narrative poem based on historical fact. There really was a Billy Dawes. He was sent on a southern route to warn colonists that the British were coming. Paul Revere went to the north. Dawes ended the night a free man. Paul Revere was captured. There was actually a third rider, Dr. Samuel Prescott, who was the only one to make it all the way to Concord.

Reading Standard 3.1 Determine and articulate the relationship between the purposes and characteristics of different forms of poetry.

The Midnight Ride of Billy Dawes

Dan Greenberg

Gather round, readers
And hear my just cause:
I tell of a hero
Named young William Dawes.
5   Of Paul Revere's ride
This much is now known:
Revere did not travel
Completely alone.
A second brave rider
10   That night rode to glory.
His name was Bill Dawes
And this is his story.
It starts out in April
Of that fateful year.
15   The folks then in Boston

TEXT REFORMULATION

Reformulate lines 1–12 as a newspaper headline.

Possible response:

Revere Is Not Alone!

Dawes Rides Too!

FLUENCY

Read lines 1–20 aloud. Pay attention to the punctuation, and pause only when you see a comma, a colon, or a period. Re-read the stanza aloud until you can read it quickly and smoothly.

Practice Read   **225**

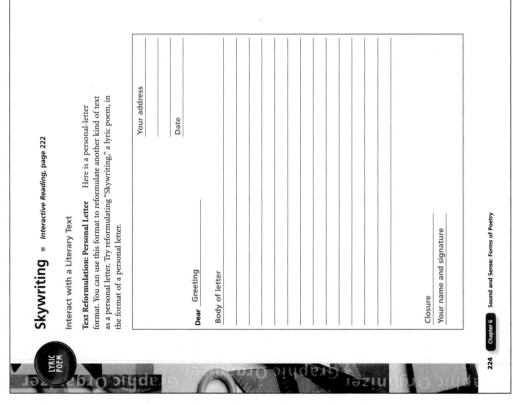

LYRIC POEM

Skywriting ■ *Interactive Reading,* page 222

Interact with a Literary Text

Text Reformulation: Personal Letter   Here is a personal-letter format. You can use this format to reformulate another kind of text as a personal letter. Try reformulating "Skywriting," a lyric poem, in the format of a personal letter.

Your address _____

Date _____

Dear _Greeting_ _____

Body of letter _____

_____

_____

_____

_____

_____

_____

_____

_____

Closure _____

Your name and signature _____

224   Chapter 6   Sound and Sense: Forms of Poetry

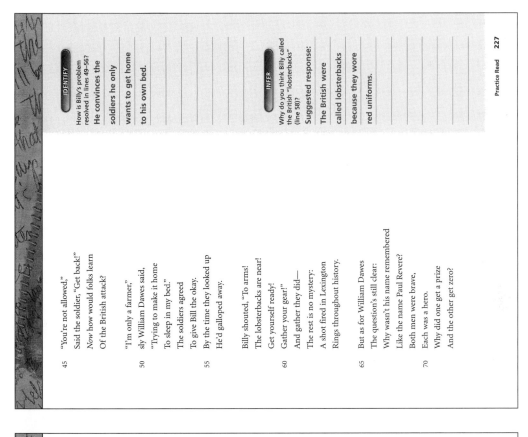

· · · · · · Notes · · · · · ·

Felt conflict and fear
The British controlled things—
And that was not right!
Sooner or later
20 It would come to a fight.

Then the word leaked out
That the British, in fact,
Were already marching—
They planned to attack!
25 There was no time to waste—
That much was clear—
So they called Billy Dawes
And his friend Paul Revere.

They said: Ride through the country
30 Make yourself heard:
"The British are coming!"
Shout out every word.
So out went Bill Dawes
And out went Revere
35 They flew down the road
On a night cool and clear.

For miles Billy raced,
Then came his big test:
"Stop!" cried the soldiers,
40 "You're under arrest!"
"Oh no!" thought young Billy,
"Is it over? Am I done?"
He looked down the barrel
Of the soldier's loaded gun.

VISUALIZE

How do you visualize the scene in lines 37–44?
Possible response: Billy is on his horse and is surrounded by several soldiers who have their guns pointed at him.

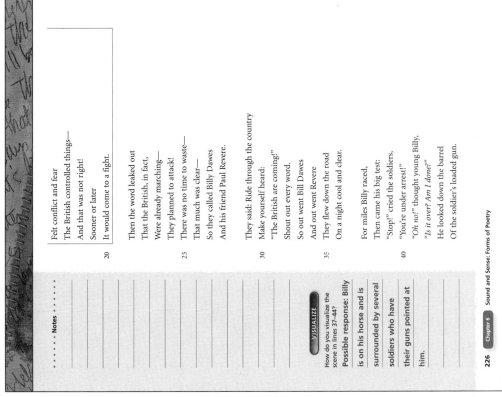

IDENTIFY

How is Billy's problem resolved in lines 49–56?
He convinces the soldiers he only wants to get home to his own bed.

45 "You're not allowed,"
Said the soldier, "Get back!"
Now how would folks learn
Of the British attack?

"I'm only a farmer,"
50 sly William Dawes said,
"Trying to make it home
To sleep in my bed."
The soldiers agreed
To give Bill the okay.
55 By the time they looked up
He'd galloped away.

Billy shouted, "To arms!
The lobsterbacks are near!
Get yourself ready!
60 Gather your gear!"
And gather they did—
The rest is no mystery:
A shot fired in Lexington
Rings throughout history.

65 But as for William Dawes
The question's still clear:
Why wasn't his name remembered
Like the name Paul Revere?
Both men were brave,
70 Each was a hero.
Why did one get a prize
And the other get zero?

INFER

Why do you think Billy called the British "lobsterbacks" (line 58)?
Suggested response: The British were called lobsterbacks because they wore red uniforms.

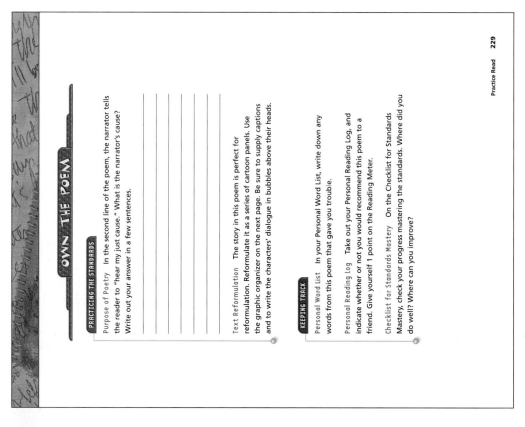

OWN THE POEM

PRACTICING THE STANDARDS

Purpose of Poetry   In the second line of the poem, the narrator tells the reader to "hear my just cause." What is the narrator's cause? Write out your answer in a few sentences.

_____

_____

_____

_____

_____

Text Reformulation   The story in this poem is perfect for reformulation. Reformulate it as a series of cartoon panels. Use the graphic organizer on the next page. Be sure to supply captions and to write the characters' dialogue in bubbles above their heads.

KEEPING TRACK

Personal Word List   In your Personal Word List, write down any words from this poem that gave you trouble.

Personal Reading Log   Take out your Personal Reading Log, and indicate whether or not you would recommend this poem to a friend. Give yourself 1 point on the Reading Meter.

Checklist for Standards Mastery   On the Checklist for Standards Mastery, check your progress mastering the standards. Where did you do well? Where can you improve?

Practice Read   **229**

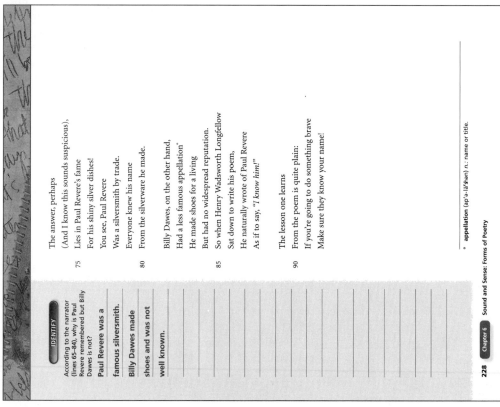

IDENTIFY

According to the narrator (lines 65–84), why is Paul Revere remembered but Billy Dawes is not?

Paul Revere was a

famous silversmith.

Billy Dawes made

shoes and was not

well known.

_____

_____

_____

_____

_____

_____

The answer, perhaps

(And I know this sounds suspicious),

75 Lies in Paul Revere's fame

For his shiny silver dishes!

You see, Paul Revere

Was a silversmith by trade.

Everyone knew his name

80 From the silverware he made.

Billy Dawes, on the other hand,

Had a less famous appellation°

He made shoes for a living

But had no widespread reputation.

85 So when Henry Wadsworth Longfellow

Sat down to write his poem,

He naturally wrote of Paul Revere

As if to say, _"I know him!"_

The lesson one learns

From the poem is quite plain:

90 If you're going to do something brave

Make sure they know your name!

° **appellation** (ap′ə·lā′shən) _n._: name or title.

228   Chapter 6   Sound and Sense: Forms of Poetry

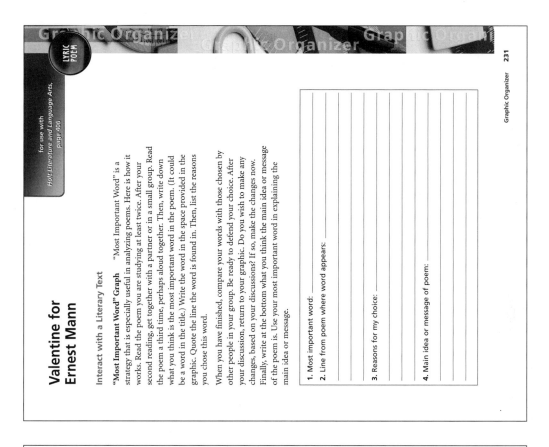

for use with
Holt Literature and Language Arts,
page 406

LYRIC POEM

Valentine for Ernest Mann

Interact with a Literary Text

"Most Important Word" Graph   "Most Important Word" is a strategy that is especially useful in analyzing poems. Here is how it works. Read the poem you are studying at least twice. After your second reading, get together with a partner or in a small group. Read the poem a third time, perhaps aloud together. Then, write down what you think is the most important word in the poem. (It could be a word in the title.) Write the word in the space provided in the graphic. Quote the line the word is found in. Then, list the reasons you chose this word.

When you have finished, compare your words with those chosen by other people in your group. Be ready to defend your choice. After your discussion, return to your graphic. Do you wish to make any changes, based on your discussions? If so, make the changes now. Finally, write at the bottom what you think the main idea or message of the poem is. Use your most important word in explaining the main idea or message.

1. Most important word: _____
2. Line from poem where word appears: _____

3. Reasons for my choice: _____

4. Main idea or message of poem: _____

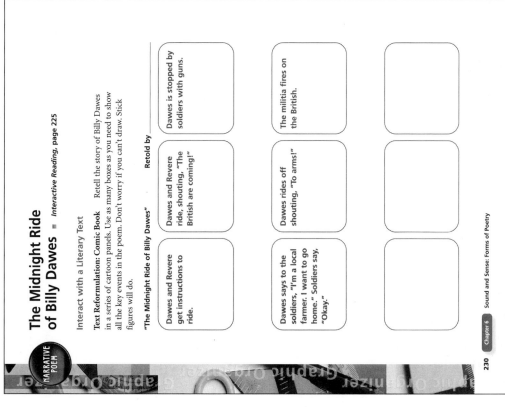

NARRATIVE POEM

The Midnight Ride of Billy Dawes ■ *Interactive Reading,* page 225

Interact with a Literary Text

Text Reformulation: Comic Book   Retell the story of Billy Dawes in a series of cartoon panels. Use as many boxes as you need to show all the key events in the poem. Don't worry if you can't draw. Stick figures will do.

"The Midnight Ride of Billy Dawes"   Retold by _____

Dawes and Revere get instructions to ride.	Dawes and Revere ride, shouting, "The British are coming!"	Dawes is stopped by soldiers with guns.
Dawes says to the soldiers, "I'm a local farmer. I want to go home." Soldiers say, "Okay."	Dawes rides off shouting, "To arms!"	The militia fires on the British.

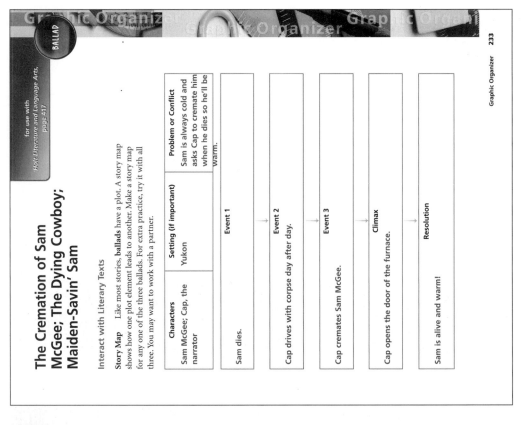

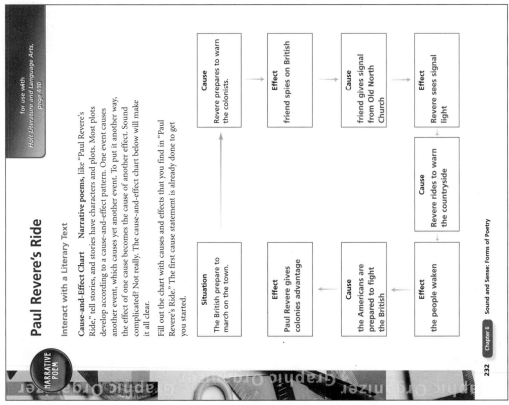

BALLAD

The Cremation of Sam McGee; The Dying Cowboy; Maiden-Savin' Sam

Interact with Literary Texts

Story Map Like most stories, **ballads** have a plot. A story map shows how one plot element leads to another. Make a story map for any one of the three ballads. For extra practice, try it with all three. You may want to work with a partner.

Characters	Setting (if important)	Problem or Conflict
Sam McGee; Cap, the narrator	Yukon	Sam is always cold and asks Cap to cremate him when he dies so he'll be warm.

Event 1

Sam dies.

↓

Event 2

Cap drives with corpse day after day.

↓

Event 3

Cap cremates Sam McGee.

↓

Climax

Cap opens the door of the furnace.

↓

Resolution

Sam is alive and warm!

Graphic Organizer   **233**

NARRATIVE POEM

Paul Revere's Ride

Interact with a Literary Text

Cause-and-Effect Chart **Narrative poems**, like "Paul Revere's Ride," tell stories, and stories have characters and plots. Most plots develop according to a cause-and-effect pattern. One event causes another event, which causes yet another event. To put it another way, the effect of one cause becomes the cause of another effect. Sound complicated? Not really. The cause-and-effect chart below will make it all clear.

Fill out the chart with causes and effects that you find in "Paul Revere's Ride." The first cause statement is already done to get you started.

Situation

The British prepare to march on the town.

↓

Effect

Paul Revere gives colonies advantage

↑

Cause

Revere prepares to warn the colonists.

→

Effect

friend spies on British

↓

Cause

friend gives signal from Old North Church

→

Effect

Revere sees signal light

↑

Cause

Revere rides to warn the countryside

↑

Effect

the people waken

←

Cause

the Americans are prepared to fight the British

232   Chapter 6   Sound and Sense: Forms of Poetry

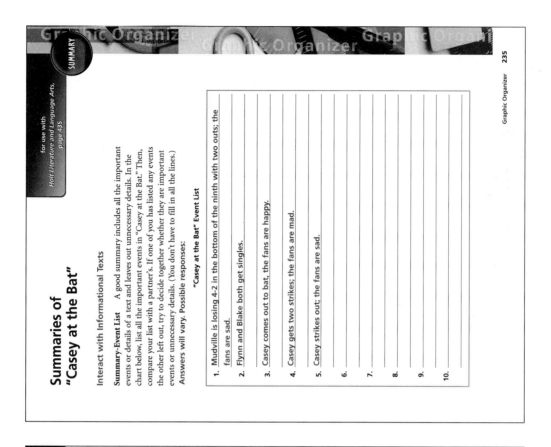

Graphic Organizer

SUMMARY

for use with
Holt Literature and Language Arts,
page 435

Summaries of "Casey at the Bat"

Interact with Informational Texts

Summary-Event List   A good summary includes all the important events or details of a text and leaves out unnecessary details. In the chart below, list all the important events in "Casey at the Bat." Then, compare your list with a partner's. If one of you has listed any events the other left out, try to decide together whether they are important events or unnecessary details. (You don't have to fill in all the lines.) Answers will vary. Possible responses:

"Casey at the Bat" Event List

1. Mudville is losing 4-2 in the bottom of the ninth with two outs; the fans are sad.
2. Flynn and Blake both get singles.
3. Casey comes out to bat, the fans are happy.
4. Casey gets two strikes; the fans are mad.
5. Casey strikes out; the fans are sad.
6.
7.
8.
9.
10.

235   Graphic Organizer

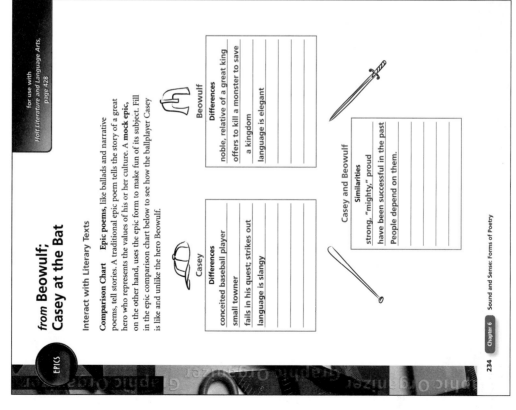

EPICS

for use with
Holt Literature and Language Arts,
page 428

from Beowulf; Casey at the Bat

Interact with Literary Texts

Comparison Chart   Epic poems, like ballads and narrative poems, tell stories. A traditional epic poem tells the story of a great hero who represents the values of his or her culture. A **mock epic,** on the other hand, uses the epic form to make fun of its subject. Fill in the epic comparison chart below to see how the ballplayer Casey is like and unlike the hero Beowulf.

Casey	Beowulf
Differences	**Differences**
conceited baseball player	noble, relative of a great king
small towner	offers to kill a monster to save a kingdom
fails in his quest; strikes out	language is elegant
language is slangy	

Casey and Beowulf

Similarities

strong, "mighty," proud

have been successful in the past

People depend on them.

234   Chapter 6   Sound and Sense: Forms of Poetry

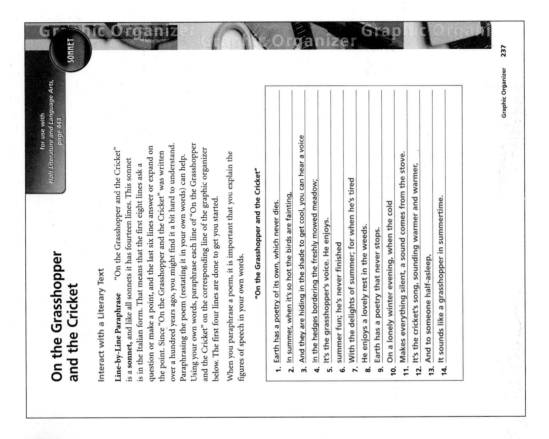

SONNET

for use with
Holt Literature and Language Arts,
page 443

On the Grasshopper and the Cricket

Interact with a Literary Text

Line-by-Line Paraphrase "On the Grasshopper and the Cricket" is a **sonnet,** and like all sonnets it has fourteen lines. This sonnet is in the Italian form. That means that the first eight lines ask a question or make a point, and the last six lines answer or expand on the point. Since "On the Grasshopper and the Cricket" was written over a hundred years ago, you might find it a bit hard to understand. Paraphrasing the poem (restating it in your own words) can help. Using your own words, paraphrase each line of "On the Grasshopper and the Cricket" on the corresponding line of the graphic organizer below. The first four lines are done to get you started.

When you paraphrase a poem, it is important that you explain the figures of speech in your own words.

"On the Grasshopper and the Cricket"

1. Earth has a poetry of its own, which never dies.
2. In summer, when it's so hot the birds are fainting,
3. And they are hiding in the shade to get cool, you can hear a voice
4. In the hedges bordering the freshly mowed meadow;
5. It's the grasshopper's voice. He enjoys.
6. summer fun; he's never finished
7. With the delights of summer; for when he's tired
8. He enjoys a lovely rest in the weeds.
9. Earth has a poetry that never stops.
10. On a lonely winter evening, when the cold
11. Makes everything silent, a sound comes from the stove.
12. It's the cricket's song, sounding warmer and warmer,
13. And to someone half-asleep,
14. It sounds like a grasshopper in summertime.

ODES

for use with
Holt Literature and Language Arts,
page 437

Oda a las gracias/ Ode to Thanks; Birdfoot's Grampa; Ode to a Toad

Interact with Literary Texts

Cluster Map An **ode** is a poem written in praise of someone or something. "Oda a las gracias/Ode to Thanks" praises the simple word *thanks.* Fill in the cluster diagram below with details that tell what the poet says *thanks* is or does.

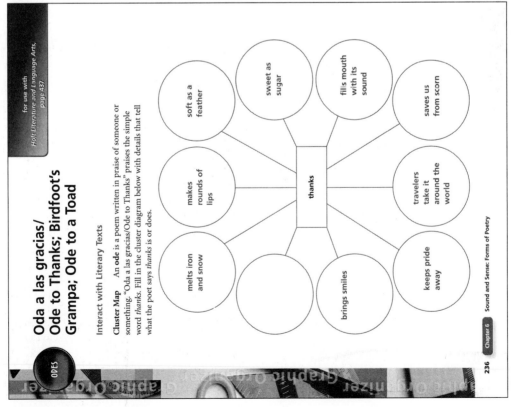

I Hear America Singing; I, Too

for use with
Holt Literature and Language Arts,
page 451

FREE VERSE

Interact with Literary Texts

Venn Diagram "I Hear America Singing" and "I, Too" are both **free-verse poems**. That means they do not follow a regular meter or rhyme scheme, though they do use strong rhythms and repetition. The two poems have other things in common. In fact, "I, Too" was written as a response to "I Hear America Singing."

The Venn diagram is useful for comparing two texts. On the diagram below, show what "I Hear America Singing" and "I, Too" have in common—and what they don't.

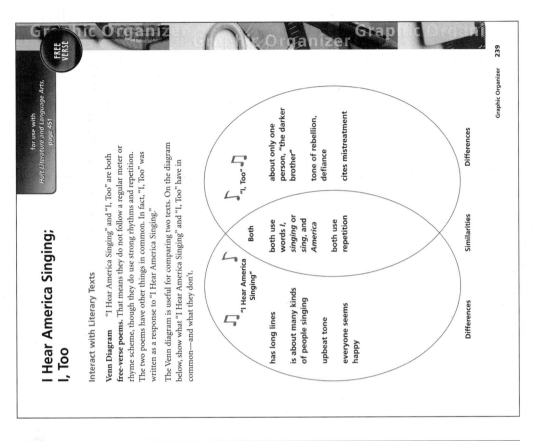

"I Hear America Singing"

has long lines

is about many kinds of people singing

upbeat tone

everyone seems happy

"I, Too"

about only one person, "the darker brother"

tone of rebellion, defiance

cites mistreatment

Both

both use words *I, singing* or *sing,* and *America*

both use repetition

Differences   Similarities   Differences

Graphic Organizer   **239**

ELEGY

O Captain! My Captain!

for use with
Holt Literature and Language Arts,
page 447

Interact with a Literary Text

Extended-Metaphor Chart "O Captain! My Captain!" is an **elegy**, or a poem in praise of someone who has died. It uses an extended metaphor. This means that throughout the poem, the captain of the ship represents President Abraham Lincoln. The ship itself represents the United States. Filling out an extended-metaphor chart can help you track the extension of the metaphor throughout the entire poem. In the chart below, the first stanza is done for you.

"O Captain! My Captain!"

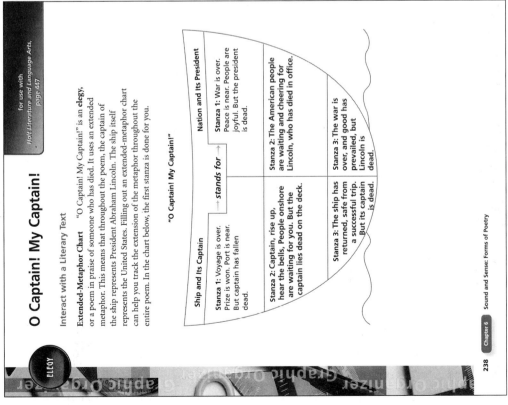

Ship and Its Captain	stands for	Nation and Its President
Stanza 1: Voyage is over. Prize is won. Port is near. But captain has fallen dead.	→	**Stanza 1:** War is over. Peace is near. People are joyful. But the president is dead.
Stanza 2: Captain, rise up, hear the bells, People onshore are waiting for you. But the captain lies dead on the deck.		**Stanza 2:** The American people are waiting and cheering for Lincoln, who has died in office.
Stanza 3: The ship has returned, safe from a successful trip. But its captain is dead.		**Stanza 3:** The war is over, and good has prevailed, but Lincoln is dead.

238   Chapter 6   Sound and Sense: Forms of Poetry

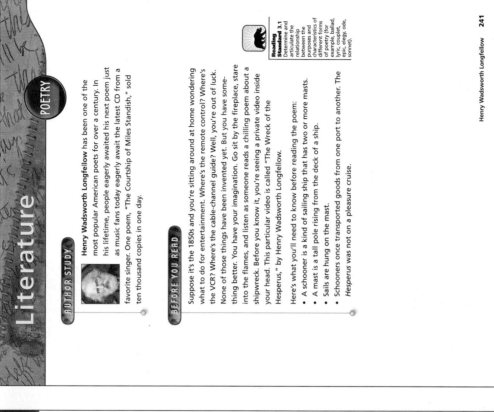

Literature

POETRY

AUTHOR STUDY

Henry Wadsworth Longfellow has been one of the most popular American poets for over a century. In his lifetime, people eagerly awaited his next poem just as music fans today eagerly await the latest CD from a favorite singer. One poem, "The Courtship of Miles Standish," sold ten thousand copies in one day.

BEFORE YOU READ

Suppose it's the 1850s and you're sitting around at home wondering what to do for entertainment. Where's the remote control? Where's the VCR? Where's the cable-channel guide? Well, you're out of luck. None of those things have been invented yet. But you have something better. You have your imagination. Go sit by the fireplace, stare into the flames, and listen as someone reads a chilling poem about a shipwreck. Before you know it, you're seeing a private video inside your head. This particular video is called "The Wreck of the Hesperus," by Henry Wadsworth Longfellow.

Here's what you'll need to know before reading the poem:

- A schooner is a kind of sailing ship that has two or more masts.
- A mast is a tall pole rising from the deck of a ship.
- Sails are hung on the mast.
- Schooners once transported goods from one port to another. The *Hesperus* was not on a pleasure cruise.

Reading Standard 3.1 Determine and articulate the relationship between the purposes and characteristics of different forms of poetry (for example, ballad, lyric, couplet, epic, elegy, ode, sonnet).

Henry Wadsworth Longfellow **241**

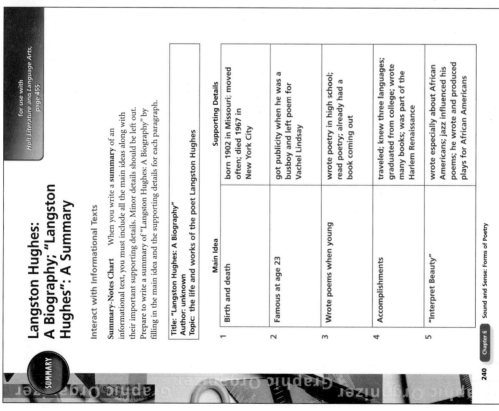

SUMMARY

Langston Hughes: A Biography; "Langston Hughes": A Summary

for use with Holt Literature and Language Arts, page 455

Interact with Informational Texts

Summary-Notes Chart When you write a **summary** of an informational text, you must include all the main ideas along with their important supporting details. Minor details should be left out. Prepare to write a summary of "Langston Hughes: A Biography" by filling in the main idea and the supporting details for each paragraph.

Title: "Langston Hughes: A Biography"
Author: unknown
Topic: the life and works of the poet Langston Hughes

	Main Idea	Supporting Details
1	Birth and death	born 1902 in Missouri; moved often; died 1967 in New York City
2	Famous at age 23	got publicity when he was a busboy and left poem for Vachel Lindsay
3	Wrote poems when young	wrote poetry in high school; read poetry; already had a book coming out
4	Accomplishments	traveled; knew three languages; graduated from college; wrote many books; was part of the Harlem Renaissance
5	"Interpret Beauty"	wrote especially about African Americans; jazz influenced his poems; he wrote and produced plays for African Americans

240 Chapter 6 Sound and Sense: Forms of Poetry

The Wreck of the Hesperus

Henry Wadsworth Longfellow

WORD KNOWLEDGE

Ope (line 8) is a shortened form of *open*, used here to fit with the poem's rhythmic pattern.

IDENTIFY

Pause at line 20. This is a narrative poem, which tells a story. Identify the characters, the setting, and the problem so far.

Characters: Skipper, his young daughter, an old sailor. Setting: schooner at sea; Problem: possible hurricane coming up.

It was the schooner Hesperus,
    That sailed the wintry sea;
And the skipper had taken his little daughter,
    To bear him company.

5 Blue were her eyes as the fairy-flax,[1]
    Her cheeks like the dawn of day,
And her bosom white as the hawthorn buds
    That ope in the month of May.

    The skipper he stood beside the helm,
10   His pipe was in his mouth,
And he watched how the veering flaw[2] did blow
    The smoke now West, now South.

    Then up and spake an old Sailor,
    Had sailed to the Spanish Main,[3]
15 "I pray thee, put into yonder port,
    For I fear a hurricane.

    "Last night, the moon had a golden ring,
    And tonight no moon we see!"
The skipper, he blew a whiff from his pipe,
20   And a scornful laugh laughed he.

1. **fairy-flax:** plant with blue flowers.
2. **veering flaw:** sudden, short gust of wind ("flaw") that changes directions ("veers").
3. **Spanish Main:** Caribbean Sea, especially the part north of South America.

    Colder and louder blew the wind,
    A gale from the Northeast,
The snow fell hissing in the brine,
    And the billows frothed like yeast.

25 Down came the storm, and smote amain[4]
    The vessel in its strength;
She shuddered and paused, like a frighted steed,
    Then leaped her cable's length.

    "Come hither! come hither! my little daughter,
30   And do not tremble so;
For I can weather the roughest gale
    That ever wind did blow."

    He wrapped her warm in his seaman's coat
    Against the stinging blast;
35 He cut a rope from a broken spar,[5]
    And bound her to the mast.

    "O father! I hear the church bells ring,
    Oh say, what may it be?"
" 'Tis a fog bell on a rock-bound coast!" —
40   And he steered for the open sea.

    "O father! I hear the sound of guns,
    Oh say, what may it be?"
"Some ship in distress, that cannot live
    In such an angry sea!"

4. **smote amain:** struck with full force.
5. **spar:** any pole holding sails on a ship.

WORD KNOWLEDGE

A simile compares two different things using a word such as *like*, *as*, or *resembles*. Underline the simile in line 27. What do you see happening?

Possible response: The ship is shaking and plunging through huge waves, as if it is a terrified horse.

INTERPRET

Why does the skipper tie his daughter to the mast (line 36)?

He wants to keep her from being washed overboard by the storm.

FLUENCY

Generations of students have recited "The Wreck of the Hesperus" and other poems by Longfellow. See how you do by reciting lines 29–48. Perhaps you and some classmates can take roles and read the passage aloud together. How many voices do you need, and whose are they?

Three voices are needed: the captain, his daughter, and the narrator.

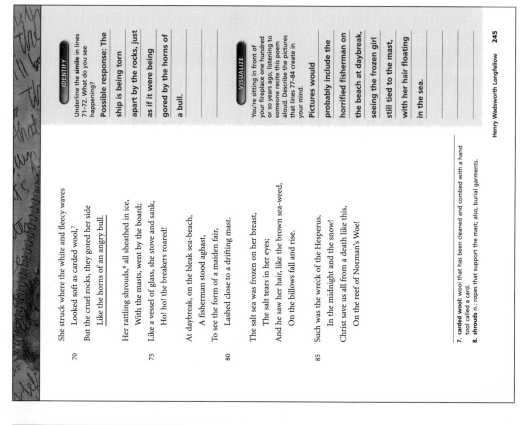

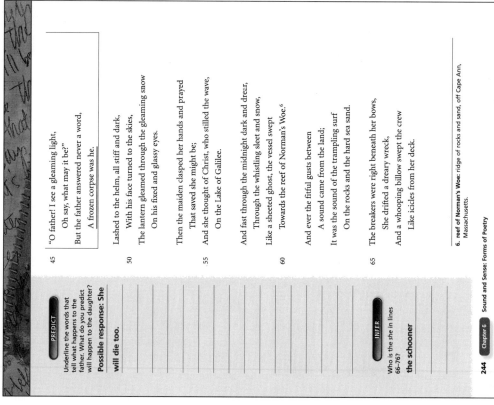

PREDICT

Underline the words that tell what happens to the father. What do you predict will happen to the daughter?

Possible response: She will die too.

45   "O father! I see a gleaming light,
      Oh say, what may it be?"
  But the father answered never a word,
      A frozen corpse was he.

50   Lashed to the helm, all stiff and dark,
      With his face turned to the skies,
  The lantern gleamed through the gleaming snow
      On his fixed and glassy eyes.

  Then the maiden clasped her hands and prayed
      That saved she might be;
55   And she thought of Christ, who stilled the wave,
      On the Lake of Galilee.

  And fast through the midnight dark and drear,
      Through the whistling sleet and snow,
  Like a sheeted ghost, the vessel swept
60   Towards the reef of Norman's Woe.[6]

  And ever the fitful gusts between
      A sound came from the land;
  It was the sound of the trampling surf
      On the rocks and the hard sea sand.

65   The breakers were right beneath her bows,
      She drifted a dreary wreck,
  And a whooping billow swept the crew
      Like icicles from her deck.

INFER

Who is the *she* in lines 66–76?

the schooner

6. **reef of Norman's Woe:** ridge of rocks and sand, off Cape Ann, Massachusetts.

244   Chapter 6   Sound and Sense: Forms of Poetry

  She struck where the white and fleecy waves
70   Looked soft as carded wool,[7]
  But the cruel rocks, they gored her side
      Like the horns of an angry bull.

  Her rattling shrouds,[8] all sheathed in ice,
      With the masts, went by the board;
75   Like a vessel of glass, she stove and sank,
      Ho! ho! the breakers roared!

  At daybreak, on the bleak sea-beach,
      A fisherman stood aghast,
  To see the form of a maiden fair,
80   Lashed close to a drifting mast.

  The salt sea was frozen on her breast,
      The salt tears in her eyes;
  And he saw her hair, like the brown sea-weed,
      On the billows fall and rise.

85   Such was the wreck of the Hesperus,
      In the midnight and the snow!
  Christ save us all from a death like this,
      On the reef of Norman's Woe!

IDENTIFY

Underline the simile in lines 71–72. What do you see happening?

Possible response: The ship is being torn apart by the rocks, just as if it were being gored by the horns of a bull.

VISUALIZE

You're sitting in front of your fireplace one hundred or so years ago, listening to someone recite this poem aloud. Describe the pictures that lines 77–84 create in your mind.

Pictures would probably include the horrified fisherman on the beach at daybreak, seeing the frozen girl still tied to the mast, with her hair floating in the sea.

7. **carded wool:** wool that has been cleaned and combed with a hand tool called a card.
8. **shrouds** *n.:* ropes that support the mast; also, burial garments.

Henry Wadsworth Longfellow   245

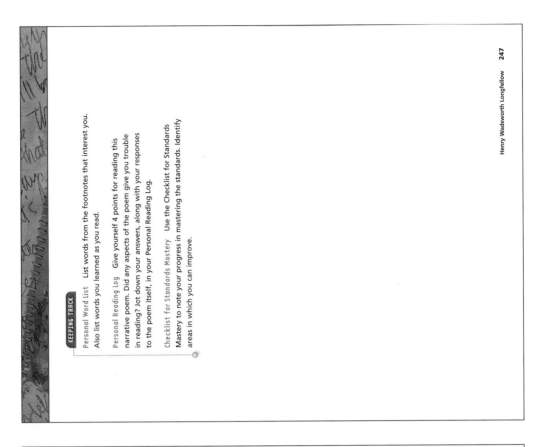

Personal Word List   List words from the footnotes that interest you. Also list words you learned as you read.

Personal Reading Log   Give yourself 4 points for reading this narrative poem. Did any aspects of the poem give you trouble in reading? Jot down your answers, along with your responses to the poem itself, in your Personal Reading Log.

Checklist for Standards Mastery   Use the Checklist for Standards Mastery to note your progress in mastering the standards. Identify areas in which you can improve.

Henry Wadsworth Longfellow   **247**

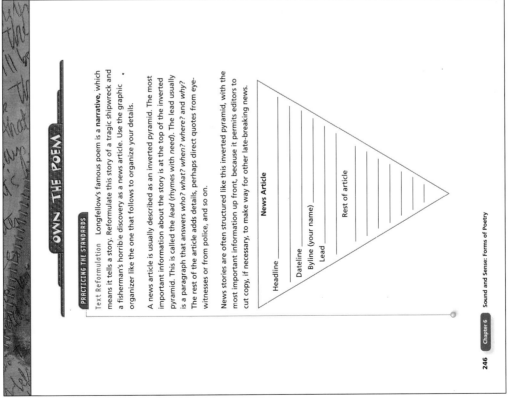

OWN THE POEM

PRACTICING THE STANDARDS

Text Reformulation   Longfellow's famous poem is a **narrative**, which means it tells a story. Reformulate this story of a tragic shipwreck and a fisherman's horrible discovery as a news article. Use the graphic organizer like the one that follows to organize your details.

A news article is usually described as an inverted pyramid. The most important information about the story is at the top of the inverted pyramid. This is called the *lead* (rhymes with *need*). The lead usually is a paragraph that answers *who? what? when? where?* and *why?* The rest of the article adds details, perhaps direct quotes from eye-witnesses or from police, and so on.

News stories are often structured like this inverted pyramid, with the most important information up front, because it permits editors to cut copy, if necessary, to make way for other late-breaking news.

News Article

Headline _____

Dateline _____

Byline (your name) _____

Lead _____

Rest of article

246   Chapter 6   Sound and Sense: Forms of Poetry

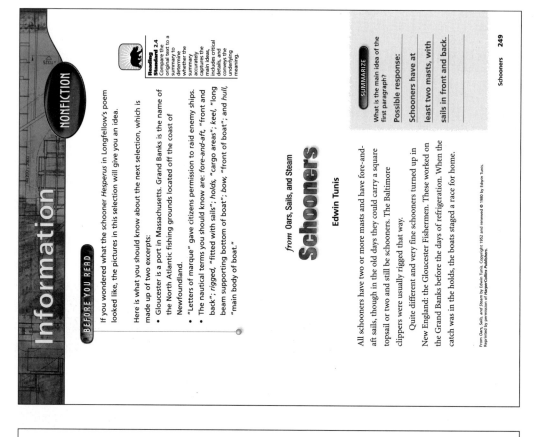

Information

NONFICTION

BEFORE YOU READ

If you wondered what the schooner *Hesperus* in Longfellow's poem looked like, the pictures in this selection will give you an idea.

Here is what you should know about the next selection, which is made up of two excerpts:

- Gloucester is a port in Massachusetts. Grand Banks is the name of the North Atlantic fishing grounds located off the coast of Newfoundland.
- "Letters of marque" gave citizens permission to raid enemy ships.
- The nautical terms you should know are: *fore-and-aft*, "front and back"; *rigged*, "fitted with sails"; *holds*, "cargo areas"; *keel*, "long beam supporting bottom of boat"; *bow*, "front of boat"; and *hull*, "main body of boat."

Reading Standard 2.4 Compare the original text to a summary to determine whether the summary accurately captures the main ideas, includes critical details, and conveys the underlying meaning.

from **Oars, Sails, and Steam**

Schooners

Edwin Tunis

All schooners have two or more masts and have fore-and-aft sails, though in the old days they could carry a square topsail or two and still be schooners. The Baltimore clippers were usually rigged that way.

Quite different and very fine schooners turned up in New England: the Gloucester Fishermen. These worked on the Grand Banks before the days of refrigeration. When the catch was in the holds, the boats staged a race for home.

From Oars, Sails, and Steam by Edwin Tunis. Copyright 1952 and renewed © 1980 by Edwin Tunis. Reprinted by permission of HarperCollins Publishers.

SUMMARIZE

What is the main idea of the first paragraph?

Possible response:
Schooners have at least two masts, with sails in front and back.

Schooners **249**

The Wreck of the Hesperus ■ *Interactive Reading, page 242*

Go Beyond a Literary Text

Author Profile Use your library and the Internet to find out more about Henry Wadsworth Longfellow. Then use your research to fill in the author profile below.

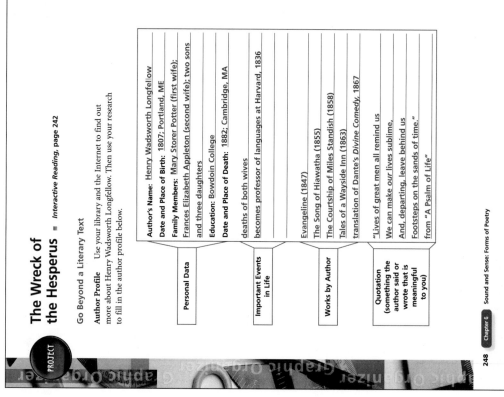

Personal Data	**Author's Name:** Henry Wadsworth Longfellow
	Date and Place of Birth: 1807; Portland, ME
	Family Members: Mary Storer Potter (first wife); Frances Elizabeth Appleton (second wife); two sons and three daughters
	Education: Bowdoin College
	Date and Place of Death: 1882; Cambridge, MA

Important Events in Life	deaths of both wives
	becomes professor of languages at Harvard, 1836

Works by Author	Evangeline (1847)
	The Song of Hiawatha (1855)
	The Courtship of Miles Standish (1858)
	Tales of a Wayside Inn (1863)
	translation of Dante's *Divine Comedy*, 1867

Quotation (something the author said or wrote that is meaningful to you)	"Lives of great men all remind us / We can make our lives sublime, / And, departing, leave behind us / Footsteps on the sands of time." from "A Psalm of Life"

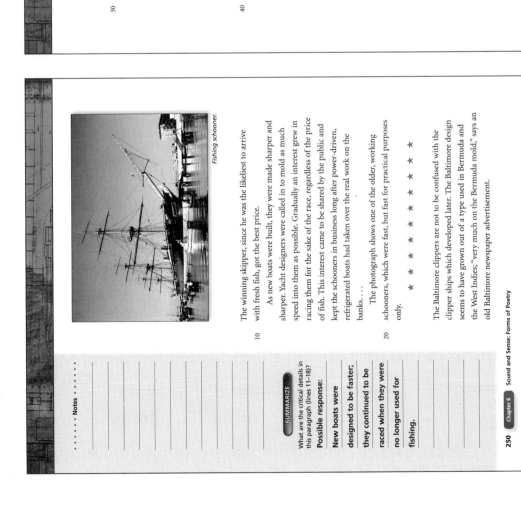

SUMMARIZE

What are the critical details in this paragraph (lines 11–18)?

Possible response:

New boats were

designed to be faster;

they continued to be

raced when they were

no longer used for

fishing.

The winning skipper, since he was the likeliest to arrive with fresh fish, got the best price.

10   As new boats were built, they were made sharper and sharper. Yacht designers were called in to mold in as much speed into them as possible. Gradually an interest grew in racing them for the sake of the race, regardless of the price of fish. This interest came to be shared by the public and kept the schooners in business long after power-driven, refrigerated boats had taken over the real work on the banks....

20   The photograph shows one of the older, working schooners, which were fast, but fast for practical purposes only.

★ ★ ★ ★ ★ ★ ★ ★

The Baltimore clippers are not to be confused with the clipper ships which developed later. The Baltimore design seems to have grown out of a type used in Bermuda and the West Indies; "very much on the Bermuda mold," says an old Baltimore newspaper advertisement.

Fishing schooner.

The clippers were superbly fast sailers, far faster than anything afloat in their time. For this reason they were much used as privateers¹ in the War of 1812 and later, for the same reason, as slavers.²

30   During that second war against England, the American government issued "letters of marque" to privately owned vessels, which then had the privilege of annoying the British. The clippers did this with great success and with considerable profits to their owners. Profits came from the sale of "prizes," that is, captured ships and their cargoes. The *Rossie*, commanded by doughty³ Joshua Barney, sank or captured fifteen British ships in forty-five days. Captain Boyle, in the *Chasseur*, declared a one-ship blockade of the

40 British Isles!

These Baltimore clippers were very sharp—long, narrow, and deep—and the keel grew deeper as it ran aft, giving them what is called "drag," but not in the sense of

Baltimore clipper schooner.

1. **privateers** *n.*: privately owned ships sent by the government to capture enemy ships, especially merchant ships, for their cargo.
2. **slavers** *n.*: ships that carried men, women, and children from Africa to be sold in U.S. markets.
3. **doughty** (dou′tē) *adj.*: brave.

WORD KNOWLEDGE

What context clues help you guess at the meaning of "letters of marque" (märk)? Underline the clues.

COMPARE & CONTRAST

How are the Gloucester schooners different from the Baltimore clippers?

Possible response:

Both had two or more

masts; both were very

fast. Gloucesters were

used for fishing and

racing. Baltimore

clippers were used as

privateers in war and

as slavers.

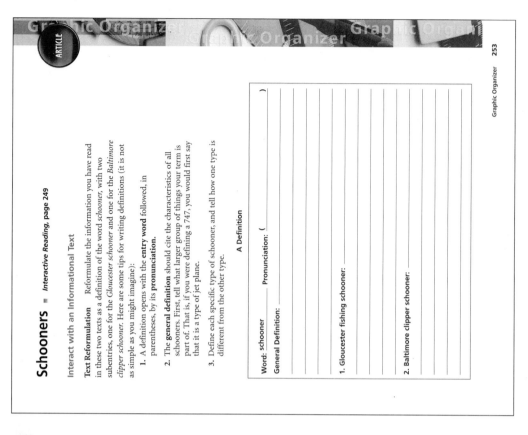

ARTICLE

Schooners ■ *Interactive Reading, page 249*

Interact with an Informational Text

Text Reformulation   Reformulate the information you have read in these two texts as a definition of the word *schooner*, with two subentries, one for the *Gloucester schooner* and one for the *Baltimore clipper schooner*. Here are some tips for writing definitions (it is not as simple as you might imagine):

1. A definition opens with the **entry word** followed, in parentheses, by its **pronunciation.**

2. The **general definition** should cite the characteristics of all schooners. First, tell what larger group of things your term is part of. That is, if you were defining a 747, you would first say that it is a type of jet plane.

3. Define each specific type of schooner, and tell how one type is different from the other type.

A Definition

Word: schooner   Pronunciation: (   )

General Definition: _____

_____

_____

_____

1. Gloucester fishing schooner: _____

_____

2. Baltimore clipper schooner: _____

_____

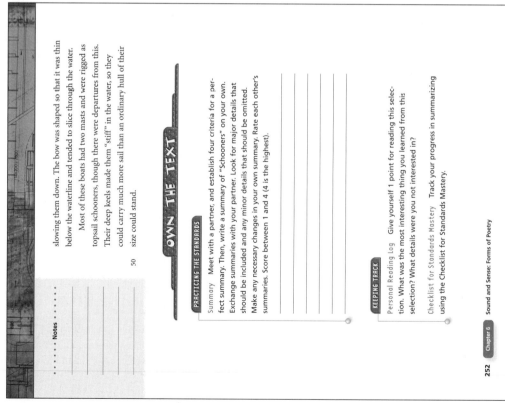

· · · · · · · **Notes** · · · · · · ·

_____

_____

_____

_____

_____

slowing them down. The bow was shaped so that it was thin below the waterline and tended to slice through the water.

Most of these boats had two masts and were rigged as topsail schooners, though there were departures from this. Their deep keels made them "stiff" in the water, so they could carry much more sail than an ordinary hull of their
50   size could stand.

OWN THE TEXT

PRACTICING THE STANDARDS

Summary   Meet with a partner, and establish four criteria for a perfect summary. Then, write a summary of "Schooners" on your own. Exchange summaries with your partner. Look for major details that should be included and any minor details that should be omitted. Make any necessary changes in your own summary. Rate each other's summaries. Score between 1 and 4 (4 is the highest).

_____

_____

_____

_____

_____

KEEPING TRACK

Personal Reading Log   Give yourself 1 point for reading this selection. What was the most interesting thing you learned from this selection? What details were you not interested in?

Checklist for Standards Mastery   Track your progress in summarizing using the Checklist for Standards Mastery.

Literature

 POETRY

Reading Standard 3.1
Determine and articulate the relationship between the purposes and characteristics of different forms of poetry (for example, ballad, lyric, couplet, epic, elegy, ode, sonnet).

BEFORE YOU READ

Langston Hughes and Carl Sandburg are two great American poets of the twentieth century. Both wrote *free verse*—poetry that imitates the rhythms of ordinary conversation.

Here is what you need to know before reading the poems:

- Langston Hughes wrote "Lincoln Monument: Washington" in 1927. The Lincoln Monument was dedicated in 1927.
- Carl Sandburg wrote "Mr. Longfellow and His Boy" in 1941, during World War II, when Franklin Delano Roosevelt was president of the United States and Winston Churchill was prime minister of England.
- Henry Wadsworth Longfellow wrote the poem that Sandburg quotes in 1849, during the Civil War, when Abraham Lincoln was president of the United States.

Lincoln Monument: Washington

Langston Hughes

Let's go see old Abe
Sitting in the marble and the moonlight,
Sitting lonely in the marble and the moonlight,
Quiet for ten thousand centuries, old Abe.
5 Quiet for a million, million years.

Quiet—

And yet a voice forever
Against the
Timeless walls
10 Of time—
Old Abe.

INFER

Abraham Lincoln died in 1865. How, then, would you explain lines 4–5?

Possible response:
It seems to African Americans that a long time has passed since Lincoln offered them freedom and equality, and they still do not have them.

"Lincoln Monument: Washington" from The Collected Poems of Langston Hughes. Copyright © 1994 by the Estate of Langston Hughes. Reprinted by permission of Alfred A. Knopf, Inc., a division of Random House, Inc.

254 Chapter 6 Sound and Sense: Forms of Poetry

Mr. Longfellow and His Boy

An old-fashioned recitation to be read aloud

Carl Sandburg

Mr. Longfellow, Henry Wadsworth Longfellow,
the Harvard professor,
the poet whose pieces you see in all the schoolbooks,
"Tell me not in mournful numbers
5   life is but an empty dream . . ."
Mr. Longfellow sits in his Boston library writing,
Mr. Longfellow looks across the room
and sees his nineteen-year-old boy
propped up in a chair at a window,
10   home from the war,
a rifle ball through right and left shoulders.

In his diary the father writes about his boy:
"He has a wound through him a foot long.
He pretends it does not hurt him."
15 And the father if he had known
would have told the boy propped up in a chair
how one of the poems written in that room
made President Lincoln cry.
And both the father and the boy
20 would have smiled to each other and felt good
about why the President had tears over that poem.

Noah Brooks, the California newspaperman,
could have told the Longfellows how one day
Brooks heard the President saying two lines:

"Mr. Longfellow and His Boy" from The Complete Poems of Carl Sandburg. Copyright © 1969, 1970 by Lilian Steichen Sandburg, Trustee. Reprinted by permission of Harcourt, Inc.

INFER

Longfellow was born in 1807 and died in 1882. What war would his son (see lines 8–11) have been wounded in?
the Civil War,
1861–1865

INFER

Why would Longfellow and his son have "felt good" that Longfellow's poem made President Lincoln cry (lines 15–21)?

Possible response:
They would have been pleased that the poem meant so much to the president.

Mr. Longfellow and His Boy 255

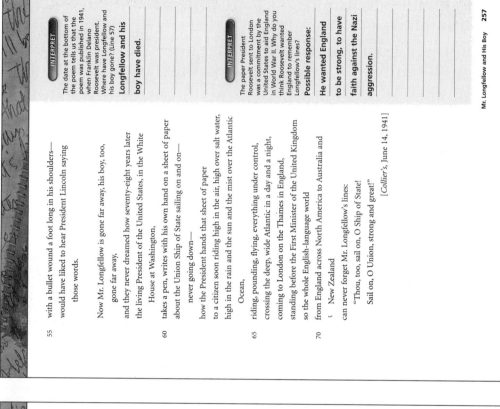

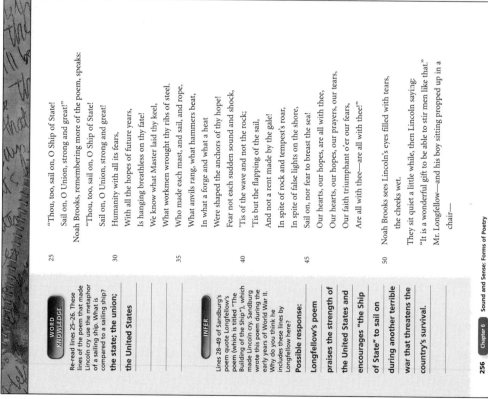

25   "Thou, too, sail on, O Ship of State!
      Sail on, O Union, strong and great!"
      Noah Brooks, remembering more of the poem, speaks:
      "Thou, too, sail on, O Ship of State!
      Sail on, O Union, strong and great!
30   Humanity with all its fears,
      With all the hopes of future years,
      Is hanging breathless on thy fate!
      We know what Master laid thy keel,
      What workmen wrought thy ribs of steel,
35   Who made each mast, and sail, and rope,
      What anvils rang, what hammers beat,
      In what a forge and what a heat
      Were shaped the anchors of thy hope!
      Fear not each sudden sound and shock,
40   'Tis of the wave and not the rock;
      'Tis but the flapping of the sail,
      And not a rent made by the gale!
      In spite of rock and tempest's roar,
      In spite of false lights on the shore,
45   Sail on, nor fear to breast the sea!
      Our hearts, our hopes, are all with thee,
      Our hearts, our hopes, our prayers, our tears,
      Our faith triumphant o'er our fears,
      Are all with thee—are all with thee!"

50   Noah Brooks sees Lincoln's eyes filled with tears,
      the cheeks wet.
      They sit quiet a little while, then Lincoln saying:
      "It is a wonderful gift to be able to stir men like that."
      Mr. Longfellow—and his boy sitting propped up in a
      chair—

WORD KNOWLEDGE

Re-read lines 25–26. These lines of the poem that made Lincoln cry use the metaphor of a sailing ship. What is compared to a sailing ship? **the state; the union;**

the United States

INFER

Lines 28–49 of Sandburg's poem quote Longfellow's poem (which is titled "The Building of the Ship"), which made Lincoln cry. Sandburg wrote this poem during the early years of World War II. Why do you think he includes these lines by Longfellow here? **Possible response:**

Longfellow's poem

praises the strength of

the United States and

encourages "the Ship

of State" to sail on

during another terrible

war that threatens the

country's survival.

55   with a bullet wound a foot long in his shoulders—
      would have liked to hear President Lincoln saying
      those words.

      Now Mr. Longfellow is gone far away, his boy, too,
      gone far away,
      and they never dreamed how seventy-eight years later
      the living President of the United States, in the White
      House at Washington,
60   takes a pen, writes with his own hand on a sheet of paper
      about the Union Ship of State sailing on and on—
      never going down—
      how the President hands that sheet of paper
      to a citizen soon riding high in the air, high over salt water,
      high in the rain and the sun and the mist over the Atlantic
      Ocean,
65   riding, pounding, flying, everything under control,
      crossing the deep, wide Atlantic in a day and a night,
      coming to London on the Thames in England,
      standing before the First Minister of the United Kingdom
      so the whole English-language world
70   from England across North America to Australia and
      New Zealand
      can never forget Mr. Longfellow's lines:
      "Thou, too, sail on, O Ship of State!
      Sail on, O Union, strong and great!"

                                      [*Collier's*, June 14, 1941]

INTERPRET

The date at the bottom of the poem tells us that the poem was published in 1941, when Franklin Delano Roosevelt was president. Where have Longfellow and his boy gone? (Line 57) **Longfellow and his**

boy have died.

INTERPRET

The paper President Roosevelt sent to London was a commitment by the United States to aid England in World War II. Why do you think Roosevelt wanted England to remember Longfellow's lines? **Possible response:**

He wanted England

to be strong, to have

faith against the Nazi

aggression.

Lincoln Monument: Washington; Mr. Longfellow and His Boy ■ *Interactive Reading, page 254*

Go Beyond Literary Texts

Poetry Dartboard Do you sometimes have trouble thinking of ideas for creative writing? Try this: Close your eyes, and put your finger on the "Subjects" dartboard. The spot your finger lands on gives you your **subject**. Next, go to the "Speakers" dartboard. This will tell you who should be the **speaker** of your poem. Put the subject and speaker together, and you're on your way.

Now, write a poem *at least* ten lines long. You will have to decide what form of poetry you'd like to write: **ballad, lyric, epic, elegy, ode**, or **sonnet**. In other words, do you want to tell a story? express a feeling or an idea? mourn someone or something that has died, or sing the praises of someone or something that is living? You will also have to decide if you want to use rhyme and meter, or if you prefer the looser form of free verse.

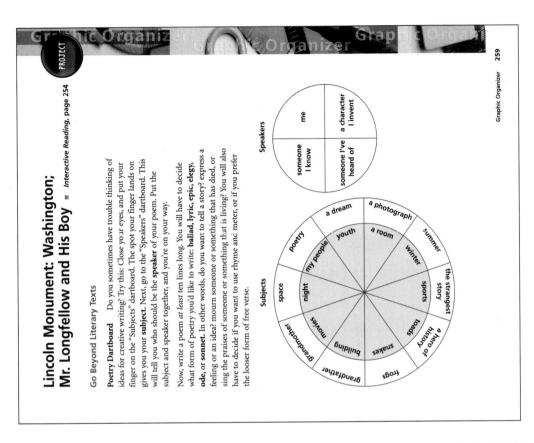

Speakers

someone I know	me
someone I've heard of	a character I invent

Subjects: a dream, a photograph, a room, summer, youth, poetry, my people, space, night, grandmother, movies, building, snakes, frogs, toads, a hero of history, the strangest story, sports, winter

---

OWN THE POEMS

PRACTICING THE STANDARDS

Fluency Prepare these two poems for a performance. You will have to work with a group and assign parts. Your first task will be to determine the number of speakers you will need. Then, make scripts of the poems, and block out each speaker's part. (You might want to use a chorus to speak the narrator's part in Sandburg's poem.) Rehearse your reading in front of a group of classmates. Ask them to evaluate your performance. When you are satisfied with your readings, take your show on the road!

KEEPING TRACK

Personal Word List Record any unfamiliar words from these poems in your Personal Word List.

Personal Reading Log Rate each poem in terms of your personal enjoyment. Why do you like one more than another? Write down your rating and your analysis of it in your Personal Reading Log. Award yourself 2 points on the Reading Meter.

Checklist for Standards Mastery Use the Checklist for Standards Mastery to evaluate your mastery of the forms of poetry.

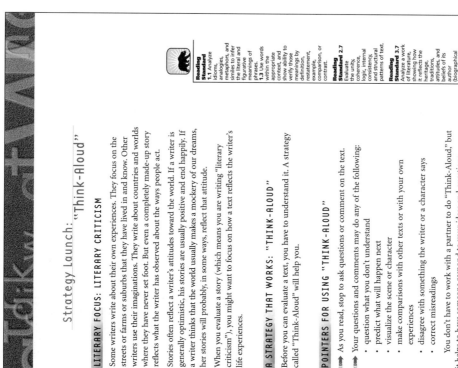

Chapter 7

Literary Criticism
The Person Behind the Text

Chapter Preview In this chapter you will—

Read: Selections	**Interact with Text:** Graphic Organizers

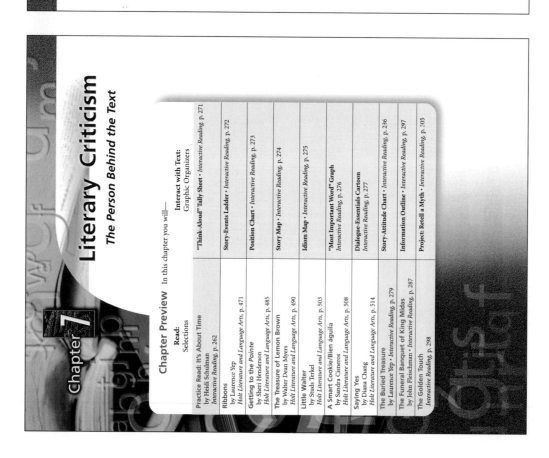

Strategy Launch: "Think-Aloud"

LITERARY FOCUS: LITERARY CRITICISM

Some writers write about their own experiences. They focus on the streets or farms or suburbs that they have lived in and know. Other writers use their imaginations. They write about countries and worlds where they have never set foot. But even a completely made-up story reflects what the writer has observed about the ways people act.

Stories often reflect a writer's attitudes toward the world. If a writer is generally optimistic, his stories are usually positive and end happily. If a writer thinks that the world usually makes a mockery of our dreams, her stories will probably, in some ways, reflect that attitude.

When you evaluate a story (which means you are writing "literary criticism"), you might want to focus on how a text reflects the writer's life experiences.

A STRATEGY THAT WORKS: "THINK-ALOUD"

Before you can evaluate a text, you have to understand it. A strategy called "Think-Aloud" will help you.

POINTERS FOR USING "THINK-ALOUD"

▶ As you read, stop to ask questions or comment on the text.

▶ Your questions and comments may do any of the following:
- question what you don't understand
- predict what will happen next
- visualize the scene or character
- make comparisons with other texts or with your own experiences
- disagree with something the writer or a character says
- correct misreadings

You don't have to work with a partner to do "Think-Aloud," but it helps to have someone respond to your ideas and questions.

Reading Standard 1.1 Analyze idioms, analogies, metaphors, and similes to infer the literal and figurative meanings of phrases.
1.3 Use words within the appropriate context, and show ability to verify those meanings by definition, restatement, example, comparison, or contrast.
Reading Standard 2.7 Evaluate the unity, coherence, logic, internal consistency, and structural patterns of text.
Reading Standard 3.7 Analyze a work of literature, showing how it reflects the heritage, traditions, attitudes, and beliefs of its author (biographical approach).

Strategy Launch **261**

Practice Read

BEFORE YOU READ

Their cultures are very different. Benny is a teenager who loves his hometown of Los Angeles. His grandparents are older people who love their tiny Mexican American village in the mountains of New Mexico. One day Benny sees their lives through new eyes.

Here's what you need to know before you begin the story:
• New Mexico was settled by the Spanish before the state became part of the United States.
• Heidi Schulman, the author of the story, once lived in Los Angeles. She now lives in New Mexico, in a little village where most of the residents are Mexican Americans.

It's About Time

Heidi Schulman

WORD KNOWLEDGE

What words or phrases in the first paragraph give context clues to the meaning of *quirk* (line 4)? Circle them.

• • • • • • Notes • • • • • •

Ever since I've been a little kid, I've had a really (strange) (habit.) Every day, while I'm having breakfast, I check the kitchen calendar to make sure I know the date. Don't ask me why. I guess you'd call it a quirk. People at school know about it, too. They say "Hey, Benny, what's the date?" and I always know. Some people think I'm doing it to (seem different,) but that's not true. If I wanted to be different, don't you think I could find a better way than memorizing the date? It just goes to show that people can be really wrong about each other.

10 Anyway, this morning, when I turned the calendar from May to June, I rolled my eyes. That's because on this

date, every year, my parents start bugging me about visiting my grandparents for my birthday.

My mother started up right on cue. "Benny, dear," she said, in a sweet tone of voice. I tried to slosh down my orange juice and zoom out the door to avoid what was next. I was getting up when my father's voice stopped me.

"Ben, son, your mother and I . . ."

20 Uh oh. My dad was pausing a lot between words. He spoke that way when he wanted me to sit down, be quiet, and listen. Since he was driving me to school, I couldn't leave without him. I was a captive audience.

"We're thinking you should visit . . ."

I didn't have to listen to the rest. Dad was about to say how great it would be to visit my grandparents at their home in Middle-of-Nowhere, New Mexico. That's not really the name of the town, of course, but when you hear descriptions of the place, that's what it sounds like. I'd bet my last dollar there's nothing to do there, not for a kid from L.A. who lives near the beach.

30 "It'll be fun, Benny," said my mother. "It's a sweet town, and your father grew up there."

"Your mother is right," said Dad, pulling me back into the room with his slow, steady words. "Your *abuelo* and *abuela* want to see you. It's about time."

I knew *abuelo* and *abuela* meant "grandfather" and "grandmother" in Spanish, but I didn't know many other Spanish words. I didn't need Spanish to play computer games or basketball or go to the beach with Tracey, the nicest girl in the whole city of Los Angeles. Come to think

40 of it, I'd be missing all of those things if I got shipped off to Nowheresville for my birthday. I'd be a prisoner in a small mountain village, population 250. I'd been able to wriggle

THINK-ALOUD

Pause at line 14. Who is the narrator of this story? How do you know the "I" in the story is not the writer?

A boy named Benny is the narrator. The writer is a woman, so "Benny" could not be the writer.

THINK-ALOUD

What details in lines 25–31 seem to link with the writer's experience?

The writer once lived in L.A., where the story's narrator lives. She now lives in New Mexico, where the narrator's grandparents live.

THINK-ALOUD

Without stopping to criticize your ideas, jot down a couple of things you predict might happen in the story.

Possible response:

Benny will go to his grandparents' house and realize he likes it after all.

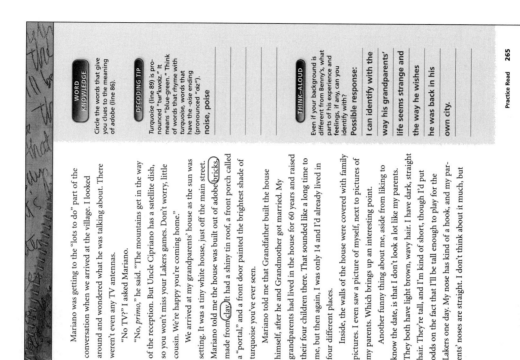

out of the trip every year or so far, but sooner or later everybody's luck runs out. My turn had come.

It takes a really long time to get from somewhere to nowhere, and don't let anybody tell you any different. Somewhere was Los Angeles. Nowhere was Tierra Linda, New Mexico.

50 *Tierra Linda* is Spanish for "beautiful earth," but names can fool you. After a three-hour drive from the airport, you turn onto a dirt road and there you are in a rundown little village in the mountains. The main street, if you can call it a street, has maybe ten houses, a post office, and a tiny general store. The houses are all different colors—pink, blue, green, you name it, and they all have tin roofs. The day I arrived, the only things moving on the main street were two beat-up old trucks and some dogs. What a yawn.

60 My cousin Mariano picked me up at the airport. He's twenty and actually pretty cool, except it's weird the way he acted like we'd known each other forever, when we'd never met or talked before.

"Hey, Benito," he said, calling me by my given name—a name I rarely used. "*Bienvenidos, primo.*¹ Everybody's waiting to meet you. *Todo la familia.*²"

Mariano spent the whole trip from the airport talking about our relatives and the village.

70 "This village was built more than two hundred and fifty years ago," he said. "Some of the people came from Mexico, and some from Spain. Our great-great grandparents were from Mexico. They still have customs from the old days. You'll get to see many things. There's lots to do."

---

1. *Bienvenidos, primo:* Welcome, cousin.
2. *Todo la familia:* the whole family.

THINK–ALOUD

What do you think so far about Benny's character?
Benny is a city boy from Los Angeles. He is of Mexican American heritage but doesn't know much Spanish. He hasn't bothered to be very close to his grandparents.

THINK–ALOUD

Comment on the writer's use of Spanish words in the story. Do you like this technique? Or does it make your reading difficult?
Responses will vary.

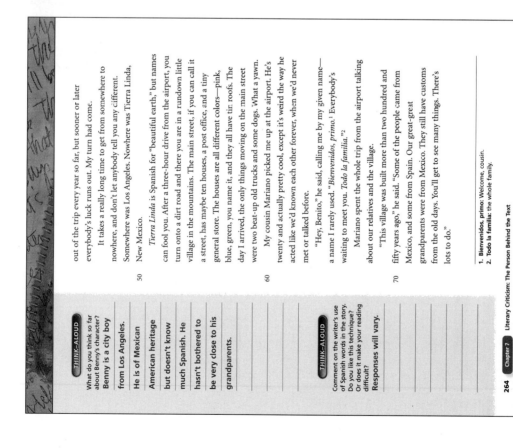

Mariano was getting to the "lots to do" part of the conversation when we arrived at the village. I looked around and wondered what he was talking about. There weren't even any TV antennas.

"No TV?" I asked Mariano.

80 "No, *primo*," he said. "The mountains get in the way of the reception. But Uncle Cipriano has a satellite dish, so you won't miss your Lakers games. Don't worry, little cousin. We're happy you're coming home."

We arrived at my grandparents' house as the sun was setting. It was a tiny white house, just off the main street. Mariano told me the house was built out of adobe bricks made from clay. It had a shiny tin roof, a front porch called a "portal," and a front door painted the brightest shade of turquoise you've ever seen.

90 Mariano told me that Grandfather built the house himself, after he and Grandmother got married. My grandparents had lived in the house for 60 years and raised their four children there. That sounded like a long time to me, but then again, I was only 14 and I'd already lived in four different places.

Inside, the walls of the house were covered with family pictures. I even saw a picture of myself, next to pictures of my parents. Which brings up an interesting point.

Another funny thing about me, aside from liking to 100 know the date, is that I don't look a lot like my parents. They both have light brown, wavy hair. I have dark, straight hair. They're tall, and I'm kind of short, though I'd put odds on the fact that I'll be tall enough to play for the Lakers one day. My nose has kind of a hook, and my parents' noses are straight. I don't think about it much, but

WORD KNOWLEDGE

Circle the words that give you clues to the meaning of *adobe* (line 86).

DECODING TIP

Turquoise (line 89) is pronounced "tur'kwoz." It means "blue-green." Think of words that rhyme with *turquoise*, words that have the *-oise* ending (pronounced "oz"). noise, poise

THINK–ALOUD

Even if your background is different from Benny's, what parts of his experience and feelings, if any, can you identify with? Possible response: **I can identify with the way his grandparents' life seems strange and the way he wishes he was back in his own city.**

Practice Read 265

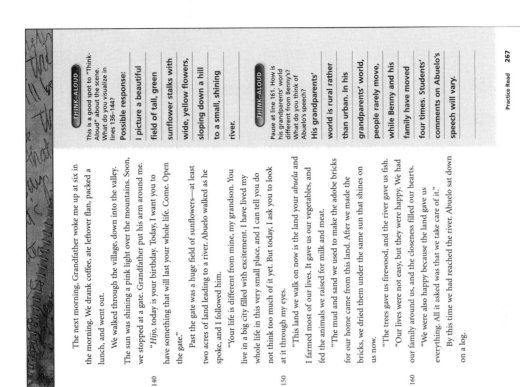

The next morning, Grandfather woke me up at six in the morning. We drank coffee, ate leftover flan, packed a lunch, and went out.

We walked through the village, down into the valley. The sun was shining a pink light over the mountains. Soon, we stopped at a gate. Grandfather put his arm around me.
140 "*Hijo*, today is your birthday. Today, I want you to have something that will last your whole life. Come. Open the gate."

Past the gate was a huge field of sunflowers—at least two acres of land leading to a river. Abuelo walked as he spoke, and I followed him.

"Your life is different from mine, my grandson. You live in a big city filled with excitement. I have lived my whole life in this very small place, and I can tell you do not think too much of it yet. But today, I ask you to look
150 at it through my eyes.

"This land we walk on now is the land your *abuela* and I farmed most of our lives. It gave us our vegetables, and fed the animals we raised for milk and meat.

"The mud and sand we used to make the adobe bricks for our home came from this land. After we made the bricks, we dried them under the same sun that shines on us now.

"The trees gave us firewood, and the river gave us fish.

"Our lives were not easy, but they were happy. We had
160 our family around us, and the closeness filled our hearts. We were also happy because the land gave us everything. All it asked was that we take care of it."

By this time we had reached the river. Abuelo sat down on a log.

THINK-ALOUD
This is a good spot to "Think-Aloud" about the scene. What do you visualize in lines 136–142?
Possible response:
I picture a beautiful field of tall, green sunflower stalks with wide, yellow flowers, sloping down a hill to a small, shining river.

THINK-ALOUD
Pause at line 161. How is his grandparents' world different from Benny's? What do you think of Abuelo's speech?
His grandparents' world is rural rather than urban. In his grandparents' world, people rarely move, while Benny and his family have moved four times. Students' comments on Abuelo's speech will vary.

Practice Read 267

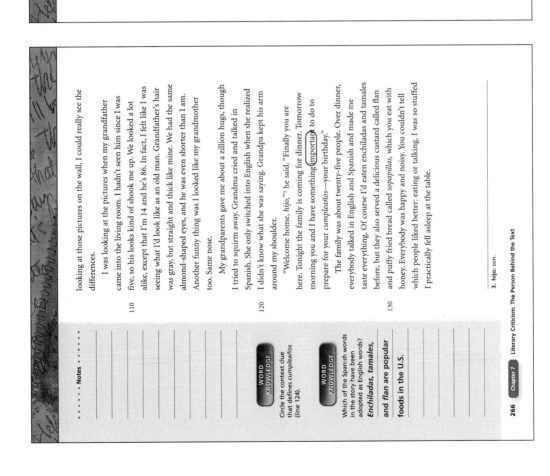

Notes

looking at those pictures on the wall, I could really see the differences.

I was looking at the pictures when my grandfather came into the living room. I hadn't seen him since I was five, so his looks kind of shook me up. We looked a lot
110 alike, except that I'm 14 and he's 86. In fact, I felt like I was seeing what I'd look like as an old man. Grandfather's hair was gray, but straight and thick like mine. We had the same almond-shaped eyes, and he was even shorter than I am. Another funny thing was I looked like my grandmother too. Same nose.

My grandparents gave me about a zillion hugs, though I tried to squirm away. Grandma cried and talked in Spanish. She only switched into English when she realized
120 I didn't know what she was saying. Grandpa kept his arm around my shoulder.

"Welcome home, *hijo*,"³ he said. "Finally you are here. Tonight the family is coming for dinner. Tomorrow morning you and I have something important to do to prepare for your *cumpleaños*—your birthday."

The family was about twenty-five people. Over dinner, everybody talked in English and Spanish and made me taste everything. Of course I'd eaten enchiladas and tamales before, but they also served a delicious custard called flan
130 and puffy fried bread called *sopapillas*, which you eat with honey. Everybody was happy and noisy. You couldn't tell which people liked better: eating or talking. I was so stuffed I practically fell asleep at the table.

WORD KNOWLEDGE
Circle the context clue that defines *cumpleaños* (line 124).

WORD KNOWLEDGE
Which of the Spanish words in the story have been adopted as English words? Enchiladas, tamales, and flan are popular foods in the U.S.

3. hijo: son.

266 Chapter 7 Literary Criticism: The Person Behind the Text

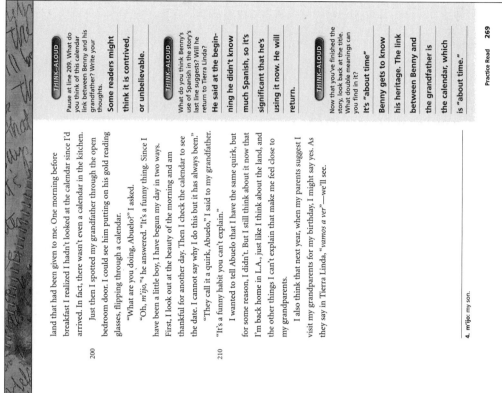

land that had been given to me. One morning before breakfast I realized I hadn't looked at the calendar since I'd arrived. In fact, there wasn't even a calendar in the kitchen.

200 Just then I spotted my grandfather through the open bedroom door. I could see him putting on his gold reading glasses, flipping through a calendar.

"What are you doing, Abuelo?" I asked.

"Oh, *m'ijo*,⁴" he answered. "It's a funny thing. Since I have been a little boy, I have begun my day in two ways. First, I look out at the beauty of the morning and am thankful for another day. Then I check the calendar to see the date. I cannot say why I do this but it has always been."

"They call it a quirk, Abuelo," I said to my grandfather.

210 "It's a funny habit you can't explain."

I wanted to tell Abuelo that I have the same quirk, but for some reason, I didn't. But I still think about it now that I'm back home in L.A., just like I think about the land, and the other things I can't explain that make me feel close to my grandparents.

I also think that next year, when my parents suggest I visit my grandparents for my birthday, I might say yes. As they say in Tierra Linda, "*vamos a ver*"—we'll see.

4. *m'ijo:* my son.

THINK-ALOUD
Pause at line 209. What do you think of this calendar link between Benny and his grandfather? Write your thoughts.
Some readers might think it is contrived, or unbelievable.

THINK-ALOUD
What do you think Benny's use of Spanish in the story's last line suggests? Will he return to Tierra Linda?
He said at the beginning he didn't know much Spanish, so it's significant that he's using it now. He will return.

THINK-ALOUD
Now that you've finished the story, look back at the title. What double meanings can you find in it?
It's "about time"
Benny gets to know his heritage. The link between Benny and the grandfather is the calendar, which is "about time."

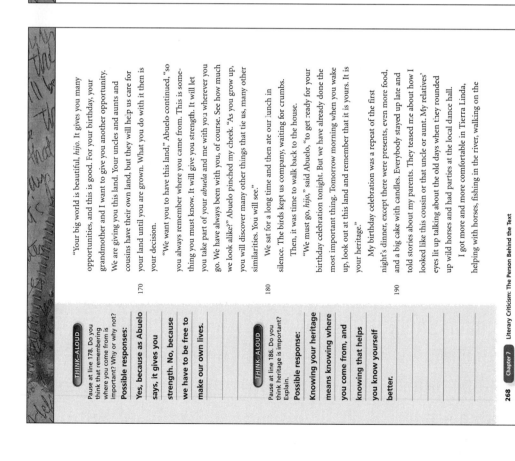

THINK-ALOUD
Pause at line 178. Do you think that remembering where you come from is important? Why or why not?
Possible responses:
Yes, because as Abuelo says, it gives you strength. No, because we have to be free to make our own lives.

THINK-ALOUD
Pause at line 186. Do you think heritage is important? Explain.
Possible response:
Knowing your heritage means knowing where you come from, and knowing that helps you know yourself better.

"Your big world is beautiful, *hijo*. It gives you many opportunities, and this is good. For your birthday, your grandmother and I want to give you another opportunity. We are giving you this land. Your uncles and aunts and cousins have their own land, but they will help us care for

170 your land until you are grown. What you do with it then is your decision.

"We want you to have this land," Abuelo continued, "so you always remember where you came from. This is something you must know. It will give you strength. It will let you take part of your *abuela* and me with you wherever you go. We have always been with you, of course. See how much we look alike?" Abuelo pinched my cheek. "As you grow up, you will discover many other things that tie us, many other similarities. You will see."

180 We sat for a long time and then ate our lunch in silence. The birds kept us company, waiting for crumbs.

Then, it was time to walk back to the house.

"We must go, *hijo*," said Abuelo, "to get ready for your birthday celebration tonight. But we have already done the most important thing. Tomorrow morning when you wake up, look out at this land and remember that it is yours. It is your heritage."

My birthday celebration was a repeat of the first night's dinner, except there were presents, even more food, and a big cake with candles. Everybody stayed up late and

190 told stories about my parents. They teased me about how I looked like this cousin or that uncle or aunt. My relatives' eyes lit up talking about the old days when they rounded up wild horses and had parties at the local dance hall.

I got more and more comfortable in Tierra Linda, helping with horses, fishing in the river, walking on the

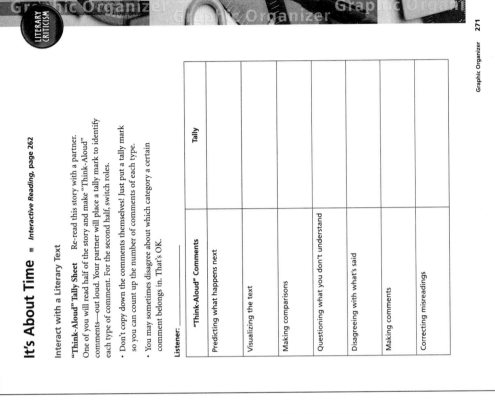

It's About Time ■ *Interactive Reading, page 262*

Interact with a Literary Text

"Think-Aloud" Tally Sheet   Re-read this story with a partner. One of you will read half of the story and make "Think-Aloud" comments—out loud. Your partner will place a tally mark to identify each type of comment. For the second half, switch roles.

• Don't copy down the comments themselves! Just put a tally mark so you can count up the number of comments of each type.
• You may sometimes disagree about which category a certain comment belongs in. That's OK.

Listener: _____

"Think-Aloud" Comments	Tally
Predicting what happens next	
Visualizing the text	
Making comparisons	
Questioning what you don't understand	
Disagreeing with what's said	
Making comments	
Correcting misreadings	

Graphic Organizer   **271**

OWN THE STORY

PRACTICING THE STANDARDS

Analyzing Literature (Biographical Approach)   Discuss with a partner what Benny learned about his Mexican American heritage in "It's About Time." Then, respond to this question: How does the writer feel about the importance of a person's heritage? Support your response with details from the story. Score each other's responses from 1 to 4, with 4 the highest score. The more details from the story you use to support your opinion, the higher your score!

"Think-Aloud" Assessment   Review the "Think-Aloud" comments you made as you re-read this story with a partner, using the graphic on the next page. Notice which comments you made most often and which ones you did not make much at all. Then, write a brief comment on this strategy by completing this statement: *Using "Think-Aloud" with this story helped/didn't help me because—*

_____

_____

_____

KEEPING TRACK

Personal Word List   In your Personal Word List, record the Spanish words in this story that have become common in English. Note any new words you learned.

Personal Reading Log   As you record this story in your Personal Reading Log, state whether or not you would recommend it to a friend. Give yourself 4 points on the Reading Meter.

Checklist for Standards Mastery   Check your progress using the Checklist for Standards Mastery.

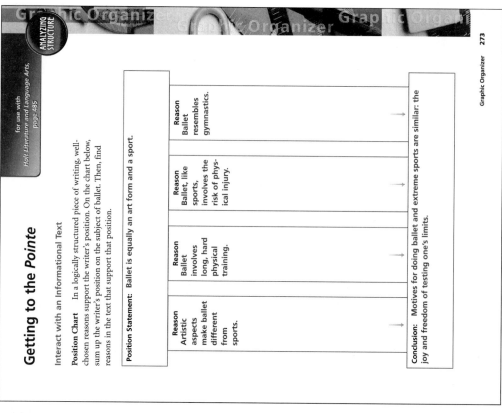

ANALYZING STRUCTURE

for use with
Holt Literature and Language Arts,
page 485

Getting to the *Pointe*

Interact with an Informational Text

Position Chart   In a logically structured piece of writing, well-chosen reasons support the writer's position. On the chart below, sum up the writer's position on the subject of ballet. Then, find reasons in the text that support that position.

Position Statement: Ballet is equally an art form and a sport.

Reason Artistic aspects make ballet different from sports.	Reason Ballet involves long, hard physical training.	Reason Ballet, like sports, involves the risk of physical injury.	Reason Ballet resembles gymnastics.

Conclusion: Motives for doing ballet and extreme sports are similar: the joy and freedom of testing one's limits.

Graphic Organizer   273

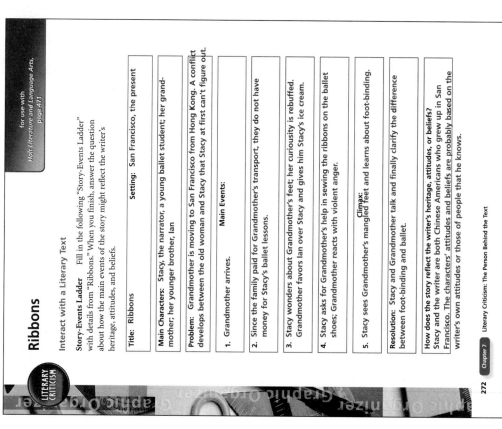

LITERARY CRITICISM

for use with
Holt Literature and Language Arts,
page 471

Ribbons

Interact with a Literary Text

Story-Events Ladder   Fill in the following "Story-Events Ladder" with details from "Ribbons." When you finish, answer the question about how the main events of the story might reflect the writer's heritage, attitudes, and beliefs.

Title: Ribbons	Setting: San Francisco, the present

Main Characters: Stacy, the narrator, a young ballet student; her grandmother; her younger brother, Ian

Problem: Grandmother is moving to San Francisco from Hong Kong. A conflict develops between the old woman and Stacy that Stacy at first can't figure out.

Main Events:

1. Grandmother arrives.

2. Since the family paid for Grandmother's transport, they do not have money for Stacy's ballet lessons.

3. Stacy wonders about Grandmother's feet; her curiousity is rebuffed. Grandmother favors Ian over Stacy and gives him Stacy's ice cream.

4. Stacy asks for Grandmother's help in sewing the ribbons on the ballet shoes; Grandmother reacts with violent anger.

Climax:
5. Stacy sees Grandmother's mangled feet and learns about foot-binding.

Resolution: Stacy and Grandmother talk and finally clarify the difference between foot-binding and ballet.

How does the story reflect the writer's heritage, attitudes, or beliefs?
Stacy and the writer are both Chinese Americans who grew up in San Francisco. The characters' attitudes and beliefs are probably based on the writer's own attitudes or those of people that he knows.

Chapter 7   Literary Criticism: The Person Behind the Text

272

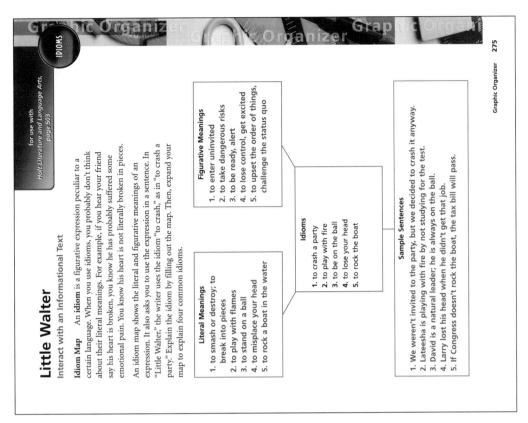

The Treasure of Lemon Brown

for use with
Holt Literature and Language Arts,
page 490

Interact with a Literary Text

Story Map Fill out the story map below for "The Treasure of Lemon Brown." Then, answer the question about how the story might reflect the writer's heritage, attitudes, and beliefs.

Basic Situation: Greg Ridley, a fourteen-year-old, is at odds with his father because of Greg's disappointing efforts in math. If Greg's next report card doesn't improve, his father won't let him join the basketball team.

Main Events

1. Greg enters an abandoned building in his neighborhood.

2. Lemon Brown, an old man who lives in the building, confronts Greg.

3. Three neighborhood men arrive to try to steal Lemon Brown's "treasure." Second conflict.

4. Lemon Brown counterattacks, and the attackers flee.

Climax

Lemon Brown shows Greg his "treasure": the "treasure" is only some yellowed news clippings and a battered harmonica that had been treasured by his son, a soldier killed in war.

Resolution

With a new sense of the value of family, Greg returns gladly to his father.

How do you think the story reflects the author's heritage, attitudes, and beliefs?

Possible response: Both the main character and the writer are African American and grew up in New York City. The writer seems to feel that young people need powerful role models in order to acquire values to live by.

Little Walter

for use with
Holt Literature and Language Arts,
page 503

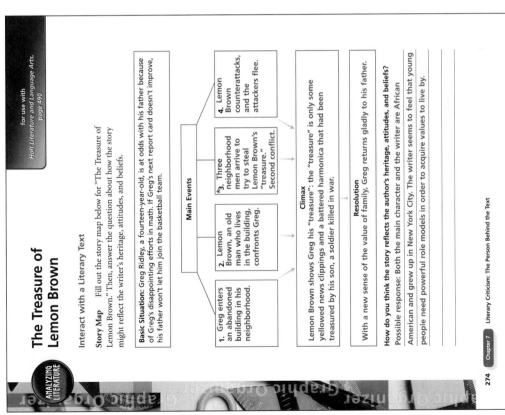

Interact with an Informational Text

Idiom Map An **idiom** is a figurative expression peculiar to a certain language. When you use idioms, you probably don't think about their literal meanings. For example, if you hear your friend say his heart is broken, you know he has probably suffered some emotional pain. You know his heart is not literally broken in pieces.

An idiom map shows the literal and figurative meanings of an expression. It also asks you to use the expression in a sentence. In "Little Walter," the writer uses the idiom "to crash," as in "to crash a party." Explain the idiom by filling out the map. Then, expand your map to explain four common idioms.

Literal Meanings
1. to smash or destroy; to break into pieces
2. to play with flames
3. to stand on a ball
4. to misplace your head
5. to rock a boat in the water

Figurative Meanings
1. to enter uninvited
2. to take dangerous risks
3. to be ready, alert
4. to lose control, get excited
5. to upset the order of things, challenge the status quo

Idioms
1. to crash a party
2. to play with fire
3. to be on the ball
4. to lose your head
5. to rock the boat

Sample Sentences
1. We weren't invited to the party, but we decided to crash it anyway.
2. Lateesha is playing with fire by not studying for the test.
3. David is a natural leader; he is always on the ball.
4. Larry lost his head when he didn't get that job.
5. If Congress doesn't rock the boat, the tax bill will pass.

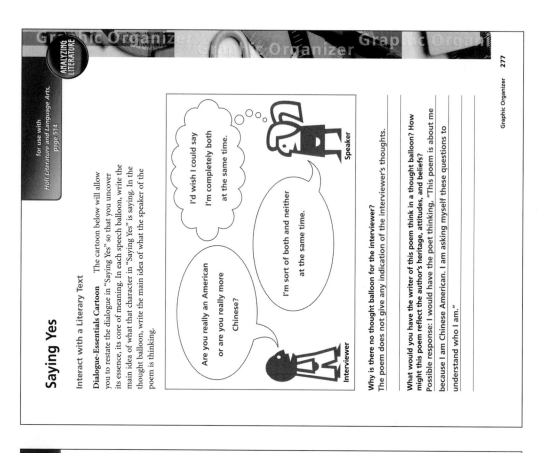

Saying Yes

for use with
Holt Literature and Language Arts,
page 514

ANALYZING LITERATURE

Interact with a Literary Text

Dialogue-Essentials Cartoon The cartoon below will allow you to restate the dialogue in "Saying Yes" so that you uncover its essence, its core of meaning. In each speech balloon, write the main idea of what that character in "Saying Yes" is saying. In the thought balloon, write the main idea of what the speaker of the poem is thinking.

Why is there no thought balloon for the interviewer?
The poem does not give any indication of the interviewer's thoughts.

What would you have the writer of this poem think in a thought balloon? How might this poem reflect the author's heritage, attitudes, and beliefs?
Possible response: I would have the poet thinking, "This poem is about me because I am Chinese American. I am asking myself these questions to understand who I am."

Graphic Organizer **277**

ANALYZING LITERATURE

A Smart Cookie/
Bien águila

for use with
Holt Literature and Language Arts,
page 508

Interact with a Literary Text

"Most Important Word" Graph When you analyze a piece of literature, you want to be sure you have grasped its theme. **Theme** is the what a story or poem or play reveals to us about our lives. Theme is usually not stated directly. You, the reader, have to read the selection carefully, look for important passages and important words, and then come up with a general statement saying what you think the text tells you about life. Try a strategy called "Most Important Word" to identify the theme of "A Smart Cookie."

Here is how "Most Important Word" works:

- Look for a word that has an impact on you as you read the story. Look for a word that is repeated or a word that is used at the beginning or end of the story and seems important to you.

- Think about how the word relates to the story's characters and to what happens to them. Fill in your ideas on the graphic below.

- Reflect on what you have written. Then, make a generalization about the theme that all of those comments seem to support.

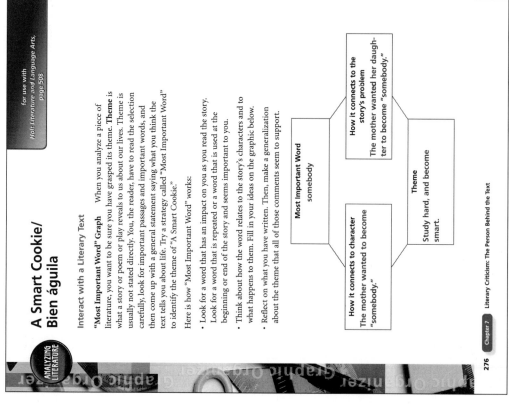

276 Chapter 7 Literary Criticism: The Person Behind the Text

Literature

FOLK TALE

AUTHOR STUDY

Laurence Yep was born in San Francisco's Chinatown in 1948. At eighteen, he had his first science fiction short story published. Today he is a well-known Asian American writer, having published many novels and short stories. He has written several books about traditional Chinese culture as well as what it is like to be a Chinese immigrant living in America. Laurence Yep has won Newbery Medals for his books *Dragonwings* and *Dragon's Gate*.

BEFORE YOU READ

"The Buried Treasure" is an old Chinese folk tale that has been retold by Laurence Yep. Yep has compiled several collections of stories based on the folk tales and legends of China. In *The Rainbow People* he retells twenty stories adapted from the recollections of Chinese immigrants living in Oakland's Chinatown. The stories were recorded by U.S. government-sponsored programs during the Depression of the 1930s. Like all folk tales, Yep's stories are full of magic and other supernatural events. Yep is especially interested in stories that help young people live between two cultures. Yep's stories have been called bridge builders because they help readers understand the ways people in this world are alike and different.

Reading Standard 3.7
Analyze a work of literature, showing how it reflects the heritage, traditions, attitudes, and beliefs of its author (biographical approach).

The Buried Treasure

a Chinese folk tale, retold by Laurence Yep

There was once a rich man who heard that there was no lock that could not be picked. So he put his money into jars and buried them in secret places. In fact, the whole town nicknamed him "Old Jarhead."

Now, Jarhead had two sons. The older son, Yüe Cang, already managed the family's lands and properties. However, the younger son, Yüe Shēng, cared neither for books nor for business. Old Jarhead scolded and begged him to change, and each time the young man promised to behave. However, he never remembered his promise.

Since Yüe Shēng was also a friendly fellow, he never turned a guest away from his door. Often he had to provide meals for three or even four guests a day. Everyone took advantage of him. As a result, his money poured through his hands like water.

One day when Old Jarhead fell sick, he **summoned** his sons to his bedside and told them the contents of his will. To the older son, he left everything. His younger son, Yüe Shēng, would receive nothing.

Hurt, Yüe Shēng sighed. "Well, it isn't as if you didn't warn me."

Alarmed, Old Jarhead tried to sit up but could not.

"I'm not trying to punish you," he wheezed. "I have money set aside for you. But if I gave it to you now, you'd spend it all. You'll get it when you've learned the value of hard work."

10

20

From Tree of Dreams: Ten Tales from the Garden of Night by Laurence Yep. Copyright © 1995 by Laurence Yep. Published and reprinted by permission of Tryll Associates, LLC.

COMPARE & CONTRAST

Pause at line 15. How do Old Jarhead's two sons differ?

One cares for business,

the other does not.

The younger son is

also very generous,

and people take

advantage of him.

VOCABULARY DEVELOPMENT

summoned (sum'ənd) v.: called or sent for.

IDENTIFY

In lines 23–26 is an important detail. When will the younger son get his money? Circle the father's words that tell you.

_____

_____

Laurence Yep **279**

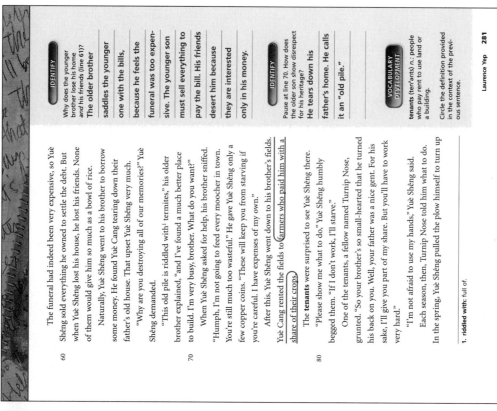

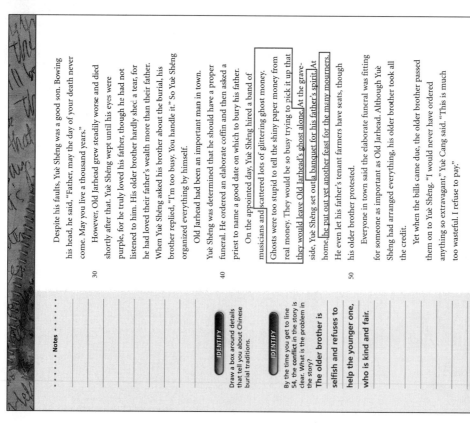

· · · · · · Notes · · · · · ·

Despite his faults, Yuè Shēng was a good son. Bowing his head, he said, "Father, may the day of your death never come. May you live a thousand years."

However, Old Jarhead grew steadily worse and died
30 shortly after that. Yuè Shēng wept until his eyes were purple, for he truly loved his father, though he had not listened to him. His older brother hardly shed a tear, for he had loved their father's wealth more than their father. When Yuè Shēng asked his brother about the burial, his brother replied, "I'm too busy. You handle it." So Yuè Shēng organized everything by himself.

Old Jarhead had been an important man in town. Yuè Shēng was determined that he should have a proper
40 funeral. He ordered an elaborate coffin and then asked a priest to name a good date on which to bury his father.

On the appointed day, Yuè Shēng hired a band of musicians and scattered lots of glittering ghost money. Ghosts were too stupid to tell the shiny paper money from real money. They would be so busy trying to pick it up that they would leave Old Jarhead's ghost alone. At the graveside, Yuè Shēng set out a banquet for his father's spirit. At home, he put out yet another feast for the many mourners. He even let his father's tenant farmers have seats, though
50 his older brother protested.

Everyone in town said the elaborate funeral was fitting for someone as important as Old Jarhead. Although Yuè Shēng had arranged everything, his older brother took all the credit.

Yet when the bills came due, the older brother passed them on to Yuè Shēng. "I would never have ordered anything so extravagant," Yuè Cang said. "This is much too wasteful. I refuse to pay."

IDENTIFY

Draw a box around details that tell you about Chinese burial traditions.

IDENTIFY

By the time you get to line 54, the conflict in the story is clear. What is the problem in the story?

The older brother is
selfish and refuses to
help the younger one,
who is kind and fair.

The funeral had indeed been very expensive, so Yuè
60 Shēng sold everything he owned to settle the debt. But when Yuè Shēng lost his house, he lost his friends. None of them would give him so much as a bowl of rice.

Naturally, Yuè Shēng went to his brother to borrow some money. He found Yuè Cang tearing down their father's old house. That upset Yuè Shēng very much.

"Why are you destroying all of our memories?" Yuè Shēng demanded.

"This old pile is riddled with¹ termites," his older brother explained, "and I've found a much better place
70 to build. I'm very busy, brother. What do you want?"

When Yuè Shēng asked for help, his brother sniffed. "Humph, I'm not going to feed every moocher in town. You're still much too wasteful." He gave Yuè Shēng only a few copper coins. "These will keep you from starving if you're careful. I have expenses of my own."

After this, Yuè Shēng went down to his brother's fields. Yuè Cang rented the fields to farmers who paid him with a share of their crops.

The tenants were surprised to see Yuè Shēng there.
80 "Please show me what to do," Yuè Shēng humbly begged them. "If I don't work, I'll starve."

One of the tenants, a fellow named Turnip Nose, grunted. "So your brother's so small-hearted that he turned his back on you. Well, your father was a nice gent. For his sake, I'll give you part of my share. But you'll have to work very hard."

"I'm not afraid to use my hands," Yuè Shēng said.

Each season, then, Turnip Nose told him what to do. In the spring, Yuè Shēng pulled the plow himself to turn up

---

1. **riddled with:** full of.

IDENTIFY

Why does the younger brother lose his home and his friends (line 61)?

The older brother
saddles the younger
one with the bills,
because he feels the
funeral was too expensive. The younger son
must sell everything to
pay the bill. His friends
desert him because
they are interested
only in his money.

IDENTIFY

Pause at line 70. How does the older son show disrespect for his heritage?

He tears down his
father's home. He calls
it an "old pile."

VOCABULARY DEVELOPMENT

tenants (ten'ants) *n.*: people who pay rent to use land or a building.

Circle the definition provided in the context of the previous sentence.

Laurence Yep **281**

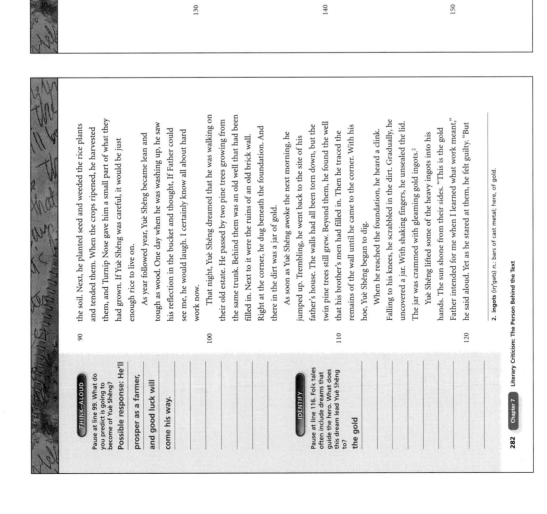

Left page (282)

THINK-ALOUD

Pause at line 99. What do you predict is going to become of Yuè Shēng?

Possible response: He'll prosper as a farmer, and good luck will come his way.

the soil. Next, he planted seed and weeded the rice plants and tended them. When the crops ripened, he harvested them, and Turnip Nose gave him a small part of what they had grown. If Yuè Shēng was careful, it would be just enough rice to live on.

90   As year followed year, Yuè Shēng became lean and tough as wood. One day when he was washing up, he saw his reflection in the bucket and thought, If Father could see me, he would laugh. I certainly know all about hard work now.

100   That night, Yuè Shēng dreamed that he was walking on their old estate. He passed by two pine trees growing from the same trunk. Behind them was an old well that had been filled in. Next to it were the ruins of an old brick wall. Right at the corner, he dug beneath the foundation. And there in the dirt was a jar of gold.

    As soon as Yuè Shēng awoke the next morning, he jumped up. Trembling, he went back to the site of his father's house. The walls had all been torn down, but the twin pine trees still grew. Beyond them, he found the well that his brother's men had filled in. Then he traced the

110 remains of the wall until he came to the corner. With his hoe, Yuè Shēng began to dig.

    When he reached the foundation, he heard a clink. Falling to his knees, he scrabbled in the dirt. Gradually, he uncovered a jar. With shaking fingers, he unsealed the lid. The jar was crammed with gleaming gold ingots.[2]

    Yuè Shēng lifted some of the heavy ingots into his hands. The sun shone from their sides. "This is the gold

120 Father intended for me when I learned what work meant," he said aloud. Yet as he stared at them, he felt guilty. "But

IDENTIFY

Pause at line 116. Folk tales often include dreams that guide the hero. What does this dream lead Yuè Shēng to?

the gold

2. **ingots** (ĭn′gəts) *n.:* bars of cast metal; here, of gold.

Right page (283)

father left the house to my older brother. By rights, the jar still belongs to him."

    The honest man put back the gold ingots and covered the jar again. Then he went to his brother's house. However, the gatekeeper would not let him inside. "I'm sorry, young master, but your brother has ordered me not to let you in. He doesn't want to see you anymore. Please don't beg."

130   So Yuè Shēng asked for ink and paper to write a note. In it, he told his brother where the treasure was. Folding it up, he asked the gatekeeper to take it to his brother.

    At first, Yuè Cang was just going to tear the note up without reading it. However, his wife scolded him, saying, "Your brother could be very sick. Imagine what people would say if we let him die?"

    Reluctantly, the older brother read the note. As soon as he finished, he jumped up and called for his servants. "What's wrong?" his wife asked.

140   The older brother rushed from the room, bellowing to his servants. Some brought his sedan chair;[3] others snatched up shovels and hoes. Cursing and shouting, the older brother guided everyone to the ruins of the old house. Getting out of his sedan chair, he went to the spot described in the note and commanded his men to dig there.

    When they had uncovered the jar, Yuè Cang told them to stand back. Then he knelt and lifted the lid. Immediately, he fell backward with a scream. When the curious servants peeked inside, they saw the jar was full of snakes. After the

150 older brother recovered himself, he straightened his

IDENTIFY

What conflict has the gold caused for Yuè Shēng?

The gold is buried in his brother's land, so he feels it belongs to his brother.

IDENTIFY

Folk tales often include supernatural events. What fantastic event has happened in line 149?

The gold has turned into snakes.

3. **sedan chair:** covered portable chair used for carrying a person, with horizontal poles that rest on the shoulders of the carriers.

Laurence Yep   283

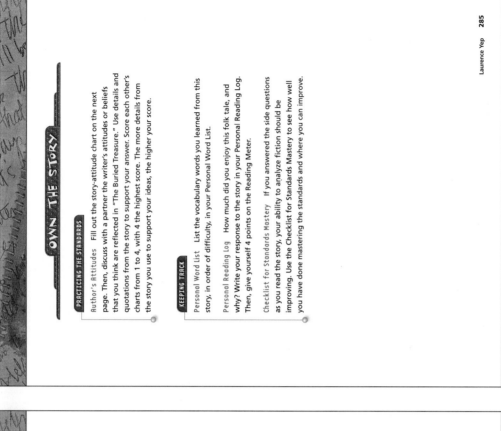

OWN THE STORY

PRACTICING THE STANDARDS

Author's Attitudes Fill out the story-attitude chart on the next page. Then, discuss with a partner the writer's attitudes or beliefs that you think are reflected in "The Buried Treasure." Use details and quotations from the story to support your answer. Score each other's charts from 1 to 4, with 4 the highest score. The more details from the story you use to support your ideas, the higher your score.

KEEPING TRACK

Personal Word List List the vocabulary words you learned from this story, in order of difficulty, in your Personal Word List.

Personal Reading Log How much did you enjoy this folk tale, and why? Write your response to the story in your Personal Reading Log. Then, give yourself 4 points on the Reading Meter.

Checklist for Standards Mastery If you answered the side questions as you read the story, your ability to analyze fiction should be improving. Use the Checklist for Standards Mastery to see how well you have done mastering the standards and where you can improve.

Laurence Yep **285**

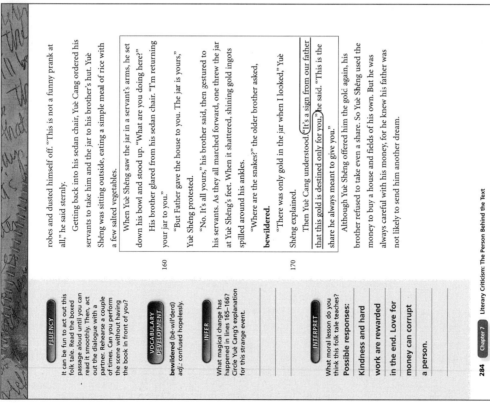

robes and dusted himself off. "This is not a funny prank at all," he said sternly.

Getting back into his sedan chair, Yuè Cang ordered his servants to take him and the jar to his brother's hut. Yuè Shēng was sitting outside, eating a simple meal of rice with a few salted vegetables.

When Yuè Shēng saw the jar in a servant's arms, he set down his bowl and stood up. "What are you doing here?"

His brother glared from his sedan chair. "I'm returning your jar to you."

"But Father gave the house to you. The jar is yours," Yuè Shēng protested.

"No. It's all yours," his brother said, then gestured to his servants. As they all marched forward, one threw the jar at Yuè Shēng's feet. When it shattered, shining gold ingots spilled around his ankles.

"Where are the snakes?" the older brother asked, **bewildered.**

"There was only gold in the jar when I looked," Yuè Shēng explained.

Then Yuè Cang understood. "It's a sign from our father that this gold is destined only for you," he said. "This is the share he always meant to give you."

Although Yuè Shēng offered him the gold again, his brother refused to take even a share. So Yuè Shēng used the money to buy a house and fields of his own. But he was always careful with his money, for he knew his father was not likely to send him another dream.

FLUENCY
It can be fun to act out this folk tale. Read the boxed passage aloud until you can read it smoothly. Then, act out the dialogue with a partner. Rehearse a couple of times. Can you perform the scene without having the book in front of you?

VOCABULARY DEVELOPMENT
bewildered (bē-wil'dərd) *adj.*: confused hopelessly.

INFER
What magical change has happened in lines 165–166? Circle Yuè Cang's explanation for this strange event.

INTERPRET
What moral lesson do you think this folk tale teaches?
Possible responses:
Kindness and hard work are rewarded in the end. Love for money can corrupt a person.

284 Chapter 7 Literary Criticism: The Person Behind the Text

Information

ARTICLE

Reading Standard 2.7
Evaluate the unity, coherence, logic, internal consistency, and structural patterns of text.

BEFORE YOU READ

King Midas was a king in an ancient country that is now Turkey. He was famous as a real king in his own time, but he has since become more famous for the myths that are told about him. In one myth, Midas wishes that everything he touches would turn to gold. He gets his wish—but what happens is not what he expected.

The following article presents some facts about the real King Midas and explains how today's scientists learned about him.

from Muse magazine

THE FUNERAL BANQUET OF KING MIDAS

John Fleischman

Hercules, they say, could kill a lion with his bare hands. The great Achilles, the story goes, could only be wounded on the heel. And King Midas turned everything he touched to gold. Well, Hercules and Achilles may have been myths, but there really was a King Midas. Recently we even found out what they served at his funeral.

The real King Midas lived in what is now central Turkey 2,700 years ago, in a kingdom called Phrygia. We know there was a King Midas because his neighbors, the mighty Assyrian kings to the east, wrote about him. They called him Mita. The Greeks, who lived west of Phrygia, also knew about him. The Greek historian Herodotus said
10   Midas was the first "barbarian" (or ~~non-Greek~~) to dedicate an offering to Apollo at his shrine at Delphi. After he died,

IDENTIFY

How do we know there was really a King Midas (lines 8–14)?

He is written about _____

by the Assyrians and _____

the Greek historian _____

Herodotus. _____

WORD KNOWLEDGE

Circle the definition of *barbarian*, which is given in context.

How do people use the word *barbarian* today?

It means "coarse," _____

cruel," and "savage." _____

The Funeral Banquet of King Midas   **287**

LITERARY CRITICISM

The Buried Treasure ■ *Interactive Reading, page 279*

Interact with a Literary Text

Story-Attitude Chart   Writers sometimes express their attitudes through what their characters say and do. But writers don't always agree with all their characters' statements and choices. Often the writer's attitudes are only implied, or suggested. The reader infers the writer's attitudes by reading between the lines. Guess at Lawrence Yep's attitudes toward life by filling in the following chart.

In the Story . . .	Possible Writer's Attitude
Yuè Shēng is humble enough to take work as a laborer.	It's good to learn to work hard.
Yuè Cang is careful with his money, but he does not show any generosity.	Generosity is rewarded; stinginess is not.
Yuè Shēng spends money, but he does not worship it. He is rewarded at the end.	It's important to learn the value of money but not to worship it.

286   Chapter 7   Literary Criticism: The Person Behind the Text

TEXT STRUCTURE

Use this map to help find Midas's kingdom, called Phrygia (frij'ē-ə). What countries are on either side of Phrygia? **Greece and Assyria**

WORD KNOWLEDGE

Circle the words that help you picture what sixty-eight meters is like (lines 25–27).

VOCABULARY DEVELOPMENT

archaeologists (är'kē-äl'ə-jists) *n.:* scientists who study the culture of the past, especially by excavating ancient sites.

Circle words in this passage that give you a clue to what archaeologists do.

excavating (eks'kə-vāt'in) *v.:* uncovering or exposing by digging.

avalanche (av'ə-lanch') *n.:* mass of loosened snow, earth, rocks, and so on, suddenly and swiftly sliding down a mountain.

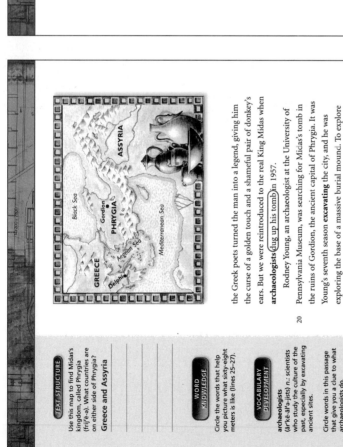

the Greek poets turned the man into a legend, giving him the curse of a golden touch and a shameful pair of donkey's ears. But we were reintroduced to the real King Midas when archaeologists dug up his tomb in 1957.

20 Rodney Young, an archaeologist at the University of Pennsylvania Museum, was searching for Midas's tomb in the ruins of Gordion, the ancient capital of Phrygia. It was Young's seventh season excavating the city, and he was exploring the base of a massive burial mound. To explore the mound without destroying it, he brought in Turkish coal miners to dig a horizontal shaft. After tunneling 68 meters (about as far as 68 people holding hands would reach), the miners struck a smooth stone wall. When they broke through, a wave of rubble spilled out, blocking the tunnel. Young had them clear as much as they could

30 without bringing down the clay ceiling. Beyond the rubble was a rough wall of heavy logs. The men sliced through that and unleashed another stone avalanche. Once it was

cleared away, they found an inner wall of beautifully crafted boxwood and cedar.

Young carefully sawed open a hatch, pushed his light into the **interior**, and found himself staring into the eye sockets of King Midas. The king was facing him, laid out on what Young thought was a bed (it turned out to be an open coffin carved from a single tree) in a tomb stuffed with
40 ancient textiles, wooden furniture, iron tripods, and bronze vessels—but not a speck of gold.

Archaeologist Ellen Kohler, who also worked on the dig, says the skeleton of King Midas rested on what looked "like a million blankets," with a cover of fine-woven linens in purple, white, and pink. When the tomb was first opened, there was a strong, clean smell of freshly cut wood. "It smelled like the inside of a cedar chest," she says. "The wood still looked freshly cut."

50 The archaeologists were astounded to find cloth and wood in such good condition because these materials usually rot quickly. Amazingly, the cloth and wood in Midas's tomb were saved by the decaying body of the king. Midas had been sealed under a burial mound of clay 49 meters high, making the tomb both dry and nearly airtight. As the bacteria that cause decay worked on his body, they also used up nearly all the oxygen in the tomb. Lack of oxygen slowed
60 down the decay process so much that the textiles and wooden furniture were preserved for centuries. Unfortunately,

> More photos and info about Midas's tomb is at http://www.museum.upenn.edu/Midas/intro.html

TEXT STRUCTURE

What are the topics of the two paragraphs beginning at line 7 and ending at line 34?

1) **The real Midas**

2) **Uncovering Midas's tomb**

VOCABULARY DEVELOPMENT

interior (in-tîr'ē-ər) *n.:* the inner part of anything. The opposite of *interior* is *exterior*.

Interior is usually used as an adjective, meaning "located within."

IDENTIFY

Describe the process that kept King Midas's burial clothes and wood in such good condition. **The tomb was airtight. Therefore, bacteria that worked on the body used up all of the oxygen. Without oxygen, the decaying process slowed down.**

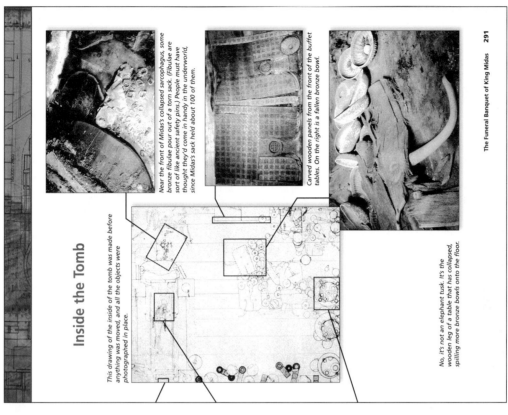

Inside the Tomb

This drawing of the inside of the tomb was made before anything was moved, and all the objects were photographed in place.

Near the front of Midas's collapsed sarcophagus, some bronze fibulae pour out of a torn sack. (Fibulae are sort of like ancient safety pins.) People must have thought they'd come in handy in the underworld, since Midas's sack held about 100 of them.

Carved wooden panels from the front of the buffet tables. On the right is a fallen bronze bowl.

No, it's not an elephant tusk. It's the wooden leg of a table that has collapsed, spilling more bronze bowls onto the floor.

The Funeral Banquet of King Midas   291

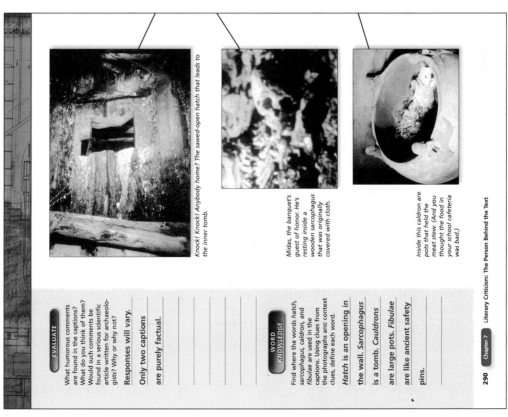

Knock! Knock! Anybody home? The sawed-open hatch that leads to the inner tomb.

Midas, the banquet's guest of honor. He's resting inside a wooden sarcophagus that was originally covered with cloth.

Inside this caldron are pots that held the meat stew. (And you thought the food in your school cafeteria was bad.)

EVALUATE

What humorous comments are found in the captions? What do you think of them? Would such comments be found in a serious scientific article written for archaeologists? Why or why not?

Responses will vary.

Only two captions

are purely factual.

WORD KNOWLEDGE

Find where the words *hatch, sarcophagus, caldron,* and *fibulae* are used in the captions. Using clues from the photographs and context clues, define each word.

Hatch is an opening in

the wall. *Sarcophagus*

is a tomb. *Cauldrons*

are large pots. *Fibulae*

are like ancient safety

pins.

290   Chapter 7   Literary Criticism: The Person Behind the Text

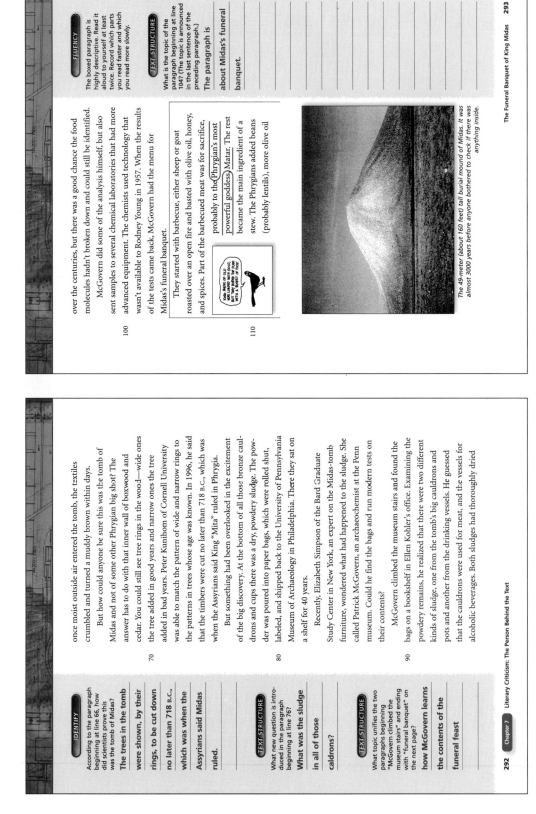

once moist outside air entered the tomb, the textiles crumbled and turned a muddy brown within days.

But how could anyone be sure this was the tomb of Midas and not of some other Phrygian big shot? The answer has to do with that inner wall of boxwood and cedar. You could still see tree rings in the wood—wide ones the tree added in good years and narrow ones the tree added in bad years. Peter Kunihom of Cornell University was able to match the pattern of wide and narrow rings to the patterns in trees whose age was known. In 1996, he said that the timbers were cut no later than 718 B.C., which was when the Assyrians said King "Mita" ruled in Phrygia.

But something had been overlooked in the excitement of the big discovery. At the bottom of all those bronze caldrons and cups there was a dry, powdery sludge. The powder was poured into paper bags, which were rolled shut, labeled, and shipped back to the University of Pennsylvania Museum of Archaeology in Philadelphia. There they sat on a shelf for 40 years.

Recently, Elizabeth Simpson of the Bard Graduate Study Center in New York, an expert on the Midas-tomb furniture, wondered what had happened to the sludge. She called Patrick McGovern, an archaeochemist at the Penn museum. Could he find the bags and run modern tests on their contents?

McGovern climbed the museum stairs and found the bags on a bookshelf in Ellen Kohler's office. Examining the powdery remains, he realized that there were two different kinds of sludge, one from the tomb's big cauldrons and pots and another from the drinking vessels. He guessed that the cauldrons were used for meat, and the vessels for alcoholic beverages. Both sludges had thoroughly dried

IDENTIFY
According to the paragraph beginning at line 66, how did scientists prove this was the tomb of Midas?

The trees in the tomb were shown, by their rings, to be cut down no later than 718 B.C., which was when the Assyrians said Midas ruled.

TEXT STRUCTURE
What new question is introduced in the paragraph beginning at line 76?

What was the sludge in all of those caldrons?

TEXT STRUCTURE
What topic unifies the two paragraphs beginning "McGovern climbed the museum stairs" and ending with "funeral banquet" on the next page?

how McGovern learns the contents of the funeral feast

over the centuries, but there was a good chance the food molecules hadn't broken down and could still be identified. McGovern did some of the analysis himself, but also sent samples to several chemical laboratories that had more advanced equipment. The chemists used technology that wasn't available to Rodney Young in 1957. When the results of the tests came back, McGovern had the menu for Midas's funeral banquet.

They started with barbecue, either sheep or goat roasted over an open fire and basted with olive oil, honey, and spices. Part of the barbecued meat was for sacrifice, probably to the Phrygian's most powerful goddess, Matar. The rest became the main ingredient of a stew. The Phrygians added beans (probably lentils), more olive oil

FLUENCY
The boxed paragraph is highly descriptive. Read it aloud to yourself at least twice. Record which parts you read faster and which you read more slowly.

TEXT STRUCTURE
What is the topic of the paragraph beginning at line 104? (The topic is announced in the last sentence of the preceding paragraph.)

The paragraph is about Midas's funeral banquet.

The 49-meter (about 160 feet) tall burial mound of Midas. It was almost 3000 years before anyone bothered to check if there was anything inside.

Page 294

In the paragraph beginning at line 104, underline the words *Matar*, *kykeon*, and *mead*, which are probably unfamiliar to you. Look for context clues, and circle them.

Sum up the main idea of the paragraph that begins on line 122. In other words, how is the question in line 122 answered?

Midas became such a legend because he was famously rich.

and honey, wine, anise or fennel, and more spices. The second sludge turned out to be from (an alcoholic drink) called a *kykeon* by the Greeks; we'd call it (punch.) It's a mixture of grape wine, barley beer, and a (fermented honey drink) known as mead. Part of this punch would have been poured out on the ground or an altar stone as an offering to Matar. All the cauldrons, bowls, and dishes that were packed away so carefully inside the tomb were used for offerings to the goddess. The food and drink were part of the religious ceremony for the dead king.

120 So how did Midas end up with a golden touch? "I think Greek myth is really hard to fathom," says archaeologist Elizabeth Simpson. She believes that any king who was as wealthy as Midas would have been seen as a great man, especially by the poorer Greeks along the coast. Long after his death, his great burial mound at Gordion

Patrick McGovern with bags of sludge from Midas's tomb. In front of him is a white plaster bust of the king—a reconstruction based on the shape of his skull.

294 Chapter 7 Literary Criticism: The Person Behind the Text

Page 295

would have impressed them. "It took a long time and a lot of precise engineering to build that," says Dr. Simpson. "I say the Gordion earthwork is the counterpart of an Egyptian pyramid."

But great monuments don't guarantee great fame. Aside from King Tut, how many pharaohs can you name? How many of the great kings of Assyria? How many emperors of Persia? But if you were asked for the kings of little Phrygia, you would remember at least one "golden" name.

130

> EGYPTIAN PHARAOHS: ZOSER, CHEOPS, RAMSES, HATSHEPSUT, TUTANKHAMON... UM—UM...
>
> PERSIAN KINGS: CYRUS, DARIUS, XERXES... UM...
>
> ASSYRIAN KINGS: SHALMANESER, ASHURBANIPAL... UM...
>
> "BUT KING UM... REALLY GOT AROUND!"

Review the article, and find its various features. What is the purpose of these features?

The photos help bring the tomb "to life"; the cartoons are amusing and related to the article's topics; the map shows the location of the city the tomb is in.

· · · · · · Notes · · · · · ·

The Funeral Banquet of King Midas 295

TEXT STRUCTURE

Graphic Organizer

The Funeral Banquet of King Midas ■ *Interactive Reading, page 287*

Interact with an Informational Text

Information Outline   Use this form to outline the supporting details for each of these main topics of "The Funeral Banquet of King Midas."

I. King Midas: Who, When, and Where
  1. Midas the myth
  2. Historical record

II. Excavating Midas's Tomb
  1. Rodney Young digs Midas's burial mound
  2. The King in his coffin
  3. Beautifully preserved cloth and wood
  4. Reason for preservation

III. How Did They Know It Was Midas?
  1. Tree ring dating
  2. Writings of Assyrians place Midas in that time frame

IV. What Is the Sludge?
  1. Simpson wonders
  2. McGovern examines
  3. The analysis

V. The Findings
  1. The banquet
  2. A theory about the myth

Graphic Organizer   **297**

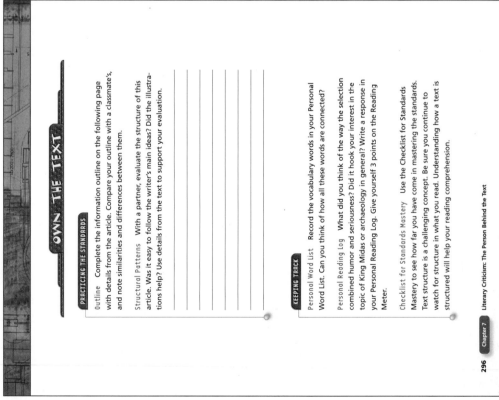

OWN THE TEXT

PRACTICING THE STANDARDS

Outline   Complete the information outline on the following page with details from the article. Compare your outline with a classmate's, and note similarities and differences between them.

Structural Patterns   With a partner, evaluate the structure of this article. Was it easy to follow the writer's main ideas? Did the illustrations help? Use details from the text to support your evaluation.

_____

_____

_____

_____

_____

_____

_____

KEEPING TRACK

Personal Word List   Record the vocabulary words in your Personal Word List. Can you think of how all these words are connected?

Personal Reading Log   What did you think of the way the selection combined humor and seriousness? Did it hook your interest in the topic of King Midas or archaeology in general? Write a response in your Personal Reading Log. Give yourself 3 points on the Reading Meter.

Checklist for Standards Mastery   Use the Checklist for Standards Mastery to see how far you have come in mastering the standards. Text structure is a challenging concept. Be sure you continue to watch for structure in what you read. Understanding how a text is structured will help your reading comprehension.

296   Chapter 7   Literary Criticism: The Person Behind the Text

Literature

MYTH

BEFORE YOU READ

You have read a factual article on the real King Midas. Now you'll read the myth about the king who was unwise in his wishes. An important god appears in this myth. Bacchus (bak'əs) is the god of wine and merrymaking. He is often shown with grapevines twisted in his hair. Bacchus's old teacher is Silenus (si-lē'nəs). Silenus is a wood-land god who has goat feet, shaggy legs, and pointy ears. (The Greek name for Bacchus is Dionysus.)

THE GOLDEN TOUCH

Greek myth

COMPARE & CONTRAST
Pause at line 16. How are Midas and Marigold different?

Midas loves money (and Marigold).

Marigold loves nature.

DECODING TIP
The flower name *anemone* (ə-nem'ə-nē') comes from the Greek word meaning "wind" (line 18). Of the two *e*'s in *anemone*, the first is short and the second is long. Watch for anemones: They appear several times in this myth.

There was once a very rich king named Midas. The columns of his palace were inlaid with gold, and his treasure room was filled with jewels. He longed for greater wealth. He did not care for music or flowers, or indeed for anything else except his beautiful little daughter and his riches.

Midas wished to give his daughter, Marigold, the finest dresses ever made, the most beautiful beads and jeweled bands for her hair. This was one reason why he longed to have gold and riches. But Marigold loved to wear a short white frock, and to go barefoot over the grass with only a band of ribbon on her head.

10 "The birds are singing," she would say, "and the very first anemones are in bloom."

She liked to feel the cool wind blow through her curls; she loved roses and violets much better than jewels. Sometimes she begged King Midas to leave his treasure room, where he liked to sit, to walk in the woods with her.

But Midas would pat her head and tell her to run out and play—just as all busy fathers have told their little girls ever since.

20 One day, as Midas sat counting his riches, a stranger walked into the room and touched him on the shoulder. Vines twined around the visitor's head, and a leopard skin hung from his shoulders.

"Who are you?" cried Midas in alarm, "and how did you pass the guards?"

"I am Bacchus," said the stranger. "I have come to thank you. Not long ago you were kind to my old teacher, Silenus. The gods do not forget such things."

30 Then Midas remembered that one evening an aged man had stumbled into the palace. Midas had given him shelter and food and fresh clothing. In the morning the king had sent him on his way with a companion to guide him.

Midas rose to his feet—as even a royal **mortal** should stand in the presence of the gods—and bowed low to Bacchus, inviting him to be seated. Bacchus looked at the chair inlaid with gold. He saw the table **strewn** with jewels and coins and glittering bowls. He shuddered and moved

40 farther away from Midas.

"I cannot stay in this room," said Bacchus. "There is no sunshine here, nor any sound of the wind in the vine leaves."

Midas looked at the god in amazement.

"You talk like my daughter, Marigold," said he. "True, there is no sunshine here, but look! See the golden lights on these bowls, and the red glow on the jewels!"

"Have you seen the colors of grapes when the sun shines through them, purple and red and amber?" asked

50 Bacchus.

VOCABULARY DEVELOPMENT
mortal (môr'tl) *n.*: here, a human being who must one day die.

What does *immortal* mean?

Immortal means "able to live forever."

The prefix *im-* means "not."

strewn (strōōn) *v.* used as *adj.*: scattered; spread about.

COMPARE & CONTRAST
Pause at line 44. How are Bacchus and Midas different?

Bacchus needs sun and nature. Midas loves gold.

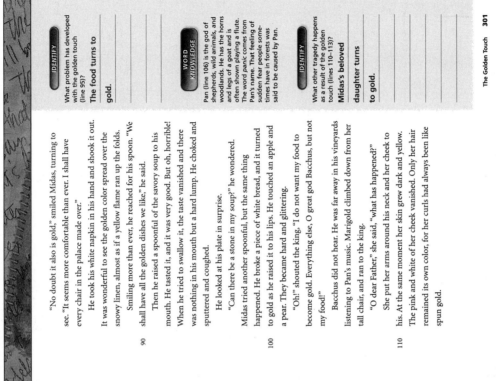

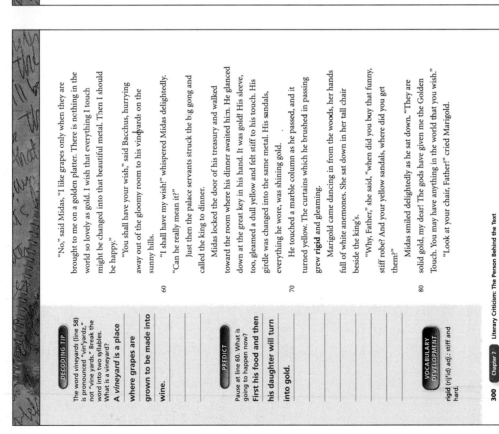

DECODING TIP

The word *vineyards* (line 58) is pronounced "vin'yardz," not "vine yards." Break the word into two syllables.
What is a vineyard?
A vineyard is a place where grapes are grown to be made into wine.

PREDICT

Pause at line 60. What is going to happen now?
First his food and then his daughter will turn into gold.

VOCABULARY DEVELOPMENT

rigid (rij'id) *adj.*: stiff and hard.

"No," said Midas, "I like grapes only when they are brought to me on a golden platter. There is nothing in the world so lovely as gold. I wish that everything I touch might be changed into that beautiful metal. Then I should be happy."

"You shall have your wish," said Bacchus, hurrying away out of the gloomy room to his vineyards on the sunny hills.

60 "I shall have my wish!" whispered Midas delightedly. "Can he really mean it?"

Just then the palace servants struck the big gong and called the king to dinner.

Midas locked the door of his treasury and walked toward the room where his dinner awaited him. He glanced down at the great key in his hand. It was gold! His sleeve, too, gleamed a dull yellow and felt stiff to his touch. His girdle was changed into the same metal. His sandals, everything he wore, was shining gold.

70 He touched a marble column as he passed, and it turned yellow. The curtains which he brushed in passing grew rigid and gleaming.

Marigold came dancing in from the woods, her hands full of white anemones. She sat down in her tall chair beside the king's.

"Why, Father," she said, "when did you buy that funny, stiff robe? And your yellow sandals, where did you get them?"

80 Midas smiled delightedly as he sat down. "They are solid gold, my dear! The gods have given me the Golden Touch. You may have anything in the world that you wish."

"Look at your chair, Father!" cried Marigold.

IDENTIFY

What problem has developed with the golden touch (line 95)?
The food turns to gold.

WORD KNOWLEDGE

Pan (line 106) is the god of shepherds, wild animals, and woodlands. He has the horns and legs of a goat and is often shown playing a flute. The word *panic* comes from Pan's name. That feeling of sudden fear people sometimes have in forests was said to be caused by Pan.

IDENTIFY

What other tragedy happens as a result of the golden touch (lines 110–113)?
Midas's beloved daughter turns to gold.

"No doubt it also is gold," smiled Midas, turning to see. "It seems more comfortable than ever. I shall have every chair in the palace made over."

He took his white napkin in his hand and shook it out. It was wonderful to see the golden color spread over the snowy linen, almost as if a yellow flame ran up the folds.

Smiling more than ever, he reached for his spoon. "We shall have all the golden dishes we like," he said.

90 Then he raised a spoonful of the savory soup to his mouth. He tasted it, and it was very good. But oh, horrible! When he tried to swallow it, the taste vanished and there was nothing in his mouth but a hard lump. He choked and sputtered and coughed.

He looked at his plate in surprise.

"Can there be a stone in my soup?" he wondered. Midas tried another spoonful, but the same thing happened. He broke a piece of white bread, and it turned 100 to gold as he raised it to his lips. He touched an apple and a pear. They became hard and glittering.

"Oh!" shouted the king, "I do not want my food to become gold. Everything else, O great god Bacchus, but not my food!"

Bacchus did not hear. He was far away in his vineyards listening to Pan's music. Marigold climbed down from her tall chair, and ran to the king.

"O dear Father," she said, "what has happened?" She put her arms around his neck and her cheek to 110 his. At the same moment her skin grew dark and yellow. The pink and white of her cheek vanished. Only her hair remained its own color, for her curls had always been like spun gold.

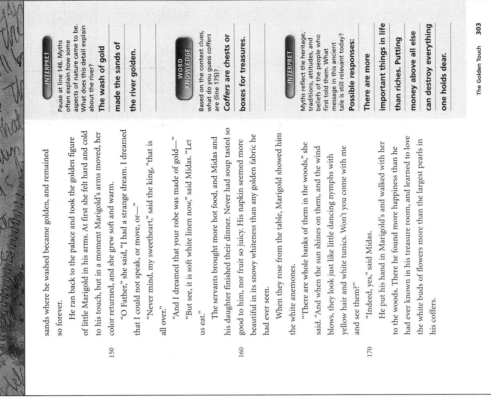

INTERPRET

Pause at line 146. Myths often explain how some aspects of nature came to be. What does this detail explain about the river?

The wash of gold made the sands of the river golden.

sands where he washed became golden, and remained so forever.

He ran back to the palace and took the golden figure of little Marigold in his arms. At first she felt hard and cold to his touch, but in a moment Marigold's arms moved, her color returned, and she grew soft and warm.

150 "O Father," she said, "I had a strange dream. I dreamed that I could not speak, or move, or—"

"Never mind, my sweetheart," said the king, "that is all over."

"And I dreamed that your robe was made of gold—"

"But see, it is soft white linen now," said Midas. "Let us eat."

The servants brought more hot food, and Midas and his daughter finished their dinner. Never had soup tasted so good to him, nor fruit so juicy. His napkin seemed more 160 beautiful in its snowy whiteness than any golden fabric he had ever seen.

When they rose from the table, Marigold showed him the white anemones.

"There are whole banks of them in the woods," she said. "And when the sun shines on them, and the wind blows, they look just like little dancing nymphs with yellow hair and white tunics. Won't you come with me and see them?"

170 "Indeed, yes," said Midas.

He put his hand in Marigold's and walked with her to the woods. There he found more happiness than he had ever known in his treasure room, and learned to love the white buds of flowers more than the largest pearls in his coffers.

WORD KNOWLEDGE

Based on the context clues, what do you guess *coffers* are (line 175)?

Coffers are chests or boxes for treasures.

INTERPRET

Myths reflect the heritage, traditions, attitudes, and beliefs of the people who first told them. What message in this ancient tale is still relevant today?

Possible responses:

There are more important things in life than riches. Putting money above all else can destroy everything one holds dear.

The Golden Touch **303**

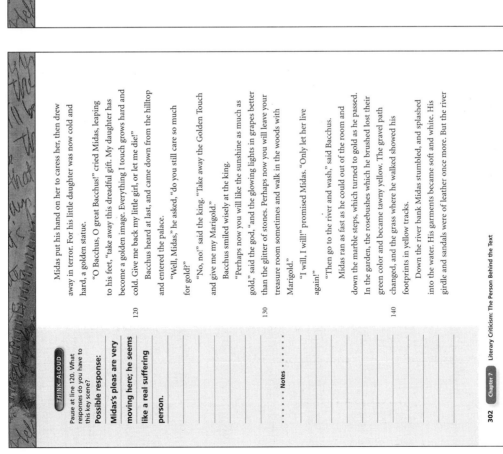

THINK-ALOUD

Pause at line 120. What responses do you have to this key scene?

Possible response:

Midas's pleas are very moving here; he seems like a real suffering person.

Midas put his hand on her to caress her, then drew away in terror. For his little daughter was now cold and hard, a golden statue.

"O Bacchus, O great Bacchus!" cried Midas, leaping to his feet, "take away this dreadful gift. My daughter has become a golden image. Everything I touch grows hard and 120 cold. Give me back my little girl, or let me die!"

Bacchus heard at last, and came down from the hilltop and entered the palace.

"Well, Midas," he asked, "do you still care so much for gold?"

"No, no!" said the king. "Take away the Golden Touch and give me my Marigold."

Bacchus smiled wisely at the king.

"Perhaps now you will like the sunshine as much as gold," said the god, "and the glowing lights in grapes better 130 than the glitter of stones. Perhaps now you will leave your treasure room sometimes and walk in the woods with Marigold."

"I will, I will!" promised Midas. "Only let her live again!"

"Then go to the river and wash," said Bacchus.

Midas ran as fast as he could out of the room and down the marble steps, which turned to gold as he passed. In the garden, the rosebushes which he brushed lost their green color and became tawny yellow. The gravel path 140 changed, and the grass where he walked showed his footprints in yellow tracks.

Down the river bank Midas stumbled, and splashed into the water. His garments became soft and white. His girdle and sandals were of leather once more. But the river

· · · · · · · Notes · · · · · · ·

302 Chapter 7 Literary Criticism: The Person Behind the Text

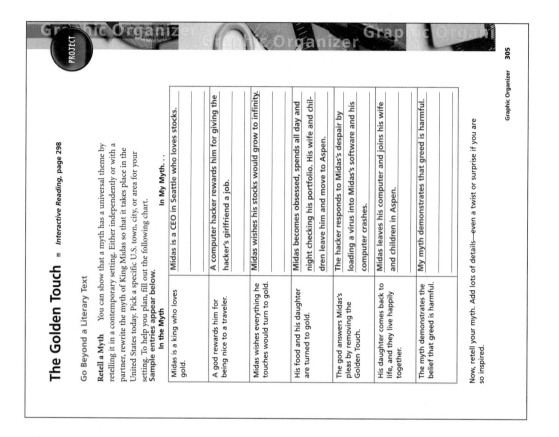

The Golden Touch ▪ *Interactive Reading, page 298*

Go Beyond a Literary Text

Retell a Myth You can show that a myth has a universal theme by retelling it in a contemporary setting. Either independently or with a partner, rewrite the myth of King Midas so that it takes place in the United States today. Pick a specific U.S. town, city, or area for your setting. To help you plan, fill out the following chart. Sample entries appear below.

In the Myth	In My Myth...
Midas is a king who loves gold.	Midas is a CEO in Seattle who loves stocks.
A god rewards him for being nice to a traveler.	A computer hacker rewards him for giving the hacker's girlfriend a job.
Midas wishes everything he touches would turn to gold.	Midas wishes his stocks would grow to infinity.
His food and his daughter are turned to gold.	Midas becomes obsessed, spends all day and night checking his portfolio. His wife and children leave him and move to Aspen.
The god answers Midas's pleas by removing the Golden Touch.	The hacker responds to Midas's despair by loading a virus into Midas's software and his computer crashes.
The daughter comes back to life, and they live happily together.	Midas leaves his computer and joins his wife and children in Aspen.
The myth demonstrates the belief that greed is harmful.	My myth demonstrates that greed is harmful.

Now, retell your myth. Add lots of details—even a twist or surprise if you are so inspired.

Graphic Organizer **305**

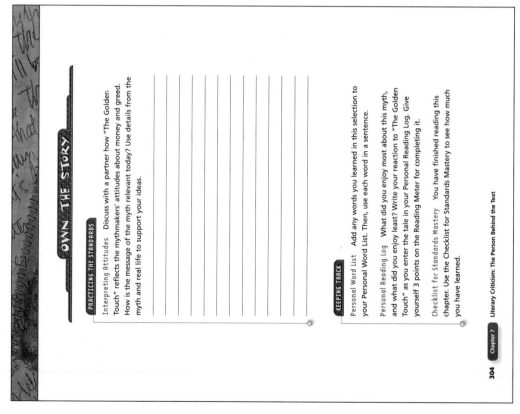

OWN THE STORY

PRACTICING THE STANDARDS

Interpreting Attitudes Discuss with a partner how "The Golden Touch" reflects the mythmakers' attitudes about money and greed. How is the message of the myth relevant today? Use details from the myth and real life to support your ideas.

KEEPING TRACK

Personal Word List Add any words you learned in this selection to your Personal Word List. Then, use each word in a sentence.

Personal Reading Log What did you enjoy most about this myth, and what did you enjoy least? Write your reaction to "The Golden Touch" as you enter the tale in your Personal Reading Log. Give yourself 3 points on the Reading Meter for completing it.

Checklist for Standards Mastery You have finished reading this chapter. Use the Checklist for Standards Mastery to see how much you have learned.

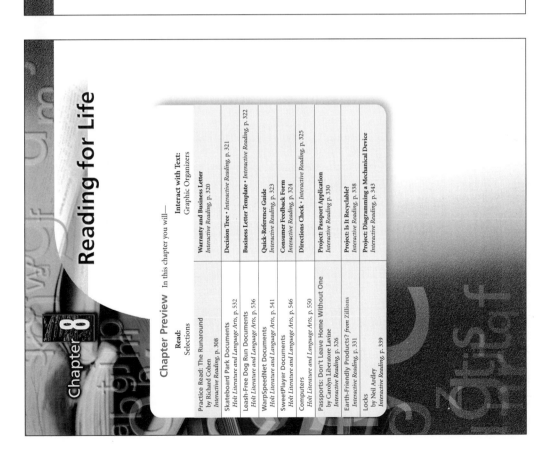

Chapter 8

Reading for Life

Chapter Preview In this chapter you will—

Strategy Launch: "Close Reading"

READING FOCUS: DOCUMENTS

You get information from documents every day.

➤ **Workplace documents** do two things: communicate and instruct. E-mail, memos, and reports communicate information you need to do your job. Employee manuals instruct you about what is expected on the job. User guides tell you how to operate equipment.

➤ **Public documents** are posted by public agencies and not-for-profit groups. They give information about voting issues, health concerns, community decisions, and various other subjects.

➤ **Consumer documents** give you product information to help you select, purchase, and use the things you buy. Instruction manuals and technical directions tell you how to set up and use products. Consumer documents such as contracts and warranties define your legal rights and responsibilities.

A STRATEGY THAT WORKS: "CLOSE READING"

When you read documents, you should read carefully and slowly. In other words, you should apply a strategy called "Close Reading."

Here are some pointers for using "Close Reading":

➤ Identify your purpose for reading the informational materials. Are you looking for instruction on how to make something, or are you trying to find out whom to contact for more information?

➤ Skim the text, and notice its features. Take note of heads, lists, and special features.

➤ Read carefully, and absorb what the text has to say. Refer to diagrams and illustrations for guidance. If a glossary or footnotes have been provided, use them.

➤ If any information is confusing, re-read to clarify.

Reading Standard 2.1 Compare and contrast the features and elements of consumer materials to gain meaning from documents (e.g., warranties, contracts, product information, instruction manuals).

Reading Standard 2.5 Understand and explain the use of a complex mechanical device by following technical directions.

Reading Standard 2.6 Use information from a variety of consumer, workplace, and public documents to explain a situation or decision and to solve a problem.

Strategy Launch **307**

mode (mōd) *n.*: state of functioning or operation.

Name some modes that a human has.

Examples of modes:

sleeping, waking,

studying, playing,

and so on

promptly (prämpt′lē) *adv.*: on time; soon.

The little ™ superscript next to the name DigiPet (line 29) indicates that the name is a trademark. Companies put the sign on their product names in order to retain ownership of the names.

A letter of complaint always has a specific purpose. Underline the words that tell what the writer wants to happen.

letting Fifi charge up for twelve hours, as your brochure recommends. Then I said to her, "Come, Fifi." To my surprise, she did not move! She remained in the sleep **mode** for nearly an hour. When Fifi did finally wake up, she ran all over the house, jumping on furniture and climbing in living room drapes. I feel that I have been shipped a defective product. I hope you will agree to repair or replace
this DigiCat **promptly**, as your advertising materials imply you will. Please let me know as soon as possible how to return the pet.

Sincerely,

Merton Morton

(Merton Morton)

20

30

Consumer Service Center
DigiPet™ Global, Inc.
8 State Highway 13,005
New Austin, TX 78700

April 10, 2053

Mr. Merton Morton
1560372 Winfrey Way
Chipsville, CA 90000

Dear Mr. Morton:

As Assistant Regional Communications Specialist for DigiPet™ Global, Inc., Consumer Service Center, I want to thank you for your recent interest in one of our DigiPets™.
Please do not return Fifi to this office. As your warranty materials indicate, the Consumer Service Center is not

40

Although years roll by, some things never seem to change. Customers in ancient Rome, for example, had to beware that sellers wouldn't take advantage of them. You may have heard the Latin phrase *caveat emptor,* meaning "let the buyer beware." A thousand years from now, buying and selling products we can't even imagine yet, people might still be having the same problems.

Get ready to read a funny story about what it might be like to be a customer in the future! This selection is organized in an unusual way—as a series of letters of complaint and a company's responses to them.

The Runaround

Richard Cohen

1560372 Winfrey Way
Chipsville, CA 90000

February 3, 2053

Consumer Service Center
DigiPet Global, Inc.
8 State Highway 13,005
New Austin, TX 78700

Dear DigiPet Global:

I recently received a DigiCat as a present and opened it as soon as I could. (I was on vacation when it was delivered. I found the box on my porch, dented on one side, when I returned.) I took Fifi out of her box and assembled the parts as the instructions showed. I inserted the batteries, plugged in the power pack, and set the switch to "On,"

10

A letter of complaint is a special type of business letter sent from a consumer to a company. Circle the address of the person sending the letter.

Underline the name and address of the company receiving the letter.

• • • • • • Notes • • • • • •

_____

_____

_____

_____

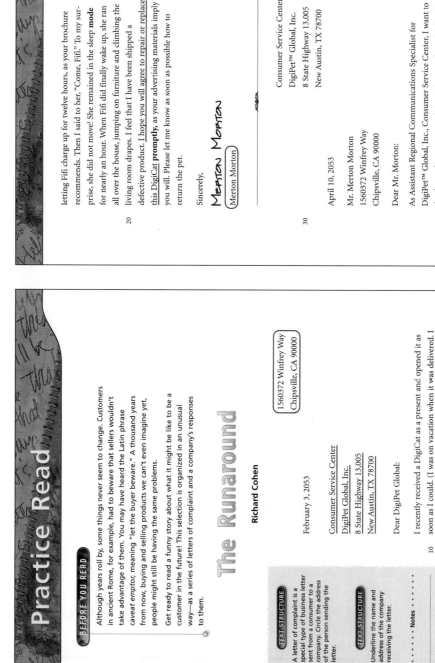

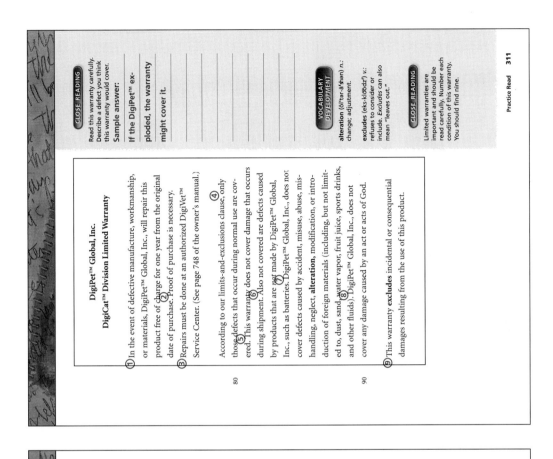

CLOSE READING
Read this warranty carefully. Describe a defect you think this warranty would cover.
Sample answer:
If the DigiPet™ exploded, the warranty might cover it.

**DigiPet™ Global, Inc.
DigiCat™ Division Limited Warranty**

①In the event of defective manufacture, workmanship, or materials, DigiPet™ Global, Inc., will repair this product free of charge for one year from the original date of purchase. ②Proof of purchase is necessary. ③Repairs must be done at an authorized DigiVet™ Service Center. (See page 748 of the owner's manual.)
④
According to our limits-and-exclusions clause, only those defects that occur during normal use are covered. ⑤This warranty does not cover damage that occurs during shipment. ⑥Also not covered are defects caused by products that are *not* made by DigiPet™ Global, Inc., such as batteries. DigiPet™ Global, Inc., does not cover defects caused by accident, misuse, abuse, mishandling, neglect, **alteration**, modification, or introduction of foreign materials (including, but not limited to, dust, sand, water vapor, fruit juice, sports drinks, and other fluids). ⑧DigiPet™ Global, Inc., does not cover any damage caused by an act or acts of God.

80

⑨This warranty **excludes** incidental or consequential damages resulting from the use of this product.

90

VOCABULARY DEVELOPMENT
alteration (ôl′tər-ā′shən) *n.*: change; adjustment.

excludes (eks-klōōdz′) *v.*: refuses to consider or include. *Excludes* can also mean "leaves out."

CLOSE READING
Limited warranties are important and should be read carefully. Number each condition of this warranty. You should find nine.

311 Practice Read

CLOSE READING
Underline the two places Mr. Morton is told to find information.

INTERPRET
How would you describe the tone of the company's letters? **polite but firm**

CLOSE READING
A limited warranty (line 59) is a guarantee of service and quality, but the guarantee has limits. What is one of the "limits" of this warranty for DigiPet™? Underline the details that state the limitation.

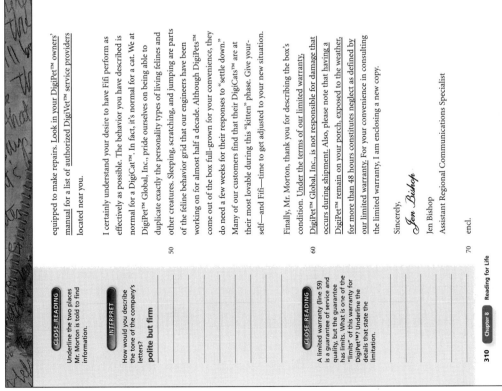

equipped to make repairs. Look in your DigiPet™ owners' manual for a list of authorized DigiVet™ service providers located near you.

I certainly understand your desire to have Fifi perform as effectively as possible. The behavior you have described is normal for a DigiCat™. In fact, it's normal for a cat. We at DigiPet™ Global, Inc., pride ourselves on being able to duplicate exactly the personality types of living felines and other creatures. Sleeping, scratching, and jumping are parts of the feline behavior grid that our engineers have been working on for almost half a decade. Although DigiPets™ come out of the box full-grown for your convenience, they do need a few weeks for their responses to "settle down." Many of our customers find that their DigiCats™ are at their most lovable during this "kitten" phase. Give yourself—and Fifi—time to get adjusted to your new situation.

Finally, Mr. Morton, thank you for describing the box's condition. Under the terms of our limited warranty, DigiPet™ Global, Inc., is not responsible for damage that occurs during shipment. Also, please note that having a DigiPet™ remain on your porch, exposed to the weather, for more than 48 hours constitutes neglect as defined by our limited warranty. For your convenience in consulting the limited warranty, I am enclosing a new copy.

50

60

Sincerely,
Jen Bishop
Jen Bishop
Assistant Regional Communications Specialist

70 encl.

310 Chapter 8 Reading for Life

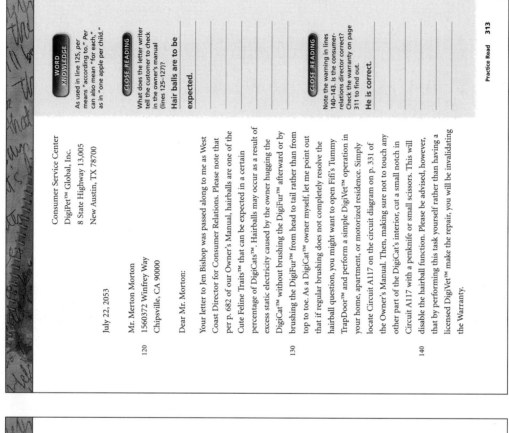

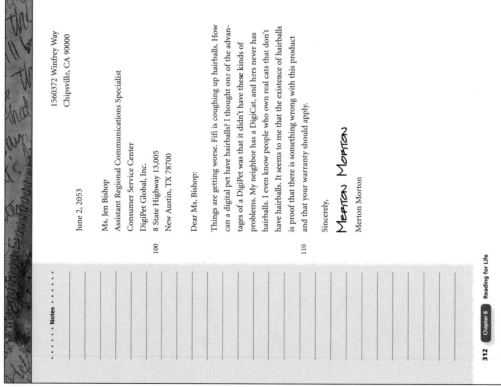

Page 312 (left letter)

• • • • • • **Notes** • • • • • •

1560372 Winfrey Way
Chipsville, CA 90000

June 2, 2053

Ms. Jen Bishop
Assistant Regional Communications Specialist
Consumer Service Center
100 DigiPet Global, Inc.
8 State Highway 13,005
New Austin, TX 78700

Dear Ms. Bishop:

Things are getting worse. Fifi is coughing up hairballs. How can a digital pet have hairballs? I thought one of the advantages of a DigiPet was that it didn't have these kinds of problems. My neighbor has a DigiCat, and hers never has hairballs. I even know people who own real cats that don't have hairballs. It seems to me that the existence of hairballs is proof that there is something wrong with this product
110 and that your warranty should apply.

Sincerely,

Merton Morton

Merton Morton

Page 313 (right letter)

Consumer Service Center
DigiPet™ Global, Inc.
8 State Highway 13,005
New Austin, TX 78700

July 22, 2053

Mr. Merton Morton
120 1560372 Winfrey Way
Chipsville, CA 90000

Dear Mr. Morton:

Your letter to Jen Bishop was passed along to me as West Coast Director for Consumer Relations. Please note that per p. 682 of our Owner's Manual, hairballs are one of the Cute Feline Traits™ that can be expected in a certain percentage of DigiCats™. Hairballs may occur as a result of excess static electricity caused by the owner hugging the DigiCat™ without brushing the DigiFur™ afterward or by
130 brushing the DigiFur™ from head to tail rather than from top to toe. As a DigiCat™ owner myself, let me point out that if regular brushing does not completely resolve the hairball question, you might want to open Fifi's Tummy TrapDoor™ and perform a simple DigiVet™ operation in your home, apartment, or motorized residence. Simply locate Circuit A117 on the circuit diagram on p. 331 of the Owner's Manual. Then, making sure not to touch any other part of the DigiCat's interior, cut a small notch in Circuit A117 with a penknife or small scissors. This will
140 disable the hairball function. Please be advised, however, that by performing this task yourself rather than having a licensed DigiVet™ make the repair, you will be invalidating the Warranty.

WORD KNOWLEDGE

As used in line 125, *per* means "according to." *Per* can also mean "for each," as in "one apple per child."

CLOSE READING

What does the letter writer tell the customer to check in the owner's manual (lines 125–127)?

Hair balls are to be
expected.

CLOSE READING

Note the warning in lines 140–143. Is the consumer-relations director correct? Check the warranty on page 311 to find out.

He is correct.

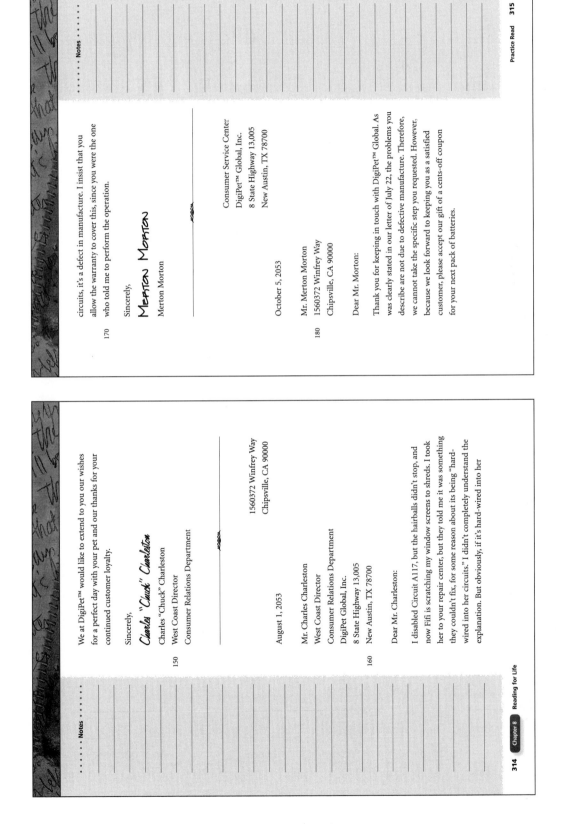

· · · · · · Notes · · · · · ·

We at DigiPet™ would like to extend to you our wishes for a perfect day with your pet and our thanks for your continued customer loyalty.

Sincerely,

Charles "Chuck" Charleston

Charles "Chuck" Charleston
West Coast Director
Consumer Relations Department

150

1560372 Winfrey Way
Chipsville, CA 90000

August 1, 2053

Mr. Charles Charleston
West Coast Director
Consumer Relations Department
DigiPet Global, Inc.
8 State Highway 13,005
New Austin, TX 78700

160

Dear Mr. Charleston:

I disabled Circuit A117, but the hairballs didn't stop, and now Fifi is scratching my window screens to shreds. I took her to your repair center, but they told me it was something they couldn't fix, for some reason about its being "hard-wired into her circuits." I didn't completely understand the explanation. But obviously, if it's hard-wired into her

· · · · · · Notes · · · · · ·

circuits, it's a defect in manufacture. I insist that you allow the warranty to cover this, since you were the one who told me to perform the operation.

170

Sincerely,

MERTON MORTON

Merton Morton

Consumer Service Center
DigiPet™ Global, Inc.
8 State Highway 13,005
New Austin, TX 78700

October 5, 2053

Mr. Merton Morton
1560372 Winfrey Way
Chipsville, CA 90000

180

Dear Mr. Morton:

Thank you for keeping in touch with DigiPet™ Global. As was clearly stated in our letter of July 22, the problems you describe are not due to defective manufacture. Therefore, we cannot take the specific step you requested. However, because we look forward to keeping you as a satisfied customer, please accept our gift of a cents-off coupon for your next pack of batteries.

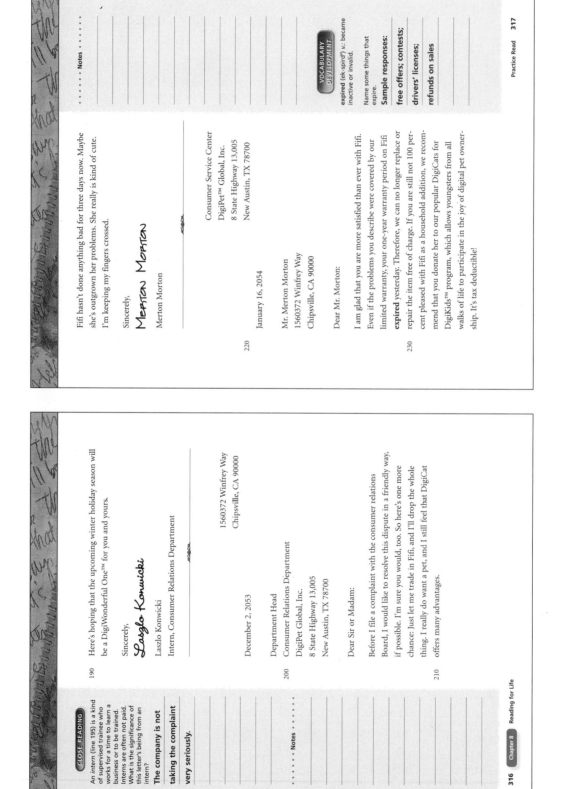

CLOSE READING

An *intern* (line 195) is a kind of supervised trainee who works for a time to learn a business or to be trained. Interns are often not paid. What is the significance of this letter's being from an intern?

The company is not taking the complaint very seriously.

· · · · · · Notes · · · · · ·

190 Here's hoping that the upcoming winter holiday season will be a DigiWonderful One™ for you and yours.

Sincerely,

Laszlo Konwicki

Laszlo Konwicki

Intern, Consumer Relations Department

1560372 Winfrey Way
Chipsville, CA 90000

December 2, 2053

Department Head

200 Consumer Relations Department

DigiPet Global, Inc.

8 State Highway 13,005

New Austin, TX 78700

Dear Sir or Madam:

Before I file a complaint with the consumer relations Board, I would like to resolve this dispute in a friendly way, if possible. I'm sure you would, too. So here's one more chance: Just let me trade in Fifi, and I'll drop the whole thing. I really do want a pet, and I still feel that DigiCat

210 offers many advantages.

Fifi hasn't done anything bad for three days now. Maybe she's outgrown her problems. She really is kind of cute. I'm keeping my fingers crossed.

Sincerely,

Merton Morton

Merton Morton

Consumer Service Center
DigiPet™ Global, Inc.
8 State Highway 13,005
New Austin, TX 78700

220 January 16, 2054

Mr. Merton Morton
1560372 Winfrey Way
Chipsville, CA 90000

Dear Mr. Morton:

I am glad that you are more satisfied than ever with Fifi. Even if the problems you describe were covered by our limited warranty, your one-year warranty period on Fifi **expired** yesterday. Therefore, we can no longer replace or repair the item free of charge. If you are still not 100 per-

230 cent pleased with Fifi as a household addition, we recommend that you donate her to our popular DigiCats for DigiKids™ program, which allows youngsters from all walks of life to participate in the joy of digital pet ownership! It's tax deductible!

VOCABULARY DEVELOPMENT

expired (ek-spīrd') *v.:* became inactive or invalid.

Name some things that expire.

Sample responses:

free offers; contests;

drivers' licenses;

refunds on sales

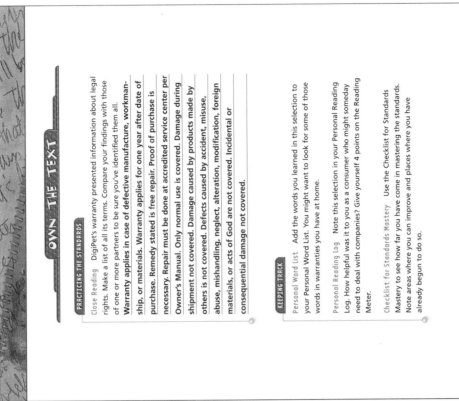

OWN THE TEXT

PRACTICING THE STANDARDS

Close Reading DigiPet's warranty presented information about legal rights. Make a list of all its terms. Compare your findings with those of one or more partners to be sure you've identified them all. **Warranty applies in case of defective manufacture, workmanship, or materials. Warranty applies for one year after date of purchase. Remedy stated is free repair. Proof of purchase is necessary. Repair must be done at accredited service center per Owner's Manual. Only normal use is covered. Damage during shipment not covered. Damage caused by products made by others is not covered. Defects caused by accident, misuse, abuse, mishandling, neglect, alteration, modification, foreign materials, or acts of God are not covered. Incidental or consequential damage not covered.**

KEEPING TRACK

Personal Word List Add the words you learned in this selection to your Personal Word List. You might want to look for some of those words in warranties you have at home.

Personal Reading Log Note this selection in your Personal Reading Log. How helpful was it to you as a consumer who might someday need to deal with companies? Give yourself 4 points on the Reading Meter.

Checklist for Standards Mastery Use the Checklist for Standards Mastery to see how far you have come in mastering the standards. Note areas where you can improve and places where you have already begun to do so.

Practice Read **319**

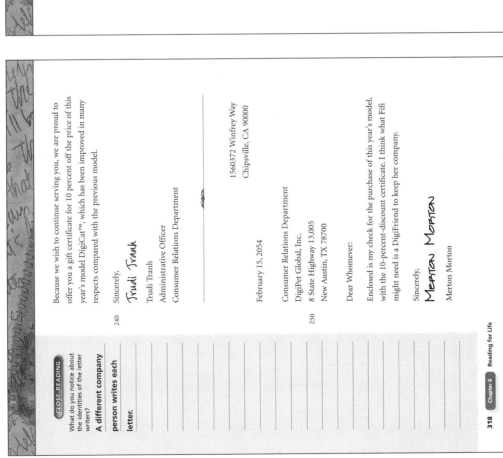

CLOSE READING

What do you notice about the identities of the letter writers?

A different company person writes each letter.

Because we wish to continue serving you, we are proud to offer you a gift certificate for 10 percent off the price of this year's model DigiCat™, which has been improved in many respects compared with the previous model.

240

Sincerely,

Trudi Tranh

Trudi Tranh
Administrative Officer
Consumer Relations Department

1560372 Winfrey Way
Chipsville, CA 90000

February 15, 2054

Consumer Relations Department
DigiPet Global, Inc.
8 State Highway 13,005
New Austin, TX 78700

250

Dear Whomever:

Enclosed is my check for the purchase of this year's model, with the 10-percent-discount certificate. I think what Fifi might need is a DigiFriend to keep her company.

Sincerely,

Merton Morton

Merton Morton

318 Chapter 8 Reading for Life

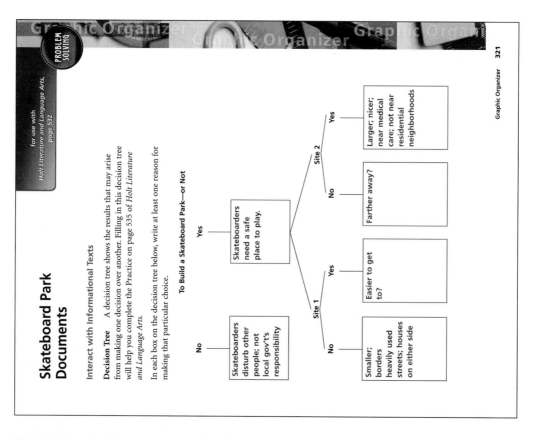

PROBLEM SOLVING

for use with
Holt Literature and Language Arts,
page 532

Skateboard Park Documents

Interact with Informational Texts

Decision Tree   A decision tree shows the results that may arise from making one decision over another. Filling in this decision tree will help you complete the Practice on page 535 of *Holt Literature and Language Arts.*

In each box on the decision tree below, write at least one reason for making that particular choice.

To Build a Skateboard Park—or Not

Yes → Skateboarders need a safe place to play.

No → Skateboarders disturb other people; not local gov't's responsibility

Site 1

No → Smaller; borders heavily used streets; houses on either side

Yes → Easier to get to?

Site 2

No → Farther away?

Yes → Larger; nicer; near medical care; not near residential neighborhoods

Graphic Organizer   321

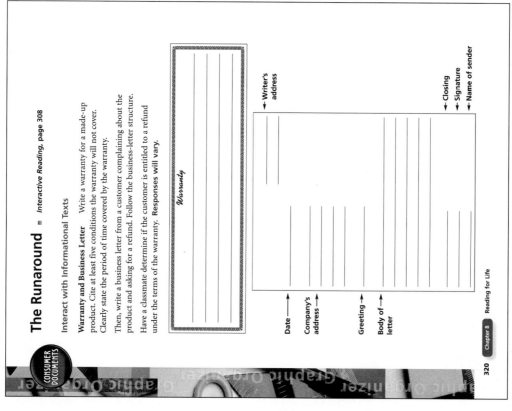

CONSUMER DOCUMENTS

The Runaround   ■ *Interactive Reading,* page 308

Interact with Informational Texts

Warranty and Business Letter   Write a warranty for a made-up product. Cite at least five conditions the warranty will not cover. Clearly state the period of time covered by the warranty.

Then, write a business letter from a customer complaining about the product and asking for a refund. Follow the business-letter structure.

Have a classmate determine if the customer is entitled to a refund under the terms of the warranty. **Responses will vary.**

Warranty

Writer's address

Date →

Company's address →

Greeting →

Body of letter →

Closing →
Signature →
Name of sender →

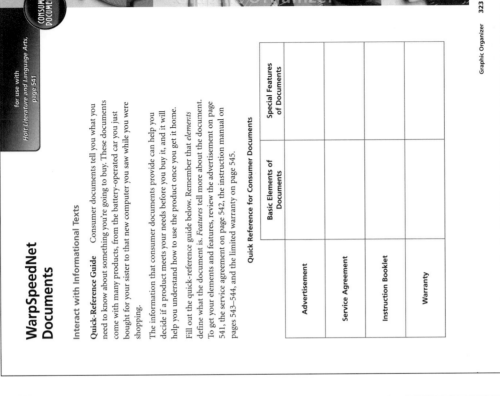

CONSUMER DOCUMENTS

for use with
Holt Literature and Language Arts,
page 541

WarpSpeedNet Documents

Interact with Informational Texts

Quick-Reference Guide   Consumer documents tell you what you need to know about something you're going to buy. These documents come with many products, from the battery-operated car you just bought for your sister to that new computer you saw while you were shopping.

The information that consumer documents provide can help you decide if a product meets your needs before you buy it, and it will help you understand how to use the product once you get it home.

Fill out the quick-reference guide below. Remember that *elements* define what the document is. *Features* tell more about the document. To get your elements and features, review the advertisement on page 541, the service agreement on page 542, the instruction manual on pages 543–544, and the limited warranty on page 545.

Quick Reference for Consumer Documents

	Basic Elements of Documents	Special Features of Documents
Advertisement		
Service Agreement		
Instruction Booklet		
Warranty		

Graphic Organizer   323

PROBLEM SOLVING

for use with
Holt Literature and Language Arts,
page 536

Leash-Free Dog Run Documents

Interact with Informational Texts

Business Letter Template   Imagine that you are T. Wagger, Director of Parks and Recreation. You want to respond to the chairperson of the Site Committee of SouthPaws. To do this, use this business-letter template. State your preferred site on the line provided. Then, write your reasons on the lines labeled "Space," "Conflicts," and "Type of Area."

2222 Central Avenue
Central City, CA 60000

December 14, 2002

A. K. Nine
Chairperson, Site Committee
SouthPaws
1111 South P. Street
South City, CA 60000

Dear A. K. Nine:

Thank you for your letter of December 12. It is important for us to work with the community in deciding where to put the dog park. Therefore, I would like to inform you that we favor the site at _Rocky Point Beach_. Our reasons, in order of importance, are as follows:

1. Space: _Rocky Point Beach's five acres are ample for this type of use._

2. Conflicts: _Rocky Point is the least heavily used of the three possible sites; fewer conflicts with families, businesses._

3. Type of Area: _The beach is best for dogs; this is nonsand beach, but dogs like climbing on rocks._

Thank you for continuing to work with us on this issue. I look forward to seeing you at the upcoming meeting.

Sincerely,

T. Wagger
Director, Parks and Recreation

Chapter 8   Reading for Life   322

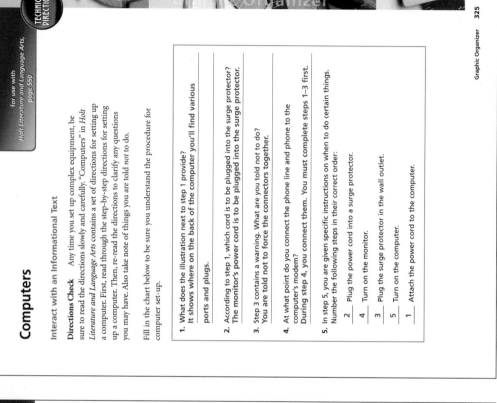

TECHNICAL DIRECTIONS

Computers

Interact with an Informational Text

Directions Check Any time you set up complex equipment, be sure to read the directions slowly and carefully. "Computers" in *Holt Literature and Language Arts* contains a set of directions for setting up a computer. First, read through the step-by-step directions for setting up a computer. Then, re-read the directions to clarify any questions you may have. Also take note of things you are told *not* to do.

Fill in the chart below to be sure you understand the procedure for computer set-up.

1. What does the illustration next to step 1 provide?
   It shows where on the back of the computer you'll find various

   ports and plugs.

2. According to step 1, which cord is to be plugged into the surge protector?
   The monitor's power cord is to be plugged into the surge protector.

3. Step 3 contains a warning. What are you told not to do?
   You are told not to force the connectors together.

4. At what point do you connect the phone line and phone to the computer's modem?
   During step 4, you connect them. You must complete steps 1–3 first.

5. In step 5, you are given specific instructions on when to do certain things. Number the following steps in their correct order:

   2 Plug the power cord into a surge protector.

   4 Turn on the monitor.

   3 Plug the surge protector in the wall outlet.

   5 Turn on the computer.

   1 Attach the power cord to the computer.

Graphic Organizer **325**

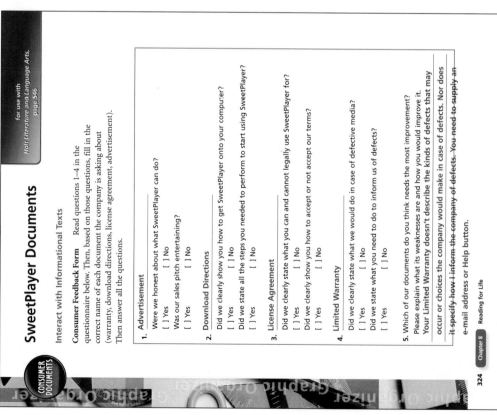

CONSUMER DOCUMENTS

SweetPlayer Documents

Interact with Informational Texts

Consumer Feedback Form Read questions 1–4 in the questionnaire below. Then, based on those questions, fill in the correct name of each document the company is asking about (warranty, download directions, license agreement, advertisement). Then answer all the questions.

1. **Advertisement**

   Were we honest about what SweetPlayer can do?
   [ ] Yes   [ ] No
   Was our sales pitch entertaining?
   [ ] Yes   [ ] No

2. **Download Directions**

   Did we clearly show you how to get SweetPlayer onto your computer?
   [ ] Yes   [ ] No
   Did we state all the steps you needed to perform to start using SweetPlayer?
   [ ] Yes   [ ] No

3. **License Agreement**

   Did we clearly state what you can and cannot legally use SweetPlayer for?
   [ ] Yes   [ ] No
   Did we clearly show you how to accept or not accept our terms?
   [ ] Yes   [ ] No

4. **Limited Warranty**

   Did we clearly state what we would do in case of defective media?
   [ ] Yes   [ ] No
   Did we state what you need to do to inform us of defects?
   [ ] Yes   [ ] No

5. Which of our documents do you think needs the most improvement?
   Please explain what its weaknesses are and how you would improve it.
   Your Limited Warranty doesn't describe the kinds of defects that may
   occur or choices the company would make in case of defects. Nor does
   it specify how I inform the company of defects. You need to supply an
   e-mail address or Help button.

324 Chapter 8 Reading for Life

Information

Reading Standard 2.6 Use information from a variety of consumer, workplace, and public documents to explain a situation or decision and to solve a problem.

ARTICLE

BEFORE YOU READ

Suppose you're planning a trip to Costa Rica this summer. What do you need to do before you get there? Buy airline tickets, arrange for a place to stay, pack your stuff, go to the airport . . .

Wait a second. Did you remember to take your passport? For that matter, did you remember to get a passport in the first place? If not, you are going to encounter a big problem at the airport in Costa Rica. The following article tells you how to avoid that problem.

from Cobblestone, December 1994

Passports: Don't Leave Home Without One

Carolyn Liberatore Lavine

If you decide that you would like to study art in Europe, pursue a career as a foreign diplomat, or simply travel abroad, you will need a passport. A passport is an official document used by both foreign countries and your birth country as proof of your identity and citizenship. It is a good idea to apply for a passport the minute you even suspect that you
10 might be traveling abroad. You will want to take off at a moment's notice when your appointment comes

IDENTIFY

What does the illustration show you? Is it drawn to actual size? Use a ruler to find out.

<u>It shows the format</u>
<u>for an acceptable</u>
<u>passport photograph.</u>
<u>It is drawn to</u>
<u>actual size.</u>

---

through as **ambassador** to Greece! Here is how to get a passport:

1. Get a passport application form. This form is available at some post offices and most county office buildings from the clerk of court. You also can get a form by writing to the
20 U.S. Department of State, Bureau of Consular Affairs, Passport Services, 1425 K Street N.W., Washington, D.C. 20524.

2. Carefully fill out the one-page form. Type or print clearly and answer *all* the questions. Ask a parent to double-check them. If you do not have a Social Security number, fill in that box with zeros.

3. Obtain an official copy of your birth certificate. Visit or write to the county office building in the county in which you were born. You must have a *certified copy* of your birth certificate (one with a raised seal on it) to get a passport. A
30 photocopy of the original will not be accepted.

4. Have two identical photographs taken of yourself alone. Check the yellow pages under "Photographers—Passport" for a photographer who knows all the rules about passport photos. Expect to pay ten to fifteen dollars for two photos. Remember to smile!

5. Take the completed application, <u>official birth certificate, and photos to the county office that sent you the form.</u> If you are under eighteen, a parent or guardian must accompany you. Your parent or guardian must show his or her driver's license or photo ID to the county clerk.
40 If the person's last name is different from yours, he or she must provide a certified copy of his or her marriage license or divorce papers and proof of his or her citizenship. (A passport can be used for this.)

VOCABULARY DEVELOPMENT

ambassador (am-bas´ə-dər) *n.:* person who represents a nation while living in another nation.

IDENTIFY

Most of the information in this document is presented in a numbered list. Why might that be?

<u>A numbered list makes</u>
<u>it easier for readers to</u>
<u>follow the directions</u>
<u>or steps being</u>
<u>explained.</u>

DECODING TIP

In "K Street N.W.," the *N.W.* stands for "Northwest" (line 20).

VOCABULARY DEVELOPMENT

obtain (ab-tān´) *v.:* get.

official (ə-fish´əl) *adj.:* having to do with a recognized authority, such as a government office.

WORD KNOWLEDGE

ID (line 40) is a shortened form of *identification.*

OWN THE TEXT

PRACTICING THE STANDARDS

Using Information from Public Documents Test your knowledge by working with a partner. Have one of you play an employee at the passport office while the other asks questions about procedures. Switch roles after five minutes.

_____

_____

_____

KEEPING TRACK

Personal Word List The vocabulary words in this selection will help you sound more official! Add them to your Personal Word List.

Personal Reading Log How well did the article do its task of showing you how to fill out a passport application? Note any especially strong or weak points in your Personal Reading Log. Give yourself 1 point on the Reading Meter.

Checklist for Standards Mastery Use the Checklist for Standards Mastery to gauge your progress in mastering the standards. Note your areas of biggest improvement and the areas you still need work on.

Passports: Don't Leave Home Without One **329**

---

6. Swear or affirm to the clerk that everything on your **application is true**—including that the photograph attached is really you. Most passport photos are notoriously unflattering.

7. **Sign your name on the application form and pay the passport fee.** If you are under eighteen, the fee is thirty dollars. Have a check or money order made payable to "Passport Office." Be prepared to pay a ten-dollar "execution fee" in cash to the county.

You can expect your passport in the mail four to six weeks later. . . . A passport for children under eighteen years of age is valid for five years. After that, a passport can be renewed for fifty-five dollars plus the ten-dollar execution fee. It is valid for ten years.

If you do travel abroad, you will want to find out about visas, too. A visa is an official document that is issued by the country to which you are traveling. It sets some limitations on the amount of time you can spend in the country. Students who go abroad to study usually must have a visa. Call the **embassy** or **consulate** of the country you plan to visit to find out more.

VOCABULARY DEVELOPMENT

affirm (ə-fûrm′) v.: say that something is true; agree.

What context clue helps you figure out the meaning of *affirm*? Circle it.

embassy (em′bə-sē) n.: offices of an ambassador and the ambassador's staff.

consulate (kän′sal-it) n.: office of the consul, the person appointed by a government to aid and serve its citizens.

COMPARE & CONTRAST

How is the information in the passage beginning on line 54 different from the information presented in the list?

This information is general; it does not involve a series of steps that need following.

CLOSE READING

If you were to go get a passport, what information would you re-read?

Answers will vary.

328 Chapter 8 Reading for Life

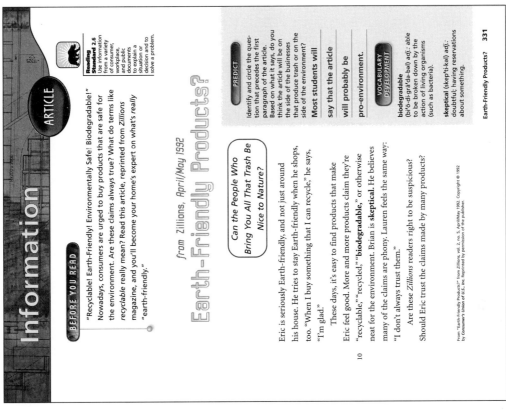

Information

ARTICLE

BEFORE YOU READ

"Recyclable! Earth-Friendly! Environmentally Safe! Biodegradable!" Nowadays, consumers are urged to buy products that are safe for the environment. Are these claims always true? What do terms like *recyclable* really mean? Read this article, reprinted from *Zillions* magazine, and you'll become your home's expert on what's really "earth-friendly."

from Zillions, April/May 1992

Earth-Friendly Products?

Can the People Who Bring You All That Trash Be Nice to Nature?

Eric is seriously Earth-friendly, and not just around his house. He tries to stay Earth-friendly when he shops, too. "When I buy something that I can recycle," he says, "I'm glad."

These days, it's easy to find products that make Eric feel good. More and more products claim they're

10 "recyclable," "recycled," **"biodegradable,"** or otherwise neat for the environment. Brian is **skeptical**. He believes many of the claims are phony. Lauren feels the same way: "I don't always trust them."

Are these *Zillions* readers right to be suspicious? Should Eric trust the claims made by many products?

From "Earth-Friendly Products?" from *Zillions*, vol. 2, no. 5, April/May 1992. Copyright © 1992 by Consumers Union of U.S., Inc. Reprinted by permission of the publisher.

PREDICT

Identify and circle the question that precedes the first paragraph of the article. Based on what it says, do you think the article will be on the side of the businesses that produce trash or on the side of the environment?

Most students will _____ say that the article _____ will probably be _____ pro-environment.

VOCABULARY DEVELOPMENT

biodegradable (bī′ō-di-grā′də-bəl) *adj.*: able to be broken down by the action of living organisms (such as bacteria).

skeptical (skĕp′ti-kəl) *adj.*: doubtful; having reservations about something.

Earth-Friendly Products? **331**

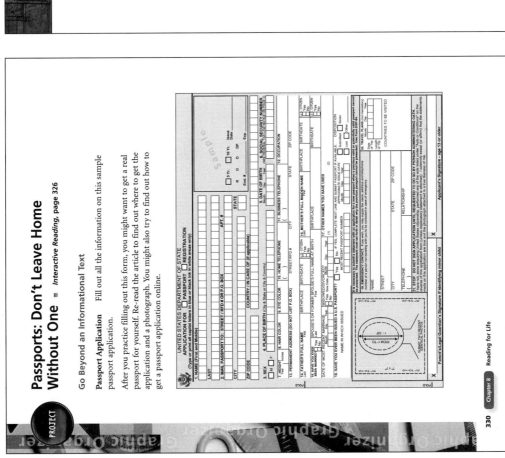

PROJECT

Passports: Don't Leave Home Without One ■ *Interactive Reading, page 326*

Go Beyond an Informational Text

Passport Application Fill out all the information on this sample passport application.

After you practice filling out this form, you might want to get a real passport for yourself. Re-read the article to find out where to get the application and a photograph. You might also try to find out how to get a passport application online.

330 Chapter 8 Reading for Life

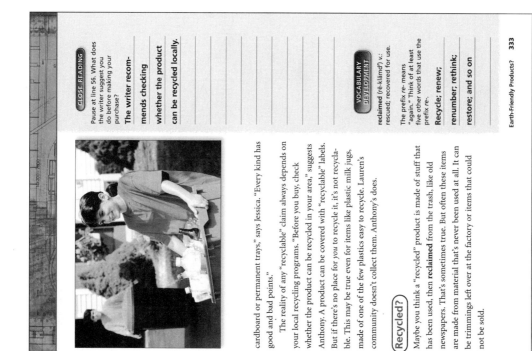

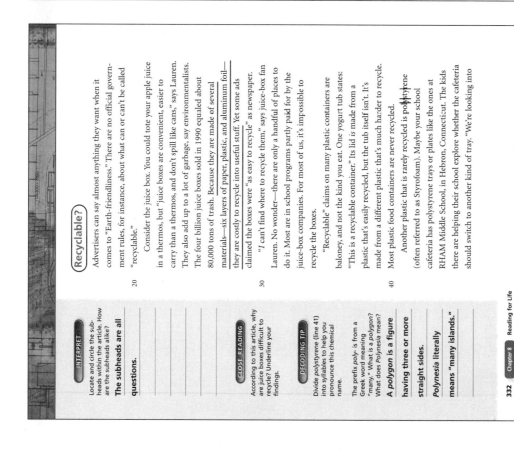

INTERPRET

Locate and circle the subheads within the article. How are the subheads alike?

The subheads are all questions.

CLOSE READING

According to this article, why are juice boxes difficult to recycle? Underline your findings.

DECODING TIP

Divide *polystyrene* (line 41) into syllables to help you pronounce this chemical name.

The prefix *poly-* is from a Greek word meaning "many." What is a polygon? What does *Polynesia* mean?

A polygon is a figure having three or more straight sides.

Polynesia literally means "many islands."

Recyclable?

Advertisers can say almost anything they want when it comes to "Earth-friendliness." There are no official government rules, for instance, about what can or can't be called "recyclable."

Consider the juice box. You could tote your apple juice in a thermos, but "juice boxes are convenient, easier to carry than a thermos, and don't spill like cans," says Lauren. They also add up to a lot of garbage, say environmentalists. The four billion juice boxes sold in 1990 equaled about 80,000 tons of trash. Because they are made of several materials—six layers of paper, plastic, and aluminum foil— they are costly to recycle into useful stuff. Yet some ads claimed the boxes were "as easy to recycle" as newspaper.

"*I can't find where to recycle them,*" says juice-box fan Lauren. No wonder—there are only a handful of places to do it. Most are in school programs partly paid for by the juice-box companies. For most of us, it's impossible to recycle the boxes.

"Recyclable" claims on many plastic containers are baloney, and not the kind you eat. One yogurt tub states: "This is a recyclable container." Its lid *is* made from a plastic that's easily recycled, but the tub itself isn't. It's made from a different plastic that's much harder to recycle. Most plastic food containers are never recycled.

Another plastic that is rarely recycled is polystyrene (often referred to as Styrofoam). Maybe your school cafeteria has polystyrene trays or plates like the ones at RHAM Middle School, in Hebron, Connecticut. The kids there are helping their school explore whether the cafeteria should switch to another kind of tray. "We're looking into

CLOSE READING

Pause at line 56. What does the writer suggest you do before making your purchase?

The writer recommends checking whether the product can be recycled locally.

cardboard or permanent trays," says Jessica. "Every kind has good and bad points."

The reality of any "recyclable" claim always depends on your local recycling programs. "Before you buy, check whether the product can be recycled in your area," suggests Anthony. A product can be covered with "recyclable" labels. But if there's no place for *you* to recycle it, it's not recyclable. This may be true even for items like plastic milk jugs, made of one of the few plastics easy to recycle. Lauren's community doesn't collect them. Anthony's does.

Recycled?

Maybe you think a "recycled" product is made of stuff that has been used, then reclaimed from the trash, like old newspapers. That's sometimes true. But often these items are made from material that's never been used at all. It can be trimmings left over at the factory or items that could not be sold.

VOCABULARY DEVELOPMENT

reclaimed (rē-klāmd′) v.: rescued; recovered for use.

The prefix *re-* means "again." Think of at least five other words that use the prefix *re-*.

Recycle; renew; renumber; rethink; restore; and so on

For example, suppose a company makes too many large rolls of paper and can't sell them all. It can grind up the leftover paper, mix it with new paper, and sell it as "recycled" paper. That's true for much of the recycled paper we buy. This sort of re-use has been going on for many years. Suddenly, however, these products have acquired a "recycled" label, so people like Eric will feel good about buying them.

70 Real wastepaper is often used in making cereal boxes and other kinds of cardboard. To tell if your favorite cereal brand uses recycled paper, just cut through a box. If it's gray or brown under the coating, it's probably made from wastepaper. White all the way through? It's fresh from the tree.

Biodegradable?

A truly biodegradable product is something like an apple core. Once it's thrown away, it breaks down (rather quickly)
80 into substances that aren't harmful to the Earth. People purchased one company's trash bags and another company's disposable diapers because ads made them think these products were better for the environment. But most trash bags and diapers end up in landfills where they are covered with piles of garbage. They are never exposed to the air, sunlight, and moisture that could make them break down.

We found a new wrinkle in environmental ad talk on a box of trash bags, which claims to be "Fighting Pollution."
90 The label boasts that these bags "will not release harmful products of **decomposition** that can contaminate underground water supplies." That's trying to get some mileage out of the fact these bags are *not* biodegradable!

WORD KNOWLEDGE
Draw a vertical line between the syllables of *landfills* (line 85). What two words make up this word? What can you guess the word means? **Land that is filled with garbage and covered with a layer of earth.**

WORD KNOWLEDGE
The idiom found in line 88 makes no sense if it is translated literally. Underline the idiom. Based on its context, what do you guess the idiom means? **"A new wrinkle" means a new problem or complication.**

VOCABULARY DEVELOPMENT
decomposition
(dē·kăm'pə·zĭsh'an) *n*.: decay; the breaking down of a substance into simple substances.
Composition, decomposition, and related words, such as *compose,* come from the Latin *componere,* meaning "put together."

Buys 'R' Us?

Finding out what's *really* better for the environment has even the experts confused. And since companies can claim almost anything, you'd have to be a wizard at environmental ad games to know what to believe. To make less garbage, just follow the three Rs:

100 **Reduce:** This is the most important of the three. If you don't need it, don't buy it. Or use it. Lauren bought a teeny hairclip, but the clerk gave her a humongous bag. "I gave it back."

Re-use: Choose products (and packages) that can be used more than once. Avoid anything used just once and thrown away, like a juice box.

Recycle: Think of this as a last resort. According to one expert: "We're recycling products we probably shouldn't be using in the first place." Make the effort to find out what
110 can be recycled in your area. (The information on the next page can help you understand plastic codes.) If you're not

WORD KNOWLEDGE
Humongous (line 102) is slang for "very large." It is probably a blend of *huge* and *monstrous.* If you didn't know its meaning, what contrast context clue would help you guess? Underline the contrast clue.

WORD KNOWLEDGE
"As a last resort," line 107, means "as the last available possibility." *Resort* here means "resource." What other meaning does *resort* have? **a place one goes for vacation**

OWN THE TEXT

PRACTICING THE STANDARDS

Using Information from Consumer Documents Now that you have read about recycling, how should this information affect you as a consumer? Write three sentences stating your response to the article.

KEEPING TRACK

Personal Word List Write the words you learned while reading this selection in your Personal Word List.

Personal Reading Log You're now wiser about recycling. Enter this title in your Personal Reading Log. Give yourself another 3 points on the Reading Meter.

Checklist for Standards Mastery The Checklist for Standards Mastery is a good tool for checking your progress toward achieving the California standards. Track your progress now.

Earth-Friendly Products? **337**

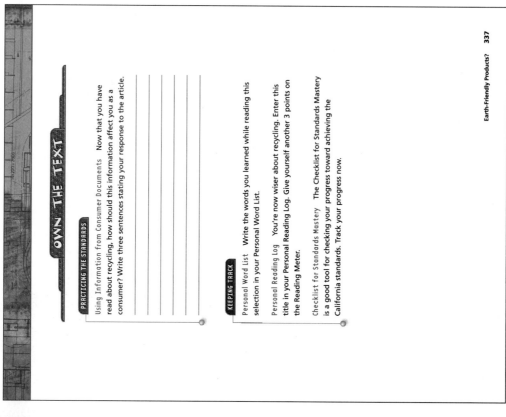

---

sure, swallow a product's environmental claims with a grain of salt. Or swallow the product. One of the world's most Earth-friendly containers is an ice-cream core.

WORD KNOWLEDGE

The idiom "take something with a grain of salt" (lines 112–113) means "be skeptical; not trusting or accepting."

• • • • • • Notes • • • • • •

Plastics Decoded

If you turn over most plastic containers, you'll see a number from 1 to 7. What does it mean? It's a code for the type of plastic used. Jessica knew that plastics with higher numbers aren't very recyclable:

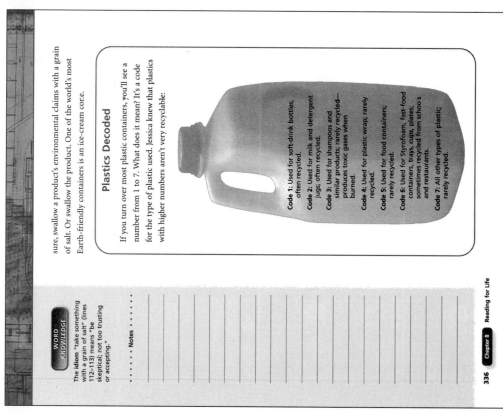

Code 1: Used for soft-drink bottles; often recycled.

Code 2: Used for milk and detergent jugs; often recycled.

Code 3: Used for shampoos and similar products; rarely recycled—produces toxic gases when burned.

Code 4: Used for plastic wrap; rarely recycled.

Code 5: Used for food containers; rarely recycled.

Code 6: Used for Styrofoam, fast-food containers, trays, cups, plates; sometimes recycled from schools and restaurants.

Code 7: All other types of plastic rarely recycled.

336 Chapter 8 Reading for Life

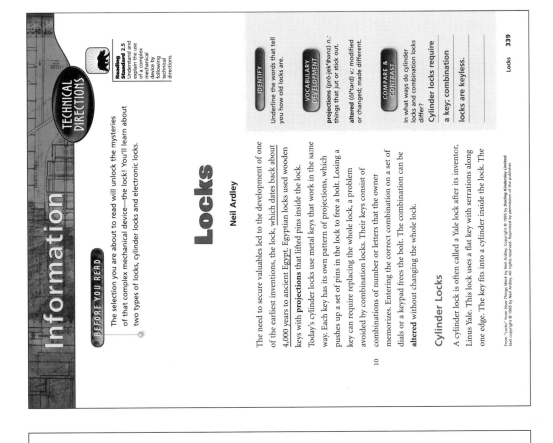

Information

TECHNICAL DIRECTIONS

Reading Standard 2.5 Understand and explain the use of a complex mechanical device by following technical directions.

BEFORE YOU READ

The selection you are about to read will unlock the mysteries of that complex mechanical device—the lock! You'll learn about two types of locks, cylinder locks and electronic locks.

Locks

Neil Ardley

The need to secure valuables led to the development of one of the earliest inventions, the lock, which dates back about 4,000 years to ancient Egypt. Egyptian locks used wooden keys with **projections** that lifted pins inside the lock.

Today's cylinder locks use metal keys that work in the same way. Each key has its own pattern of projections, which pushes up a set of pins in the lock to free a bolt. Losing a key can require replacing the whole lock, a problem avoided by combination locks. Their keys consist of
10 combinations of number or letters that the owner memorizes. Entering the correct combination on a set of dials or a keypad frees the bolt. The combination can be **altered** without changing the whole lock.

Cylinder Locks

A cylinder lock is often called a Yale lock after its inventor, Linus Yale. This lock uses a flat key with serrations along one edge. The key fits into a cylinder inside the lock. The

IDENTIFY

Underline the words that tell you how old locks are.

VOCABULARY DEVELOPMENT

projections (prō-jĕk′shanz) *n.*: things that jut or stick out.

altered (ôl′tard) *v.*: modified or changed; made different.

COMPARE & CONTRAST

In what ways do cylinder locks and combination locks differ?

Cylinder locks require a key; combination locks are keyless.

Locks **339**

PROJECT

Earth-Friendly Products?   ■ *Interactive Reading,* page 331

Go Beyond an Informational Text

Is It Recyclable?   Using the "Plastics Decoded" feature in the "Earth-Friendly Products" article, do your own study of the plastic containers you use. Do this independently or with a partner.

First, find ten or more different plastic containers for products. Make a list of the code numbers that you find on each container. If you can't find enough containers at home, go to the grocery store, and take notes about the containers there. Then, find out which code numbers indicate plastics that can be recycled in your community. To do this, you may need to call your community recycling center or sanitation department.

Finally, present your findings in a visual form of your choice, perhaps as a chart or graph such as the ones shown below. Show the number and percentage of each recycling code among the containers you surveyed. Also show which ones are recyclable in your community.

Many students will choose bar graphs or pie graphs for their visual presentations. These are probably the two most convenient forms to use for this type of information.

Sample bar graph

Sample pie graph

cylinder has a cam at one end that grips a bolt. Turning the key rotates the cylinder so that the cam pulls back the bolt and the door opens. However, the cylinder cannot rotate unless the right key is inserted. The cylinder and body of the lock have a set of holes that each contain a pair of pins and a spring. The pins block the gap between the cylinder and the body of the lock, preventing the cylinder from rotating. When the key is inserted, its **serrated** edge pushes up the pins by different amounts. This causes the gap in

· · · · · · Notes · · · · · ·

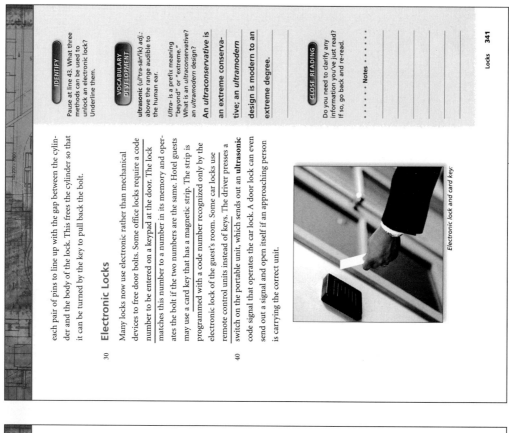

Upper pin in each pair obstructs gap between cylinder and body

Bolt

Cam

Springs

Body of lock

Cylinder

Gap between pins in each pair lines up with edge of cylinder

Cylinder and cam turn, pulling bolt back

Key

each pair of pins to line up with the gap between the cylinder and the body of the lock. This frees the cylinder so that it can be turned by the key to pull back the bolt.

Electronic Locks

Many locks now use electronic rather than mechanical devices to free door bolts. Some office locks require a code number to be entered on a keypad at the door. The lock matches this number to a number in its memory and operates the bolt if the two numbers are the same. Hotel guests may use a card key that has a magnetic strip. The strip is programmed with a code number recognized only by the electronic lock of the guest's room. Some car locks use remote control units instead of keys. The driver presses a switch on the portable unit, which sends out an **ultrasonic** code signal that operates the car lock. A door lock can even send out a signal and open itself if an approaching person is carrying the correct unit.

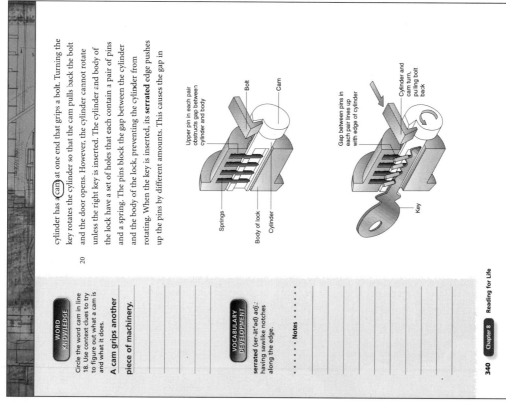

Electronic lock and card key.

· · · · · · Notes · · · · · ·

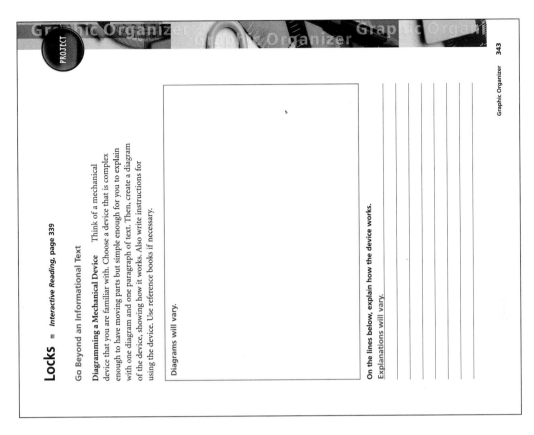

PROJECT

Locks ■ *Interactive Reading,* page 339

Go Beyond an Informational Text

Diagramming a Mechanical Device Think of a mechanical device that you are familiar with. Choose a device that is complex enough to have moving parts but simple enough for you to explain with one diagram and one paragraph of text. Then, create a diagram of the device, showing how it works. Also write instructions for using the device. Use reference books if necessary.

Diagrams will vary.

On the lines below, explain how the device works.
Explanations will vary.

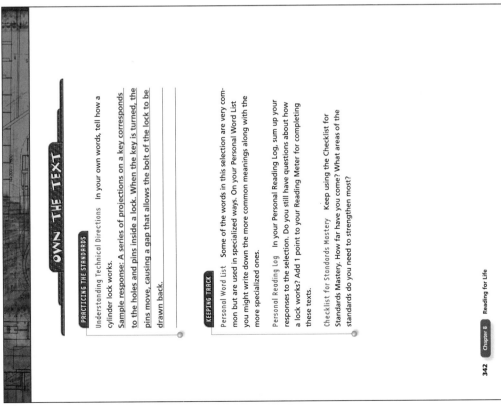

OWN THE TEXT

PRACTICING THE STANDARDS

Understanding Technical Directions In your own words, tell how a cylinder lock works.
Sample response: A series of projections on a key corresponds to the holes and pins inside a lock. When the key is turned, the pins move, causing a gap that allows the bolt of the lock to be drawn back.

KEEPING TRACK

Personal Word List Some of the words in this selection are very common but are used in specialized ways. On your Personal Word List you might write down the more common meanings along with the more specialized ones.

Personal Reading Log In your Personal Reading Log, sum up your responses to the selection. Do you still have questions about how a lock works? Add 1 point to your Reading Meter for completing these texts.

Checklist for Standards Mastery Keep using the Checklist for Standards Mastery. How far have you come? What areas of the standards do you need to strengthen most?

Section Three

Graphic Organizers

- GRAPHIC ORGANIZERS FOR READING STRATEGIES

- GENERIC GRAPHIC ORGANIZERS

Name _____ Date _____

Selection Title _____

"Somebody Wanted But So" Chart

Somebody	Wanted	But	So

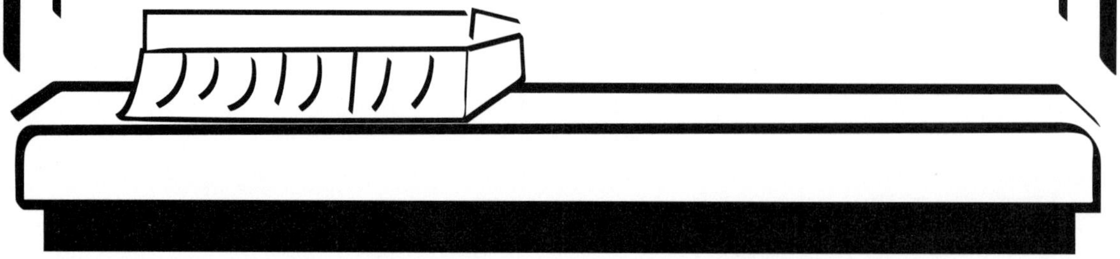

Name _____   Date _____

Selection Title _____

Comparison and Contrast
Venn Diagram

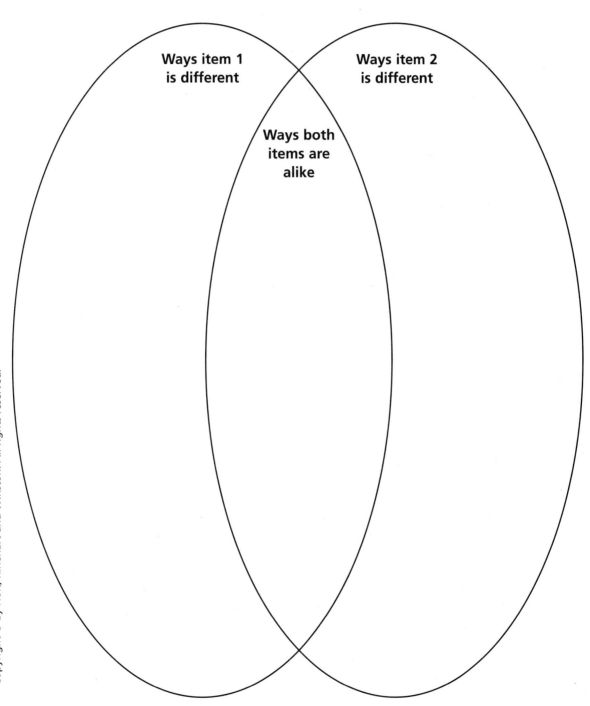

**Ways item 1
is different**

**Ways item 2
is different**

**Ways both
items are
alike**

Name _____ Date _____

Selection Title _____

"Sketch to Stretch" Canvas

Setting Words	Title

Write an explanation of your sketch.

_____

_____

_____

_____

_____

Name _____ Date _____

Selection Title _____

"Save the Last Word for Me" Cards

Chosen Passage:

_____
_____
_____
_____
_____
_____
_____
_____
_____
_____
_____
_____
_____

Comments About the Passage:

_____
_____
_____
_____
_____
_____
_____
_____
_____
_____
_____
_____
_____

Name _____   Date _____

Selection Title _____

Literary Devices Chart

Repetition	Figurative Language	Imagery	Irony	Sentence Length and Structure
_____	_____	_____	_____	_____
_____	_____	_____	_____	_____
_____	_____	_____	_____	_____
_____	_____	_____	_____	_____
_____	_____	_____	_____	_____
_____	_____	_____	_____	_____
_____	_____	_____	_____	_____
_____	_____	_____	_____	_____
_____	_____	_____	_____	_____
_____	_____	_____	_____	_____
_____	_____	_____	_____	_____
_____	_____	_____	_____	_____
_____	_____	_____	_____	_____
_____	_____	_____	_____	_____
_____	_____	_____	_____	_____
_____	_____	_____	_____	_____
_____	_____	_____	_____	_____
_____	_____	_____	_____	_____
_____	_____	_____	_____	_____
_____	_____	_____	_____	_____

Name _____   Date _____

Selection Title _____

Text Reformulation Chart
Newspaper Article

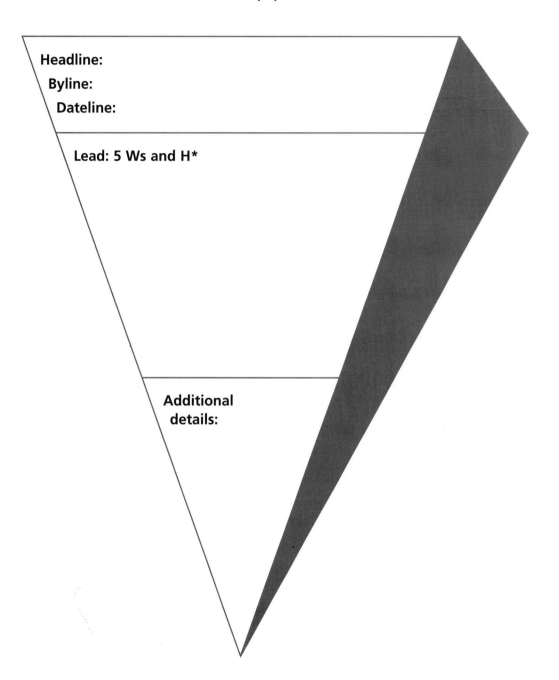

Headline:

Byline:

Dateline:

Lead: 5 Ws and H*

Additional details:

***What** happened? **Whom** did it happen to? **When** and **where** did it happen? **Why** did it happen? **How** did it happen?

"Think-Aloud" Assessment Sheet

While I was reading, how often did I use these strategies?

	Not much	A little	Most of the time	All of the time
Making and revising predictions				
Forming mental pictures				
Connecting what I read to what I already know				
Asking questions				
Making comments				
Identifying problems I have in understanding the text				
Fixing the problems				

Name _____ Date _____

Selection Title _____

"Close Reading" Chart

	Public Document: Advertisement/ Notice	Workplace Document: Letters and e-mails	Consumer Document: How-to Instructions
Key Information			
Key Information			
Key Information			
Key Information			
Key Information			

Plot Outline

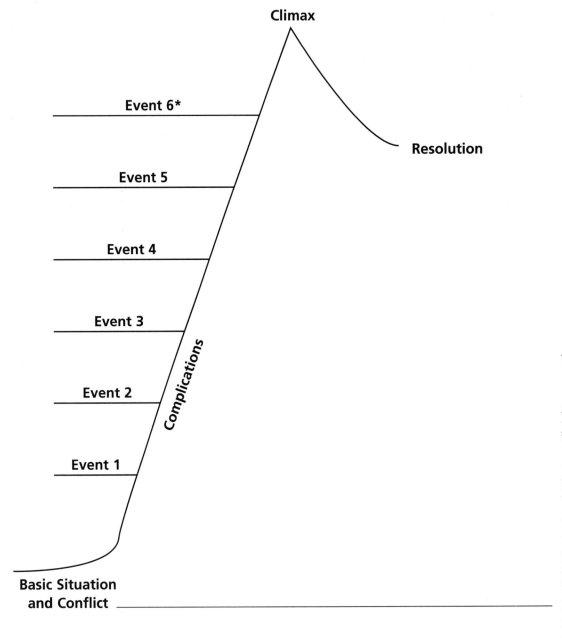

Climax

Event 6*

Resolution

Event 5

Event 4

Event 3

Complications

Event 2

Event 1

**Basic Situation
and Conflict** _____

***Number of events will vary.**

Story Map

Characters	Setting

Problem/Conflict

↓

Major Events

1.

2.

3.

4.

5.

↓

Climax

↓

Resolution

↓

Theme

Character Analysis

Character _____	Passages
Words	
Actions	
Appearance	
Thoughts	
Effects on Other People	
Direct Characterization	
Analysis of Character	

Name _____ Date _____

Selection Title _____

Word Map

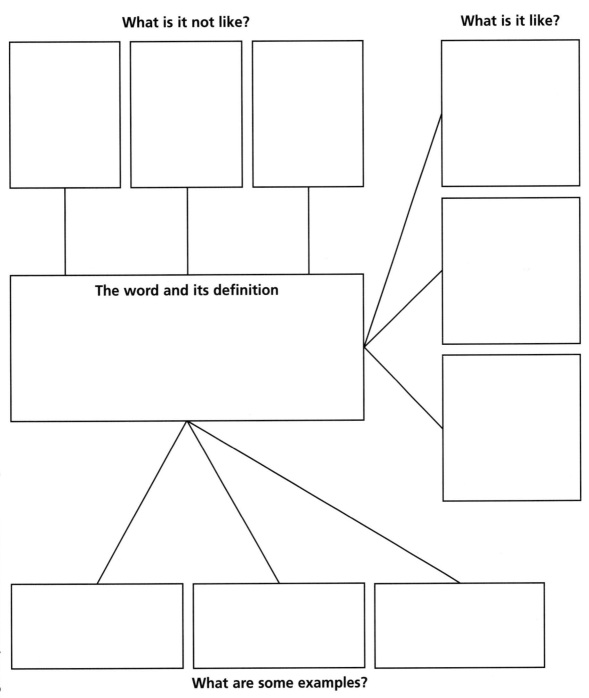

What is it not like?

What is it like?

The word and its definition

What are some examples?

Name _____   Date _____

Selection Title _____

KWL Worksheet

K What I know	W What I want to find out	L What I learned and still need to learn

Name _____ Date _____

Selection Title _____

Main-Idea Web

Supporting Detail

Supporting Detail

Supporting Detail

Supporting Detail

Main Idea

Name _____ Date _____

Selection Title _____

Proposition/Support Outline

Topic

Proposition

Support

| 1. Facts |
| 2. Statistics |
| 3. Examples |
| 4. Expert Authority |

Name _____ Date _____

Selection Title _____

Chronological Sequence Chart

Topic

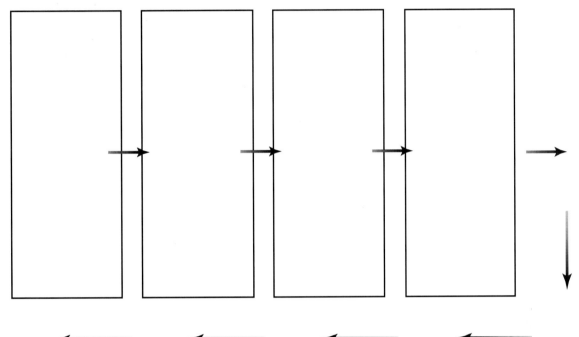

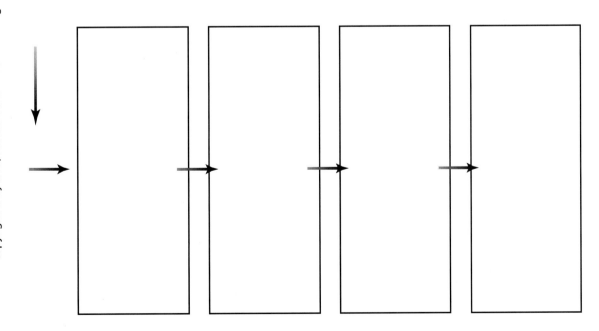

Name _____   Date _____

Selection Title _____

Comparison-Contrast Chart

Features	Selection 1	Selection 2
1.		
2.		
3.		
4.		

Name _____ Date _____

Selection Title _____

Causal Chain

Cause

↓

Effect
Cause

↓

Effect
Cause

↓

Effect
Cause

↓

Effect

Name ———————————————————— Date ————————————

Selection Title ————————————————————————————————

Cause-and-Effect Charts

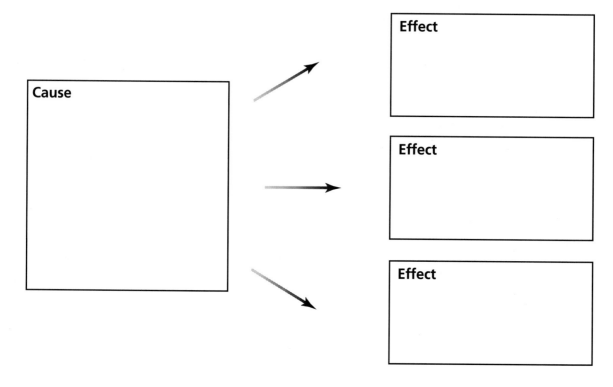

Cause

Effect

Effect

Effect

Cause

Cause

Cause

Effect

Evaluation Chart

	Response	Support from Text
Figures of Speech (originality, power)		
Believability of Plot		
Believability of Characters		
Clarity of Writing		

Certificate of Achievement

★

Congratulations!

You have achieved 100 Points for reading about 45,000 words.

_____
Student

_____
Teacher

Section Four

Transparencies
for
Modeling Instruction

The Princess and the Pea

Once upon a time, a prince wanted to marry, but only a genuine princess would do for *his* wife. He searched the world over, but he could find no one to suit him. He began to despair.

Then, one dark, stormy night, a knocking was heard at the palace gate. The prince went to investigate. A princess stood there, but she was a soggy mess. The water ran down her hair and clothes and into her shoes, but still she claimed to be a genuine princess.

"We'll soon find that out," thought the old queen, as she helped prepare the bed for the visitor. She piled on mattress after mattress; then, she placed a tiny pea underneath them.

The next morning, the royal family asked the princess how she had slept.

"Horribly!" exclaimed the princess. "I hardly slept all night. I'm black and blue from lying on something as hard as that was!"

> Now they knew she was a real princess. Nobody but a real princess could be as sensitive as that.

So the prince took her for his wife, and the pea was put in a museum, where it may still be seen if no one has stolen it.

My "Last Words" on Choosing the Passage

"This is the most important passage because it shows how the true test of something is not always in its appearance."

"This passage is also important because it resolves the major question in the story: Is she or isn't she a true princess?"

The Mermaid in the Sea

Long ago and far away, a sailor sailed his boat to sea. A poor man, he hoped to fill his nets with so many fish that his nets would be overflowing. In a kingdom under the sea there lived a beautiful mermaid with hair as golden as the rays of the sun. She loved the sea, but she longed for a true love. Every evening, she sang a song of longing, and her haunting voice filled the night. The poor sailor heard her song. So distracted was he that when a big wave came along, it overturned his boat. Down, down, under the sea he went. The mermaid saw him, hoping he would turn out to be her true love. But instead of love, she saw fear in his eyes and so saved him, carrying him up to the top of the waves. The sailor gratefully drank in the air and found his boat. Though he was grateful for his life, a part of him longed always for the beautiful mermaid under the sea.

Connect Literary Devices and Author's Style

- I put a sticky note next to this passage because I liked the way it sounded. When I re-read the passage, I realized that the writer used a simile that made the mermaid's beauty very vivid.

- I chose this passage because it seemed out of the ordinary. I discovered when I re-read it that the writer used unusual word order "So distracted *was he*. . . ." This word order makes the story seem classic, or old-fashioned. When I re-read the whole story I also found other instances of word inversion. The author probably used this style of writing to give this tale a traditional feel.

Strategy: Think-Aloud

from Little Red Riding-Hood

When Red Riding-Hood came to her grandmother's cottage, the place was strangely silent. No birds chirped. No squirrels skittered on the roof. No dog barked on its chain outside.

Maybe the birds and squirrels left because they saw the wolf. But what happened to the dog? Maybe the wolf killed it.

"Hello, is anybody home? Grandma, are you there?" she called out. There was no answer, but when she let herself in, Red Riding-Hood saw the lumpy bulk of a living body on the bed, moving under a thick gray blanket that completely hid it from view.

"Oh, Grandma, there you are. We heard you were sick, so Mom sent you stuff to eat." She rummaged around in her basket. "Let's see, we have some chicken and poblano pepper enchiladas in an ancho chili sauce, some black beans sautéed in rosemary olive oil, and a light sprinkling of goat cheese . . ."

What are all those foods? I bet the author just put this description in for a laugh.

Red Riding-Hood heard a groan arise from the bed. "Never mind the fancy cuisine, child. Come here and let me feast my eyes on my wonderful granddaughter."

Red Riding-Hood went obediently to the bedside. The blanket slipped slightly down off the patient's head, and Red Riding-Hood saw two huge, red-rimmed eyes blazing at her as if burning from fever. She saw gray fur falling over a long snout that ended in two wet, whiskered, black, bulging nostrils.

"Grandma," said Red Riding-Hood, thinking fast, "What big eyes you have." . . .

Is she fooled by the wolf, or is she just stalling for a way to escape? This is funny.

Strategy: Close Reading

Classic Pasta

Fill a large, heavy-bottomed pot with 6 quarts of water. Add 1 tbsp. salt. Turn heat on to high. When water comes to a rapid, rolling boil, add contents of 1 16 oz. package of spaghetti. Return to boil. Boil for 8 minutes for *al dente,* or longer for softer spaghetti. Stir occasionally to prevent strands from sticking.

Taste for doneness. Do not overcook; cooking continues after heat is turned off. When spaghetti is cooked to your liking, remove from heat and drain into a large colander. Rinse with cold tap water to stop cooking. Pour immediately into a large bowl, or into the cooking pot, and toss with 2 tbsp. butter or olive oil. Add your favorite sauce and grated parmesan cheese, and serve at once. Serves 6.

Glossary

> **tbsp.** tablespoon
> **tsp.** teaspoon
> **oz.** ounce

"Close Reading" Questions:

- What is your purpose for reading?

- What information is revealed by skimming the text? By scanning the text?

- Where might you look to learn what "tbsp." and "oz." stand for?

- What sections might you re-read to clarify information?

The Legendary Davy Crockett

Davy Crockett was both a real man and a legendary one. He was born in Tennessee in 1786 and had a tough childhood. By age thirteen he had left home to make his way in the world. Between 1811 and 1813, Crockett fought under General Andrew Jackson in the Creek War. He quickly established himself as a fierce fighter and frontiersman. Although he was admired for being strong and tough, Crockett's gift for storytelling and his common sense helped get him elected to Congress three times.

Crockett became a bona fide hero in 1836, when he lost his life while defending the Alamo during the battle for Texas's independence from Mexico.

Questions:

- How did historical events help shape Davy Crockett's life?

- If Davy Crockett had lived in the late twentieth century, how might he have reacted to historical events?

- What other figures from past history remind you of Davy Crockett? Did any of those figures become legends?

- What figures from modern history remind you of Davy Crockett? Might any of those figures become legends?

Strategy: Sketch to Stretch

Pinocchio "Sketch to Stretch" Example

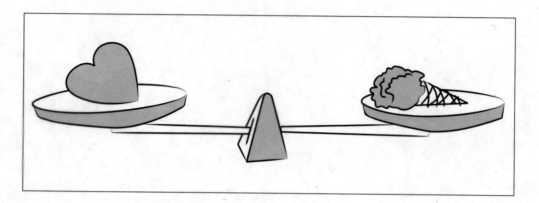

Explanation of Sketch

My sketch shows Pinocchio weighing his choices. On one side of the scale is the possibility of becoming a real boy. This is represented by a heart. On the other side is a life spent in mindless self-indulgence. This is represented by the ice cream cone. Pinocchio's dilemma can be seen as a struggle between these opposing forces.